PEN REPAIR
THIRD EDITION

A practical guide for repairing collectable pens & pencils with additional information on pen anatomy and filling systems

Jim Marshall
Laurence Oldfield

This book is a special tribute to Arthur Twydle

APPRECIATION

1st Edition

Pen repairing is one of the most co-operative activities we know. Knowledge is openly shared and techniques are divulged in magazines, on the internet and over the phone. In such circumstances such a book is never produced without consciously or subconsciously benefiting from other people's suggestions and ideas. We fully appreciate these influences.

Our acknowledgements to all these influencers and with regard to makers especially Letta Grosskemper, Ray Bailey and Lois Hagan for Sheaffer matters; Dave Ruderman and The Parker Pen company for their permission to use material and diagrams from their manuals and especially Osman Sumer for his contribution on European pens.

Our thanks for specific images to Steve Hull, Peter Ford, Azad Sadollah, David Shepherd, The Parker Pen Company and Roger Wolfe for special pen parts. You may notice that many different hands, often ink stained and scarred, feature in this book; Arthur's, our own, Peter Crook's and a few guest hands posing as models! We also have included images of typical customer's pens and other repairers tools, which has added to the variety; finally Terry Shepherd for her most helpful suggestions on layout and Jane for her patience and typing.

2nd Edition

We are very grateful for the constructive and helpful comments received from collectors in response to the first edition. Comments from professional repairmen have been added where possible and this has led to a significant improvement in the descriptions and techniques presented - our very grateful thanks.

3rd Edition

After 4 years we did not expect to be producing a third edition but it illustrates that pen repair is alive and well. There have been a few changes in our hobby over a relative short time and perhaps the two most important have been improved communication or searching for information and the availablility of parts and tools. Shows are still popular and Ebay and websites continue to thrive; books on pens continue to be published and there are now well attended repair courses in the UK under the umbrella of the Writing Equipment Society. Sadly there are still few specialist auctions but the beginner does have plenty of opportunity to buy at shows in all continents. It is truly a global hobby but the shows need your support. The learning experience can be profound when you buy at a show compared to the internet.

We again thank our readers for the constructive comments on the second edition. We truly do value such a response and we have included most of these in the third edition. We have added a few more pens and techniques but the structure is essentially the same. The knowledge base is however expanding and we are delighted to recommend other wizards at work, who are unselfishly sharing their expertise and experience.

We hope our book will help you to repair and become more adventurous with more complex pens. There is always more help available somewhere if you need it.

'A pen repaired is useful, a pen unrepaired just looks useful'

Jim and Laurence

PART ONE

Introduction to repair procedures, pen anatomy, tools, parts and components

Appreciation	2
Contents	3
Preface	4
Introduction	6
Ready to repair	10
What goes wrong	11
Anatomy of a fountain pen	12
More complex parts	13
Filling system classification	14
Pen terms and classification	16
Pen Components	17
Nib	17
Feed/Breather tube	18
Nib/feed as a unit	19
Gripping section/Nib housing	20
Barrel	21
Cap	22
Clip	24
Pressure bar/lever/button	25
Tools	27
Facilities	30
Sacs	32
Repair Procedure -General	33
Specific Procedures	
Removing a section	34
Removing a nib	35
Replacing a nib	36
Checking space for a nib	36
Selecting sac size	37
The section peg	37
Fixing a sac	38
Replacing a clip	39
Testing and tuning a pen	40
Filling a pen	44
Ink capacities	45
Spares & Parts	46
General classes	48
Lever fillers	49
Lever dismantling	50
Lever variety	52
Button fillers	53
Body reservoir	54
Screw piston fillers	55
Cartridges/Converter	56
Converters	57
Ball pens	58
Pencils	60

PREFACE

Arthur Twydle in his Pen Museum Workshop listening to Glenn Miller

This book originally involved our dear friend Arthur Twydle, who having worked with major pen companies, provided a unique distillation of 60 years of repairing and teaching how to repair fountain pens. For almost 11 years Jim and Arthur agonised how best to pass on the basic elements of pen repair and in 2005 Laurence became involved to add his input and energy.

Arthur died at the end of 2005 just as we were about to start, but his spirit and teaching is on every page and as two of his students, our efforts and this book are a dedication to Arthur.

His energetic, enthusiastic and generous contribution to all students of pen repair and his inspiration will continue to influence most practising repairers. As a repairer he was without equal and we only hope this book does justice to his legacy as a teacher.

The general aim of the book is to help enthusiasts repair pens and pencils more confidently by emphasising practical points that are rarely included in the repair procedures in the manuals. Furthermore not all manufacturers published manuals so we hope some of these observations and notes will fill some gaps.

As we live in the UK we repair a lot of pens made there. This includes indigenous makes such as Swan, Wyvern, Onoto, Ford, Conway Stewart, Unique, Burnham. However, most of our repairs are on pens made by Parker, Sheaffer, Eversharp, Watermans and Montblanc.

We are not starting from scratch because apart from manufacturers' manuals, Frank Dubiel's book is the inspiration for many repairers. It has been successful worldwide and Pendemonium, who own the copyright, have reprinted it. Jim was instrumental with the help of Susan Wirth in promoting Frank's book in Europe. Just before Frank's death, Arthur and Jim were helping him to compile new chapters on European pens for the 3rd Edition. In this light, our efforts should be viewed as complementary, with more attention devoted to pens manufactured in the UK.

We have tried not to reproduce what is readily accessible from workshop manuals but we emphasise that such procedures usually requires a bench of appropriate tools and a readily available stock of replacement parts. We know that this is often not the case, so practical solutions are offered to get a pen working again without the luxury of a quick replacement part fix. Nevertheless, the ultimate references are the manuals and where these are available they should be consulted.

The book is laid out in three parts.

First we outline general procedures, including pen and pencil anatomy and the tools required to start repairing.

Second we refer to the repair of some specific makes and models of fountain pen, and because we are faced with ballpoint pens and pencils as part of a day's work, we have included some guidance on these.

Finally we delve into more advanced repair techniques, which often require special procedures or tools.

Highlighted 'wisdom boxes' offering TIPS, INFORMATION and CAUTION are scattered throughout the book. We have added a new box titled WEB NOTES because at times we have not had the space to explain procedures in sufficient detail. Further working notes are given on our web sites.

The joint authorship has allowed us to combine experience and, as one might expect, to have differing opinions on some repair procedures. This emphasises that there is usually more than one way of doing a repair and at times options are presented.

The format of this book is important, and if such a book is to be useful, it should be a convenient size to have on a desk or bench and stay open for easy reference.

Perhaps the final word has to be about the internet; there is so much free information that it makes one think twice about writing a book. However a book is easy to read on a workbench and few workshops have computers sharing space with tools, water, chemicals and an ultrasonic bath.

So we resisted the temptation to surf the net; we repaired those old Swans, Onotos and Burnhams, filled them with blue-black Stephens ink, and as Arthur would have wished -'we wrote the book'.

We hope you will enjoy it.

Jim Marshall and Laurence Oldfield

To get more information on a topic highlighted by this box - go to either www. penpencilgallery.com or www.penpractice.com and click on this box located on the website homepages.

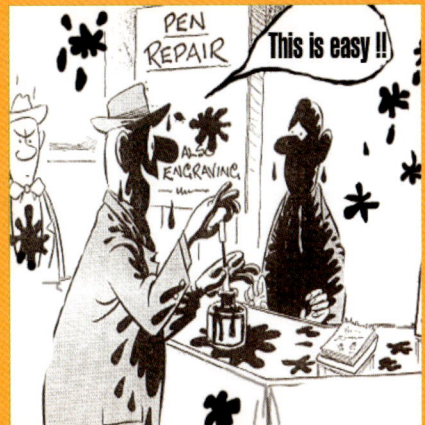

Repairing pens should be fun and usually is until you start repairing other people's pens. Only then do you appreciate what you don't know.

Arthur Twydle

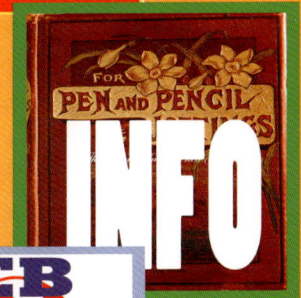

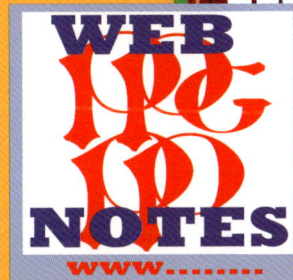

INTRODUCTION

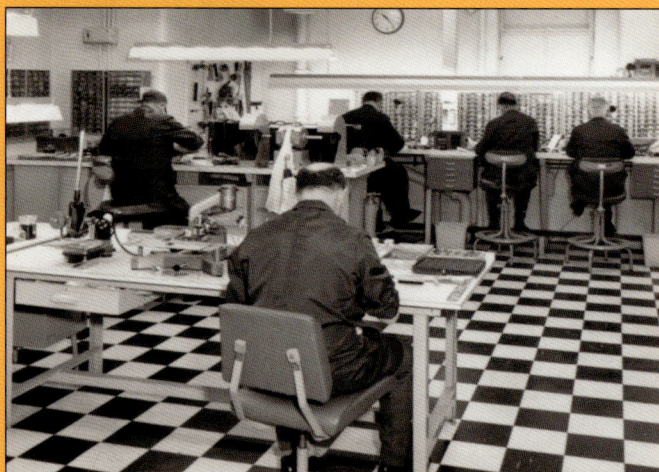

Parker service workshops in the basement of Bush House 1952

THROUGH A REPAIRER'S EYES

Our focus is repairing rather than collecting fountain pens. The dominant interest of a restorer is with the design, materials of construction, mechanisms and the weaknesses and quirks of a pen or pencil. However it is important to know the history of fountain pens and the changes that have occurred over the last 100 years. There are many good books on collecting fountain pens, which are regularly used by repairers for identification and background (see Bibliography).

Early Years

The earliest fountain pens of the late 19th century were black hard rubber eye droppers with only 5 parts: a barrel reservoir, slip cap, screw in section, nib, feed. Repairing them was simply replacement of parts and tuning the ink flow.

As pens became more popular, the range of material, design and decoration introduced more complexities for the repairer. Metal overlays, chatelaine chains, coloured hard rubber and different feed designs and nibs demanded more spare parts stock. Probably the biggest changes came with the introduction of self-filling pens. The variety of filling systems is a subject

on its own for pen collectors, but the repairer was fortunate, in that only two or three reliable systems were used by the big manufacturers. The pen barrel was still used as the ink supply in some pens, but the use of thin rubber sacs was a milestone in pen design and adopted by most pen makers. The means of compressing the sac varied. Consequently, repairers were not only required to stock sacs of different sizes and shapes, but also to ensure they had the appropriate levers, buttons and pressure bars. The repairer's skills were broadening, but although pen clips, introduced in 1906, created some additional headaches, most pens were easy to repair (excluding a few piston and safety pens).

1920s – '30s

In the early 1920s the main material for making pens was still hard rubber, but advances in polymer chemistry stimulated Sheaffer and other pen companies to adopt new 'coloured ' materials, which was another milestone in pen making. Lever and button fillers had attained a dominant position over piston fillers. The new challenge for repairers came with the fashion for ink visibility and the introduction of new plastics as these could be more temperamental than hard rubber. At the end of the 1920s the depression created changes

in all manufacturing industries. A generalization might be that most pens became smaller and more compact. Less expensive components such as clips were frequently slotted into caps. Nevertheless innovation was not suppressed and new advances with piston and pump systems were adopted and this created more complex activity for the repairer.

1940s – '50s

The war catalysed many changes including the use of alternative materials. Eversharp Wahl produced total metal lever pens in 1924 but few manufacturers had used metal, other than for overlays over hard rubber foundations. This changed dramatically in the 1940s as Parker, Watermans, Eversharp and Sheaffer all designed pens with metal caps; some with metal connectors and barrels. The repairer had to deal with new plastics, which were injection moulded rather than turned. Pen parts were often assembled in a 'permanent' manner and crimping, adhesives or push fit assembly replaced labour intensive screw fitting and riveting. It became more involved for the pensmith to make complex shaped replacement parts on a lathe, even if he could get the pen apart without breaking it. Pens were now rarely designed with repair in mind but most quality pens still retained some threaded assembly.

The demise of the fountain pen/growth of the ball point pen

The ball pen had a few technical and marketing teething troubles in the 1940s. However by the mid 1950s the impact on fountain pens was significant, causing a number of UK companies, such as Mabie Todd, Onoto and Summit, to cease manufacturing. By 1960 only the 'big boys' were left making quality fountain pens. The closure of UK companies created situations where sole agents were appointed to service past makes. For example Reg Phillips took over the repairing of Swan and Onoto and acquired the residual stocks of parts and pens. He also employed ex-Swan nibsmiths to make and stamp Phillips nibs. Sadly some UK companies such as Conway Stewart,

tried to compete with ball pens by compromising on quality. So much so that the pens produced from 1960 were hardly worth repairing.

Modern times

From 1960 to the early 1980s only well marketed decent quality or very cheap school fountain pens were successful. Ball pen sales rocketed with 'Jotters', 'Reminders' and 'No-Nonsense' pens being supplied as corporate gifts. There were some excellent, now classic collector's pens, such as the Parker 51, 61, 65, 75, the first Limited Editions, Sheaffer's PFM and Targa, Pelikan's 400 series and the Meisterstück range. Repairing was changing from intricate dis-assembly and replacing a small part to complete unit replacement, and the company manuals reflect this.

The resurgence of interest in fountain pens from about 1980 was primarily due to an increasing interest in status pens and collector items. New pens based on old heritage designs proved popular, while older pens became fashionable with frenetic interest at specialist shows and auctions. Old pens, that worked, were of higher value than those that did not, and there was a dramatic growth in restoring pens to use. This created a new business of restoring vintage pens as the collector market grew dramatically from 1990. It arguably peaked around 1999 but continues to be a significant hobby market today.

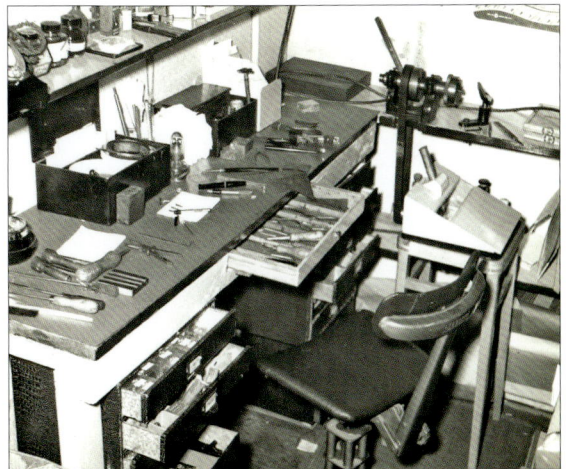

A repair bench at Reg Phillips -Oxford 1956

8

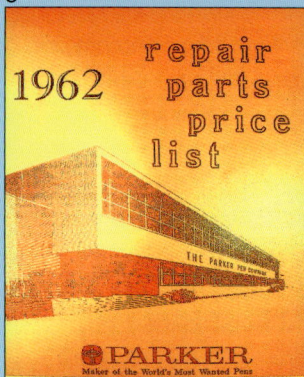

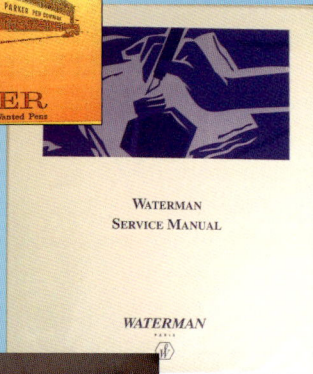

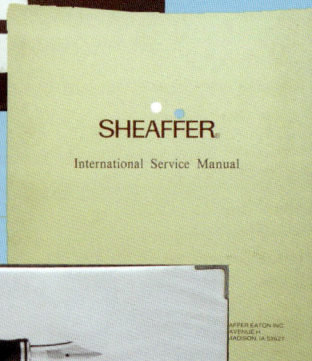

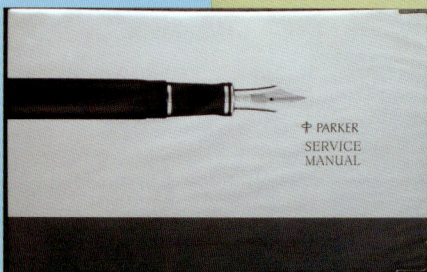

Manufacturers and repair

Manufacturers have always been aware of the importance of service and repair and initially they were the first and only 'point of call' for repair. From the earliest days they offered guarantees to promote their pens, sometimes lifetime, which was a rather ambiguous offer. Nevertheless until the 1950s they catered for all their current and past products. Even companies that had withdrawn from manufacture made sure that service arrangements were in place to attend to past customers.

Large repair units existed on factory sites but regional or city centres were set up and offered a quicker, more convenient repair service to customers. Parker, for example, established a major service centre in the basement of Bush House in London.

Many repairs were simple. Consequently, almost all pen companies offered training courses, manuals and spare parts to 'trade outlets' and encouraged them to offer a personal repair service. Staff from pen shops were trained to carry out fundamental repairs, and service centres such as Bush House were used for such courses. Arthur was coached there in the late 40s and in the 1950s; he also attended similar training courses with Montblanc and Sheaffer.

Industrial changes in the UK from the 1960s forced companies to rationalize their manufacturing activities. 'Industrial Engineering' focused on process, stock control and 'non core' diverting operations. Surplus stocks of parts for older pens were regarded as an unnecessary cost, as was the repair of such older pens. Obsolete parts stock was simply disposed of. This policy meant that companies not only did not wish to repair pens older than 15 years, but could not, because there were no spares.

Parts have always been a key factor with repair. Lists of redundant parts are still offered to the trade and diligently scoured for that 'treasure' but the 'old' parts have long gone. Makers still retain a small repair staff today to attend to modern manufactured items. However a lot of the repair experience and tools have been dispersed or simply lost as operations downsize, move or sites are closed. Today almost all 'vintage' repair work is carried out by third parties.

Classic and collectors fountain pens are perhaps not as buoyant as ten years ago but pen shows still surprise and excite enthusiasts. Books continue to appear with revelations previously untold; Ebay has a few thousand pens to sell each day and the 'Enthusiast Societies' are very active in the UK and USA.

From a repairer's viewpoint there is no shortage of work and although some parts are unobtainable, innovators adapt other units or have parts remade. Only twenty years ago Visofils, Ink Vues, Nozacs and Onotos were regarded, by many, as unrepairable and of little value; today these are pens that are in regular use and most 'old' repairers can't even remember why they were regarded as difficult.

The current scene

The larger pen manufacturing companies have had a turbulent time during the last 15 years. However, there are some promising signs; companies such as Conway Stewart and Onoto have re-established UK manufacturing; Italian companies such as Visconti, Montegrappa and Omas have significant international presence; Montblanc, Pelikan, Lamy and Faber Castell produce quality items and new products are regularly introduced by Parker, Watermans and Sheaffer.

A fountain pen is not challenged by environmental issues, health risk or oil prices; it can be a thing of beauty, true sentiment and, providing it has been repaired properly a 'thing o' purpose' TO USE!

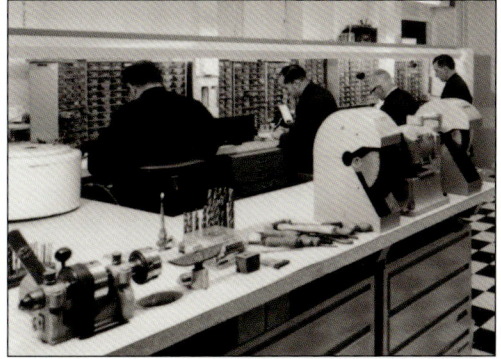

Parker's workshops in Bush House

Reg Phillips pen repair area in 1956 in Oxford

Letta Grosekemper cutting nibs in Ft Madison

Osman Sumer getting ready to repair at the LA Show

READY TO REPAIR

We must put ourselves in the position of the handyman who is expected to get things working again. Our task is to diagnose the problem propose a solution and correct the fault. To do that we have to have knowledge, dexterity and judgement which can only be achieved with experience.

Do I appreciate what the problem is?
Does the pen require dis-assembly?
Can I get it apart without breaking it?
Do I have the parts and skill to correct the fault?
Can I put it together again so that it works as it was meant to!

Do I know what I'm doing?

It is very important to know what you are doing, particularly if you are entrusted with a customer's pen to repair. There are well documented procedures for repairing. You must examine, record and diagnose before you decide to operate! Furthermore you must judge if you have the ability and resources to effect a complete recovery! If you do not then you had better not start! It can be great fun repairing pens but it can be embarrassing and expensive to make a mistake on someone's sentimental treasure! Believe us, things can break and mortification is a real issue in professional pen repair! For this reason we suggest that the early months, and possibly years, are spent working on your own pens before you ever think of embarking on a career in pen repair.

There are seven stages of repairing, which apply to amateurs and professionals.

Receipt and recording
Examination and Diagnosis
Dismantling
Repair/Replace parts
Assembly
Testing
Updating records, despatch or storage.

Knowledge, experience, patience, humility and honesty are vital. It is just as important to know your limitations as it is to continue learning. This book may help you try new things but do not rush at a pen without a clear appreciation of how it is constructed.

The first steps are to understand the designs, to appreciate what is inside a pen, and to find out why it stops working.

Arthur's bench ready to start in the morning and a familiar sight for his many 'students'

WHAT GOES WRONG

Bonzo's Pen

A few casualties, including the results of an attack by 'Bonzo' on Grandma's 1927 Watermans

To correct a filling problem requires a knowledge of the systems and mechanisms. Frequently the non filling is due to deterioration of a renewable part such as a seal or a rubber diaphragm or sac.

To make a pen write properly involves an understanding of nib, feed and ink flow. The most common problems are nib damage, clogged feeds or dried ink debris.

To rebuild or restore a pen with serious structural damage demands an intimate knowledge of pen materials and construction because parts may have to be remade.

Old pens, which have not been used for many years, may present a different repair challenge compared with a working pen, which has developed faults. In the first case, the old pen may simply need careful cleaning and the replacement of deteriorated renewable parts.

'In use' pens may still require dismantling but often only require adjustment. These usually arrive with a description of what is wrong. However, take care because the lay description of 'leaking' can mean at least five different things to different people.

A practical point is that most owners send the pens without being emptied. Beware of this if you unwrap your pens on the dining room table!

REPAIRING A PEN IS ABOUT RESOLVING PROBLEMS WITH
FILLING   WRITING   APPEARANCE
There isn't anything else!

ANATOMY OF A FOUNTAIN PEN

The main process in a fountain pen is the controlled transfer of ink from a bulk reservoir to writing. The ink moves through parts of a pen and the repairer must become familiar with these parts.

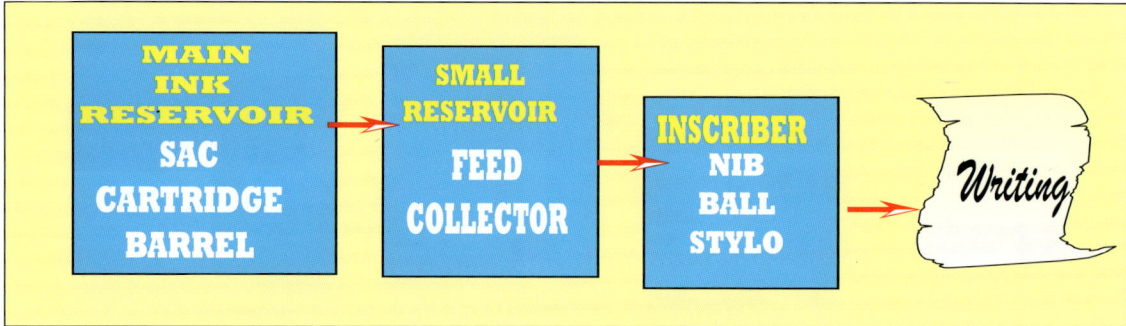

BASIC PARTS

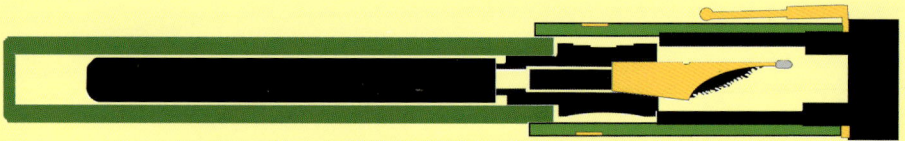

The fountain pen can be separated into 3 units

FOR WRITING
nib, feed, collector.

FOR FILLING
ink reservoir, (barrel) and all the paraphenalia for filling

FOR CARRYING AND PROTECTING
cap, clip, trim, barrel

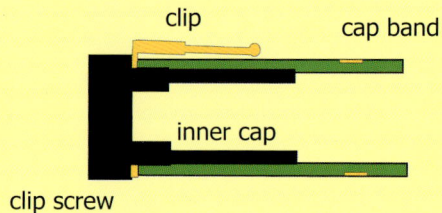

MORE COMPLEX PARTS

It is easy to understand the basic parts of a pen but when one is repairing more complex systems it can become a little confusing. For example with piston pens, safety pens and pencils there are spirals, screws, followers, pegs, seals of many different designs. Consequently we have presented diagrams to define some of the words that we use in this book to describe less familiar parts of a pen. More detailed explanations will be given in Section Two but this introduction should help clarify, for example, the difference between a piston seal and a barrel seal or a propelling spiral and a follower.

Piston pens and upfillers

The filling processes are explained in detail elsewhere but the action of filling is related to a piston, which moves up and down a cylinder (pen barrel). The piston has a seal, which is fixed to the piston body by a screw or push peg; the movement of this piston is effected by pushing, pulling or screwing a knob on the barrel top. There is no top seal because ink does not normally pass the piston.

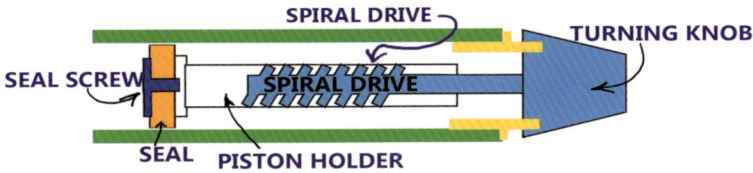

Vac fil and rod downfiller

These have a piston with a washer seal but also a barrel seal to give an ink tight reservoir. The rod pushes the piston and the vacuum is broken at the release groove.

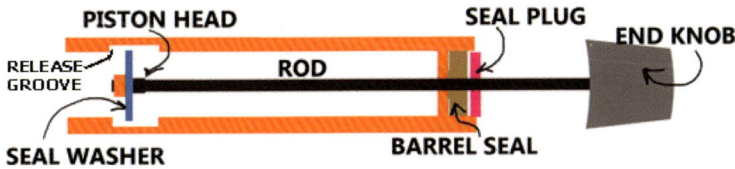

Safety pen

These pens have a retractable nib/feed holder which emerges from the barrel propelled by a spiral and drive pin, when the top turning knob is rotated. The tracking groove keeps the nib straight. The barrel seal is similar to the 'vac fil' as an ink tight seal.

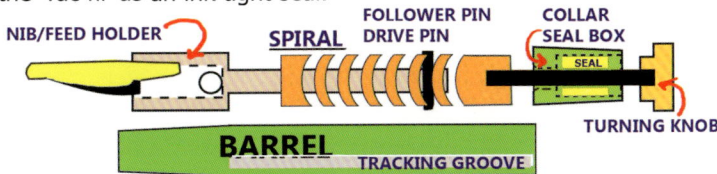

Bulb fillers

These include Vacumatics, and Ink vues that draw ink into the barrel by flexion of a rubber bulb.

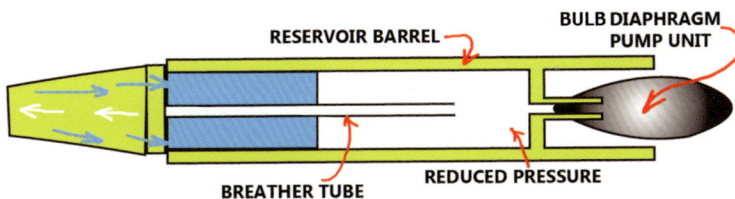

Lever and Button fillers have no complex parts.

FILLING CLASSIFICATION

Self-fill pens work by the creation of a difference in air pressure, but there is a variety of mechanisms that can be employed to utilise this effect.

Sac pens

Perhaps the simplest filler is based on a flexible sac that can be squeezed to eject air, and then released to create a low pressure volume into which the ink flows. A variety of mechanisms have been employed and they may be put into two categories, the ones that use a longitudinal bar to squeeze the sac laterally, and those that use other means. Levers, buttons and press bars are all mechanisms that use lateral pressure on the sac; they have been used on reservoir pens over a long period (Conklin crescent filler (1897) and Parker 51 aerometric (1948). Some sac squeezing mechanisms use longitudinal compression by means of a button (Swan Visofil V); others use air pressure (Sheaffer TD, Chilton).

Rigid reservoir pens

In the 1930's many refinements were added to pen design, the chief of these being ink visibility. This quality can be achieved with sac pens (e.g. Sheaffer transparent sections, Parker 51 transparent ink sacs and Visofil V transparent buttons), but it is better with a transparent barrel, something that was made possible with the advent of advanced plastics. Ink capacity is potentially much greater than for a sac pen. The mechanism for filling the barrel may be by piston or by diaphragm.

Diaphragm fillers use the pen barrel as the ink reservoir. The diaphragm is typically a rubber bulb fitted to the end of the barrel; this is squeezed to eject air that is subsequently replaced by ink as the bulb returns to its normal configuration. The Dunn pen achieves the same effect by means of two telescoping cylinders. Pens will not take up much ink unless a means is provided to operate the bulb through several cycles without ejecting it again between cycles; the solution is to fit a breather tube connected to the ink channel so that air can escape from the end of the pen as the bulb is compressed. The pen will then fill to the end of the breather tube. The Parker Vacumatic is a bulb filler; in this example the bulb is turned inside out and compressed end wise. The Blackbird Topfiller and the Visofil VT are variations on the same theme. The Watermans Ink-Vue is another variation, but it uses a lever to squeeze the side of the bulb. This class of pen is very sensitive to air pressure and temperature variations, and they can easily empty their contents into the owner's pocket during a flight.

Piston fillers are upfillers (syringe) or downfillers (vacfillers). The advantage of piston fillers is that there are no flexible components, so pens are less likely to leak due to air pressure variations; however, they are sensitive to temperature variations unless they are doubly insulated. Vacfillers rely on the creation of a vacuum in the barrel end as the piston is pushed down, followed by the sudden release of the vacuum as the piston seal enters a groove near the barrel mouth. The idea dates from a 1905 UK patent. Vacfillers had a remarkable run of success; lasting with their main protagonists (Onoto, Sheaffer and Eversharp) until around 1948. The main disadvantage was unreliability in filling, which is critically dependent upon high quality seals. The barrel seal must hold a vacuum, and the piston seal must do the same on the down stroke and be flexible enough to allow fluid to pass it on the up stroke.

The **syringe technique** is perhaps the obvious way to fill a pen, but unless the barrel is very long, the problem remains of what to do with the withdrawn piston rod. One of the best syringe fillers was introduced as the Ford Patent Pen in 1934. The Ford uses an ingenious sliding seal that allows the plunger to be returned without emptying the pen. Typically, three operations of the plunger are required for complete filling of the reservoir, the ink being able to bypass the seal at the end of each stroke. It is probably the only self-filling system where it is possible to completely fill a full-length reservoir. A screw operated telescopic syringe fill system, where the piston is a two part assembly that retracts within itself, (e.g. Nozac and Mont Blanc 149) is now the method of choice in many modern pens. These pens typically lack the double insulation and the full barrel ink capacity of the Ford.

The **capillary filling** system (Parker 61) was a brave attempt to produce a self filling pen. It uses a roll of thin surface-profiled plastic sheeting contained within a rigid open-ended tube, the end being sealed in use by a valve in the pen barrel. By placing the open end into the ink, the pen fills by capillary action into the spaces between the layers of sheeting. The method has very good double insulated properties, but it suffers from low ink capacity, can dry out and lacks a method to flush and clean the reservoir.

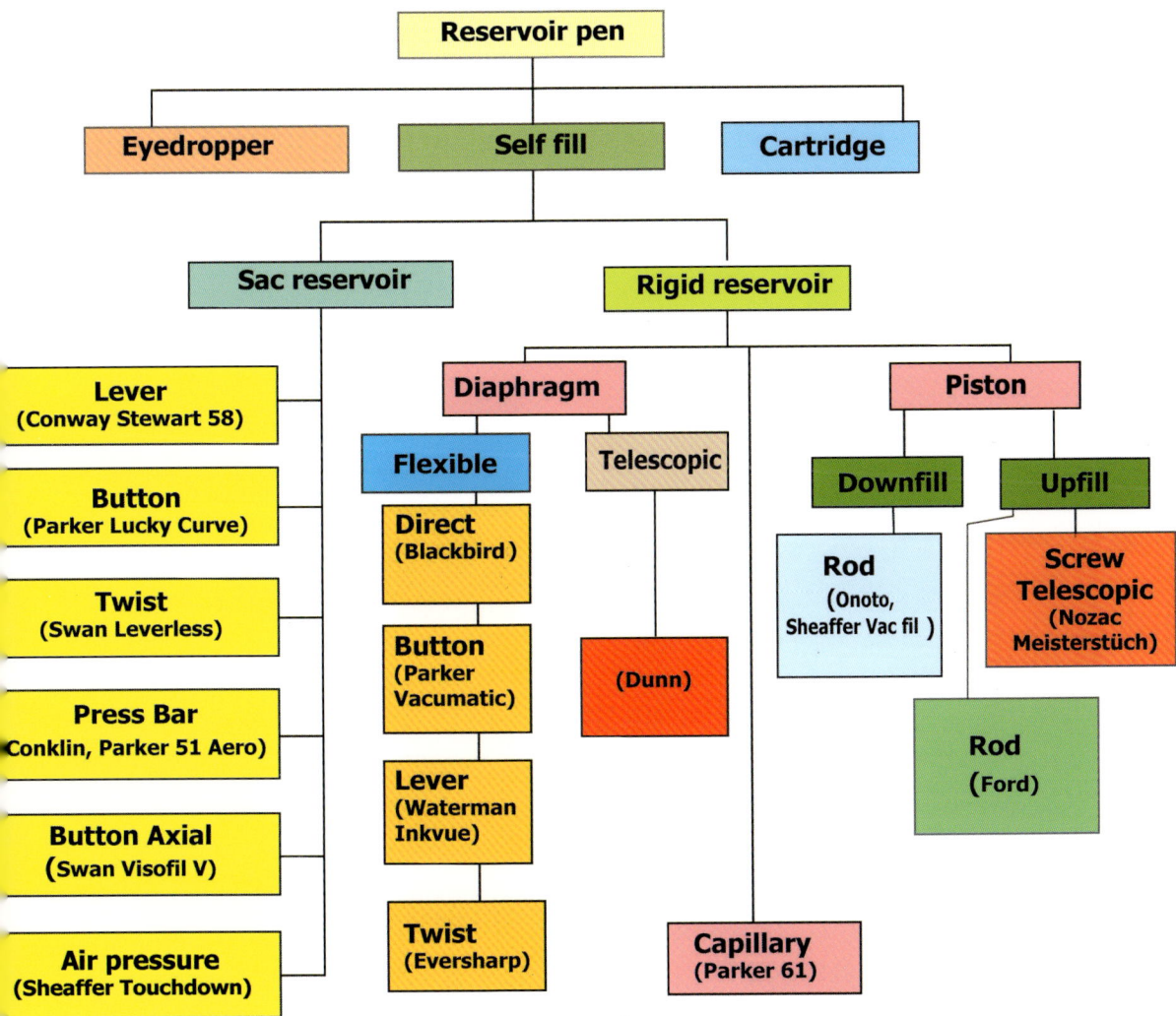

```
                          Reservoir pen
        ┌─────────────────────┼─────────────────────┐
   Eyedropper              Self fill              Cartridge
                      ┌────────┴────────┐
               Sac reservoir      Rigid reservoir
                                ┌────────┴────────────────────┐
  Lever                    Diaphragm                        Piston
(Conway Stewart 58)    ┌───────┴────────┐              ┌───────┴───────┐
                    Flexible       Telescopic       Downfill        Upfill
  Button
(Parker Lucky Curve)   Direct                        Rod         Screw
                     (Blackbird)                   (Onoto,       Telescopic
  Twist                                          Sheaffer Vac fil)   (Nozac
(Swan Leverless)       Button                                    Meisterstüch)
                      (Parker        (Dunn)
  Press Bar           Vacumatic)                                  Rod
(Conklin, Parker 51 Aero)                                        (Ford)
                       Lever
                      (Waterman
  Button Axial        Inkvue)
(Swan Visofil V)
                       Twist
  Air pressure       (Eversharp)      Capillary
(Sheaffer Touchdown)               (Parker 61)
```

The Family of Filling Systems

PEN CLASSIFICATION

Classification is a means to make a large variety of items more comprehensible. Pens can be classified in many ways: Makers, Models, Filling Systems, Country, Size, Material, Style, Age, and so on. Within these classes there are many terms, which are used to describe individual aspects of pens. A few of these are mentioned to illustrate the variety. Most collectors use maker and filling system to organise their treasures.

EYE DROPPER

Fills with a pipette that was used to put drops in eyes. It emphasises the importance of filling systems, in that, the earliest pens were classified by 'How they fill!'

nib, feed, under/over, barrel, trim, taper cap, chatelaine, 'lucky curve', overlay, gripping section,

VINTAGE PEN

Normally refers to early pens made until about 1930.

piston, lever, button, sleeve, collar, safety, clip, post, pump, twist, plunger, blind cap, shut off, spiral, turning knob, head, crescent, stud, match, coin, blow, radite, flat top, streamline.

CLASSIC PEN

Pens of distinction made from the late 1920s until the 1960s. They include the bulk of collectable fountain pens.

Vac fil, Vacumatic, all manner of colours and patterns:-onyx, turquoise, ripple, cracked ice, tassie, roller clip, spring clip, touchdown, Snorkel, Viso and Vue, connector, collector, breather tube, manifold, maniflex.

MODERN PEN

From the late 60s until today. This includes Limited Editions, cartridge pens and most ball point pens. The collectability of modern pens has had an amazing growth in the last 5 years.

shell, point end, cartridge, converter, ornament, pierce tube, ratchet.

Examples illustrated are Parker Jointless, Onoto sterling silver London 1912 , Conway Stewart 60 Executive Cracked Ice, Montegrappa sterling silver hexagonal.

NIB

PEN COMPONENTS

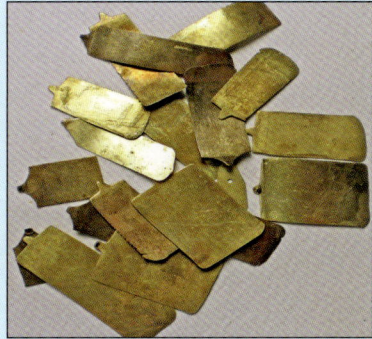

A fountain pen nib and feed must be considered together. The breakthrough of a practical fountain pen is credited to Waterman's design of the feed which stimulated others, such as Parker, to explore alternative designs. The nib evolved in association with these various feeds.

In the 1880s nibs for fountain pens were supplied by gold dip pen makers such as Foley, Mabie Todd and Bard and John Holland, who were probably making fountain pens before Watermans. Nibs in early eyedroppers were gold with 'iridium' tips, with no vent hole and frequently long slim tines, separated by a long slit. The flexibility of gold allowed the tines to spread open and also move away from the feed to give a distinctive 'wet' calligraphic script. This was not to everyone's taste and more rigid nibs were made with thicker gold and different shapes. Thicker shoulders, vent holes and shorter nibs, more suited to under feeds rather than under/over feeds, were introduced to influence flow.

By the early 20th century the 'tip' profile was being modified by makers, who were offering ranges of nibs from extra fine to double broad italic.

Little changed for almost 20 years other than the decoration of nibs with the application of platinum and palladium to give two tone nibs. At the end of the 1930s the development of tubular nibs by Sheaffer and smaller 'wrap around' nibs for the Parker 51 dramatically changed the design of pens.

The shapes of nibs were now designed together with newly developed feed systems and new materials. From the 1950s onwards small cleated nibs, pointed stylo shaped nibs, 'integrated' nibs and gold and white metal nibs inlaid into plastic were all in the shops. Traditional style nibs still existed but usually on expensive flagship pens with elaborate stamped or engraved decoration.

Nib blanks in 14ct gold

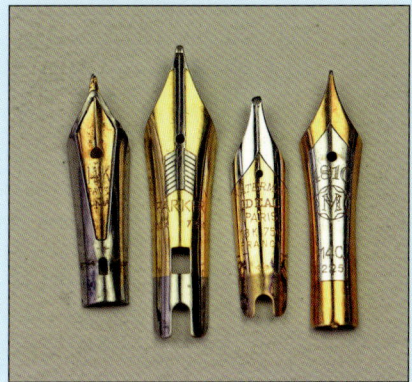

Two colour nib decoration; note unusual Skyline overlay

Smaller nibs from 1950 onwards

Problems with nibs
General damage including
- missing tips
- deformed nib tails
- cracks usually from vent hole
- plier marks

INFO *For more information on nibs including nib repair see PART THREE*

Classic pen nibs ; Swan eyedropper, Parker Big Red, Sheaffer Lifetime, 1940s Swan, Watermans 7 Red.

FEED / BREATHER TUBE

The feed both supports the nib and facilitates regular ink flow. Hard rubber was an excellent choice of material for nib feeds, mainly because of its chemistry and wetting properties. It was also relatively easy to machine and its ability to be adjusted with heat made tuning the flow of ink quite easy.

The variety of early feed design with cavities, scallops, channels and combs is diverse and makers adopted characteristic shapes. The function of a feed is to allow constant flow of ink to the nib. The surface chemistry and hydrodynamics can now be explained but in the 1880s it was an experimental hit and miss development. Whether all the claims made could be substantiated is very doubtful, but the advertising of Parker's 'Lucky Curve' and 'Christmas tree' feeds was obviously appealing. By the end of the 1920s comb or ladder feeds were used by most makers and breather tubes were attached to the feed during the 1930s.

Breather Tube

The breather tube allows more of the ink reservoir to be filled by providing an additional path for the escape of air. Without it, pens are 'one stroke' fillers because a second stroke of the filling mechanism starts by extracting ink already in the pen. The breather tube internal diameter is such that air flows down the tube more readily than ink flows down the feed channel. Capillary action in the tube ensures maintainance of the air pressure difference required to keep the ink in the pen during writing.

With the introduction of hooded pens and newly designed ink collectors the feed became a simple grooved rod. 'Collectors' are really part of the feed system. Initially they were separate units which were assembled into a shell, called in some maker's technical manuals 'the collector housing'. In time this slitted structure was built into the housing or combined with the feed shaft. Modifications had to be made to cater for cartridge pens. One end of the feed was thin, designed to fit intimately into the cartridge through the pierce unit and the other end was a bulbous support unit

Parker -two designs of Lucky Curve feed, Waterman eyedropper feed, Swan, Sheaffer, Pelikan and modern Watermans feeds

with grooves to secure the nib. In some cases the pierce unit was part of the feed (Sheaffer). The channels in the feed were usually large to ensure good ink flow from a cartridge.

The moulding of the collector and feed together created a unit, which is now standard in most pens. These are often shaped to accommodate nibs with flats or to fit into shaped sections. Some feeds fit into a collar which in turn screws into the gripping section or shell.

Sheaffer Triumph nibs demanded unique feeds and the Snorkel systems made these even more complex. In some cases the nib is fixed to the feed, in others, to the housing or shell. This makes a Sheaffer more 'interesting' to tune as there are usually seals and O-rings to add delight for a repairer.

The tolerance in the manufacture of feeds is critical. On a micro level surface roughness can produce air locks and irregular flow. Most manufacturers have at one time struggled with the performance of plastic feeds.

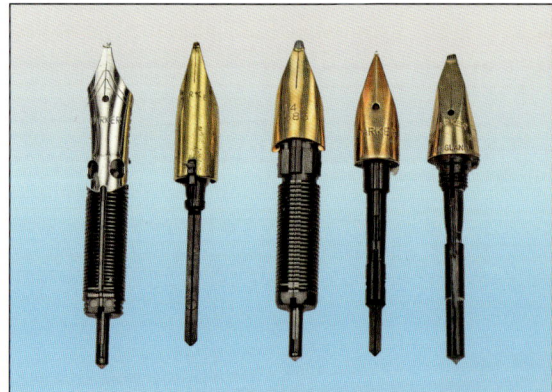

Parker cleated nibs; Sonnet, Rialto, 105, 75, 65

NIB/FEED AS A UNIT

Controlled ink flow is the fundamental property of a pen and this is influenced by how the nib and feed 'come together' as well as the individual design of each part. Most early pens had nibs located in a split feed (under-over) but this changed to an under feed by about 1915. The nib and feed were 'jammed' together and the intimacy of that association dramatically affects how a pen writes (see Tuning).

The size of the feed channels is designed to supply sufficient ink to the nib and maintain the reservoir in the combs and scallops. A double broad nib will 'use' more ink than an extra fine and some companies produced nibs with larger channels for very broad nibs (Ford and Parker).

Parker's 1960 UK Mechanics guide devotes a full page of explanation of the Duofold combs and half moon intermediate ink storage. This was introduced to compensate for surges of ink due to hand heat. This manual also contains instructions on the use of a 'Go No Go' tool for 51 collectors and a brass nib gauge for positioning nibs correctly; past practices that are rarely if ever used by any of today's repairers.

Modern nib and feed adjustment is not left to chance, notches, grooves, cleats and prongs ensure the nib and feed are in the correct position. e.g. Parker 61, 65, 75, Sheaffer lady and 444.

From a repair stand point the cleanliness of feeds is vital and the channels must be clear. A nib wedge or fine scalpel or feeler gauge is ideal for cleaning.

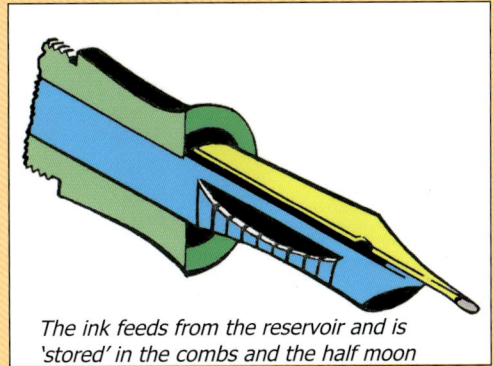

The ink feeds from the reservoir and is 'stored' in the combs and the half moon

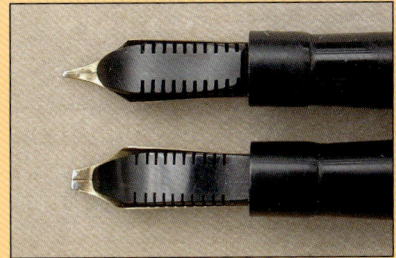

Two extremes of Ford nibs

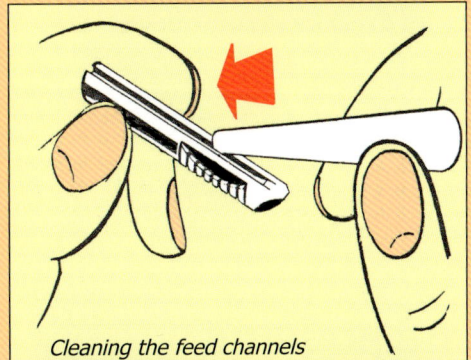

Cleaning the feed channels

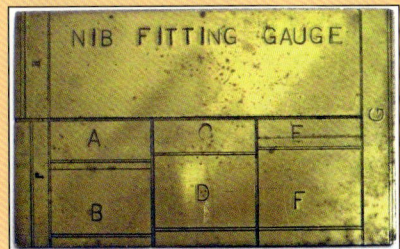

NIB FITTING GAUGE

Problems with feeds

- Restrictions in channels or breather hole due to sediments from ink drying out
- Greasy feeds; they must be clean!
- Broken combs
- Damage by vandal repairer, plier marks, drift marks, breather tube hole damaged
- alignment

Sections to Nib tips		
Line A	Demi Duofold – Victory V	
" C	New Duofold – Victory IV	
" E	Senior Duofold – A/F Duofold	
A1	Slimfold	**Feed to Nib tip**
Line B	Demi-Duofold – Victory V – Slimfold	
" D	New Duofold – Victory IV	
" F	A/F Duofold – Senior Duofold	
" J	Parker "21"	
Line G	Parker "51"	**Shell tip to Nib tip**
" H	Parker "21"	

GRIPPING SECTION

Note the changing shapes from streamlined to stub, with edges for sealing against the inner caps and pegs for sac attatchment.

Early fountain pens had a short plug to seal the barrel/reservoir; this was drilled out to accommodate the nib and feed. The nib was wedged firmly in position by the feed and gripped by this section, which in time became known as the 'gripping section' or shortened to 'section'.

The design of the section developed along with other pen parts. Originally sections were tapered to fit inside slip caps; in time sections were ridged to reduce slip cap cracking. Screw fitting and inner caps influenced the shape of sections and a broad flange was required to give a good seal with the inner cap. The greatest change to section shape came with the adoption of rubber sacs as ink reservoirs because a peg or nipple was required for attaching the sac.

Most early sections screwed into the barrel although some did push in e.g. the Parker jointless. The threaded section gave a reasonably good ink-tight seal but with the introduction of sac reservoirs it was no longer essential for the section to be ink-tight with the barrel. Push in sections were therefore adopted by most pen makers, but some continued with screw fit sections, so there is a mix even in the same company e.g. Duofold senior flat top (thread); streamline (push).

Note that there is sometimes a weakness if there is insufficient material between the internal section threads and external cap threads. Barrel reservoir pens require a screw fit but do not need a sac peg e.g. Vacumatic and Ink Vue sections. Other pens incorporate internal modifications e.g. to 'shut off' the ink when not used, but in general the section was a simple stepped structure accepting a sac and a feed/nib. The design is essentially the same today but often with a metal tube to support a cartridge and an inner thread to accommodate a 'screw in' nib.

CAUTION

> **Problems With Sections**
> - plier marks and chips
> - loose feed
> - broken peg

NIB HOUSING

Sheaffer nib unit and Parker 45 illustration

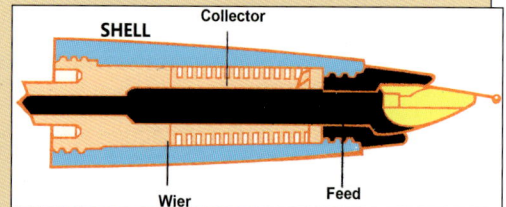

SHELL
Collector
Wier
Feed

There had to be some more appropriate terminology with the advent of the Parker 51 and it's challengers. There was no longer a section but a shell or housing which contained a collector, nib and feed, that was attached to the barrel by a connector. Housings became more and more complex with the 1950s and 60s developments of cartridges and converters. Injection moulded housings were shaped internally to facilitate the correct positioning of components such as collectors, seals, snorkels, cartridge sleeves and pierce units. The proliferation of designs meant that the 'innards' of every housing were different and the pen repairer had to treat each pen with careful reference to the manuals.

The housings in some cases had the nib screwed onto or inlaid into the shell (Sheaffer) and in some cases the shell was the nib (Parker Falcon, T1). Special tools were frequently required to unscrew internal parts.

The barrel as a handle

The pen barrel is the 'handle' of the pen. It is the largest part of the pen; it's colour and shape influence the customer while the dimensions and weight dramatically affect the appeal of the pen.

The barrel as a reservoir

Eyedropper pens use the barrel as a reservoir, as do bulb fillers and piston pens of all types. If there are any moving parts for filling systems, seals may be required (e.g. Onoto, Sheaffer Touchdown). The replacement of barrel seals is one of the most frequent repair tasks.

The barrel as a cover

This is a protection for the reservoir such as cartridges, converters or aerometric systems. In these cases, the barrel is removable to access the filling system. Alternatively the barrel is fixed, and consequently is fitted with a lever, pump, button or piston. In some cases more complicated filling mechanisms are built in (Snorkel, Visofil, Safety pens).

Blind caps/turning knobs

These are streamlined to the barrel shape and are either fixed to a piston rod, or screw off to expose a button, pump or turning knob.

The barrel attachment

To the cap - most barrels are threaded to accommodate the cap or, if not, there is a threaded barrel ring (Sheaffer) or a shaped barrel ring to click fit with the cap.

To the section - the inner barrel can be smooth or ribbed to accommodate push in sections, or threaded for a section or connector. There is quite a variety of threads, which include early single start and multi-start (see Threads). Later pens such as the Parker aerometric range require the barrel to be removed for filling.

Both internal and external threads can wear and suffer damage by cross-threading or stressing. Barrel cracks are a serious repair defect; not only for attachment of caps and sections but for ink and air leakage from the barrel reservoir (Vacumatic pens, piston pens and air pressure pens (Sheaffer Touchdown).

Decoration with overlay (Waterman, Stylochap); engine turning (Onoto, Sheaffer, Parker) and painting (Sheaffer)

Mixed barrel types; Crocker hatchet, Ford cover, Watermans pump, Croxley lever and Parker button.

Examples of barrel reservoirs; Waterman, Pelikan, Parker, Onoto, Sheaffer, Eversharp.

Barrel decoration

This is the largest part of the pen to see and to hold so it is frequently decorated by chasing, fitting gold bands, overlays or lacquer painting. Blind caps are often in contrasting colours or adorned with metal trim and decals.

Barrel shape

Earliest barrels were simple cylinders and streamlined shapes were introduced at the end of the 1920s. The style and shape of a pen is important for its appeal. Flat top, streamlined or asymmetric curved shapes have all been used.

Barrel dimensions

It is not by accident that most pens are 15cms long and 1.2cm diameter, because these are the most comfortable dimensions for most writers.

Barrel weight

Most of the weight of the pen is in the barrel and pens which are either too heavy or too light are tiring to use. Preferences vary, but most popular pens weigh 15-25 gms. The balance of a pen is a subjective term but shape and weight have a major influence on why a pen suits an individual.

Problems with barrels

- material discolouration, shrinkage and in some cases splits along spiral lines.
- crystalisation of barrels (some Dorics, Sheaffer and Waterman 100 year)
- stretching or gaping of the lever slot
- cracks in barrel threads
- cracks in barrels (Sheaffer PFM, Touchdown)
- worn threads
- wear due to posting

Pen weight gms with cap; Parker Big Red=25gm ; Parker 61=18gm -Sheaffer Snorkel=19gm; 1910 eyedropper=10gm; Flighter 51=24gm; Montblanc149=30gm

CAP

Caps initially had one function - to protect the nib. In time they developed into the foundation unit for the clip and the means of maintaining the pen 'ready to write'.

Most caps were push on 'slip' caps until the early 1900s and were superceded by threaded (safety) caps. Screw on caps were used by most makers until push on caps were re-introduced at the beginning of the 1940s. Today pens are produced with both push-on and screw caps.

Early push-on caps

The earliest caps were a cylindrical tube with breather holes and a slight inner taper to fit

tapered pen barrels. Caps were susceptible to splitting if pushed on to the pen too firmly, so reinforcing bands were added to strengthen the cap lip, and in time these became distinguishing and decorative features.

Early eyedroppers were prone to leakage or seepage if not kept upright, consequently pouches in leather and metal were made to carry the pens in a pocket. The Waterman riveted clip cap was patented in 1905 and from that date the cap became the location for clips with a variety of designs and fittings.

Threaded caps

Threading the cap and barrel was an obvious step

Inner caps and springs
Parker 75, 51, 61cloud,
Lucky curve Duofold

Decoration on caps and different clip positions; Aurora, Stylochap, Swan, Hancock, Watermans, two Eversharp.

to keep both parts together in the pocket. Caps were bored from rod and threads cut near the cap lip. Two-piece caps with a plug at one end were favoured by some makers (Parker). This made it quite easy to fit 'washer' clips or create an inner cap.

The inner cap

This was introduced to prevent the pen from drying out when not in use. This was usually a cylindrical insert, which was designed to give an air tight seal with the section lip. Parker used the cap screw to form the inner cap but Waterman and Sheaffer made inserts which were pushed in to the cap. Some inner caps had a secondary function of securing the clip e.g. Conklin.

From the 1940s plastic moulded inserts replaced the old style rigid inner caps and they remain a vital part of today's pens.

Push on metal caps

Most caps were screw on hard rubber or synthetic until the advent of the Parker 51 and metal caps. Sheaffer continued to use threaded closure with metal inserts and metal threaded barrel rings but Parker and Waterman moved to push on caps which contained a clutch to hold the cap on the pen. These caps engaged with a ring on the barrel or had a ledge in the inner cap which clicked over a profiled section.

Cap decoration

Undoubtedly part of cap decoration and appeal is the clip, but the body of the cap, like the barrel, is a visual item. Metal caps were engine turned, lined, hammered, lacquered, polished, etched, colour patinated and made in gold, silver and other metals. Many pens had plastic barrels with contrasting metal caps. Plastic caps offered a variety of colour options and were decorated with bands.

The clip screw offered further scope for decoration and like the blind cap it was often a contrasting colour.with ornate shapes or set with a pearl tassie.

Cap bands

From the 1920s cap bands have adorned most caps. Broad, thin, single double, triple and deco were part of a pen and a way to date it. Cap band replacement is a frequent repair.

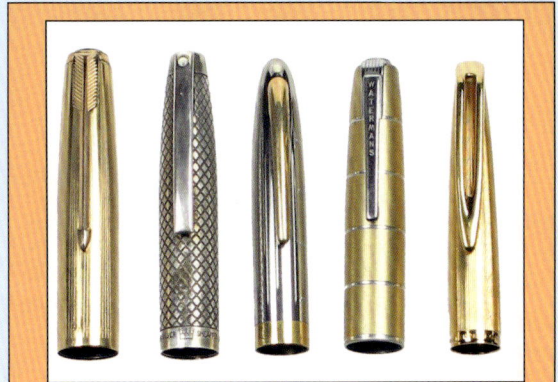

Metal caps with a variety of decoration; Parker Sheaffer, Waterman

Ring clips Conway Stewart, Parker, Wyvern with a variety of cap bands

Air Holes reduce condensation and if blocked can cause overpressure and ink can be 'vacuumed' out when a pen is uncapped.

Cap Problems
- dents, cracks, chips
- torn out clips, rings missing
- shrinkage, unwinding spirals
- threads worn, innercap split
- clip turning marks
- cap bands missing

THREADS -an effective way of cleaning barrel threads is to use a toothbrush with stiff bristles cut down to 3mm and for inner cap threads use a stiff small bottle brush.

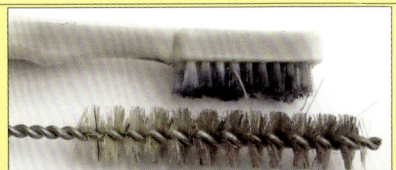

TIP

CLIP

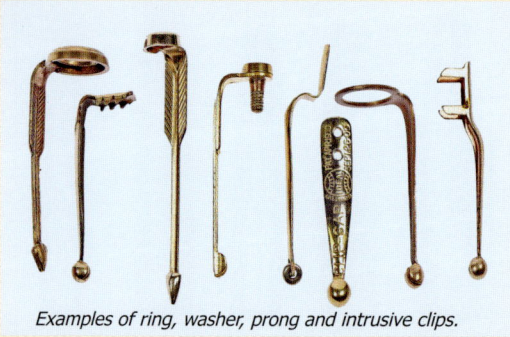

Examples of ring, washer, prong and intrusive clips.

Early pens had no clips and even today a number of pens are made without clips. The majority of pens were designed for the pocket and consequently 'clipped'. The clip is the logo or identity badge of a pen. The range is enormous and even in a single company the variety is often surprising. Clips are an important aid in dating pens.

The cap was the obvious place for the clip. Initially accommodation clips were fitted to eye droppers. In 1905 Watermans patented the 'Clip Cap' and these were riveted on to the pen but it was not long before a wide range of different designs were being used.

Early Swan, Waterman and Onoto accommodation clips

Clips can be classified by their attachment to the cap. In broad terms they are attached 'onto' or 'into'; the majority attach by some screw mechanism to the top of the cap.

Washer clips

These are secured through a ring by a single or complex clip screw unit. From the 1920s Parker used the washer clip with an integral inner cap and vulcanite clip screw and this system was copied by many UK manufacturers until the 1950s. Makes such as Mentmore, Wyvern, Valentine (pre and post Parker), Stephens, Onoto all used 'washer' clips.

By the 1930s pens had progressed to more streamlined shapes and the washer clips became smaller in diameter and consequently required a stronger fitting. Threaded brass bushes secured the clips, which were disguised with a tapered 'tassie' or clip screw.

Riveted and pronged clips

Watermans used the riveted clip until the 1930s and then opted for pronged clips, but by the 1940s they also had adopted a screw clip. Sheaffers first clips were pronged, protected by an inner cap. In the 1940s they moved to intrusive clips secured by a clip spring.

Intrusive clips

Swan and early Conway Stewart clips fitted through slots in the cap and were secured by small plates on the inside; early Eversharp, Sheaffer and Conklin used clips that were secured by the inner cap and this principle was still in use in the 1990s with the Parker 25. By the late C20[th] the Parker Duofold, the Waterman Man100, Montblanc 149 and Sheaffer's Targa had progressed all the way back to washer clips.

Tassies and clip screws

They are important in repairing because frequently tassies are missing and may have to be made. Brass bushes have different threads (Parker conveniently approximate to odd numbered BA sizes and hard rubber clip screws are usually 36tpi (see Replacing a clip).

> **Clip problems**
> - broken, brassed or twisted
> - clip rotation marks the cap
> - no spring
> - loss of temper due to soldering repair

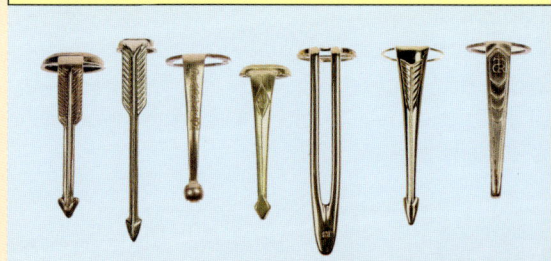

Top mounted clips are the most common -Parker (4), Waterman, Conway Stewart and Onoto.

Variety is the spice of life when it comes to levers, buttons and bars. It is vital to know the main types but you will at some time encounter a new variant.
(See section on lever and button fillers for details on removal and replacement).

Simple bars

A **V Type** – a simple piece of sprung steel, both legs of equal length.

B/C **Crookbar** – the crook being anchored in the bottom of the pen barrel. A single piece of sprung steel shaped like a shepherd's or bishop's crook (J-bar).

D **Two piece crook** – Spring steel with support bar, slotted to allow a lever operation, which improves sac compression.

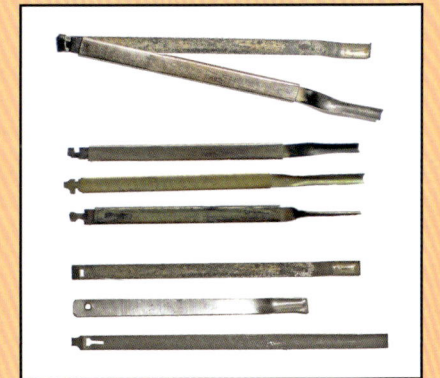

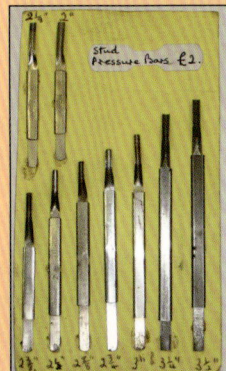

Slide bars

Used in better quality Conway Stewarts, some Watermans and Eversharps. It is a solid rail in which one or two tabs are cut and stand proud. These restrict the distance along which the bar is allowed to move, when engaged with the 2 hooks on the lever.

Angle bars

Used in Swan leverless pens. A solid bar attached to the twist button and angled off-centre, which when turned anticlockwise flattens the sac against the barrel wall. Removal and replacement of the angle bar requires a special Swan tool. Take care when removing the old sac not to damage the angle bar as it can snap off.

Anchor bars

Used in Parker Duofolds. A three piece pressure bar; the third leg contains a hook which anchors on the end of the barrel and is held in place by the button. The pressure legs can be made from standard button bars cut near the pressure plate.
Anchor bars do not require the back resistance from the section and are ideal for push fit sections.

From the top
A collection of different designs of J-bar

Two Swan leverless angle bars;

A variety of anchor bars .

Four different length slide bars

A collection of Arthur's button bar parts for sale.

Waterman lever, box and swing bar; 3 sizes of lever box; 4 button designs.

Button bars

Are the most widely used and consist of a 2 piece bar, viz; a solid bar attached to a longer sprung bar (these were made in various lengths from 40mm to 84mm).

On depressing the button the resistance of the anchor point (in most cases beside a threaded section or sac peg) causes the spring to bow and pushes the solid bar out, thereby compressing the sac. (It is useful to measure bars for future reference. e.g. AF Duofold 62mm, Big Red 82mm).

Buttons

- **Plastic buttons** – used in cheaper/wartime school pens; the button is threaded for half its length and screws into the bottom of the barrel. After the threads disengage it becomes a normal push button.
- **Top hat button** – also used in cheap/but postwar school pens. Fitted through barrel mouth and anchored with a flat collar.
- **Twist button** – a Swan patent used in Swans and Blackbirds. A screw cam action moves the bar down towards the nib end and compresses the sac. Part of the section thread is cut away to allow the conventional pressure bar to sit inside the thread (the twist button on leverless Swans is a different design and is attached directly to the angle bar).
- **Brass button** – the most popular type which is sprung through the bottom of the barrel.
- **Aluminium button** – part of an assembly secured to the two postwar Parkers – Victory and Duofold. The button is fitted into a collar which is secured in the plastic barrel.
(Note. Some Conway Stewart button fillers have a total bar assembly screwed into the button end hole from the inside; the Stephens button socket is threaded in and tightened with a small C spanner).

Levers

A lever is a simple 'key' anchored into an opening cut in the side of a pen barrel. Its function is to actuate a pressure bar which squeezes the rubber sac. The shape is usually a U channel bar , drilled in one or two places (to suit the varying barrel diameters of different models) with a thumb tab, which is often stamped with a logo. There are long levers such as hatchet fillers but most have a dimension about double the barrel diameter and are pivoted at a point that allows full sac compression.

Pivots

The bar rotates on a pivot which can be
- a C-clip which fits into an internal groove or two or three coils (Conway Stewart).
- a barrel pin, which fits into a pre-drilled hole in the barrel (Conklin).
- a pivot pin, which fits into the sides of a lever box (Watermans).

Attachment of the pressure bar to the lever

- None but the end of the lever rides on the profiled pressure bar.
- Through protrusions on the end of the lever (Waterman, Conway Stewart)
- Direct attachment through a loop or tab (Swan).

Problems with bars, levers and buttons

Bars - corrosion; loss of flexibility

Levers - broken tab, particularly Conway Stewart
- broken pivot; - broken lever box (Waterman)
- deformed barrel caused by too strong a J-bar or too strong a C-clip
The slot is a point of weakness and some pens such as Swallows and Conway Dinkies are rarely found without a stretched barrel.

TOOLS

This section lists the hand tools that you should have to repair pens and also some useful tools that make it easier.

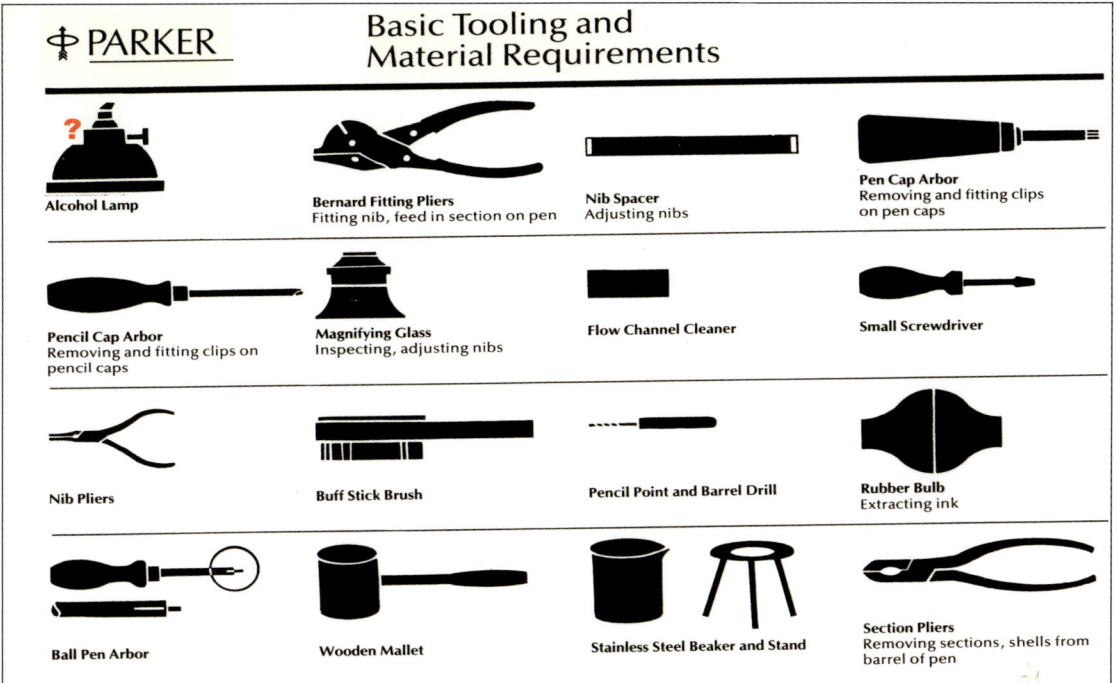

♦ PARKER

Basic Tooling and Material Requirements

Alcohol Lamp

Bernard Fitting Pliers
Fitting nib, feed in section on pen

Nib Spacer
Adjusting nibs

Pen Cap Arbor
Removing and fitting clips on pen caps

Pencil Cap Arbor
Removing and fitting clips on pencil caps

Magnifying Glass
Inspecting, adjusting nibs

Flow Channel Cleaner

Small Screwdriver

Nib Pliers

Buff Stick Brush

Pencil Point and Barrel Drill

Rubber Bulb
Extracting ink

Ball Pen Arbor

Wooden Mallet

Stainless Steel Beaker and Stand

Section Pliers
Removing sections, shells from barrel of pen

Most repair manuals have a silhouette of tools required for repair and there is no limit to the number of useful tools one can assemble. Professional repairers rarely hesitate spending money on tools which will save them time and help them to do a job with less risk of damaging a pen. Repairers often make their own tools; it is essential to be able to make widgets for specific jobs. Some repairers enjoy making tools more than repairing pens!

Basic tools

The basic tools you cannot do without are
Section pliers
Dental picks
Small files
Knocking block and rods
Small screwdrivers
Long nose pliers
An eyeglass
Hot air supply

Section Pliers

The section pliers are most important. Plug lead pliers work but better friction is obtained with rubber and the factory designed pliers. These have curved jaws and use rubber tube. More than one set can be useful with very tight joints.

Pliers of all sorts

Small pliers for removing pins, parallel pliers for removing snorkel tubes or fitting nibs; nib pliers for straightening nibs; long nosed pliers for fitting pressure bars; for pencil nozzles, clip screws. Most pen repairers have a plier fetish!

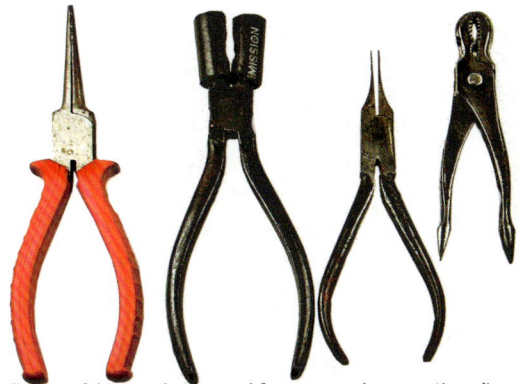

Four useful items; long nosed for pressure bars, section pliers ex factory, nib pliers with notch to avoid tip, pencil pliers.

Variety of rubber tubes

Knocking block plates and rods

Adjustable heat hairdryer

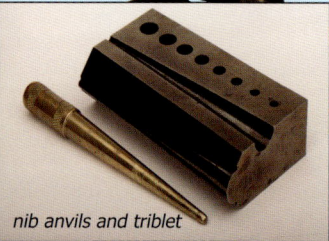
nib anvils and triblet

Scraper for sac residue

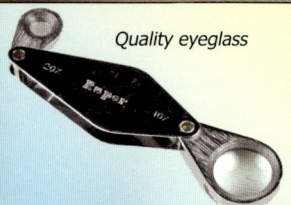
Quality eyeglass

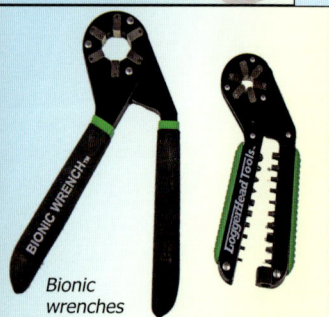
Bionic wrenches (loggerhead pliers)

Screwdrivers

Most screws are slotted and a range of driver sizes is essential; e.g. unscrewing clip bushes, fitting end knobs on Sheaffer. Spanning screw drivers are important for clip work but if made by grinding a notch out of a normal driver, they should be tempered otherwise they might bend.

Punches

A wide range of diameters of round punches for pin or section removal and also a small chisel punch for clip removal (e.g. Jotter and Falcon clips). Pieces of tube can be utilised for section drifts.

Knocking block

There are various options. One can easily make a block with different hole diameters. Wood with metal plates and nylon blocks fitted into tube are two examples that can be purchased or can easily be made. Metal drill gauges, gem gauges or sewing machine templates provide a greater variety of sizes and are very useful for pencil and ball pen repairing.

Drills and Dremels

A good set of 'number' drills and letter drills can serve as measuring gauges. A drill used in a pin vice is a very good way of cleaning out debris such as blocked pencil nozzles and air holes. The use of a big drill is sometimes necessary to remove broken parts but small drills or engraving or dental burrs are more likely to be used. Most small scale tasks such as removing rivets from clips or the ball from a Vac pump can be achieved without a Dremel but it can make it much quicker.

Scrapers, files and dental picks

Scrapers are vital for removing hardened sacs from pegs and old triangular files ground down make superb hand scrapers. Dental picks are another adaptable item and they can be heated and bent to make tools for scraping barrels, removing seals, fitting O-rings and general cleaning of metal surfaces. A set of 'Swiss files' is invaluable for cleaning surfaces, enlarging round holes and rectangular slots, cleaning threads ...etc

Surface plate

A heavy metal plate gives stability when removing sections or removing pins from barrels or knobs.

Clamps

The investment in a variety of clamps for Parker and Sheaffer pens with different collets is only justified if one is intending to repair a lot of pens. Many clamps can be made easily or economic ones purchased on the internet. They undoubtedly make some jobs easier

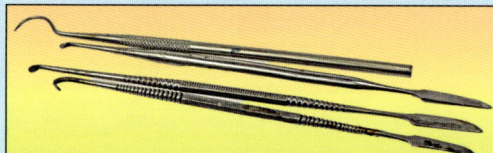
Dental picks and probes

Inner cap depth gauge

Easily made from a piece of rod and tube. It is an important tool when refitting nibs and one rarely referred to in any manual.

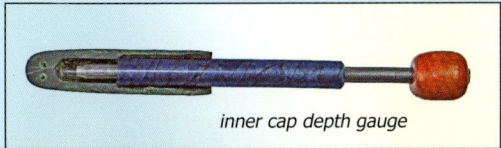
inner cap depth gauge

Cap arbor

This is a rod with a tapered end, which holds the cap firmly and makes it easier to work on the cap. It is particularly useful when dealing with metal caps. The Parker ratchet tool for ball pens is simply a slotted rod.

Parker clamp set

thread cleaners

Measuring equipment

Digital callipers are useful for measurements of sections and feeds; anyone using a lathe will have their own sophisticated kit.

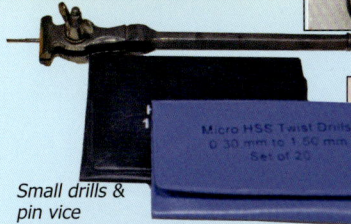
Small drills & pin vice

Inspection lamp

For examination of the insides of pens a fibre optic inspection lamp is invaluable. There are various models of these available from the internet or your local hardware store.

watchmakers staking punch

Glasses and magnifiers

An range of eyeglasses for examination and an illuminated head lens for intricate work.

Feed adjustment clamp

Proprietary tools.

The number of proprietary tools is endless and how much effort you spend in acquiring a range of tools depends upon the extent of your repairing activity. Investment in a speciality inner cap puller may not seem justified if you rarely service Sheaffer, Waterman, Swan or older pens.

Some tools are essential e.g. for removal of Parker 65 collectors or refitting Sheaffer Reminder springs (see Section Two).

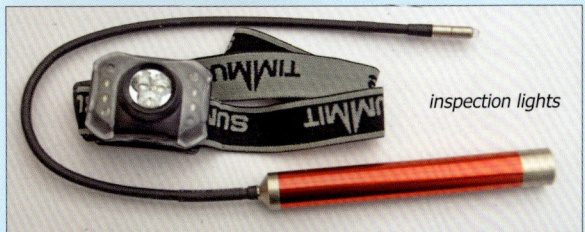
inspection lights

range of bottle brushes

A gas torch

Invaluable for modifying dental picks, removing metal cap inserts, re-annealing lever box lugs and clip prongs, soldering pencil tubes and burning plastic to get metal spares from scrap pens!

Dremel plus burrs

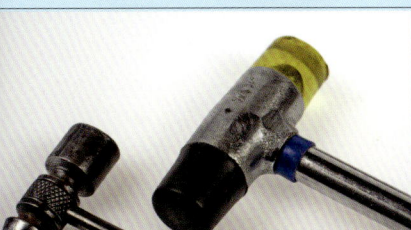
light hammers wood, plastic rubber and fibre as well as metal are useful

FACILITIES

Many pens can be repaired with basic tools on a kitchen table and this is illustrated by the show repairers who arrive with their small bag of tools. However repairing can be a messy business and if a lot of repairing is planned, try and set up a dedicated area.

The work bench and dismantling.

There should be sufficient space for spreading out trays or boxes and storage for parts and tools. How one works is very personal - the 'corporate' photos show tidy benches and minimum tools but in the frenzy of doing 40 repairs a day, it is rarely like that and benches do become cluttered. However it is nevertheless important to try and maintain at least one 'clutter free' area for dismantling. Pen parts are small and they can easily 'disappear' beneath a debris of tools and containers.

Good discipline is to have a dismantling tray with small containers for parts. Repairers are often urged to work on one pen at a time but it is often more efficient to do similar operations in parallel providing one has a set of labelled containers.

Light

Good general lighting is essential and an angle poise lamp with magnifier can be ideal for close work.

Warmth and water

One cannot underestimate the importance of soaking to facilitate dismantling. It may be tempting to 'attack' a pen quickly, but dry pens break and soaked pens come apart. It may be necessary to soak overnight, but take care because some black hard rubber pens will discolour and casein pens (Conway 550 and some Burnhams) catch an incurable swelling disease. You do not have to completely immerse a cap to soak the

inner cap; stand it up in a polystyrene block with the breather holes plugged up! The availability of running water is a boon for washing out ink filled caps and barrels; the process is aided by a stiff bottle brush. Make up brushes are excellent for cleaning out sections.

Warm water

Many pens were assembled with adhesive sealant and this must be softened. Sheaffer adhesives, in general, soften at 140°F (60°C). It is virtually impossible to dismantle tubular nibs and sections without soaking them at 150-160°F.

Untrasonic bath in deep tray   Electric heater with cast iron pan and sifter   Gas torch

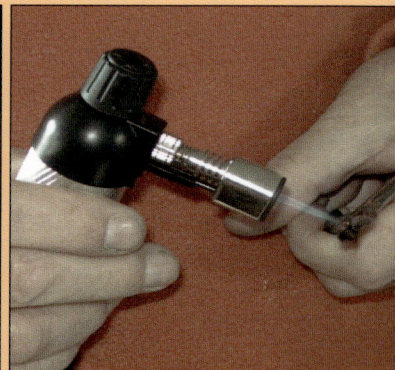

An electric heater and sturdy pan with a thermometer will provide all you need. Do not guess at the temperatures because if you go above 160^{0}F certain plastics will become irreversibly opaque and the pen will be spoiled. Sometimes boiling water has to be used, for example to tune a hard rubber feed to a nib, but never boil a complete plastic pen!

pH

As most inks are acidic, cleaning is best effected using a basic solution, but do not go to extremes. A pH of 14 will burn your fingers and cause untold damage to pens. Aim for pH 10, which is best achieved by ammonia or a small amount of well dissolved detergent washing powder.

Drying

Shaking, absorbent paper or pipe cleaners will dry most pens. If you have an airline use it.

Ultrasonic bath

A good quality bath with timer and stainless steel inner is preferable. This is no longer an expensive investment and will make life a lot easier. We glibly say this but Arthur never needed one! Use a mesh frame so that pens can be vertically positioned in the bath; a detachable gauze container (such as an in line fuel filter) is very useful for nibs and feeds. Small beakers

containing oil or solvent facilitate the release of corroded metal parts.

Heat/warming parts of a pen

The early 1930s manuals invariably show a spirit lamp being used to warm a pen. It definitely works, but without experience, your valuable pen can provide a sparkling display! The source of focused heat nowadays is either a hair dryer or a paint stripper, but take care, because heat can easily destroy. Most of us have learnt the hard way!

Vice

We cannot imagine working on pens, pencils and ball pens without having a good vice. It does not have to be a large one, but it has to be firmly mounted so that it can be used for sawing, riveting or soldering.

Storage of parts

Boxes, drawers, filing cabinets, tool chests are vital! Repairers all have a box fetish but mark the parts drawers or boxes clearly to make it easy to access them without wasting time. ! Keep frequently used parts such as sacs close to hand.

FINALLY - A big rubbish bin but not located where parts can accidentally fall into it!

A selection of Laurence's tools

A useful carousel for frequently used tools

SACS

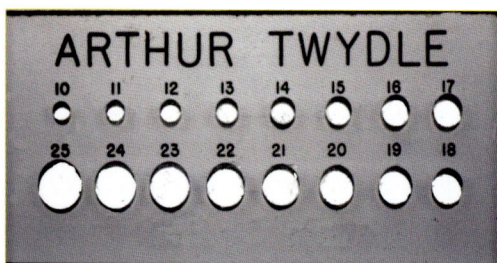

Flexible ink reservoirs made from cat gut were patented by Scheffer in 1819 but it was not until the 20th century that flexible rubber tubes became a vital component of fountain pens. Plastic tubes had a major impact from the 1940s but rubber continued to be used in convertors. Sac manufacture was a major business from the 1920s until the 1950s, but the demise of the fountain pen and the use of plastic reservoirs and cartridges reduced production to almost zero.

The revival of pen sac manufacture by The Pen Sac Company in the late 1980s has been one of the most significant milestones in vintage pen repair. Pen sacs are now available in almost all the traditional sizes and as straight, tapered, necked and in complex shapes.

The size of a pen sac is defined by the outside diameter expressed as 64ths of an inch and the length in inches. So an 18 sac x 2 ½ has an outside diameter of 18/64th and a length of 2 ½".

Straight sacs are used on most pens mainly because they can be cut to different lengths.

Necked sacs are used to fit small section pegs and give a good ink capacity or ensure a very tight fit inside a barrel (leverless Swan).

Tapered sacs are used in Skylines, for refurbishing convertors and suggested for aerometric replacement in Parker 21, 41 and 51.

Specific shaped sacs for Ink Vue (2 sizes), Vacumatic (3 sizes) and Sheaffer Imperial are all available.

An invaluable reference booklet was produced by The Pen Sac Company detailing which sac for which pen. It refers to the USA but for UK pens the majority of lever and button fillers use straight sacs (sizes range from 15 to 19; 13 or 14 for Conway Stewart Dinkies.) Swan leverless use necked sacs of different lengths to suit the models.

Plastic sacs as used by Parker in their aerometric systems have to be sealed with a good adhesive; nail varnish works very well.

Determining the sac size for a pen

An obvious way of determining the sac size is to measure the peg diameter with callipers and fit a sac one size less; there is a formula that has been proposed by The Pen Sac Company which makes it more accurate and that is included in their booklet.

An imperial drill stand offers a very useful way of measuring peg sizes.

Cutting a sac to length

It is critical to have a sac cut to the correct length. This is best done by sliding a sac into the barrel of the pen and then with the section next to the barrel (fitted position), cut the sac to fit. With button fillers the sac should never be flush with the end of the barrel but approximately 2mm clear. This allows the pressure bar to enter and the button to work freely.

Miscellaneous

Concertina/accordion sacs are not available so straight sacs have to be used with a spring.
Use thin walled sacs for Sheaffer Touchdown and Snorkels as they are more sensitive to the plunger pressure.

REPAIR PROCEDURE- GENERAL

We frequently hear from enthusiasts that it is their intention to set up a pen repair service when they retire. Many have already done this and most services on the web sites are provided by such persons.

Receipt and recording
Examination
Diagnosis
Dismantling
Correction
Assembly
Testing
Updating records
Despatch or storage.

Some of the next sections are directed at those who might have aspirations to do commercial repairs. The procedures we describe are also for the collector who might never wish to repair, but wants to have a good idea of what is involved. In fact most collectors are as adept at examining pens for defects as repairers themselves.

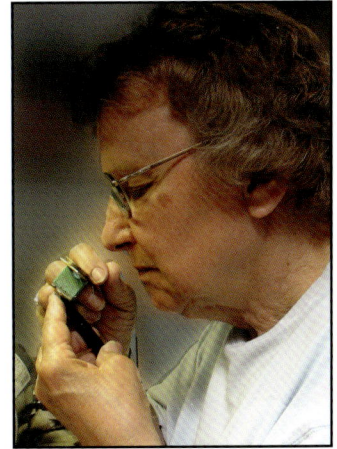

Recording

Having received a pen for repair the first step is to record: when it arrived, the owner's name and if it came with a letter, what the owner wants done to the pen; finally do they require contacting with a quote and how do they want it sent back.

Examination

The next stage is to examine the pen, initially without dismantling it. This is a vital step and important because most owners are unaware that a crack or two may have some serious consequences.

It is also essential to examine the state of a pen for ones own security. Most of us are familiar with the problems of pens arriving from Ebay and 'one man's perfect is another man's dross'. The same applies to pens for repair, and remember that pens can get damaged in the post.

Although the owner's letter may only request a new sac if you have some doubts about the pen, it is a good idea to check it. If the pen has a major defect that is not mentioned in the letter or enclosed note, make sure that you talk to the customer. Tell the owner that you have looked at the pen, and did he know that it had a cracked barrel thread or the cap was wrong or whatever.

It saves misunderstanding later if the owner is made aware of the problems.

This first examination should be detailed. The sequence is up to you but it should include a visual and eyeglass search for defects. If you have a system that includes notes then the details should be recorded.

It is not long before such an examination becomes routine and the more you see the more you know.

Delay dismantling the pen until you have completed the initial examination. Sometimes a repair is so obvious that secondary defects are overlooked, and in the end these turn out to be more significant. This is often the case with leaks. A Parker 61 will leak if the connector has decomposed but you cannot presume that is the only reason until you have examined the shell and the converter very carefully. Why an item does not fill involves an holistic examination although you know that the snorkel O-ring is the problem!

Having finished the preliminary examination, it will invariably be necessary to dismantle the pen in order to confirm in detail what repairs are required.. - You can start **DISMANTLING!.**

SPECIFIC PROCEDURES

Few repairs are possible without dismantling a pen. There are various operations in dismantling that must become routine. After the pen is in pieces, cleaned and repaired it is then put together again. These next sections illustrate the most common basic procedures .

Removing a section

Section pliers and a firm grip. A feel develops with experience.

A fibre hammer a knocking block with good edges and a solid surface. The drift rods can be made from nails and tubes. Do not use too small or too large a rod for obvious reasons.

This is usually the first step; it is the separation of the writing unit from the barrel, where the main aim is to access the nib, feed and whatever else is hidden in that part of the pen. The barrel is put aside while the 'heart of the pen' is dealt with.

Sections of traditional open nibbed pens can be push or screw fit. More than one manual recommends the gentle tapping of the barrel joint with a fibre hammer to break the shellac seal but this is not endorsed with an 80 year old pen!

The first stage is to soak and pull the section out or unscrew it using good section pliers. It is said that it rarely does harm to use a screwing action with section pliers even with a push on unit. This is probably correct, however it is better to know your pen as some pens may have innards that will twist out of shape (Visofil V) or have left hand threads (Wyvern 303).

Soaking in an upright position is preferable rather than soaking the whole pen. The use of an ultrasonic bath can aid the re-dispersion of dried ink residues.

Most sections move easily after cold water soaking but if not, heating is recommended to facilitate the removal of many parts. Too much heat will deform the pen and too little will not work, but with experience one can decide how far to go. It can, in rare cases, take days to 'release' a pen but patience is preferable to breaking it. Repeated warmth, water and ultrasound usually prevails. The section pliers are the most important tool and sometimes it is necessary to hold the barrel firmly with a small rubber sheet.

The gripping sections of later pens may have shells and hooded nibs or tubular nibs (Sheaffer) The principle of dismantling is the same, namely to use soaking and warming. Many pens were assembled with 'reversible' adhesive and this must be softened with air heating or warm water. (most adhesives soften between 140° and 150°F.)

Replacing a section

Probably more barrels are cracked putting sections back in than taking the sections out.

Frequently very tight sections require heat to remove them from the barrel and when the section is offered up cold it does not fit. The section can be 'eased' with emery paper but this is not good practice. If it came out it should go back, and it will, provided it is preheated in the same way as it was, while being dismantled. (The same procedure of using heat to put together also applies to fitting difficult feeds and nibs into sections!)

Most plastics are less brittle when warm and therefore less susceptible to cracking. Most sections are replaced resacced and that may present a problem if the sac is thick and binds against the barrel. In this case you may have to turn the peg down or find a thinner sac.

At least 50% of sections screw in and the sac may snag or twist on the pressure bar. In such situations talc is used as a lubricant (graphite is also extremely effective).

If the sac is the correct size and there is still a problem use a rod to support the sac. In this case the nib will be fitted after the section is in place.

There is a tendency to avoid such problems by simply fitting a smaller sac but this is wrong. It not only stretches the sac to extremes on the peg but reduces the ink capacity and filling efficiency. Plastic rods of a diameter 4-5mm or knitting needles are easily made into sac supporters. (see Leverless Swan)

Removing a nib

Once the section or point end unit is removed the next task is to get the nib out. With conventional pens this involves knocking out the feed.

Make sure that the section has been soaked, and is positioned firm against the knocking block and use a rod or tube of smaller diameter than the feed.

A fibre hammer or a small tack hammer is adequate. Sections that have breather tubes can be removed with a tubular drift rod but it is usually easier to pull out the tube first.

Nibs can be pulled out in some cases and the trick of working a nib from side to side with your thumb nail is worth practising as it can save removing an aerometric sac protector and plastic sac (UK 1950s Parkers).

Removing nibs from tapering sections can be a problem. Most of these pens such as Waterman Taperite, Summit and Wyvern have good fitting feeds which require solid support to drive out the nib and feed. Makers supplied clamps for such pens but it is easy to make one from wood. The clamp is made in two halves in order to release the shell section after the feed is knocked out.

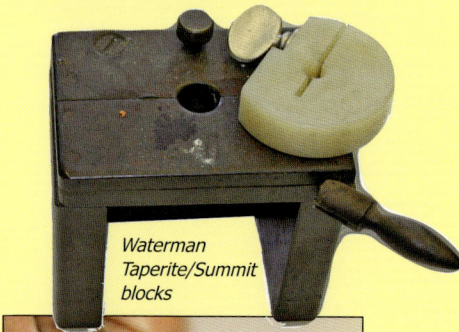

Waterman Taperite/Summit blocks

Sheaffers modified parallel pliers for nibs

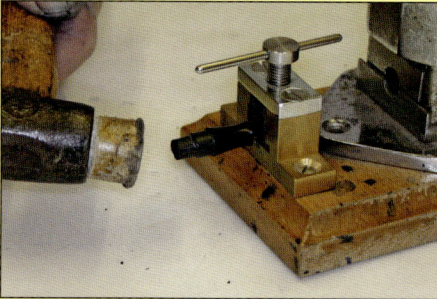

nib clamp

A nib depth gauge being used to ensure that the nib will fit within the inner cap

Use a scraper to remove the hard rubber residue - finish it with wire wool.

Replacing a nib

Manuals refer to nib position on the feed and suggest the use of parallel jaw pliers with felt or nib gripping clamps but fail to mention that the section is probably slightly oval due to enthusiastic section plier work. Furthermore the nib may well have created it's own bed so it pays to examine the inside of the section and try to refit the nib in its original position. (It is helpful to use a piece of masking tape and mark the line of the nib slit on the tape during dismantling).

The nib and feed together are pushed into the section by hand or with a pair of parallel pliers and if necessary finished off with a nib clamp.
If a nib is difficult to fit remember to use hot air to facilitate assembly. If a nib is too loose then either use a better fitting section or paint the inside of the section with shellac and leave to dry before refitting the nib and feed.
Never try and push the nib and feed further in to the section to secure the nib because it will create future problems.
The nib should 'look right'; the tapered waist of the nib should be well gripped by the section. During fitting a nib/section, if the nib is stressed by pushing too hard or with a twisting action, the nib edges can buckle or the tail of the nib can crack
However with all makes of pens, how far the nib should protrude is a little subjective. If the feed underside is marked with a notch then it gives a guide or if the section is profiled internally then the feed (presuming it is the original feed) will only go in as far as the stop. Most sections do not have stops and most feeds are without notches so the nib must be fitted so that it looks good and in proportion to the pen and does not foul the inner cap.

Checking the space for a nib

We have been surprised that many repairers who are meticulous in most matters do not routinely check the cap/nib fit with an inner cap depth gauge.
Even if the nib/feed is set to what appears to be the correct depth within the section, it is still necessary to check that there will be adequate

room for the nib when the cap is screwed on. The inner cap may be damaged or shortened and the cap or barrel threads may have been adjusted to ensure that the cap engages more threads on the barrel.

Arthur used to say that this is the most important tool in the repairer's box; it is also the easiest to make, so there is no excuse if you bend an expensive nib!

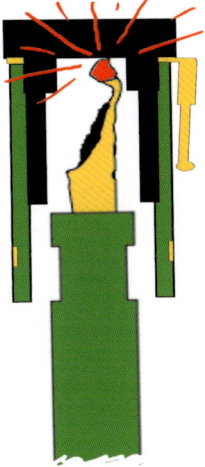

If the tool indicates that the space is inadequate, the nib can be pushed further down in the section or the inner cap can be replaced with one of the correct length. Lengthening the inner cap is preferable, but it will probably result in the cap threads failing to engage, or the cap becoming tight after less than one turn (see cap threading). If this happens, the section can be shortened, or the first few threads on the barrel can be removed if they are not engaging due to wear. It is sometimes possible to lengthen the inner cap by boring it a little deeper. The best solution for a particular pen may be a compromise between these approaches.

With the section and nib sorted out the attention is now on fitting the sac prior to refitting the writing unit into the barrel. So our attention returns to the section.

The section peg

Most sacs fit onto a section peg or nipple, which must also be completely cleaned of rubber residue. This usually chips off with a strong short bladed knife, or you can easily make a purpose scraper from an old triangular file. Take care with some pens, particularly Swan, because the peg can easily break . The nipple shapes are usually quite simple, but some pens have flanges or ribbed nipples to help improve the sac adhesion. Finishing off with fine wire wool gives a clean and receptive surface for adhesion.

Repairing a broken peg

Frank Dubiel recommended a quick solution using a cut down ink cartridge and certainly this works, but it can mean that the feed has to be shortened and in some cases the flow can be affected. The procedure we recommend is the same in

A replacement nipple fitted.

principle, but uses a brassl tube which is glued into a recess drilled into the section. This means that the feed does not have to be altered and the section peg is as good as new. The replacement peg can be made from hard rubber rod or alternatively can be cannibalised from another section. The brass tube or sheet can be obtained from any hobby shop.

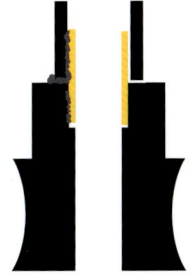

Selection of the right sized sac

It is desirable to have the correct sized sac to give the original designed ink capacity (see Sacs). Smaller sacs have the advantage of an air gap between the barrel and the sac to create some insulation and reduce the effect of external heat. However too small a sac can create a vulnerable area near the peg to tear when a button pressure bar is introduced. Sacs that are too large may come off the peg or make insertion of the pressure bar difficult.

A good compromise is that the outer sac diameter

A good fit is essential. (X) - too large or too small will give problems. Pens with small pegs and wide barrels favour the use of necked sacs.

should be the same as that of the peg. The sac can then be stretched onto the peg and sealed. Sac stretchers can be used and are useful for necked sacs but most sacs can be fitted by hand.

Sealing and fixing the sac

Shellac was the traditional material used for early fountain pens and is a good adhesive for flexible rubber onto hard rubber. Contact adhesive (rubber solution), waterproof PVA adhesive (wood glue) and varnish are also quite effective. Solvent adhesives (such as nail varnish) are required with the transparent plastic sacs and these should usually be left for a few hours before fitting into the pen. One may encounter pens with metal bands or wire to ensure good sealing of the sacs on the peg. Swan and Le Boeuf are examples of these. A different challenge with sac adhesion is presented with pump/twist fillers such as A A Waterman and Gold Starrys because they use tubes joined to a section and a plug or 'pump'. Rubber adhesive is suggested together with a crimped band or fine thread/wire. This is only recommended if there is twisting or pulling stress.

The procedure for fitting a sac;
A match the size of the sac to the peg
B push the sac half way onto the peg
C apply the adhesive
D push the sac well onto the peg ensuring that the adhesive, whether it is shellac, rubber solution or varnish, is between the rubber sac and the peg.
Capillary forces will pull a low viscosity glue into the sealing area but a syrupy mix, although it looks good, is less effective. Leave the adhesive to dry before fitting the unit back into the pen.

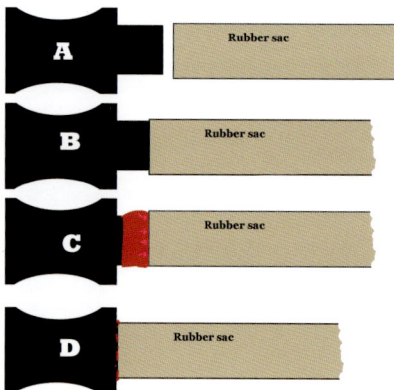

A Rubber sac
B Rubber sac
C Rubber sac
D Rubber sac

Cleaning the barrel/sac protector

Having fitted the sac onto the section it is ready to be fitted in a cleaned barrel. The old sac must be completely removed. This is usually dry and is easy to clean but sometimes it can be a gooey mess inside the barrel or at the other extreme the rubber has become so hard that it cannot be penetrated. Lighter fuel has been proposed to soften hard rubber residue but we have had little success with it.

Scrapers or dental picks can clean the majority of the debris from barrels or tubes (such as Snorkel or Touchdown tubes) and a bladed scraper or woodcarving gouge is sometimes useful with Vacumatic pens. Wire brushes or bottle brushes can be used to give a final cleaning and gun cleaning brushes are particularly useful for stubborn residues.

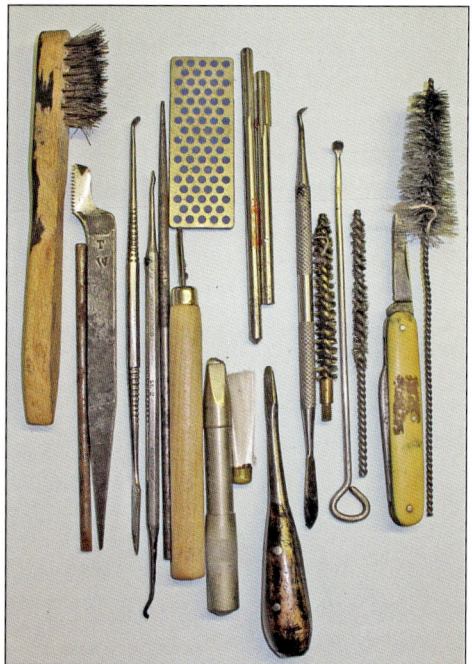

Cleaning out the old sac residue is critical and requires a range of scrapers and probes. Modified dental picks, gun brushes, reamers, probes, files, glass fibre, wire wool and wire brushes all have their place.

Replacing a clip

This is a general introduction; specific clip types are considered in section Two

Having dealt with the writing end we can now attend to other pen matters, one of which is the repair of the cap and clip. The majority of clips have screw attachments of one form or another. Early Parkers had hard rubber clip screws; 1930s models had recessed crowns with brass bushes and decorative clip screws and more modern pens had intrusive clips fixed by screws. Sheaffer and Waterman had a variety of riveted and pronged clip attachments. Early Conklin, Eversharp, Swan and Conway Stewart all had intrusive clips. Broken or missing clips means dismantling.

Dismantling

Washer clips require the hard rubber top to be removed. This involves warming and unscrewing with a pair of section pliers. Many clip screws are tapered and hard rubber jawed pliers can slip off, so a piece of rubber tube will improve the grip. Plier marks infuriate repairers and naked jaws are never justified! The new circular 'loggerhead' pliers are very effective used with a strip of fine emery paper, for such clip screws.

Examine the cap to determine whether the clip is recessed into a notch in the cap. If it is, then the clip must be held very firmly when unscrewing the retaining unit to prevent chipping the cap top, especially Swan.

Later ring clips with recessed brass bushing require removal of the 'clip screw trim' or tassie. These can be very stubborn but it is worth persevering in order to remove them in one piece. A friction pad of some sort is necessary and usually this is a rubber sheet, bung or adhesive tape. If the top does shear off then it can still be re-used with glue or replaced (see Parker 51) After accessing the metal clip bush, unscrew it and remove the clip.

Intrusive clips

Conklin, Sheaffer, Waterman and early Swan require the removal of the inner cap (see Pullers) and then either the retaining plate is removed or the prongs are released; after which the clip or remnants can be taken out. Later Swan clips are simply prised out with a screwdriver after heating (see Mabie Todd pens).

The main tools required for clip repair are screwdrivers, rubber grips and hot air.

Removing a clip is like hide and seek – the aim is to find the screw! Parker screws hide behind trim; Waterman and Conway Stewart hid the screws or threaded retaining collars inside the cap. Sheaffer Targa's screws reside behind polythene inner caps.

Small screws corrode, spacers rust and in such circumstances releasing oil can help. If extreme heat is the only solution try a clean soldering iron tip; it can often provide enough expansion to get a collar or screw started.

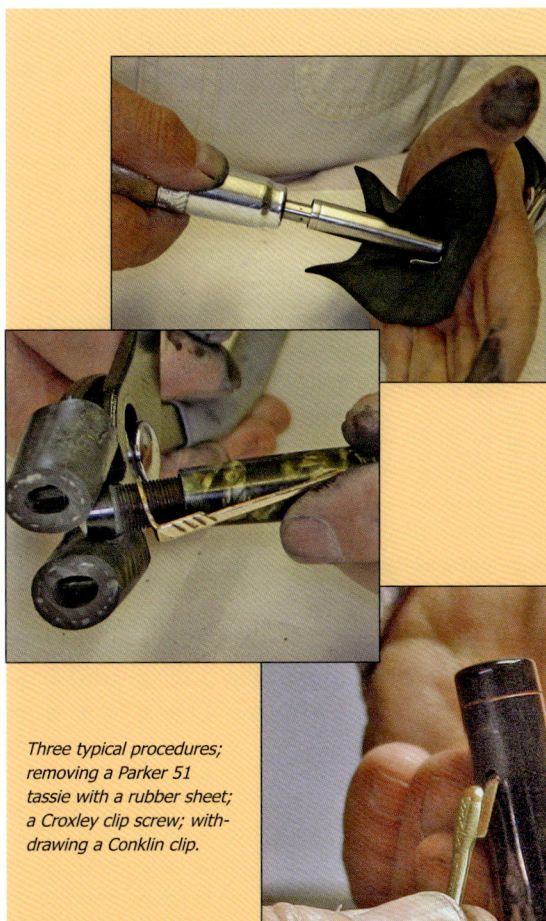

Three typical procedures; removing a Parker 51 tassie with a rubber sheet; a Croxley clip screw; withdrawing a Conklin clip.

TESTING AND TUNING A PEN

The pen should write on its own

Test, tune, test, tune, test.....................

When a pen has been dismantled, parts replaced and reassembled, it must be checked to see that it works. We regard this as the most important step in finalising the repair process.

The purpose of doing the repair was to get the pen to fill and to write; this testing is the quality control step in the process and it also offers a good opportunity to tune the pen for optimum performance.

Check that it fills

The first thing you must do is ensure that the pen fills properly and that sufficient ink actually goes in. If you have an instruction leaflet do use it; the correct and recommended procedure is important. Perhaps it is obvious, but complete writing tests can only be performed with a filled pen (see Filling and Ink capacity).

Writing

The next step is putting pen to paper by writing with the pen.

When we pick up a pen and write with it, we have an immediate reaction it. A smooth pen is a delight and a scratchy, noisy pen is one that will never be used.

Free weight test - A pen should write on it's own without any pressure.

The first test with a filled pen is the 'free weight

test'. Rest the pen in the hand, between the first and second fingers and in the crook of the thumb and as you move the pen it should draw a good line. This is not an 'in use' test but is a preliminary indicator of ink flow.

In use test

Make up a writing test page with a series of directional lines, loops and patterns that you repeat with each pen. One example is illustrated but as long as it contains up and down strokes and left to right and right to left it will tell you all you need to know about the pen.

This test page MUST be followed by at least one or two paragraphs of words written at speed. This is

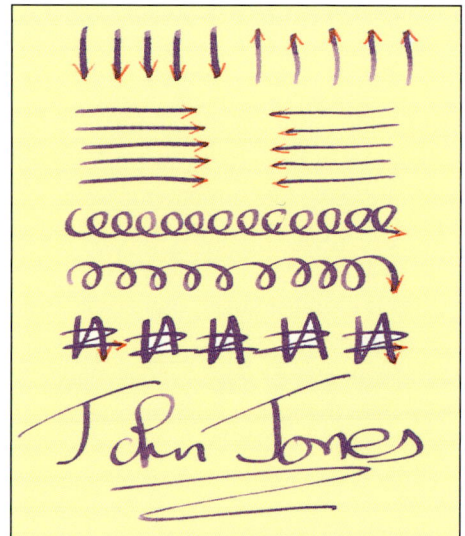

important; finally write with a light hand and then a firm (heavy) pressure. If you are ambidextrous try a few left handed strokes for completeness.

A typical evaluation could be

Flow from 'free weight test' rather faint. In use testing: scratches on the up strokes, skips after two lines, spatters a little on the left hand horizontals, rather slow to start.

Attention must now be given to correcting these defects by adjustment.

Ink Flow Adjustment

Irregular ink flow can be for a number of reasons. With an unrestored pen it can be a old sac, poor seals, dirt, sac too large for the barrel, cracks in the barrel or nib and so on as well as nib/feed adjustment. With a restored pen however, in most cases the problem is only nib/feed adjustment.

The defects are manifest as skipping, drying out, too wet, blobbing.

Nib/feed position

If the feed is too far into the section relative to the nib, the ink will not reach the nib evenly. If the feed extends too far, the ink will flow too freely and the pen will blot. The correct position is for the shoulders of the feed to be in line with the shoulders of the nib. In other words, when looking at the nib from the front, the feed should not be visible - but only just.

Correct position of nib; too much ink flow and too little.

Nib/feed setting

Manuals show you how to do this, but most have terrifying diagrams of methylated spirit heaters and potential flaming sacrifices of your recently repaired fountain pen. However, it really is quite simple to tune a fountain pen.

For even flow of ink it is essential that the feed should lie snugly against the nib. Check this by the paper test

OK

X

Slide a piece of paper between the nib and the feed. If the paper cannot be inserted, the adjustment is probably correct. But if there is a gap and the paper slides behind the feed, then the gap must be reduced by resetting the feed.

Resetting

Most feeds are made of hard rubber or vulcanite, which becomes very flexible in hot water and can be easily adjusted towards the nib. Simply immerse the nib and feed ONLY in very hot water (just off the boil) for about 10 seconds and then

gently press the feed towards the nib and hold the pressure for about 10 seconds. The gap will have been reduced and the paper test should now show the feed is snugly against the nib. If not, repeat the warming and adjustment procedure until the paper cannot be inserted. You only need a gentle pressure on the feed

Nib adjustment

Having adjusted the feed to the nib, any further adjustment necessary must be made to the nib itself. Ink flow can be regulated by adjustment of the nib tines.

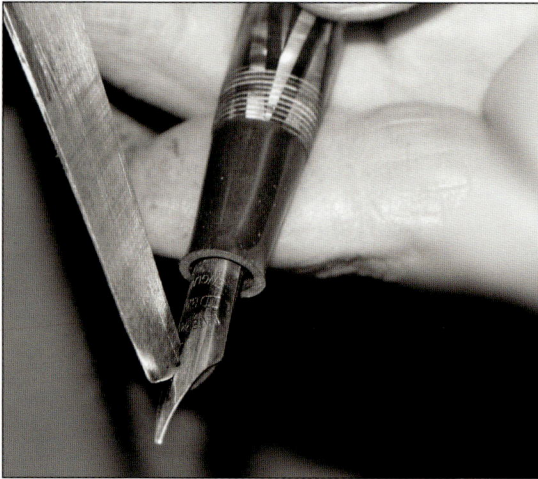

Too dry A wider gap between the tines increases the flow; adjustment is simply by inserting a nib spacer (a heavy razor blade or fine penknife) in the vent hole and moving it gently towards the tip. This will increase the gap and consequently the ink flow.

New nibs are strong, and the iridium tip welded firmly in place, but older nibs are often brittle, and care must be taken not to break off the iridium. Have a good look at the tip with an eyeglass first and, if there is any risk, start from the vent hole but stop short of the tip.

Too wet

If the pen writes too wet it may be because the gap between the tines is too great and must be reduced. The best, permanent way of doing this is to remove the nib and adjust the gap by flexing the tines over each other (like crossing your legs) until the gap is narrowed all the way along the slit.

To carry out a slight adjustment without removing the nib, hold the pen in your right hand and rest the side of one tine on a sharp, firm edge of your workbench. With your left thumb catch the upper tine and press over and down. This will cross the upper tine over the lower, and when you examine the pen point you will find the slit spacing has been decreased. Move the pen to your left hand and rotate the pen so that the other tine is laid on the bench edge, and repeat with your right thumb to cross the opposite tine.

During all these adjustments the pen is being tested by writing.
It takes a considerable time to adjust and then dry off and then fill with ink and then retest, and if necessesary do it again.   Do not cut it short!
It is vital procedure, but alas, most customers do not appreciate that correctly adjusting a pen can take longer than a repair.

Alignment

Once the nib has been properly spaced this should correct the ink flow, but inspect the tines to see if they are in line at the writing surface. If they are not, the pen will not write smoothly, so further adjustment may be required. For best performance, the slit edges should be straight, with tines making light contact with each other at the tips.

If the tine gap does not have parallel sides, then the nib body should be squeezed or opened out to correct the fault.

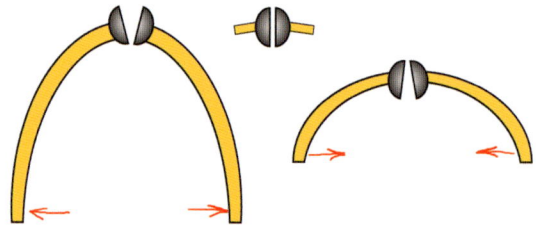

Nibs with non parallel tines; gap should be corrected as indicated

Roughness or scratchiness

Old pens rarely have virgin tips and usually have flats due to past use. This can be improved by writing on Arkansas stone, foam backed abrasive sheet or Jeweller's rouge paper. The foam backed sheets are available in a range of grades from 600 to 12000.

Draw some figure eights with light pressure, rolling the pen between the thumb and finger. This will take the hard edges off the flats on the nib.

However everyone has a slightly different way of holding a pen so what is a smooth nib to one person may be scratchy to another. The final tuning must still be performed by the owner.

Alteration of nib cut

Tool sharpening stones can be used to convert nibs to italic or oblique if there is sufficient width and thickness of iridium on the points. Grinding wheels have their place but only after a lot of practice. Destruction is always a likely outcome! (see Nib Grinding)

In all tests use smooth writing paper (not the textured surface designed for ballpoints). Finally appreciate that there is a world of difference between the modern more rigid nibs and the older highly tempered flexible ones; there is no way that you can make one into the other.

SUMMARY

1. **Position the nib correctly with respect to the feed.**

2. **Ensure the tip of the feed is snug to the nib.**

3. **Adjust the tine gap.**

4. **Smooth the tip using fine abrasive.**

5. **Use writing tests for final assessment.**

FILLING A PEN

It is surprising how many pen owners do not know how to fill their pen properly. This can be critical and although the instruction leaflets tell you how to do it, they are rarely read.

Do not mix inks

Find an ink that you like and stay with it. If you wish to change make sure that you flush the pen out before transferring to the different ink. Futhermore be prepared to make a nib adjustment to get satisfactory flow.

Give the pen time to fill

Leave the pen in the ink for at least 10 seconds after you have released the lever, button or finished plunging or twisting the filling or converter knob. It takes time for atmospheric pressure to force liquid uphill into a reservoir especially through the small orifices. Ensure that the nib unit or snorkel unit is well immersed in the ink. The ink level must be at least above the vent hole to be effective. Some ink bottles are not suitable for filling pens when the ink level is low. Waterman bottles are designed so that one can fill the pen even when the bottle is almost empty.

Press with knowledge!

Piston downfillers such as Sheaffer, Eversharp and Onoto require a firm but steady downward stroke. Do not pump, these are not pump pens and if you pull the piston back with a full ink barrel it can stress the cork or rubber seals.

If your downfiller pen only fills half the reservoir do not return it to the repairer. For most downfillers it is not theoretically possible to fill the reservoir more than about 60%. This is because the air volume between the release groove and the end of the ink channel can never be removed. This air can be compressed if the downward stroke is vigorous and since this air will be released into the newly created vacuum, the ability of the pen to draw in ink is severely reduced (a Sheaffer Vac Fil shows nearly a 40% reduction compared to a steady stroke). Conversely a very slow stroke will also reduce filling efficiency if there is any leakage in the seals (there usually is!).

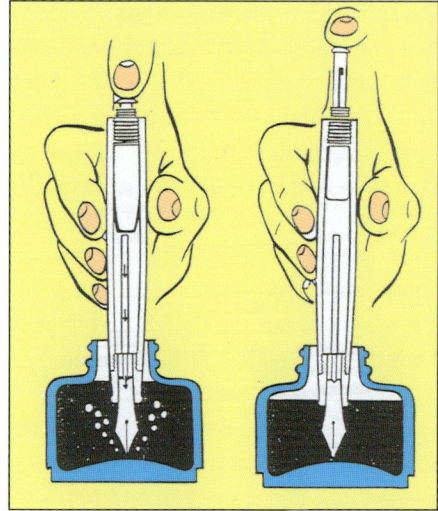

Illustrated procedure for vacumatic filling

Touch-down and Snorkels can be pumped without stressing anything but this is not really necessary as a firm stroke and a patient wait of 8–10 seconds will give a very good fill.

Overfilling

Piston upfillers such as Montblanc, Pelikans and piston converters can fill the whole reservoir including collector feeds and fins. This can cause a small leakage into the cap which is irritating. Consequently, the instructions usually suggest turning the filling knob after filling to emit one or two drops, which releases the excess ink.

Breather tubes (see also Feeds)

A pen with a breather tube will hold more ink than one without. In an experiment the capacity of a Parker Lucky Curve Senior Duofold was increased from 2.1ml to 3.5ml, when fitted with a sac length breather tube.

There is no benefit from operating a lever, button or diaphragm more than once if the pen has no breather because the ink taken in on the first stroke will be expelled on the second. A breather tube allows air at the end of the reservoir to be expelled in preference to ink already in, so a pen can be filled to the end of the breather tube by operating the filling system through several cycles. In the case of a Parker Vacumatic it is usually 7 to 8.

INK CAPACITIES

Ink capacity has frequently been used to promote the potential of a pen to write for a longer time between filling, and consequently, it is a measure which can be used to indicate the efficiency of a restoration. It would be ideal to compare fountain pens on the basis of the number of words they could write, but as any fountain pen nib can be adjusted for stingy or generous ink flow, a ranking of pens in these terms is almost meaningless.

The capacity of various pens have been measured after their repair and this has provided a data base for comparison. It is regrettable that many modern pens hold so little ink in comparison with their ancestors and thereby compare unfavourably with ball-point rivals.

Make	Date	Model	Filler type	Vol. (ml)
Conklin	1934	Nozac Jnr	Piston upfill	1.46
Conklin	1934	Nozac Snr	Piston upfill	1.93
Conway Stewart	1951	28	Lever/sac	0.95
Conway Stewart	1938	700	Piston upfill	1.25
De la Rue	1944	6233/64	Piston downfill	1.62
De la Rue	1948	Magna	Piston downfill	3.3
De La Rue	1950	K Series	Piston Upfill	1.12
Dunn	1924	Small	Telescopic diaphragm	1.3
Dunn	1924	Dreadnaught	Telescopic diaphragm	2.65
Eversharp	1937	Doric Standard	Piston downfill	2.05
Ford	1933	Magnum	Piston upfill	7.25
Ford	1933	Short Standard	Piston upfill	3.36
Goldfink	1970?	0B	Piston upfill	1.15
Mabie Todd	1935	Blackbird Topfill	Diaphragm	1.78
Mabie Todd	1935	Visofil V	Button/sac	1.6
Mabie Todd	1937	Visofil VT	Diaphragm	2.35
Mabie Todd	1946	Leverless No4	Bar/sac	1.00
Montblanc	1959	22	Piston upfill	1.15
Montblanc	1970	149	Piston upfill	1.6
Osmia	1933	Supra Progresstet	Diaphragm	2.85
Parker	1928	Lucky Curve Senior	Button/sac	2.1
Parker	1934	Vacumatic Oversize	Diaphragm	3.25
Parker	1935	Vacumatic Standard	Diaphragm	2.7
Parker	1937	Vacumatic Maxima	Diaphragm	2.5
Parker	1946	51 Vacumatic	Diaphram	1.22
Parker	1952	Maxima	Button/sac	1.45
Parker	1958	51 Aerometric	P bar/sac	1.2
Parker	1975	61 Aerometric	P bar/sac	0.8
Parker	1990	International	Piston upfill	0.75
Pilot	2006	Custom 823	Piston downfill	1.55
Sheaffer	1936	Balance 350 Lady	Piston downfill	1.42
Sheaffer	1938	Balance 1000 Senior	Piston downfill	2.7
Sheaffer	1945	Tuckaway 875	Piston downfill	0.76
Sheaffer	1950	Touchdown	Air pressure/sac	0.64
Stylomine	1938	303V	Button/sac	1.74
Sheaffer	1960	PFM	Air pressure/sac	0.85
Waterman	1936	Ink vue (Standard ray)	Lever/diaphragm	2.5
Waterman	1936	Ink vue (Lady)	Lever/diaphragm	1.7
Waterman	1937	Ink vue Mk 2	Lever/diaphragm	2.5

Measuring method : Using water, the volume quoted is the maximum in ml that can be extracted from the full pen. Measurements were made with a fine-needled medical syringe graduated in 0.02ml intervals. To facilitate comparison with previously published data on ink capacities, the conversion factor from ml to drops is between 20 and 25, (drop volume will vary, depending on the surface tension of the ink and on the geometry of the nib).

SPARES & PARTS

From the 1930s most manufacturers offered a lifetime guarantee and consequently, even though pens became obsolete, they still were repaired in the factories. As parts were depleted it became impossible to repair some pens but most makers had a list of competent private repairers, who would cannibalize older pens to effect repairs. (Arthur was such a person).

Pen repairers associated with shops or companies, had access to parts directly from the factory, but most also purchased old pens in quantity, when possible, to allow them to repair the older models. This became increasingly important from the 1990s as classic and vintage pens became popular as practical writing instruments.

Major pen makers showed little interest in older pens so most 'out of date' stock was sold to dealers or at auction. This created problems as the stock ended up in a small number of dealers/repairers hands. It also created a new market in spares. Parts appeared on sale at pen shows and companies produced regular disposal lists of spare parts for their agents and stockists.

There is very good cooperation between the few professional repairers in the UK, but the person who has the spares has a real advantage in the repair business. Consequently few repairers sell spares to hobbyists, because they know that they will be unlikely to be able to restock.

So where does the amateur pen enthusiast get his spares?
The best way is to purchase lots of old pens. The internet is a source, as are shows but gone are the days of 5 tables at a pen show competing to sell spares and bags of parts pens, which was the norm in the mid 1990s. It is worth buying bagged lots for spares at specialist auctions.

The value of a pen for parts may be a surprise! We chose a Parker 51 as an example and with the supposition that the parts were in acceptable condition, the pen was 'virtually' dismantled and the separate parts valued on a £ basis.

This illustrates that a Parker 51, which you might buy on Ebay for £35, is worth between £42 and £98 for parts, providing of course that you use them all. This is an academic exercise but spares have a value and there are parts that are very much in demand.

One can still occasionally discover new old stock and it pays to know the parts that are hard to find.

The parts illustrated on the next page are just a few of the rare parts for popular collector pens. A few dozen boxes of each would gladden the heart and pocket of any repairer.

£ VALUE OF PARTS	
Barrel	5-10
Shell	5-10
Foundation unit	3-6
Collector	2
Feed	1
Breather tube	1
Nib	5-20
Ring	1-2
Cap tube	5-25
Clip	10-15
Tassie jewel	3-5
Brass bush	1
TOTAL	**£42-£98**

Prices of parts of a Parker 51

Generic Spares

Not all fountain pen users want a pen to be as original. Many want a pen to work and have no concern about the use of very expensive parts. It is a good idea to assemble a range of 'generic' spare parts such as clips, clip screws, feeds and sections and also some steel or gold plated nibs. The advantage of such parts is that they are often excellent quality but a fraction of the price of branded items.

SPARES WANTED

PFM nibs and barrels

Onoto rods

61 shells with arrows

PFM sac protectors

CF converters

VP filling units

Duofold clips (streamline)

Lady Sheaffer nib units

Targa nib units

51 clips (3 sizes and blue diamond)

Parker 51 jewels

51 Broad and stub nibs

Patrician clips, decals, lever boxes

Conway Stewart 58/60 clips

50's Duofold Maxima feeds, nibs

Sheaffer point holders 444

Brown Falcon (50) nib units

Small Sheaffer Reminder cams

Conway Stewart No 5 nibs

Onoto No 6/7 nibs

and a lot more.

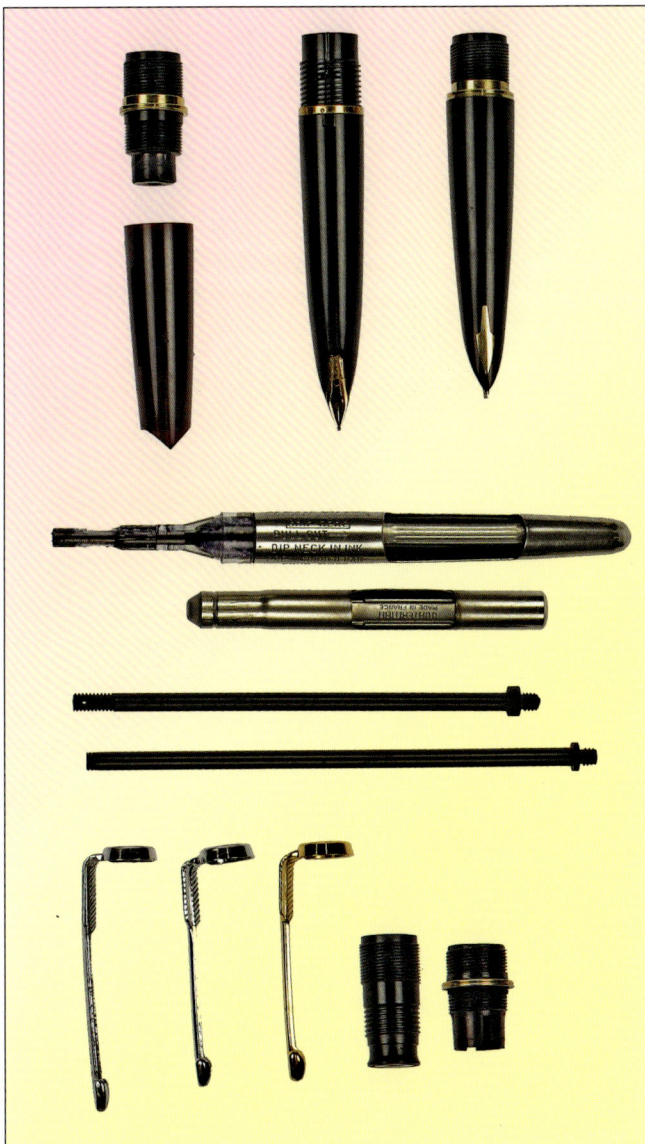

Removing old parts from pens

As a professional repairer it pays to accumulate drawers of pens for dismantling. A fountain pen scrapyard! It may hurt to cut up a black pen that works but sadly black pens are not collectors items unless they are Senior Duofolds, Patricians or Fords. A gold filled Waterman leverbox and clip is worth more than a working, black, worn out 52. The value of gold seems unlikely to drop and the scrap value of gold nibs is now significant so there are likely to be more nibless pens for sale in the future. If you are about to ravage a bundle of pens for spares, our suggestion is to be ruthless and cut the precious items out. Do not risk breaking lugs off lever boxes or bending levers or damaging clip screws by approaching the task as if you were about to repair Auntie Marjorie's pen. Cut and burn! This may seem an exaggerated and trivial point but more damage can be done to parts by trying to lever them out or remove them as if it was a repair task. To get the spare in the best possible state use the saw, Dremel and the torch!

GENERAL CLASSES

A collector usually refers to the maker first and then frequently refers to the filling system to describe a pen. Consequently we are continually referring to Parker Vacs, Sheaffer Snorkels, Conklin Crescent, Swan leverless and so on. Such pens are specifically dealt with in Section Two.

However we frequently use general groupings based on filling systems such as body reservoir, lever fill, piston and so on and there are many common repair procedures within these groups that we do not want to be repeating time and time again in Section Two.

The following pages detail some of the problems and procedures that are common to these classes or groups of pens. Our headings are arbitrary and chosen simply to assemble repair procedures that are frequently required. Our first attention is given to rubber sac reservoir pens and then to body reservoir.

Crocker red/black mottle blow filler and a decorated Williamson (Janesville) pen

Dual coin filler and matchstick filler above and a peg filler below.

RUBBER SAC COMPRESSION

The introduction of the rubber sac as an ink reservoir was one of the milestones in pen design and it triggered off patent and design activity to compress the sac and then release it in order to fill the pen.

A simple system was the blow filler, which simply involved compressing the sac by blowing into the barrel through an end vent hole. Crocker and Williamson were very successful with these somewhat unhygienic pens.

Most compression systems involved a mechanical action. From the beginning, early examples used some form of pressure bar to protect the sac from damage and this bar was depressed often by direct finger pressure.

The most simple systems exposed the pressure bar by sliding a sleeve or rotating a collar and this was used by Waterman with their sleeve fillers. Some examples required matches or pegs, others used coins and Waterman even supplied the coins with their logos stamped on them.

Perhaps the best known in this pre-lever period was the Conklin crescent (1897) but other companies such as Evans, Jaxon and Grieshaber were all successful with similar pens.

The repair of all such pens is very simple as the bars are easily removed from the body and sac replacement is the main task. The pressure bar became a standard component and the next milestone was the lever.

Jaxon Stud filler with rotating plate to secure the bar

Evans with a solid lug and a slimmer hard rubber securing ring

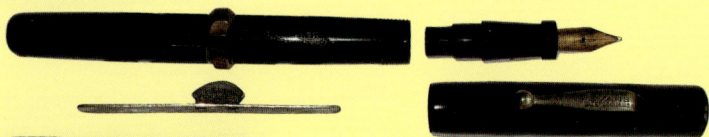

Conklin Crescent with a crescent bar removed. The rotating barrel ring is hard rubber

Cut away, to show the lever slide bar system on a Conway Stewart.

C-clips of different diameter

The idea of a lever to activate a pressure bar for compressing and relieving rubber ink sacs was introduced by Sheaffer in 1908 and eliminated the awkward crescent and peg protuberances. This system was probably the most common filling system from 1910 to 1950 and is a vital area of pen repair.

Pivots The lever requires a pivot, so that raising one end depresses the pressure bar that is connected to the other end. Lever pens differ in the way the pivot is mounted in the pen.

Watermans, De La Rue, and older Conway Stewart use a lever box that is held in a slot in the barrel by metal tabs. The lever box has the advantage that the entire mechanism is self-contained and it only requires a slot for mounting. For this reason lever box pens are the easiest to repair if a replacement box is available. Hatchet fillers usually have a box pivot.

Sheaffer and Eversharp pens often retain the lever with a metal pivot pin contained within a hole drilled across the lever aperture. The use of this method is readily apparent from the filler covering the ends of the hole on either side of the lever. Long levers such as the Crocker 'hatchets' have a barrel pin.

Conway Stewart, Swan and most other lever pens have a circumferential slot in the inside of the barrel to accommodate a spring steel ring that provides the pivot for the lever.

A lever with only minor problems, such as a bent lifting tab, can be repaired in the pen, but more serious problems require lever replacement.

Problems
- broken tabs
- lever detached from pressure bar
- lever does not lock and stay down
- lever remains proud
- lever does not lift all way up
- broken pivot pin

Dismantling
Before serious work can commence on the lever the slide or pressure bar should be disconnected if that is possible.

Removal of pressure bars
J-bars
On some pens the pressure bar is spring-loaded and not connected directly to the lever. This type of bar is called a 'J-bar'. In most cases it is desirable to remove this before the new lever is installed.

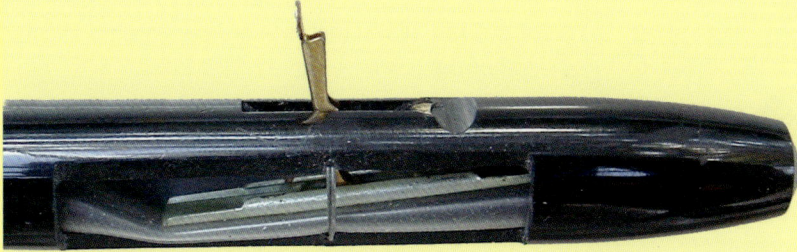

J-bar removal is not always easy, but by pressing a screwdriver blade firmly into the foot of the 'J', the grip can usually be weakened so that the bar can be pulled out with long nosed pliers. In some Sheaffer pens the foot is mounted immovably into the barrel end by a thin strip of metal; the only option then is to twist the bar until this metal strip breaks. Too strong a J-bar can deform the end of the barrel.

Slide Bars
Major pen makes such as Watermans and Conway Stewart use a lever with a forked end that engages slots in the sides of a straight pressure bar. The slide movement is restricted by one or two tabs. Disengaging the bar from the lever

Cutting the C-clip with a Dremel is the easiest way and does not stress the barrel. You can cut through the lever in a closed position ; use a small diameter wheel

Conway Stewart with lever stop in front of the lever tab

Variety of J-bars

Press the tab down to release the pressure bar.

is achieved by pushing a fine screwdriver blade through the lever slot into the tab in the pressure bar just in front of the open lever. The depression of this tab allows the pressure bar to slide off the end of the lever.

Dismantling the lever unit

Lever boxes can often be removed by using a sharp bladed fine screwdriver to lift the front inner barrel retaining tab. Be careful not to raise the tab more than necessary, because they are easily broken off. If the box has been broken or badly damaged, it is often possible to save the lever and mount it in a new box. This is a fiddly operation involving removal of the pivot (see Waterman boxes).

Levers held by a pin across the slot are removed by pushing the pin out with a fine drill; they are unlikely to be glued in, so this is in principle a simple task. However in practice it depends upon the condition of the pen and the pin material. If it is a steel pin then it could have rusted and removal may be a serious problem. In such cases soaking in a releasing agent such as WD40 may help. Take great care with red hard rubber which is notoriously brittle. Furthermore the drill must be the correct size (typically 1.0mm diameter) and the barrel MUST be firm otherwise it can chip.

Removal of C-clip levers

Try pushing the lever into the barrel whilst rotating it; often this will cause the ring to pop out of its slot so that the damaged parts can be easily removed. When this does not work, the best approach is to use a small abrasive disk in a Dremel type tool to cut through the top of the lever and the ring. The remnants of corroded C-clips must be removed from the inner groove.

Other pivots or stops

Both Swan and early Conway Stewart have 'catches' to hold the lever down. Swans have a second C-Clip which acts as a latch for a notch in the lever; Conway Stewart have a metal support which grips protrusions on the lever (this can be very awkward to refit as it is crimped into recesses in the barrel). Waterman levers also 'snap' into the lever box.

Removing a J-Bar with a screwdiver

Donor levers

The easiest way to remove a ring-held lever from a donor pen is to saw the barrel in two with a small hacksaw at the pivot point, being careful not to damage the lever or the ring. It may help to anneal the lugs on a box to make them less likely to break off during refitting.

Re installing levers and bars.

Having removed the damaged parts, and most importantly having found replacements, the next step is to test for a satisfactory fit. It should not be assumed that all pens from a given manufacturer followed the same dimensional specification, so the availability of a set of needle files will help in making any small adjustments. The position of the pivot hole also varies with barrel diameter and should be checked.

Refitting the Lever

Lever boxes can usually be fitted without any

Refitting a Swan lever and bar through the barrel

problem, but they should be firmly mounted; this being achieved by pressing the box into its correct location whilst flattening the tab to the inside of the barrel with a large diameter metal rod.

Levers held by a pin are also easily installed, but it is probably wise to seal the ends of the pin with a spot of shellac to ensure that the pin does not fall out.

Ring-held levers are the most difficult and there are a number of options, depending on the size of the tab and method of attachment of lever to pressure bar.

Through the slot

Start with the ring threaded centrally through the hole in the lever and the lever axis perpendicular to the barrel axis so that the end of the lever and the ring can be inserted through the barrel slot. In the ideal case, a firm 90^0 rotation of the lever around its axis will complete the job as the ring falls into its retaining slot. In some cases the ring will need assistance to find its proper location: a coat hanger wire with a right angle bend at the tip used in conjunction with a fibre optic light source will aid the process.

Through the open barrel end

This is the only method for Swan combined bar/levers but it can be used for C-ring levers if the tab is small; with practice it is not difficult. Using long nosed pliers the lever is fed into the barrel and through the slot. A narrow spatula inserted at an angle through the slot can help 'thread' the lever through the slot, so it can be pulled into position. The C ring can be manoeuvred into the inner grooves.

Refitting the bars

J-bar insertion is not difficult, but it must be done accurately. It is not always easy to rotate it if it does not align properly with the lever. With a simple J-bar the foot of the J-bar must be bent such that it grips the barrel tightly and also provide upward pressure on the lever to keep it closed within the barrel. Other variants such as Sheaffer double slotted bars have a cylindrical end, which is also pushed into position but it must be exactly aligned because the lever operates through a slot in the bar.

A slide bar must have the tab or tabs pressed out and then by holding it in long nosed pliers, advance it into the barrel with the lever raised by about 30^0. It may take a little patience to get the forks aligned in the grooves in the pressure bar, but when you have, you will feel a slight click as the bar tab is pushed down by the forks. The bar should now slide between the stops and stay attached to the lever lugs by the channel on the edge of the slide.

If the lever has broken or damaged forks, or was never designed for a slide bar then a J-bar must be fitted.

Using graphite powder lubricant (for locks) will make the lever operation and the slide bar movement much smoother.

TIP

LEVER VARIETY

There are many designs of lever, some of which were designed specifically to circumvent the original Sheaffer patent. The standard Swan, Conway Stewart and waterman box levers have been dealt with. The ones on this page are rather different variants.

Eisenstadt and So Simple reverse levers

Reverse levers

The advantage of this lever is that it will not snag when put into a jacket or shirt pocket and that can avoid ink leaking into the cap. There is perhaps also less strain on the sac peg joint but the design of the pressure bar has to be different for such lever pens. It is mounted into the barrel with a cylindrical support, which causes it to pivot at the nib end. In fact it seems a much better lever direction but it was rarely used. Eisenstadt had this characteristic lever, as did the Newhaven brand N.I.B So-Simple, which had an unusually long lever. An interesting variant was the Snapfil (see below). This has a lever, which after lifting up, has a tab, which folds down and is then used to depress the pr

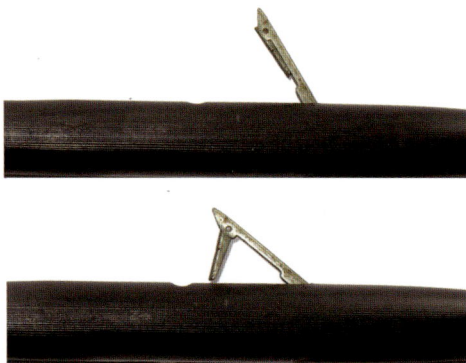

Snapfil lever with pivotted tab to depress lever, after filling it is folded back and the lever closed

John Holland 'hatchet'

This initially looks as though half the lever is missing and what at first appears to be half a lever swivels at the pivot and the shaped lever pushes down the pressure bar. This model was made in a number of sizes and also with rather expensive silver overlays.

John Holland hatchet filler

Crocker 'Ink Tite'

The 1916 patent illustrations below from Seth Crocker's company show the detail of the lever system and the importance of pressure bar design and alignment to make these systems work. If these were not correct the leverage could easily pull the sac from the peg.

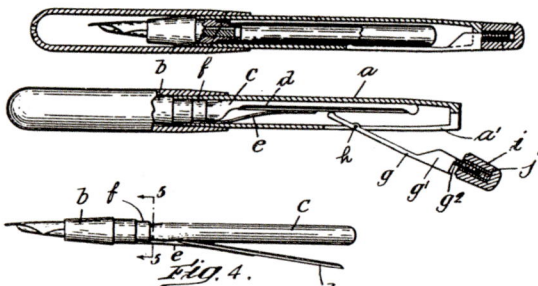

Diagram from Crocker filler patent

General repair Most lever pen sections are push fit so resacing is straight forward but the removal and replacement of pressure bars requires a strong hook. The levers are pinned and some examples have a frame for added strength (John Holland).

BUTTON FILLERS

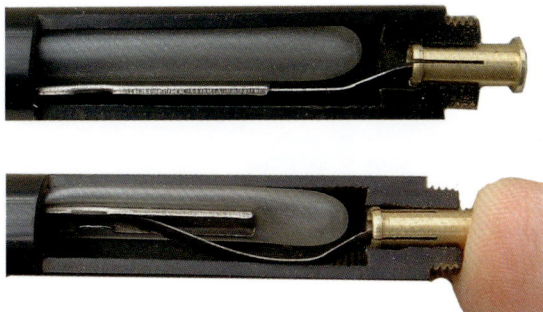

Button bar in action, compressing the sac

Four examples ; two Valentine, two Parker

The button filling system was adopted by Parker and used almost exclusively by them for some 50 years. The simplicity of the system has much to commend it, and for the repairer, button fill pens are the least challenging.

The heart of the filler is the spring steel strip that is compressed in length by operation of the button. The resulting sideways movement pushes the pressure bar against the sac.

In the majority of pens, the pressure bar will be found serviceable. Fortunately, there is a ready supply of reproduction bars, should a replacement be required.

Buttons usually benefit from a clean up, but they rarely need replacement.

Dismantling

Confirm that the button is not secured by a thread and then it should be removable by simply exerting a strong pull. There is frequently a lot of corrosion or sac debris so the pressure bar is best removed through the section end.

Where the button is part of a bush that is screwed into the end of the barrel, like the AF Duofolds, it should also pull out. However if the mechanism involves turning a knob then this is not a simple button filler.

Replacement

If the bar has to be replaced then make sure it is the correct size. It is important to ensure that the range of movement of the button results in the maximum range of movement of the pressure bar. Bars can be un-crimped and shortened by cutting the solid and the 'flexy' bar and then recrimping. They can be extended a little by using cotton

bud shafts if marginally too short. The end of the button socket can also be plugged with a piece of the stick or lead shot.

Assembly

The preferred method of assembly for most button fillers is by insertion of the pressure bar after the sac and section have been fitted. With the button removed, the top of the sac will be visible so the pressure bar can be inserted down the side, being careful not to push in the end of the sac. The button can then be pushed home. The skirt lugs of the button can be widened with a blade.

Some later button fillers departed from the simple and elegant design. Parker aluminium buttons can be difficult to remove. Sometimes pens must be assembled with the sac rotating against the pressure bar. The sac may become twisted as the pen is assembled and the pen will not fill. Another variation involves a slot in the section to receive the end of the pressure bar. This rotates with the sac as the section is screwed in.

Again there is potential for twisting the sac, so the button end of the bar is sometimes fitted with a metal cap so that it can rotate easily inside the button housing as the pen is assembled. A sac supporter will help to prevent the sac from twisting (see Leverless Swan).

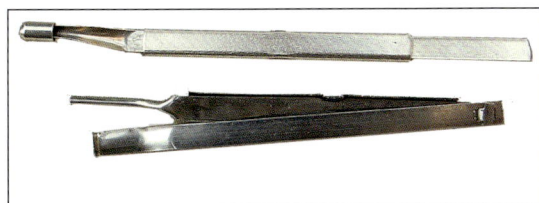

Anchor bar and button bar

BODY RESERVOIR

Wyvern syringe filler piston pen. probably made in the late 1920s

In the C18th and C19th earliest fountain pens such as the Bion and Scheffer used the body as an ink reservoir. At the end of the C19th stylographs and eyedroppers made from hard rubber were the first commercially successful fountain pens. The disadvantage was that the pen had to be dismantled for filling and also care had to be taken with the storage of the pen, when not in use. However self filling systems were not long in appearing.

Early self-filling syringe pens The first simple pens were piston upfillers and used a syringe system with cork seals. These pens were very popular, economic and worked well.
The Wyvern self-filler from the 1920s above illustrates the simplicity of a shaft and piston that when pulled back 'sucked' in ink. The main repair task was replacing the cork seal, which was fitted to the piston with a screw plug. Dismantling and reassembling is easy. These pens were criticised because the plunger rod takes up a lot of space

but quite a range of such pens was made all over the world. They often have lovely flexible nibs, ideal for calligraphy. In fact Pitman recommended such pens for shorthand.

Piston downfillers. From 1905 downfillers such as Onoto and later Eversharp and Sheaffer were very successful. These body reservoir pens are often referred to as vac fillers. The repair problems centre on two seals: replacing the plunger washer seal and replacing the end barrel seal. Examples of all three are included in Section Two.

Diaphragm fillers
There is a large group of body reservoir pens, that are not piston based; these include bulb fillers, the Vacumatic, Dunn and the Ink Vue. All variations involve breather tubes and a variety of 'pumping mechanisms' located at the top of the barrel. They are explained in the filling section and are dealt with individually in Section Two.

1910 Pitman fono fountain pen

 There are also piston/plunger pens that are not body fillers, such as the Touchdown. The principle of air compression was used in the original Crocker Inktite blowfiller, which in turn led to Seth Crocker's Chilton. All these pens have sacs.

SCREW PISTON FILLERS

Three typical piston pens; Osmia open nibbed pen with a twistknob under a blind cap; a glass nibbed Palmboom pen and a stylographic drawing pen. The first two use corks seals and the more modern 'stylo' uses a plastic gasket.

The main remaining class of body reservoir pens are 'piston' pens, which use a rather more complex syringe based on a screw mechanism. Kovac's patents of the 1920s proposed a pen which moved the piston by a screw. This was exploited by Pelikan and Conklin and further developed as a 'telescopic' by Montblanc in the 1930s. Most makers of piston pens opted for the 'double' screw system and the principle is still being used today. Germany particularly adopted piston mechanisms for pens. The majority of piston pens encountered for repair are of European origin from Pelikan, Montblanc, Soenneckan, Osmia, Geha, Lamy and Matador. The repair of these pens involves two aspects - the maintenance of the piston moving mechanism. - the replacement of piston seals which are the main parts exposed to friction and abrasion.

A number of piston pens are considered in detail in Section Two, but the disciplines which must be applied, are common to all. The key step is to access the seals and that usually involves some degree of dismantling followed by making cork seals.

Dismantling

Patience as well as water and warmth is emphasised again. It is important to get water into the barrel to loosen the parts and ink residues. This may be facilitated by removing the nib and feed or the section.

If the section comes off it may allow access to the seal without further dismantling, but in many cases the mechanisms must be withdrawn. That can be time consuming, but if you know what you are doing, it is not difficult.

Making corks is straightforward with the right technique (see Cutting seals). Piston pens can be a delight if they work well; they may appear mysterious with hidden parts but they are no more difficult than any other pen.

Focused heat and good section pliers are essential

Three different Montblanc telescopic mechanisms

CARTRIDGES

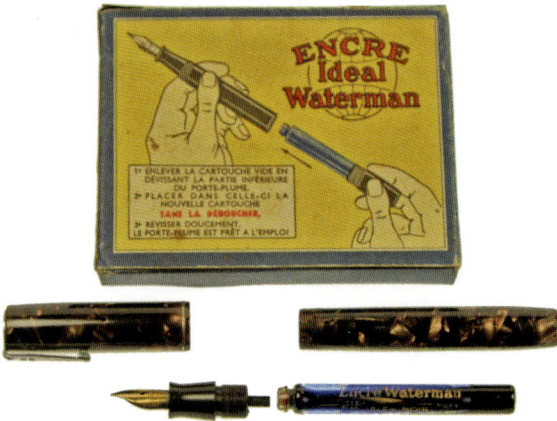

Glass cartridges were introduced in the late C19th by the Eagle Pen company and again tried in the 1930s by Waterman with little success. Plastic cartridges were developed by Aurora in the late 1940s and in 1954 Waterman were granted a patent for a plastic cartridge.

It was an interesting period, with the explosion of the ball point pen, and cartridges must have been regarded with the potential to combat the ball pen. The Waterman CF (Cartridge Filler) was launched in the USA and was perhaps not as successful as might have been expected. Parker first introduced a cartridge pen as a Parker 51 in 1958 and introduced their first completely cartridge pen, the Parker 45, in 1960. It was a convenience, which became a milestone in the design of fountain pens and was perhaps their saviour.

Modern cartridges are injection moulded plastic tubes filled with ink and sealed with a plastic bead or thin membrane. Pens that use cartridges have a sharp peg or tube, which can displace or rupture the seal and allow ink to flow to the writing unit.

Standardisation with Euro cartridges (mainly short) was adopted quite quickly, but major makers also developed their own proprietary designs.

Cartridges are firmly held in position by the extension tube protruding from the gripping section.

The pierce unit

A piercing tube exists to pierce the cartridge and is located at the bottom of the cartridge tube holder. Originally these were metal and cut at an angle to facilitate piercing; the fitting recommendation was to insert the cartridge with downward pressure using a twisting action. Barrels were designed to ensure that the cartridge fitted tightly over the pierce unit tube. Screwing the barrel on could force the cartridge into position but this could also stress plastic threads.

Piercing units from CF Waterman, Parker 61, Lady Sheaffer, Sheaffer Imperial.

Waterman and Parker located the early pierce 'tubes' in the connectors but in time pierce pegs became part of the shell or collector moulding (Parker 45). Sheaffer used a short tube fitted into the feed to act as the pierce spike. Their Skrip cartridge was a simple plastic cylinder that often required considerable force to pierce. Sheaffer recommended screwing the barrel down to fit the cartridge (but they had metal threads!).

A variety of cartridge shapes

It is no longer possible to purchase the correct cartridges for some vintage pens. In such cases it is necessary to fill old cartridges with an eyedropper or syringe.

CONVERTERS

Cartridges are an expensive way of 'running' a pen so converters are usually supplied with new pens. These convert the pen to a reservoir pen, which can be filled from an ink-bottle. The first converters were based on the aerometric principle with a sac, sac protector and a nipple arrangement similar to a cartridge. The major companies commissioned their own converters and the variation of converter length, diameter and nipple design make it almost impossible to adapt converters for other pens. Some will fit onto other piercing pegs but are too wide to fit the barrels; some have too wide an orifice and leak; some are too long.

Recently small converters with a syringe action have been available and they can sometimes be adapted for smaller pens and also for the Waterman CF.

The availability of converters can influence the value of classic pens e.g. the Waterman CF has a reduced value because both converters and cartridges are hard to find.

Many repairs involve adapting converters to suit other pens or refurbishing converters for old pens. Euro converters have a large diameter support band below the reservoir that can be turned down on a lathe as required.

Six different designs of Parker converter

Repairing early converters

Waterman CF, Parker, Sheaffer converters can all be refurbished .

It would have been unthinkable to repair a converter even as late as the 1990s but old metal converters are now expensive or impossible to find.

The most common is the tapered Parker aluminium 'aero' convertor. This can be easily restored by carefully removing the plastic 'peg' and replacing the sac with a 16 1/2 tapered sac cut to size. First examine the peg to make sure it can be reused and is not enlarged or damaged; if it is, then a different one will be required. Warm the metal and pull/wiggle the peg from the metal sac protector. After fitting a new sac push the unit back into the metal case and crimp.

Sheaffer and Waterman converters can be refurbished in a similar way, but with these it is easier to knock out the nipple. With the Sheaffer, cut the top off the converter near the top to avoid cutting the pressure bar; the plastic sac easily pulls off and the nipple can be pushed out with a plastic rod. Sheaffer's crimps are tenacious so it may need knocking out with the correct diameter punch. The sac nipple may require some slight reduction if the rubber or plastic sac is thick walled.

The same procedure can be used for the Waterman CF. When refitting a sac reduce the nipple diameter slightly; clean the sac protector orifice with a round file, Alternatively make a simple plastic plug for the top to keep the pressure bar in position. The CF converter metal is quite thin and can split so progress slowly and use a thin wall sac.

BALL POINT PENS

Examples of Biro & Wyvern clip actuation, US button, Montblanc lever, Biromatic early and later Parker cap actuation.

Ballpoint pens have a fascinating history (see G.Hogg-Bibliography) and had an explosive growth once the technology and product development was sorted out. Laslo Biro is credited as the inventor of the modern ball pen but until satisfactory inks and accurate ball units were available, the ball point was a marketing disaster. Reynolds and Eversharp never recovered from their promotion of non-working pens, and in 1950 the ball point was near death. However by 1954 it had recovered and had overtaken fountain pens in sales and had become the most used writing instrument of all time.

We can classify ball pens into two groups

'Stick' pens, which have a barrel containing a reservoir, writing unit, barrel and cap;
'Actuated' pens, which have a retractable writing unit protruding from a nozzle.

The fundamental part of the pen is
The **Writing unit** (or refill), which consists of a sealed ink reservoir and a dispenser/writing point.
The **Body**, which is the support for the writing unit and exists in many different forms.

The earliest ballpoint pens were stick pens similar in shape to fountain pens. The writing unit either screwed or pushed into a gripping section and exposed the writing tip.

Actuated pens were patented in 1945 and available from the early 1950s. The body of these pens was essentially a tube containing a spring and fitted to a top, which included some mechanism to move the writing unit down against the spring. All the 'magic' happens in the top end and it is usually this actuation mechanism that presents most repair problems.

Clip actuation
The most basic actuator is the Biro bayonet catch pen where the clip simply presses down into a slot. Twenty years on Sheaffer used a more complicated press clip in the Reminder pen.

Button actuation
Parker, Sheaffer, Papermate and Eversharp introduced button action pens and these were mainly generic models. The early examples could be quite complex, but the simplicity of Parker's 'Jotter' made it the most successful ball pen ever.

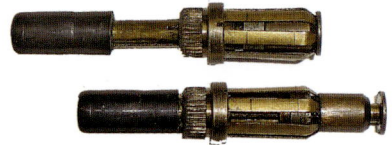

Early Sheaffer button mechanism engaged and released. Note complicated claw system, prone to release problems

Lever actuation
An example of a lever actuator was the Mont Blanc 1970s ball pen where the lever is centred in the clip.

Cap actuation
This involved pressing the cap down. The early Biromatic is unlikely to be encountered today but cap actuated Parker ball pens, made to match fountain pens, are probably the most frequent repair task.

Twist actuation
The invention of a small unit, which allowed the top half of the pen to be turned to propel the writing unit. This was a major advance and it was adopted by most pen makers because it simplified the manufacturing assembly process.

The Writing unit

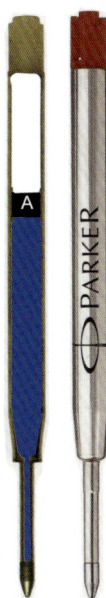

The principle of the ball pen is the control and even transfer of a viscous ink mix to paper via the rotation of a ball writing point. The ball is fitted into a special housing which is attached to the ink reservoir.

The original reservoirs were complicated spirals, tubes or capillary systems in plastic, which progressed to metal housings and finally back again to plastic. Refills are now usually 4mm in diameter, with a grease plug A to seal the ink top surface (see image).The success of the ball pen has proliferated an enormous range of shapes and styles and frustratingly rapid obsolescence. This can make an attractive pen useless because no refills are available (to our knowledge no service is offered for refurbishing old ball pen refills) It is possible to adapt some writing units to fit other pens but this is not very common. In general if 'refills' are not available the pen is a museum piece as far as using it is concerned.

The Body-Stick pens

These have a housing for the writing unit and a cap or cover to which a pocket clip can be fitted. They look like a fountain pen. Eversharp used the case of the Fifth Avenue fountain pen, which was a failure, as a housing for their ball pen in 1946. The 'traditional' fountain pen shape did not favour the 'refills' of the day. Inversion in the pocket caused the ink to drain away from the ball tip, causing air locks.

A few expensive stick ball pens were made like the Parker 105 and the Sheaffer Nostalgia but the great impact of such pens was with the cheaper Parker 'Big Red' and Sheaffer's 'No Nonsense' corporate gifts pen.

Rollerball and fibre tipped pens were made in stick form because both of these writing units 'dried out' and the cap retarded this. Parker, Waterman, Montblanc and Sheaffer all have stick rollerballs in their most expensive ranges, e.g. Edson, Duofold, International and Sheaffer Nostalgia

The Body -Actuator pens

There are two parts - **the lower barrel**, made from metal or plastic with a nozzle tip. The lower barrel usually contains the coil spring.

The **upper part or cap** incorporates the actuator system.

The two parts are usually screwed together with a threaded portion in the actuator (Parker) or a threaded metal bush in the cap (Sheaffer).

The correct spring is vital and should always be used, otherwise it can lead to malfunction or over-stressing the joining threads.

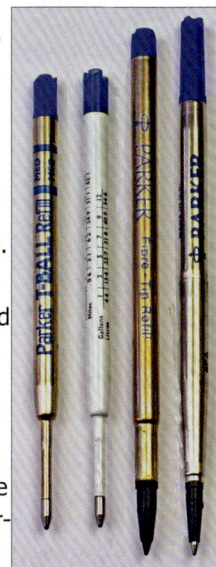

Refills

Actuator systems

Actuator design played a major part in the success of a pen. There is a wide variety of these mechanisms. The writing unit is propelled out of the nozzle and 'catches' so that pressure exerted on the ballpoint during use does not push it back into the barrel.

When the pen is not in use the 'catch' can be released and the pen returns into the barrel due to the barrel spring.

Parker's 'simple' ratchet for button and cap and Papermate's button were so reliable, while Sheaffer and Waterman battled with mini engineered springs and grips which were too complex and expensive.

Ball pen problems

- writing unit leaking at the top, which can gum up the actuator system
- springs damaged
- refills do not propel or return to barrel
- clips broken and jammed mechanism
- threads stripped or broken off actuator ratchet
- nozzle damaged and fouling 'refill'

The repair of ball pens is not complicated but usually requires special tools and a good knowledge of the innards.

Expensive stick pens often look like fountain pens and it is an option to convert them by fitting a nib unit. However all is not what it seems as there is usually an insert in the barrel, which has to be removed or the barrel has to be drilled or reamed out to accept an ink converter.

CAUTION

PENCILS

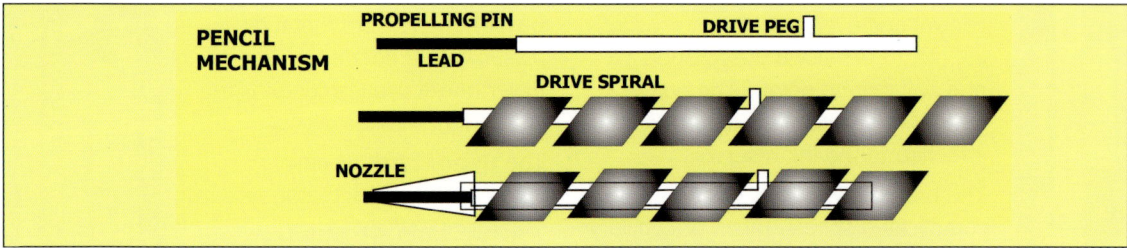

PENCIL MECHANISM

PROPELLING PIN

LEAD

DRIVE PEG

DRIVE SPIRAL

NOZZLE

Mechanical pencils were established long before the fountain pen became popular but the pencil became a partner for the pen in the early C20th. The pen and pencil 'set' was promoted and became a desirable present of the early C20th. Pencils were made to match the pens in style and colour and they remained as a 'twosome' until displaced by the ball point in the 1960s. There are two types of pencil; the rotary and the clutch.

Rotary pencil

The aim is to propel a lead holder up and down a tube. The simple way of doing this is to use a spiral and put a peg on the tube. They are easy to work on, once they are dismantled!

There are other systems such as 'the spiral outer tube' used by Eversharp but most makers such as Parker, Sheaffer and Waterman used the peg and inner spiral.

The anatomy of a rotating pencil is based on a series of concentric tubes. The lead carrier tube slides up and down a slotted guide tube which is usually fixed to a nozzle. The spiral rotates around the guide tube and is geared into the lead holder drive peg. The spiral frequently has a serrated bush which can be fixed to the outer casing. When it is attached to a cap or a turning knob the spiral responds to rotation by propelling the carrier tube with the pencil lead. The outer case can be metal or plastic. (see detailed mechanisms in Parker Pencils)

Clutch pencil

The action is derived from old porte crayon holders that used a split tube and a ring. In more modern pencils there is a chuck like holder, which opens as the lead is propelled forward and which closes to re-grip the lead as the propelling action is released. Sometimes these are called continuous or repeater pencils.

What goes wrong with pencils

Usually not a lot! They get blocked and few owners seem to realise that powdered carbon and clay (lead) makes a good cement when compressed. Often a small drill and a pin vice can clear a blocked pencil in seconds. A set of small drills ranging from 0.5mm to 1.5 is a must for any pencil restorer.

Mechanisms do get stripped, and some of the older pencils develop splits in the inner brass tubes, but most can be repaired.

Leads

The older standards were 1.1 to 1.2mm and this is still the Yard-o-led grade. By the 1960s the European and East Asian standardisation pushed pencil makers to adopt 0.9mm first and then progressively down through 0.7 and 0.5 to 0.3mm. Sheaffer and Eversharp had opted for 'Fineline' 0.9mm early in the 1940s, but all the classic pencils of the 1920s and 1930s are 1.1mm. Supplies of all leads are readily available including the unusual Faber Castell sizes 1.4mm and 1mm leads that Parker used for a brief period.

Nozzles

The lead should be firm in the nozzle. If it is loose it will be uncomfortable to use and will frequently break leads. There are a variety of different sized nozzles, with different diameters. Some screw on to the barrel and some screw on to the mechanism and act to secure it in the barrel.

Metal pencils often have soldered nozzles. Nozzles get lost and are a frequent repair request, so maintaining a collection of different nozzles is important for the professional repairer. It is usually possible to match up a nozzle or in the extreme case make one.

Dismantling

Pencils from the 1920s had quite large mechanisms, usually made of brass tube and consequently the pencils are large in diameter. The outer cases were normally a tube, which was attached to a big nozzle and at the other

end there was a turning knob with eraser and cap. Most pencils were assembled with screw threads, although some 1930s pencils had push fit mechanisms; these have to be knocked or pulled out. This takes confidence if it is a moss agate Patrician pencil but most dismantle with a little warmth and patience.

Few tools are necessary for taking a pencil apart, but a pair of good small pliers is essential. There are a number of sloping and conical shapes to deal with; Arthur used to drill holes in pliers to suit a particular purpose. Cone or nozzle removing pliers can easily be made by filing out a nozzle shape in a pair of pliers and lining them with a sheet of rubber. As with pens, warmth is essential to soften adhesives.

Caps

The cap is a friction fit and pulls off. The cap inner tubes are usually fixed in by the clip screw. These can be changed to suit different diameter mechanisms. In some cases the same caps can be used for pencils and ball points.

The most complex maintenance to the cap is probably changing a clip.

Servicing

The problem with pencils is rarely technical. Our guestimate is that 50% of pencil problems can be resolved with cleaning the nozzles and the propelling mechanism. However most pencils demand an inordinate time to dismantle and reassemble. With ones own items this is rarely an issue but in a commercial situation pencils can be a time consuming and expensive repair.

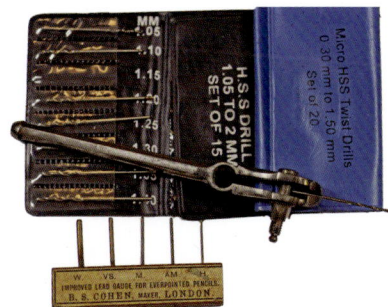

Perhaps the most important tools for pencil repair- a set of drills a pin vice and a nozzle gauge

Eight Parker pencils and eight different nozzles

The variety of leads and erasers for classic pencils

Parker Duofold button filler	64
Parker Vacumatic	66
Parker 51 Vacumatic	70
Parker 51 Aerometric	72
Parker 61 Capillary	74
Parker 61 Aerometric	76
Parker 61 Capillary Conversion	78
Parker 65	80
Parker 1950s Duofold	82
Parker 17	83
Parker VP & VS	84
Parker 75	85
Parker 25, 45	86
Parker Falcon/Osmia 96	87
Parker Modern	88
Parker ball pens	90
Parker Pencils	94
Webnotes	97
Sheaffer lever	98
Sheaffer Vac-Fil	100
Sheaffer Touchdown	106
Sheaffer Snorkel	108
Sheaffer PFM	112
Sheaffer Imperial I	114
Sheaffer Imperial Range	115
Sheaffer 444, 506	116
Lady Sheaffer	117
Sheaffer ball pens	118
Sheaffer Targa/Modern	119
Watermans eyedroppers	120
Watermans pump	121
Watermans 1920s-40s	122
Waterman sleeve filler	123
Watermans Ink vue mk1	124
Watermans Ink vue mk2	126
Watermans CF	128
Watermans modern	129
Watermans clips	130
Waterman pronged & ring clips	132
Watermans lever boxes	133
Watermans overlays	134
Watermans Emblem/100year	135
Mabie Todd eyedroppers	136
Mabie Todd lever	138
Mabie Todd Swan leverless	140
Mabie Todd button bar	142
Swan Visofil V	144
Swan Visofil VT	146
Swan Visofil New York	150
Blackbird Topfiller BT	152
Stylomine/Gold Starry	155
Wahl Eversharp Doric	156
Wahl Eversharp Decoband	158
Wahl Eversharp Oxford	160
Eversharp Skyline	162
Eversharp 5th Avenue	164
Eversharp pencils	165
Conway Stewart	166
Conway Stewart CS 700/800	168
Onoto piston	170
Onoto Magna	173
De La Rue lever/Elfin	176
Onoto Minor	177
Onoto K series piston	178
Onoto Ink pencils	179
Onoto pencils	180
Knight Rider/ Onoto tit-bits	181
British pens	182
Ormiston & Glass/ Croxley	183
Burnham	184
Perry/Unique/Curzon/Summit	185
Macniven & Cameron	186
Mentmore/Platignum	187
Valentine	190
Wyvern	191
Stephens/National Security	192/3
Ford	194
Pullman and Brenna	198
Pelikan	200
Montblanc piston	203
Soennecken	206
Dunn	208
Chilton	210
Conklin Nozac	211
AA Waterman	212
Eagle	213
Esterbrook	214
Japanese piston/Utility	216
Omas/glass nibbed pens	217
Safety Pens	218
Stylographic pens	222
Demonstrators	224
Yard-o-led pencil	226
Filling Instructions	228

See inside front cover or index for alphabetical list

PARKER DUOFOLD BUTTON FILLER

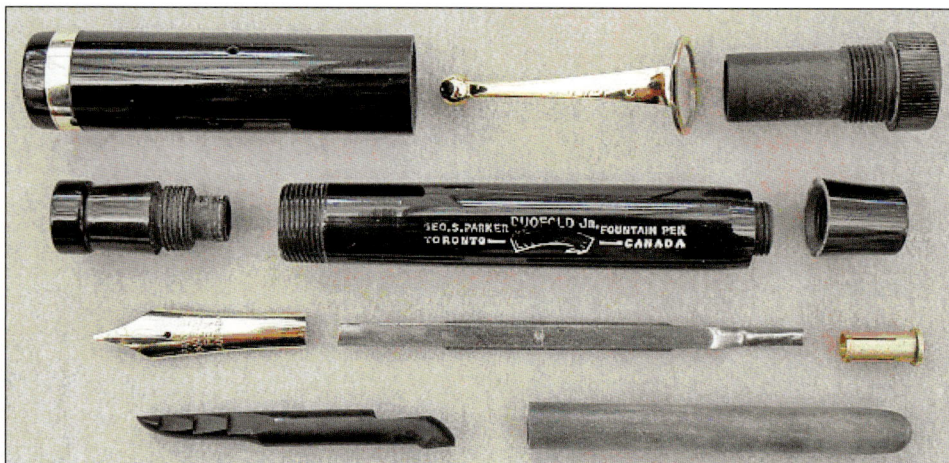

Lucky Curve Junior about 1926

The press button fill method was introduced in about 1917 and remained the favoured method for filling Duofolds until about 1948 on UK models. The Lucky Curve Duofold (main picture) remains the iconic vintage fountain pen, largely because of its elegant style. These pens are amongst the easiest to service and there are few inherent problems. There are a few model-specific aspects worthy of mention.

Lucky Curve

The Lucky Curve feed was designed to enable ink in the nib/feed area to return to the sac more easily when the pen was placed in the pocket, and thereby reduced the risk of leaking into the cap. There is no evidence that this idea worked, but the name was a good marketing ploy.

The sections come out on a screw thread, usually without a problem, but the usual soak and hot air is recommended. The curve on the end of the feed does give rise to some servicing problems because it cannot be knocked out without risk of damage. These feeds were originally fitted from the back, so they should be removed from the back. This operation requires the nib to be removed first. After a good soak and some hot air the nib should be rocked free with the fingers so that the feed is free to move.

Parker service engineers were advised to cut the end off the feed so that it could be knocked out in the conventional way. This is why it is now comparatively rare to find an unspoiled Lucky Curve feed.

A sacced section must never be screwed in with a pressure bar in place otherwise it will become twisted. The pressure bar is always fitted after the section is screwed in.

Parker made a tool for fitting the bar, but it is quite possible to do the job without it if the bar is pushed firmly towards the inside wall of the barrel.

If the Lucky Curve feed retains its original profile, it is important to insert the bar in line with the nib, otherwise it may foul the feed.

If the pressure bar needs to be replaced it is important to make it the correct length because the range of movement of the button is not large. A pair of tin snips can be used to trim the front of the bar, but do not leave the edge sharp for fear of tearing the sac. When finally fitting the button it is good to expand the slots with a knife blade so that it will not have a tendency to fall out.

Streamline

The Streamline pens were marketed in the USA from 1929 until about 1932, but pens of similar design and dimensions were produced in the UK until 1945. These pens have a fragile washer clip, a conventional feed and a push fit section; otherwise they are similar to the Lucky Curves and present no special problems in servicing.

Due to a possible risk of pushing the section out when operating the button, the pressure bar mounting was changed in the Streamline pens, but this brings no extra problems. The three types (see picture) are interchangeable in practice because the sections fit so tightly that they are not pushed out by the filler button.

NS Duofold

The New Style (NS) Duofolds appeared in the UK in 1946 and lasted only until 1948. The main changes were the incorporation of a jewelled tassie and a clip derived from the early Vacumatic pens. Sections push in.

AF Duofold

The Aluminium Filler (AF) Duofolds were marketed between 1948 and 1950. The aluminium button assembly can be removed from the pen using the Vacumatic pump tool, and the pressure bar can then be inserted from the end like other button fillers. Failing removal of the button, a sac one size smaller than normal will have to be fitted or it will become twisted when the section is screwed on.

Duofold clips

The early models have an integral blind cap and clip screw, that screws out. The AF Victory pens have smaller clip screws but present few problems and the NS are like Vacumatics and 50s Duofolds with a small clip screw or tassie and a threaded brass bush.

A Duofold Streamline Senior (UK)

A New Style Duofold Senior (UK)

A Victory AF from 1948 (UK)

Problems with Duofolds
- weak streamline clips
- brassed gf trim
- corroded AF buttons
- discloured blind caps
- crack through barrel threads

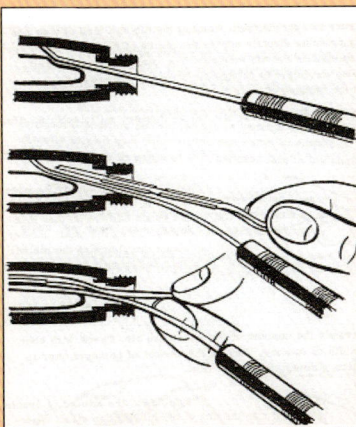

Parker's drawing of the pressure bar insertion tool

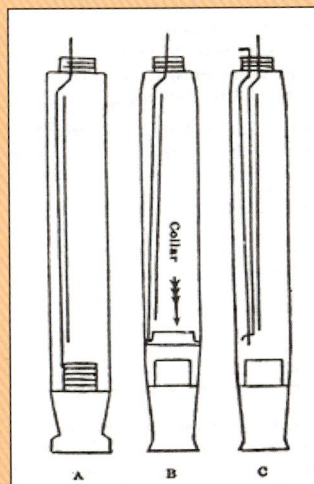

Three types of pressure bar installation. Type A presses on the section, type B presses on an internal collar and type C presses on the barrel end.

PARKER VACUMATIC

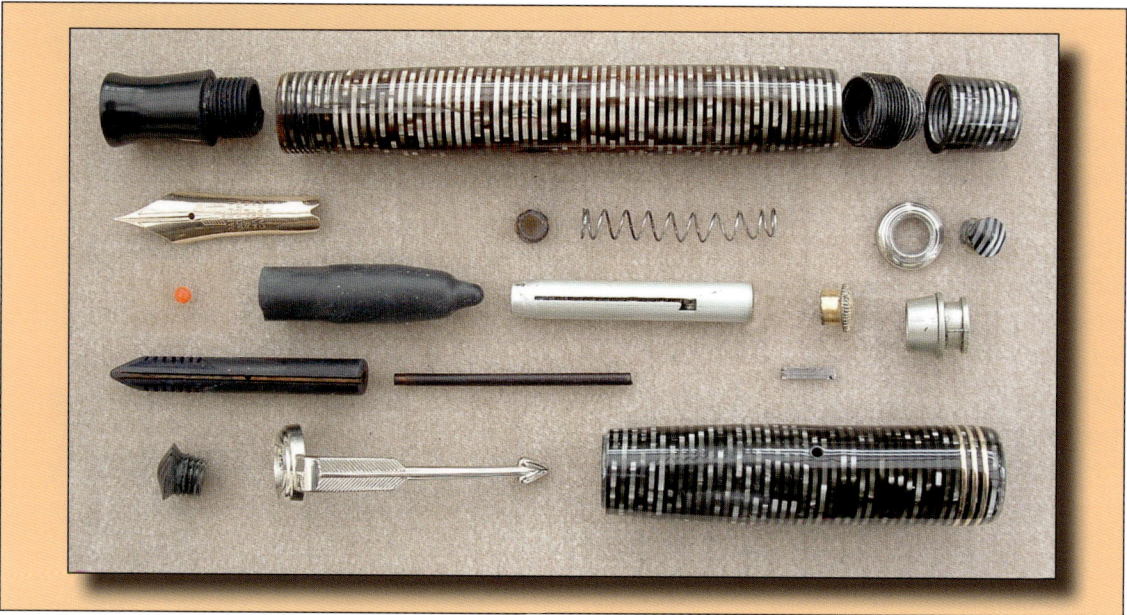

The Vacumatic first appeared in 1932 following extensive research by Parker in developing patents published by Dahlberg and others in the 1920's. The popularity of Vacs lasted until about 1947.

How a vac works

Vacs work on the bulb-filler principle where ink is drawn into the barrel by relaxation of a bulb-shaped diaphragm connected to a plunger mounted on the end of the barrel. A breather tube, fixed to the back of the feed, allows air to be expelled from the barrel. Several filling strokes are required to fill the barrel.

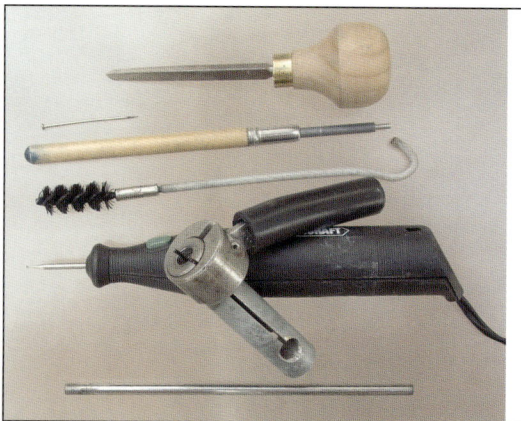

Some tools used in Vac repair

Problems

- tendency to blob
- pump shaft wears
- speedline corrodes
- tassies come off
- barrel snaps
- some plastics develop fine cracks (Golden Web)

Repair

The main task in repairing Vacumatics is to refurbish the pump system. This is fairly straightforward if the correct tools are available and there are no damaged components. The early Vacs used a high quality mechanism made of metal that could be locked down to enable a small blind cap to be used and thus utilise the full length of the barrel. Later models used a similar mechanism, but without the lock-down capability and thus requiring a much longer blind cap. The final phase of production used a mechanism with a plastic plunger rod, which was never intended for repair; these are easily damaged and require careful treatment. Imperial Vacs have a one-piece barrel and section, but others have a black hard rubber section with a right hand thread and sealed with a mild temperature sensitive adhesive.

Dismantling

With the aid of a little heat, unscrew the section and then the filler using a Vac servicing tool to grip the threads of the mounting bush (do not grip the bush harder than necessary for fear of making it oval). Simple tools exist e.g. a C ring gripped with pliers. A few of the later pens used a bush made of plastic. As these bushes are almost impossible to remove without damage to the threads the repair involves pulling the plunger out (breaking it) so the bush can be drilled out. A replacement metal unit can then be fitted.

If the filler is the lock down type, be sure to unlock it first. It pays to mark the alignment of the barrel and the bush so that when it is refitted,

Simple C-clip tool for gripping pump bush

it will be to the same depth as before. This also means that the blind cap will still have the same orientation to the barrel. If you do not do this, you will risk a slight misalignment of the blind cap with the barrel due to imperfect concentricity in the original manufacture. This is particularly

The three types of filler -locking; speedline; plastic

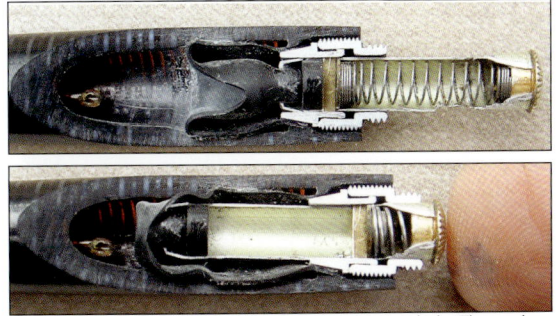

Sectioned filler showing it relaxed and extended. The end of the diaphragm is held by the aluminium cone against a tapered surface inside the barrel.

noticeable with the long blind caps on speedline fillers (and Parker 51s). Parker manuals say that any such misalignment should be polished out and they provided hand scrapers for use on the lathe to take out any unevenness. Having unscrewed the bush, the mechanism rarely comes out; this is because the old diaphragm has hardened and acts as a cement to hold everything in place. Never pull the filler shaft; use a flat ended rod to break the bond by pushing from the barrel throat.

In most cases a sharp tap from a light hammer will be required: do this with the bush screwed a few turns back into the pen so that the bush rests on the knock out block rather than the fragile barrel end. With the seal broken unscrew the bush and unit will usually drop out.

Preparing the barrel

With the barrel now open at both ends, you have the perfect opportunity to clean it thoroughly and restore much of the original transparency. A tool for scraping the barrel may be required to remove any hardened rubber (e.g a small wood carving gouge).

The important area to clear is the collar at the bottom of the filler unit threads because this is the sealing surface for the open end of the diaphragm. Debris left here may cause the pen to leak, not fill properly and prevent full insertion of the pump so that the blind cap will not pull up to the barrel.

A light source inside the barrel will enable the collar to be inspected, and it will guide the cleaning/scraping operation. A special tool can be made for this, but an old triangular file ground with a curved end is a good alternative if used with care.

The filler unit

Now turn to the filler and clean any debris from the aluminium cone that provides the other sealing surface within the barrel. Remove the old pellet and debris from the nose of the plunger. With metal fillers this can be achieved with a pin, but it is scarcely possible to do this on plastic fillers without risk of serious damage to the socket (they were disposable in the old days!). A better strategy is to use a small engraving tool to break up the pellet so that damage to the edges can be avoided.

Repair and Re-assembly
Fitting the diaphragm

Diaphragm folded into correct position

The new diaphragm must be cut to a maximum length of 30mm in order to avoid it fouling the breather tube when the plunger is depressed. Make sure that the diaphragm pellet is in place and then grip the diaphragm firmly just behind the nipple between the nails of the thumb and forefinger, whilst tightening the nipple over the pellet as much as is required for it to be able to pass through the hole in the plunger. This process is made easier with a pellet pusher.

The handle of the pusher, (or a suitable pencil), should be covered in talc and then pushed into the open end of the diaphragm (also covered in talc)

Pellet pusher

so that it can be folded back on itself onto the cone. Be sure that the end of the diaphragm rests comfortably up to the shoulder on the cone, not over it. There is no need to apply adhesives to the diaphragm or the cone, but a little silicone grease should be applied to the outside of the diaphragm to prevent it sticking to the inside of the barrel and becoming twisted when the filler bush is screwed

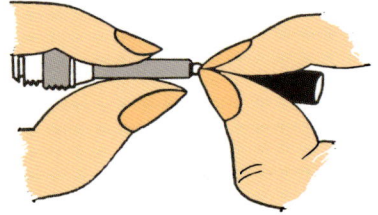

in. Do not over-tighten the bush.

Testing

The installation must now be tested to ensure that the seal is good and that there are no holes in the diaphragm. Arthur used to push the plunger in and then place the end of the barrel on the inside of his lip. If the barrel stayed there, the seal was good. If you do not like the taste of ink, you can do the same with a wetted finger. A more rigorous test of the efficiency of the seal can be performed with a rubber bulb and water immersion. The section can now be re-attached, but first make sure that all the components are clean and the nib setting is correct. The breather tube must be checked for blockages. Make sure that it is long enough to be just clear of the diaphragm when the plunger is fully depressed. There is no need to use adhesives for fitting the section; silicone grease will be sufficient to prevent ink leakage when the section is tightened moderately after gentle heating with hot air.

Cap, clip and trim

The main cause of difficulty is loss of jewels and the metal tassie rings from the end caps. Tassie rings can often be made from the tops of broken clips.

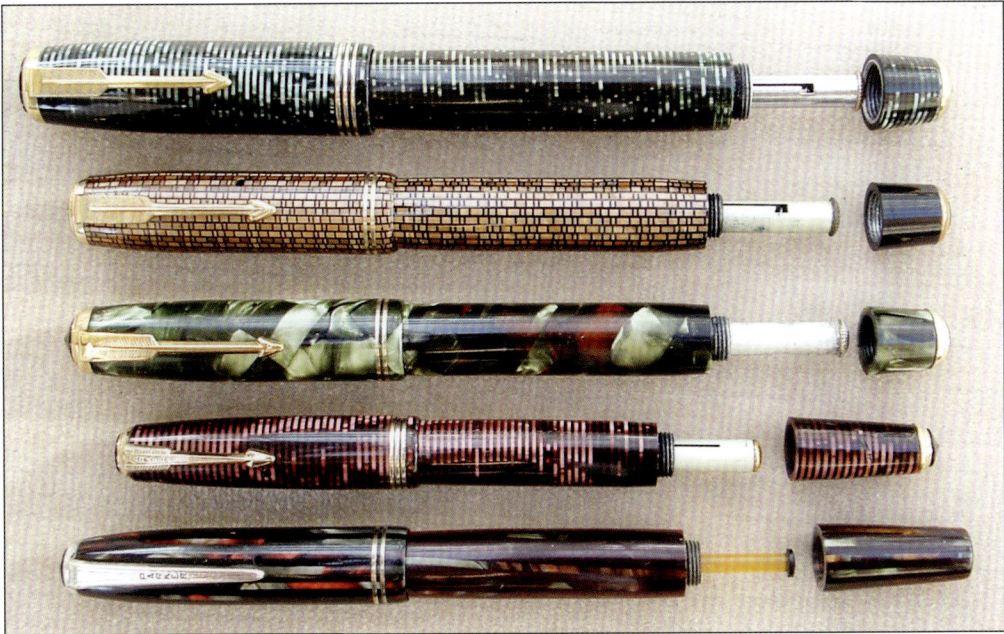

A collection of the some of the classic Vacumatics; Oversize, Golden Web, Green Marble, Burgundy pearl and striated, illustrating the three different pump types and lengths of blind caps

SPECIFIC PROBLEMS WITH FILLER UNITS

Lock-down plunger does not lock

The lockaway unit was originally made of brass and plated and was quite robust but the later shafts were made from aluminium and the lock away notch was quick to wear away and make the pen unserviceable. The shafts are the same diameter for all models (but there are 4 sizes of blind cap bushing) so good shafts can be interchanged.

Try using a needle file to reform the locking slot in the plunger, but bear in mind that the plunger will now not lock down as far as it did and the end of the plunger may contact the inside of the blind cap. If this does not work then it will be necessary to change the shaft.

Plunger does not hold the pellet securely

This does not need to be a tight fit, but if in doubt glue it in with rubber cement or shellac.

Parts of the filler assembly are damaged, e.g. the shaft or the blind cap threads

Metal Plunger - dismantle by pushing out the metal tab. Replace any damaged components. Use a thin blade inserted into the plunger slots to depress the spring before reinserting the tab, remembering that it fits between the spring and the pellet cavity washer. If the brass end cap needs replacement remember that it is a push fit and it needs to be tight.

Plastic plunger -can be dismantled after removing the nose, but it will be glued, so a breakage is likely. The spring end is held where it enters a hole drilled in the rod at the point where the nose is attached, and this is where the rod is weak.

PARKER 51 VACUMATIC

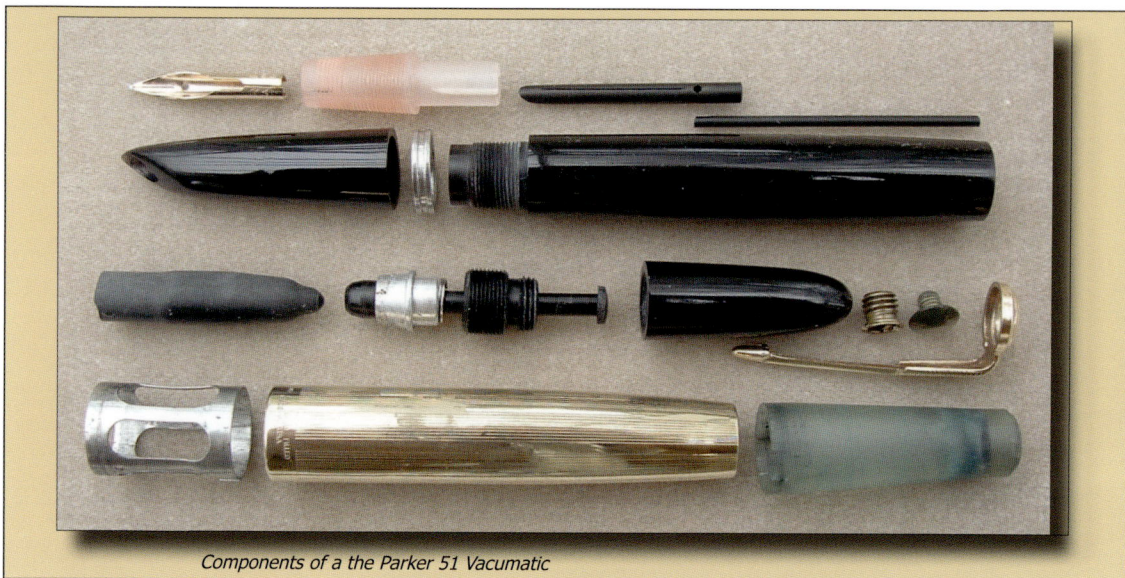

Components of a the Parker 51 Vacumatic

The Parker 51 was introduced in 1941 after extensive research to develop a more reliable and stylish pen to suit the emerging age of technology. The first models, including the Demi size used the same filling mechanism as the later Vacumatics.

Problems
- filling
- chipped and cracked shells
- cap and clip damage
- some colours difficult to match

The 51 vac is a sturdy pen and the main problems are related to filling. The repair procedure for the pump is the same as for the later Vacumatics.

Dismantling
The barrel and shell are made of Perspex (Lucite), and unlike the Vacs, they are unharmed by hot water immersion. In fact, one way to soften the sealant that holds the shell on the filler unit is to place the shell in boiling water. Most shells will unscrew easily after this treatment, but if

Removing a nib unit with a piece of rubber tube

assistance is required, be sure not to apply gripper force to the middle region of the shell because it may distort or crack.

A piece of sponge rubber tube gives an excellent grip on the shell, and Parker produced such a 'tool' with serrations for this purpose.

At this point it is useful to mark the barrel (a line drawn on a piece of masking tape is a good way to do this) so that the nib tip alignment with respect to the shell can be retained. The collector, nib and feed may now be pulled out of the barrel by finger grip, taking care not to damage the delicate fins on the collector. If the collector is stubborn soak it again and as a last resort use section pliers. The feed and nib should easily pull out of the collector.

Clean all the components, making sure that the breather tube and the fine channel on top of the feed are both clear (a fine wire and a feeler gauge are useful here).

Different feeds were fitted to Parker 51s; the early ones had no channel but the official statement is that either work well. Ensure that they are clean before reassembling.

Re assembly

No special tools are mandatory for re assembly of the nib unit. Hold the nib and feed together in alignment and push them back into the collector, making sure that the broad channel in the collector is above the top surface of the nib. Screw the shell back on again using heat; it is rarely necessary to reapply any adhesive. A little silicone grease or rosin based thread sealant at the top end of the threads where the shell meets the clutch ring is a good insurance policy against leaks. If when tightened, the tip of the shell does not align precisely with the nib, the shell must be removed again and the nib unit rotated in the barrel until it does. It is often necessary to repeat this tedious procedure several times.

The pen will work best if the shell tip makes contact with the top of the nib. To adjust this spacing, immerse the tip in hot water and squeeze the tip to the nib as it cools.

The Vacumatic filling system may require about 10 to 12 operations of the plunger to fill the pen. Give the pen a little time to drink after each operation. To empty the pen depress the plunger slowly; several cycles are needed and even then a small residual amount remains in the pen.

Cap, clip and trim

Cap servicing requires removal of the jewel (see Caps). The cap clutch must be removed if any work is required on the inner cap. Special tools are required for this, but it can often be useful to dismantle the cap completely so that it may be cleaned properly and any dents removed (see Dents). Often the mouth of the inner cap is cracked and can scratch the shell.

WRONG   RIGHT

FEED BAR WITH CHANNEL

FEED BAR WITHOUT CHANNEL

Be careful with the selection of blue diamond clips for the 51. From the front they look identical, to the 1940s Vacumatic pens but the crown diameter is slightly smaller.

Converting an Aerometric Parker 51 to a cartridge pen

In the 1990s The Pen Exchange in London's Chancery Lane sold a lot of vintage Parker 51s. There were frequent requests to convert the classic conventional aerometric Parker to a cartridge pen. Parker had produced a cartridge 51, which was one of the first pens to use modern cartridges, but it had a short 3 year life and was discontinued in 1962. Arthur had a passion to reintroduce this pen so a connector was designed, with the help of Bexley. The Parker 51 is dismantled and the foundation unit is replaced with the connector. The breather tube is cut to length so that it fits just below the pierce tube. The collector is fitted into the connector, the nib aligned, the barrel ring is fitted to the connector and the shell screwed on. Voila! A cartridge 51!

A Parker 51 dark blue cartridge/ converter pen

The all important connector

PARKER 51 AEROMETRIC

Dismantled Parker 51 made in UK with early sac protector

The Aero 51 appeared in 1954 in both full and Demi size.

Despite the claimed longevity of the Vac diaphragms, they aged at a similar rate to conventional sacs, so a new material was developed for the 51 Aero. The novel plastic (Pli-glass) added an attraction of transparency making the sac pen more desirable. Parker adopted the direct pressure bar and included a breather tube to give almost complete filling of the sac.

Problems with 51s

P51s rarely need much maintenance and should not be dismantled unless a nib change or adjustment is required or they are clogged with ink that cannot be removed by ultrasonic treatment. Early models used nickel-silver breather tubes that are subject to corrosion. A test for corroded, blocked or detached breather tubes should be made before deciding on dismantling. The pen should expel air for 5 squeezes of the pressure bar – if it does not, there is a problem.

Dismantling

This follows the procedure for the 51 Vac pen, but you do not have the pen barrel to provide a grip when unscrewing the shell. The process is made easier using the special clamp tool that enables the foundation unit threads to be gripped. The thread is 48 turns per inch three-start, so do not use the Vac thread gripper which is 36 per inch single start.

51 Shells

The shells of Vacs and Aeros are not the same. Aeros carry an O-ring seal between the filler and the shell and the shell lip is thinned to accommodate this. If you have to fit a Vac shell to an Aero, you must omit the O-ring.

The breather tube differs from the one used in the Vac in that it is much longer and it has a tiny hole in the wall (0.43mm, drill #77) about 7mm before it enters the feed. This hole provides a means to equalise the internal and external air pressures and thereby prevent leaks when the pen is clipped vertically in a pocket. If a breather tube has to be replaced make sure it is fitted the right way round.

Different clamps for holding the foundation unit ; smaller examples require plier grips.

If you do not have the special clamps, a simple tool can be made using an old barrel glued inside a tube of metal or plastic. This may be slit as shown and gripped with pliers

TIP

Removing the sac protector

If this has to be removed it is easiest done by warming the nipple and rocking and pulling (see sequence below). Use the Parker clamp to grip the sac protector.

1

2

Sequence for removing sac protector

4

3

Replacing a sac

The Pli-glass sac is extremely long lasting and although a rubber sac can be substituted the correct sac should be used. The factory adhesive was solvent based and was left for 5 hours to set. Nail varnish is an effective adhesive for such sacs. The protector is simply pushed over the sac onto the peg.

Re-assembly

Assembly and testing is similar to that for the Vac 51. The nib and feed should be fitted in the collector such that the wide channel is above the top of the nib, but this alignment does not seem to be critical. Add some silicone grease to the O-ring.

Cap, clip and trim

Good caps are becoming harder to find so it is important to know how to refurbish and restore older caps and clips. Plating clips does improve them but this usually requires a professional chrome plater. Gold plating is well within the repairer scope. Cap dents can be dramatically improved and a mild shot blasting can add icing to the cake (see also Dents).

Barrel dents are more difficult to fix because the insert needs to be removed first. US made pens used a soft soldered brass collar, which is easy to remove. UK made pens have a plastic full barrel insert which is glued in and can only be removed destructively. After the insert has been removed and the barrel restored a relacement threaded collar can be turned down from an old 51 barrel.

TIP

Collar made for metal barrel 51 -see webnotes for procedure

WEB NOTES www.........

Sac protectors are usually push on but some of the early US models were threaded.
Metal breather tubes corrode and are best replaced by plastic ones
Nibs vary a little; some have pierce holes others do not and also the feed design is with and without channels.
Threads on Mk1 and 2 pens are 48tpi 3 start for the barrel and single start for the shell.
Mk3 foundation unit threads are 32tpi (dual start for the barrel and single start for the shell). They also have a different barrel ring and a truncated barrel end (which can be confused in shape with a Parker17)

INFO

- Do not use section pliers to grip the sac protector if you want to remove the shell – it may distort, and it may slip on its mount as it is not glued on
- Be sure to clear the vent hole in the end of the barrel in order to keep the ink flow stable
- We do not regard the Parker 'hook' nib remover as a sensible tool - all too often the nib is damaged. We suggest you dismantle the unit to remove the nib!

CAUTION

PARKER 61 CAPILLARY

Parker 61 capillary

The Parker 61, introduced in 1956, was intended to be the successor to the 51 and adopted some of the Mark 3 parts, such as cap and barrel shape. An innovative capillary filling system was used.

Problems
- filling problems if left to dry out,
- shell shrinkage,
- the arrow trim falls out,
- clutch prongs can distort and mark the shell.

Filling and Cleaning
A frequent repair request is that the pen does not fill, and often this is because it has been left for a considerable period full of ink and has dried out.

Flushing a capillary unit with a rubber bulb and the original Parker ink ejector. Do not flush from the nib end until the flush from the other end is working as it can clog up the capillary.

The pen can usually be brought back into working order by flushing the pen out as illustrated with a bulb. Parker made a specific tool with a threaded barrel attached to a bulb, but a pipette bulb works very effectively with a cut down barrel and can be used to flush from both ends.

The pen fills when inverted into ink. (see 'filling classification')

Dismantling
Barrel
The construction is more complex than it appears in that it contains a spring loaded cup seal for the capillary unit. If this seal has to be replaced it can be pulled out with difficulty using a dental pick, but it is easier to knock it out after removing the pearl tassie and trim. Use a rubber bung and if the tassie is stubborn warm it gently. They have an ACME thread (32tpi).

Flighter, Insignia and precious metal pens have a plastic insert which may require replacement. It can rotate inside the metal barrel and consequently need regluing. If the plastic threads have stripped the liner must be removed; it is usually easier to burn it out. The inside of the capillary barrel liner is specially shaped to receive the capillary cup seal.

The Writing Unit
This comprises: the capillary unit; collector; trim ring; connector; nib; and shell.

Removing the shell

Parker 61 shells are made from a soft plastic and they are susceptible to damage and deterioration with heat and certain inks. They shrink onto the collector and can be very difficult to remove. Unlike Parker 51 shells , hot water must not be used to dismantle! Good shells are valuable, so if there is little shrinkage and the arrow is still in

Three clamps for capillary and aerometric 61

place then effort should be made to remove the shell without damage. However, if the shell is badly distorted cut it off with a fine piercing saw. A spiral cut is easiest and, if done with patience, causes no damage to the collector.

Soaking is important and particularly warming the shell near the connector threads to soften any adhesive. Take care with the use of an ultrasonic bath as it can often dislodge the arrow from 61 shells.

Use a clamp if possible or section pliers with an old barrel to grip the connector, and a rubber tube for the shell. The removal of 61 capillary shells is rarely easy.

Normally, the capillary unit stays in the shell as the connector screws out and is withdrawn over the capillary tube. Further soaking and movement will remove the capillary unit from the shell.

Do not use pliers which will scratch the PTFE coated capillary case. The only function of the

hydrophobic coating is to 'run' the ink off and give a dry surface following filling.

The capillary unit comes out as one piece and the nib easily detaches from the collector and feed.

Regenerating the capillary unit

In the 1962 Parker Spares manual all the component parts of a capillary unit are listed. This might indicate that the repair of capillary units was common practice but we would hesitate to recommend dismantling unless parts are broken (even if all the parts were available). The collector is fragile and even with heat can easily snap in two.

New capillaries are unavailable, but with plenty of flushing with a good detergent mix and heavy ultrasonic to disperse the particulate material, most capillary units can be regenerated. The task is to remove the debris from the foam pad at the top and from the interstices of the rolled capillary element.

A low electrolyte mix with synthetic detergent is most effective. Use warm dishwashing liquid adjusted to pH 10/11 with dilute caustic and immerse in an ultrasonic bath for a number of cycles before flushing. Use the bulb on the top end and flush out through the collector end to avoid building up deposits into the foam pad (use rubber gloves as the mild caustic may cause some skin irritation!). Repeat this a few times and your capillary unit will work again!

Cap/Clip -see 'Parker 61 Aerometric'.

Reassembly

Refit the nib. Take care to put the connector the right way round and replace the plastic seal. PVA waterproof adhesive is sparingly added to the connector threads.

When replacing a liner in Flighters or Insignias, it is important that it is firmly fixed in position and this can be aided by ensuring the tassie screws firmly into the barrel liner. This can be facilitated by cutting a slot into the tassie as shown, and using a slim screwdriver to tighten the tassie liner joint. It is also a useful practice with later model plastic or metal tassies.

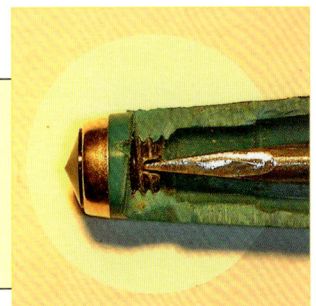

PARKER 61 AEROMETRIC

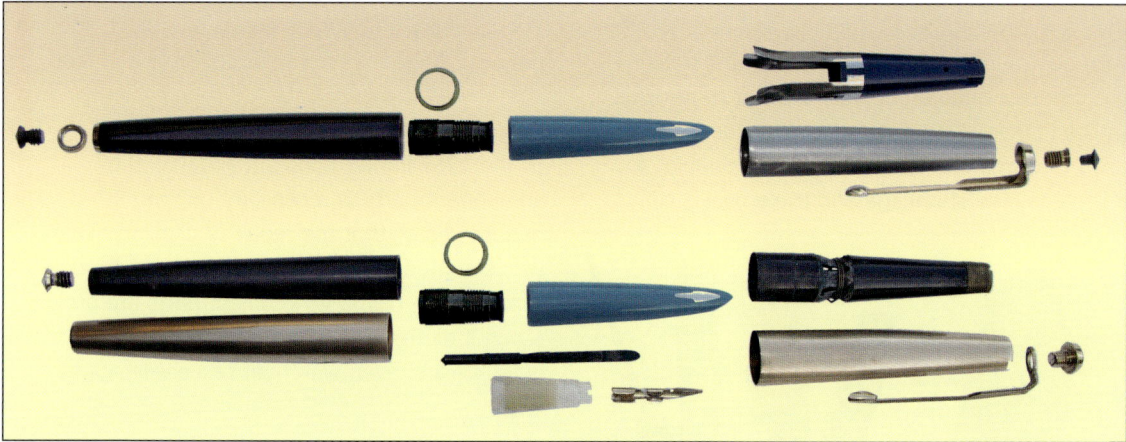

Exploded Parker 61 illustrating Mk1 plastic and Mk2 insignia with differing trim/clip

Capillary filling was not a great success and cartridges were the new fashion, consequently Parker completely modified the 61 and it was introduced as a cartridge/convertor pen. The Mark 2 had modified trim and clip. The Cloud series had a different inner cap.

Problems
- the shell arrow still dislodged
- the pens developed leaks due to connector deterioration
- the barrel trim worked loose

Dismantling
The barrel screws off; the writing unit comprises a connector with incorporated piercing unit, collector, feed, trim ring, nib and shell; the cap is metal with a plastic inner cap and clutch.

Barrel
The barrel has a fine internal thread (48tpi 3 start) and these are not interchangeable with capillary barrels. The Mk1 has a pearl tassie and trim and later Mk2 had a metal tassie Barrels did not need to incorporate a capillary unit seal and were thinner walled. The metal barrel aero 61s have fine threaded liners.

Dismantling the writing unit
The connector must be removed and this is usually straight forward after soaking and warming. A correctly threaded clamp is most practical if the connector is to be used again or good section pliers with a cartridge, convertor or wooden plug in place to support the thin connector wall. Unfortunately connectors frequently shear at the top of the shell and have to be removed. This can be a tedious digging and filing job but a suitable plug tap usually gives a good enough grip to screw out the remnants.

For some reason there is excessive material degradation of the 61 connector and this invariably occurs at the base around the piercing unit and gives rise to leaking. It appears to be some sort of chemical or ageing defect and is quite a serious '61 disease' as the shell is also affected. The solution is simply to replace the connector and new metal connectors are recommended.

Connectors from l to r -original Parker, Model 1 (1998); model 2 (2004); Deteriorated example

Once the connector is removed the feed and nib should simply drop out of the shell. Sometimes shell shrinkage makes this tricky and the collector has to be forcibly withdrawn. Take out the feed and with the use of a long fine wood screw, pull out the collector and nib. Be careful because the feed has an oval locating lug, which fits into a recess in the collector; this should not be damaged. The lug/recess ensures that the nib lines up correctly with the feed.

Reassembling the writing unit

Slide the feed into the collector, locating the lug, and push on the nib; this is then aligned and pushed into the shell. A piece of metal tube can be used to push it into the right position (the internal part of the shell is shaped so that the nib collector can only fit in one position). Refit the trim ring on the connector with the flange on the nib side and screw in the connector using a small amount of shellac or PVA.

The new metal connectors are better than the earlier coated ones because they accept all sizes of converter. The early examples would not take the larger converters. If there is any movement of the nib then the assembly is incorrect.

The connector should be checked to ensure that the barrel screws on easily. It is not impossible, with the metal connectors, to cross the threads particularly if there is no cartridge in place to ensure alignment. Plastic barrels are rarely a problem but the fine threads on a Flighter or Insignia can cross thread quite easily. A small amount of silicone grease can facilitate fitting.

Replacing a clip

With Mk1 pens this involves removing the pearl clip screw or tassie and the brass bush.

Later and early 61 clips/tassies

Use a rubber bung and a little heat to remove the pearl tassie and then a screwdriver for the bush. If the pearl has broken in the bush it may be necessary to cut it out a little until the screwdriver fits into the bush slot. The remnants of the jewel can be burnt out.

The Mk 2 has a metal clip screw and sometimes this is difficult to remove without damaging the screw - warm the cap by inverting the end in hot water and unscrew with a piece of rubber tube or small padded pliers.

Reassembly

The clip is lined up with the cap prong and the bush and clip screw are refitted. A holding arbor makes it easier to tighten the screw without dislodging the clip.
The Mk2 clip slots into the cap first and the clip screw is tightened again with rubber tube.
Always examine the inner cap and clutch when changing a clip!

Replacing the arrow
Clear away any residues in the recess with a pin, noting that arrows were never glued on. Find some clear adhesive tape and stick the arrow face down on it. Stick it on the pen carefully making sure that the arrow lies fully in the recess. Press the tape firmly down on all edges and then lift one side just sufficiently to be able to see under the arrow. Apply a thin coat of warm epoxy with a cocktail stick and press the tape down again. When dry, remove the residue from the shell using abrasive sticks and polish, bearing in mind that the arrow is gold plated - not solid gold.
Removing the recess
BEFORE AND AFTER

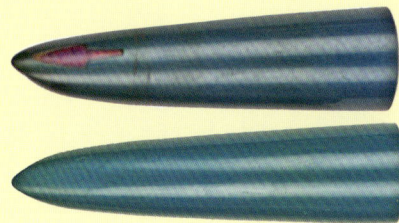

It is possible to make a Parker 61 shell with missing trim look more presentable by removing the recess. This is easily done with a 4 grade nail board and polishing. Another option is to fill the recess with gold paint.

PARKER 61 CAPILLARY CONVERSION

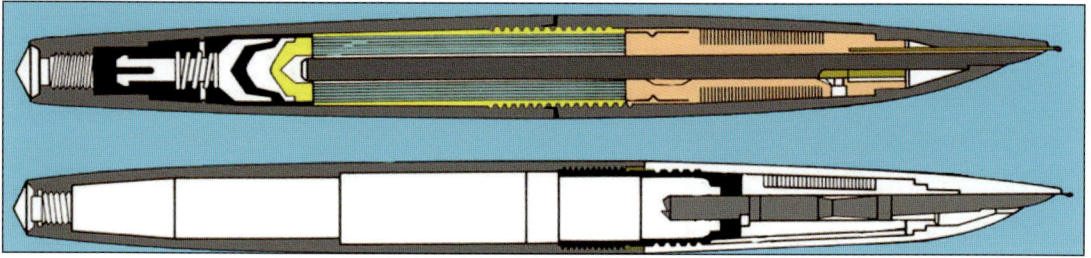

Comparison of capillary barrel and shell with a cartridge converter model

For many, the 51 'aero' system was preferable to dipping a pen upside down into a bottle of ink, so when Parker provided this with a redesigned Parker 61, it reinforced the perception that the capillary pen was useless. This was compounded when Parker also offered a conversion service for capillary 61s.

When this conversion service was discontinued, private repairers such as Arthur Twydle were recommended to those who wanted a conversion. Initially this conversion involved changing the barrel, internals and using only the customer's shell and nib, which was a costly conversion in terms of parts. By the 1990s parts for 61s were hard to find so a conversion system using most of the existing capillary parts was devised. This entailed the manufacture of a new connector with ACME threads so the original pen parts can be used.

Modifying the barrel

Material must be removed from the barrel to accomodate a cartridge or converter because the capillary barrel has a different internal profile. Before any reaming can be carried out the the spring seal system must be removed. It can sometimes be pulled out with a modified dental pick. However we normally sacrifice the end pearl and knock it out or alternatively use a small drill (1mm) and drill through the pearl and then knock out the seal. The hole can be filled later with grey epoxy.

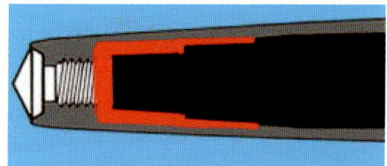

The material which has to be removed to accomodate a cartridge or converter.

Reaming can then be carried out by hand or with a slow speed drill fitted with a 6mm reamer. The depth (69mm) should be accurately marked with tape to ensure that the reamer does not break the barrel. Take care at the final stages as the barrel wall is quite thin.

The writing unit

Remove the shell and begin to dismantle the capillary unit. The collector, feed and trim ring are going to be used again so use plenty of warming and patience. Sacrifice an unwanted part in order to get the part that is going to be reused out in one piece e.g. cut the metal tube and withdraw the feed and collector; the feed withdraws easily. Take care because the collector is brittle. The parts are now ready to be adjusted.

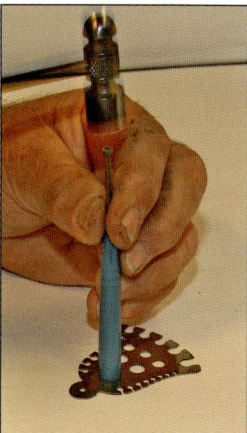

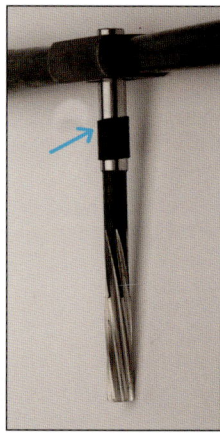

Knocking out the capillary seal unit and reaming the barrel either with a drill reamer or with the hand reamer. Note the depth guide!

Modifying the feed and collector

It is easiest to fit a Mk2 feed and collector but we presume that most enthusiasts do not have a stock of parts so the solution is to adapt the existing parts.

The feed must be cut to a length of 45mm and then chamfered slightly at the top. The capillary feed has two fine channels running down the length of the rod. With a sharp knife blade enlarge these channels as far as the scalloped part of the capillary feed. This helps improve flow from the cartridge/converter into the collector.

The collector is cut to a length of 23mm with a piercing saw or a cutting disc at slow speed. Take your time because these are acrylic and brittle. Ensure the cut is square to the collector length.

First fit the nib into the collector with the wide channel underneath. The feed is now fitted into the modified collector. The cleats ensure the feed is aligned correctly.

There is a possibility that the modified feed can move in towards the cartridge as there is no flange on the feed. (In the case of the Aerometric feed the locating flange is pressed down by the connector and there can be no movement.) Initially we used to pin the modified feed through the bottom breather hole in the collector but all we now do is ensure the nib cleats are a tight fit on the feed and put a drop of shellac between the underside of the feed and the collector.

Assembly

This is exactly as one would assemble an ordinary cartridge/converter 61 but using the special connector with ACME threads for barrel and shell. Position the assembled collector/feed/nib in the shell and push into position with a small tube. Fit the barrel trim ring to the connector and screw into the shell, using shellac on the threads.

The stages of conversion
- remove the barrel seal
- ream out the barrel
- modify the collector and feed
- fit the 'special' connector

The only special tools required are a reamer and a fine saw or Dremel.

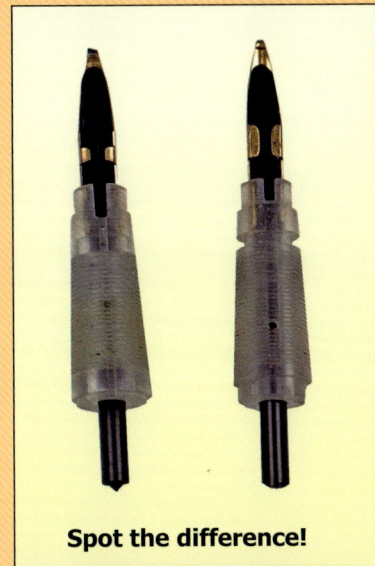

Spot the difference!

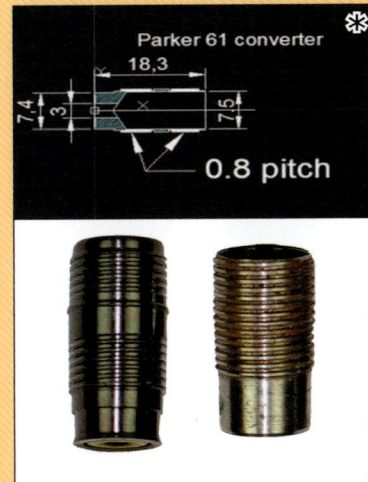

Parker 61 converter
18,3
0.8 pitch

Conversion connector with coarse threads compared with the original connector

The modified feed compared to normal

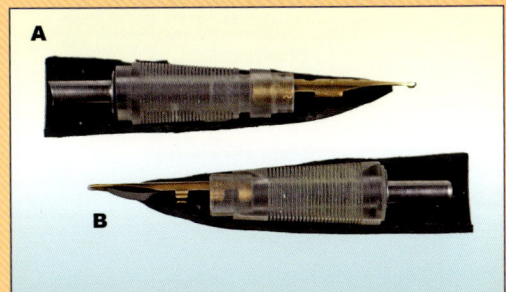

The position of a modified A and an aerometric B collector, feed, nib and piercing unit within the shell.

* Courtesy Roger Wolfe

PARKER 65

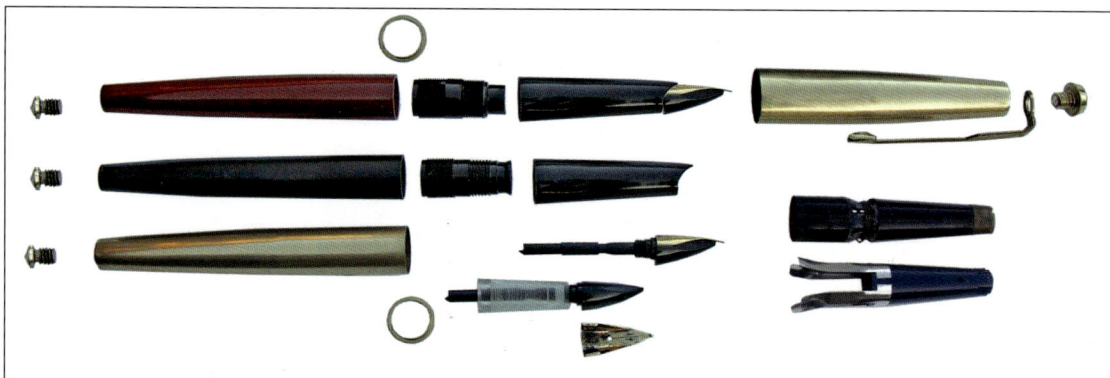

The illustrated Parker 65s have the two styles of collector and the fine and coarse threaded shell. The two inner caps were used with the Cloud series of 65s. The Insignia barrel has a plastic liner.

There are three versions of the Parker 65 which all appear to have been influenced by other pens and pen parts. The main consumer attraction was the large exposed gold nib.

The 'fixed filler' model was exclusively distributed to export markets. It had a Parker VP filler unit and VP style feed with a short stub feed to fit into the filler unit protrusion. These pens are included in the Parker pen mechanics guide but are rare. The two later models adopted the 61 barrel style and connector. The writing unit housing contained a new collector design, a longer feed with the VP style nib. The connector with integral piercing unit was at first fine threaded for both barrel and shell. The Parker 61 connector was used for later pens. Consequently, the later 65 shells have a coarse thread and cannot be used with the early connectors. The collectors required different tools to dismantle them.

The metal nib, with a spade shape and two cleats, was common to all models.

It is important to emphasise these variations because parts for Parker 65s are now in very

Mk2 & Mk3 connectors with fine and coarse threaded shell-threads; both barrel threads are fine. The right examples have been remanufactured recently.

short supply and few realize that although the two convertible models look the same from the outside they are composed of totally different parts..

Dismantling

The barrel is the same as the Parker 61 Aerometric.

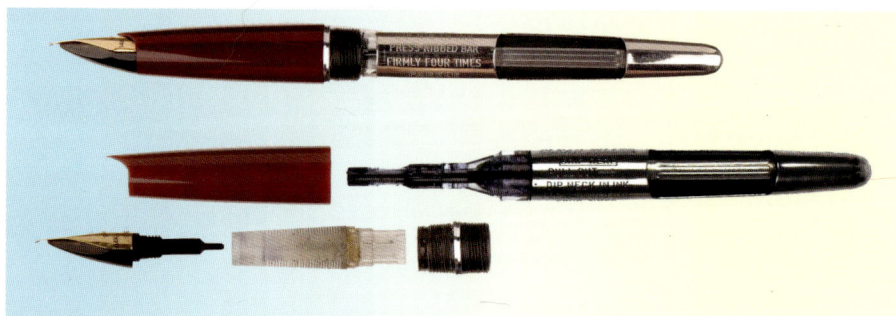

This was the model for export and designed to accept the VP reservoir. Note the unusual connector.

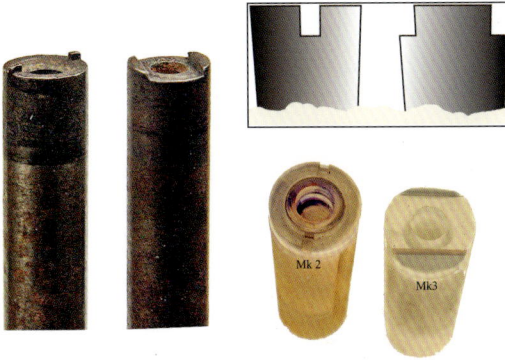

The two designs of connector have to be unscrewed to release the nib unit. The two tools are illustrated

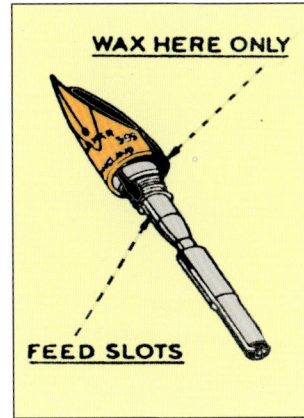

The writing unit

Soak, warm and then remove the connector with an appropriate clamp or good section pliers. A piece of rubber tubing gives a good grip on the shell.

The collector has to be unscrewed from the feed with the appropriate tool. The two types are illustrated together with the appropriate tools. Take your time, particularly if the collector is being difficult. Do not chew up the slots or flanges otherwise you will be making a pronged removal tool! Shells do shrink and it may be impossible to release the feed and collector- in such cases the shell will have to be cut off with a piercing saw. When the collector is completely unscrewed the nib unit is easily pulled out.

Replacing a nib

The nib can be removed from the feed with a piece of rubber gently pushing the nib backwards out of the two grooves. Do not try to lever the cleats or use pliers to pull the nib. The nib can be worked on or replaced and is fitted on to the feed by putting the cleat into one side slot and pressing firmly down on the top of the nib until the other cleat clicks into the other retaining groove.

Reassembly

One of the critical steps is to seal the base of the feed and shell. Dental wax or soft wax is rolled into a thin ribbon and placed in position before the nib/feed assembly is pushed into the shell. The wax must only be on the underside of the feed otherwise flow will be impeded. The collector is then dropped over the feed and tightened until the excess wax squeezes out – this seal is vital otherwise the pen will leak.

Finally the trim ring is refitted to the connector, which is screwed in with a small amount of adhesive sealant such as shellac or PVA. Connectors and shells are not interchangeable, but collectors can be used in either pen.

Both the VP nib unit (A) and the 65 export model (B) have short stub feeds to fit into the 'VP' reservoir unit. The later 65 cartridge/ converter model (C) has the long feed to fit into the pierce cutter.

Never try and unscrew the nib or twist it even slightly! There is an internal peg on the inside of the shell inner which aligns the feed and keeps the feed in position. If this snaps off the shell is useless as the nib will turn during use. The collector must be removed completely before pulling the nib out, which must also be in a straight line without twisting.

CAUTION

PARKER 1950s DUOFOLD

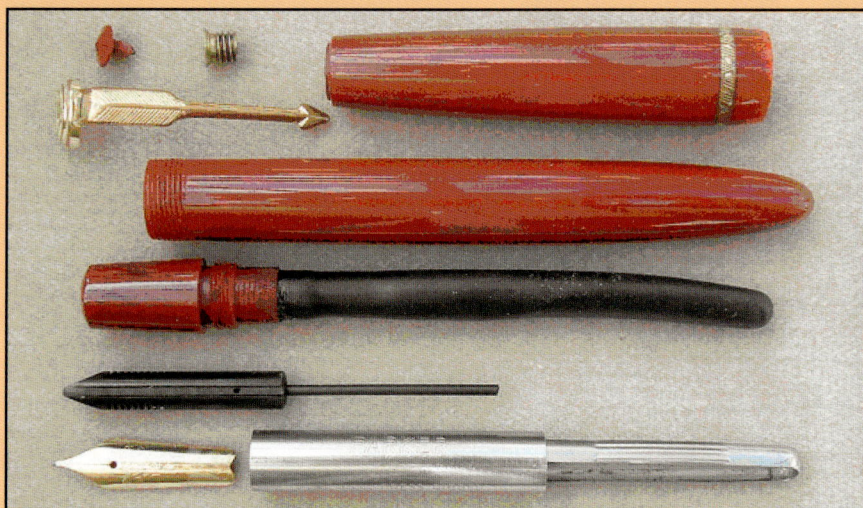

The popular Duofold school and student pen of the late 1950s

The 1950s Parkers were a natural development from the NS and AF Duofolds and the Parker 51. The new pen combined the advantages of the 51 Aero filling system with the more traditional style having a plastic cap and barrel and an attractive, open nib. These pens appeared in 1953, and were so successful, that by 1962 seven different sizes were being sold, all constructed to the same design.

Problems
- thin cap lips that chip and crack
- feed loses fins
- tassies split
- normal accidental damage of clips and nibs

These pens are extremely reliable, and because of their use of the pli-glas sac, they rarely need servicing.

Servicing
Sac replacement
If a sac needs to be replaced, the sac protector must be taken off. The sac protector is a press fit on the back of the section and will require some heat to assist with its removal (see Aero 51). A Parker clamp can be used but section pliers are just as effective. Remember to grip over the section nipple so that the protector is not distorted.

If the nib has not been removed take care to protect the breather tube when removing the sac. New sacs should be glued on with solvent based adhesive rather than shellac.

Nib
It is best not to disturb the sac, so the nib and feed should be pulled out.

The section must first be soaked to make removal easier. Most feeds are a good fit in these pens so warming is essential. Try 'walking' the nib out first. This involves pressing the shoulder of the nib up and across and then repeating that from the other side. This process is often successful after about

A nib vice for pulling the nib and feed

CAUTION The Slimfold Lady and Parker 17 pens have a loosely fitting rod within the sac; it is there to break down surface tension that tends to hold the ink in suspension in the sac.

10 or so presses. If a clamp has to be used ensure that it will not distort the nib or damage the delicate fins in the feed. It is best if the grip is between a piece of flat firm rubber against the feed, and soft rubber against the nib. Parallel pliers with soft rubber or the nib clamp are both effective. Pull straight! Twisting may well remove the nib but with the risk of deforming the sides.

Assembly

If the nib/feed has been a challenge to remove then reassemble with heat. If you have never used heat when you put a pen back together, you will be very surprised how much easier it makes the process. Make sure that the feed is clean before putting it back. Dried deposits from syrupy ink can be very stubborn, so use a thin wedge to clean the channels.

Testing

The pens contain a breather tube, so typically four squeezes of the filler are required to fill the pen.

PARKER 17

The Parker 17 was introduced in 1962 with a large beak nib but was modified to the hooded version in 1964. It had a slip cap and a small gold nib. The wide band deluxe model had more elegant trim and a small model akin to the Slimfold, the Lady 17, was popular. These are very functional pens but have never had the collectors appeal of the Duofold range

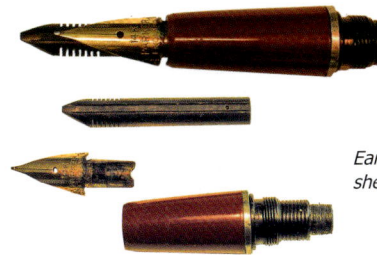

Early Parker 17 shell, feed and nib

Problems
- foundation unit splits
- caps become loose

Dismantling

This is easy with section pliers or a piece of soft rubber tube and heat/soak. There are a few sizes so make sure that your replacement parts are for the correct pen. Sac replacement is the same as for the Duofolds but nib replacement is a little more complex as the small nibs must be pulled out. Use soft jawed pliers or a clamp.

Neither of these are practical for the beak nib. There is no way this nib will come out undamaged without soaking and heating. A tapered section clamp is essential and the final stages of removal involve heating and pushing with a rod. Hot air is essential to assist replacement.

CAUTION

Exploded Parker 17 De Luxe and Standard model with small nib and hooded section

PARKER VP

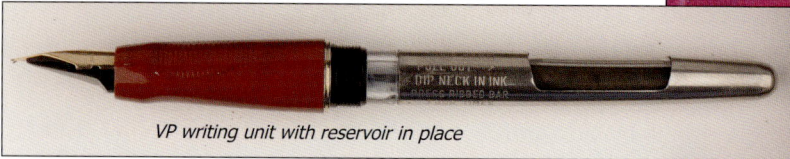

VP writing unit with reservoir in place

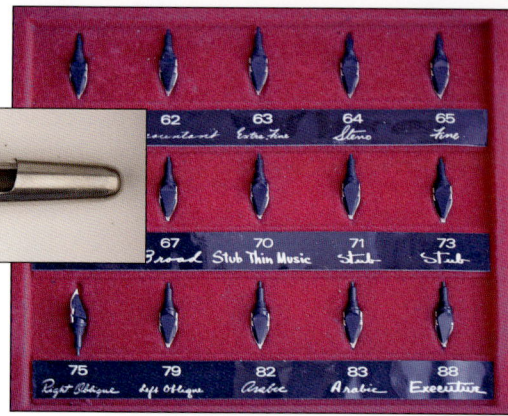

Range of nibs for Parker VP

Introduced in 1962, the VP had a contoured grip that was supposed to be more practical for writing at different angles. The pen had a short nib and feed which screwed into a collector, which was specially designed to accommodate a new design of acrylic removable reservoir. The proposal was to fill the reservoir and then insert it into the pen. However the reservoir was rather fragile and sadly snapped easily, often leaving part of it in the collector. There were ambitious marketing intentions for the VP as a writing instrument and the range of nibs was extensive.

Exploded view of writing unit with short stub feed, collector and connector

Dismantling

The barrel is removed and the converter pulled out with care. The connector is then unscrewed, which exposes the collector. With the aid of a star shaped screwdriver is inserted into the collector hole to unscrew from the nib unit. The collector pulls out and the nib is released.

Reassembly

The nib is fitted into the shell and the collector is screwed onto the feed threads. With the barrel ring in place the connector is refitted with a small dab of shellac, taking care not to add too much so that it fouls the collector. The acrylic reservoir is refitted.

PARKER VS

Three slightly different models , one with an aerometric filler and two button fillers, one fitted with an AF button

An interesting post war open nibbed pen which originally was a button filler but there were obviously a number of versions as the aerometric example illustrates. The early models had plastic threaded blind cap nipples. The cap has a short Parker 51 style clutch and this fits on to a barrel ring which is identical to the 51. It presents no hazards of repair but use a tube to knock the feed out, so as not to damage the breather tube orifice. It has a large 6mm diameter feed, which we are told was originally transparent lucite.

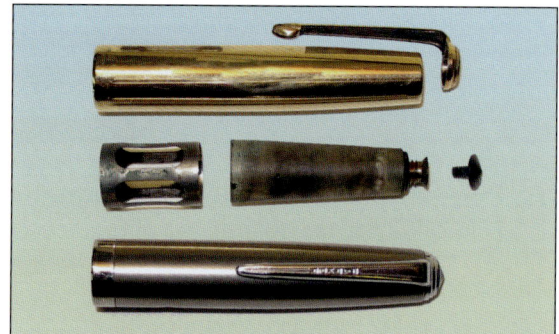

Parker VS cap

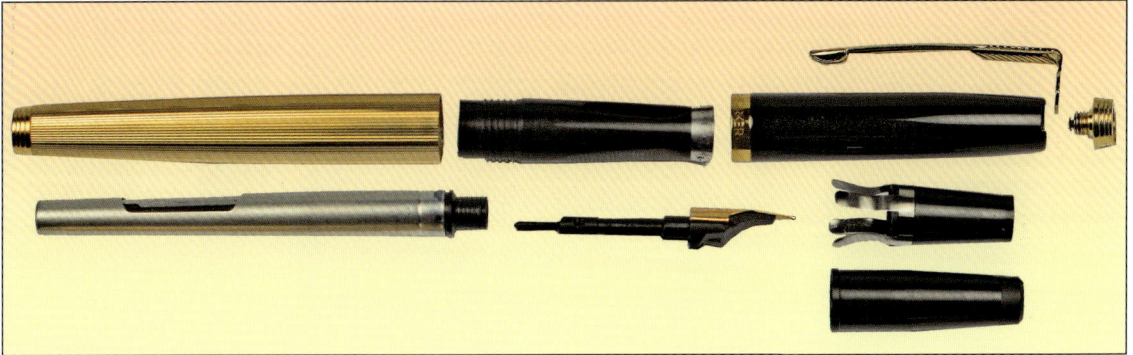

The Parker 75 was introduced in 1974 and was an attractive medium sized pen. The first limited Edition was produced as a Parker 75. There is little to go wrong with them and repairing is essentially replacing damaged parts

Nib section unit

There are four types of trim on the section and two different feeds. It can be quite difficult to remove the nib from the feed but if this has to be done; warm the unit and use a rubber bung and work it or walk it off; a thumbnail works well!

Walking a 75 nib off the feed

They were never meant to be taken off the feed but good nibs are hard to find! The nib is refitted by sliding it back onto the feed. The nib units are common to the Premier range .

There is quite a variety of 75 shell trim

Inner clutch

The two types of inner cap clutch are illustrated.

Replacing a clip

Cisele, Independence, Queen Elizabeth

The clip screw is loosened with shaped rubber grips or a piece of rubber tube to avoid scratching the clip screw (not pliers!). The inner clutch is depressed and the clip can be removed. Parker used some different clips and clip screws for unusual models such as the limited editions and special makers models like the 14ct gold Tiffany. The first year models had a smooth top, which was superceded by the recessed design. (Beware of shorter smaller clip screws turned down to look like first year!).

The two nib supports ; the later design with the collector as part of the support. (In the early models the collector is moulded as part of the shell).

PARKER 25

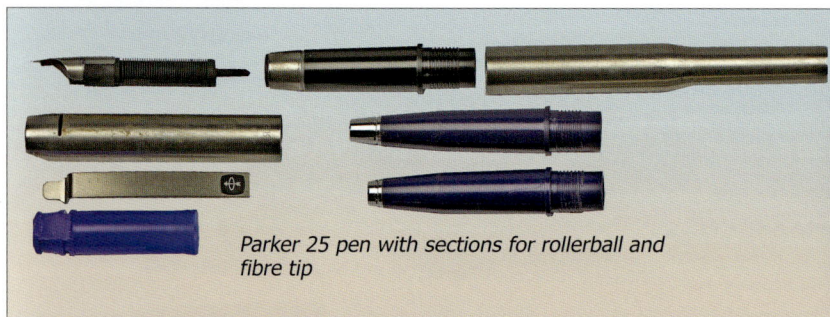

Parker 25 pen with sections for rollerball and fibre tip

Parker 25 pen and ballpen caps are the same size with different inners.

Parker had some very sturdy pens and the 25 was one of the best. Easy to service and economic. There is little that goes wrong with this pen. The Stainless steel 25s had push in steel nib units with the nib crimped to the feed. The section colour matched the trim on the cap (inner cap) and the clip logo disc. The colours were black, blue and the much rarer green and white. The range icluded pens, ball pens, roller balls, fibre tiped pens and pencils using a ratchet lead insert in a cap actuated ball pen.

Dismantling the cap/ clip repair/ ratchet replacement

The same procedure applies to all models. In order to change a clip or access a ratchet one has to knock the inner-cap or ratchet out with a small wooden peg -the stepped clip can be unhooked. The ratchet removal is a little trickier because the cap must be positioned over an exact diameter hole in a knocking block to allow the ratchet to be displaced.

PARKER 45.

Parker 45

The 45 was Parker's first completely designed cartridge pen and it has now had over 40 years in production. The flighter barrels were a little unusual in that the steel overlay was secured by a top trim screw; this was also the case with the elegant gold filled clipless pens. The 45 nibs were in 14ct gold or 'Octanium' and held in a collar which screwed into the gripping section. The nibs are very easy to change by screwing the unit out.

Parker 45 nibs and carrying unit with threaded collar

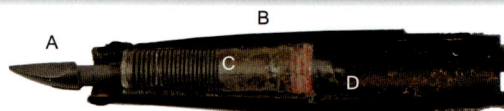

The internal design is similar to the early Parker 75 pens in that the collector C is fixed in the gripping section B and accommodates the slim feed shaft AD. The pierce cutter is metal. These are regarded as cheap pens but this is quite a complex assembly operation and must have been costly. Fortunately the nib is small which would have offset some of the costs.

Repair work other than on the nib is essentially replacing parts.

PARKER 50 (FALCON).

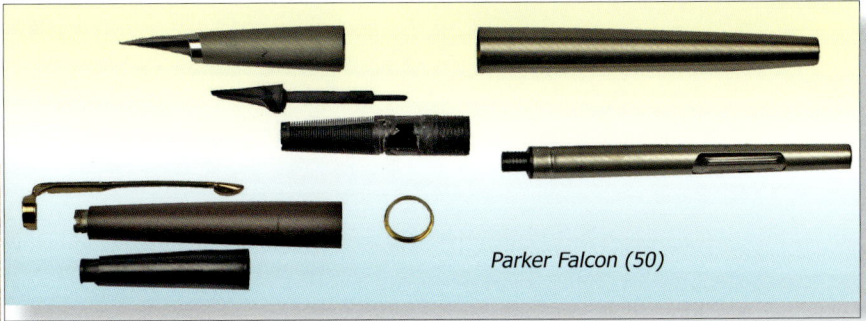

Parker Falcon (50)

The Falcon was a space age design of pen similar to the T1 with a nib formed from the metal shell. There were four versions, black, gold filled, brown and brushed steel. Ball pens and pencils were made to match.

The only problem with the pen is that the the clip cracks at the ring/arrow joint. The metal trim disc is removed and the plastic bush pulled out. The clip is pushed on and secured by a new plastic bush.

OSMIA PROGRESS 96

Osmia quality diaphragm fill pen

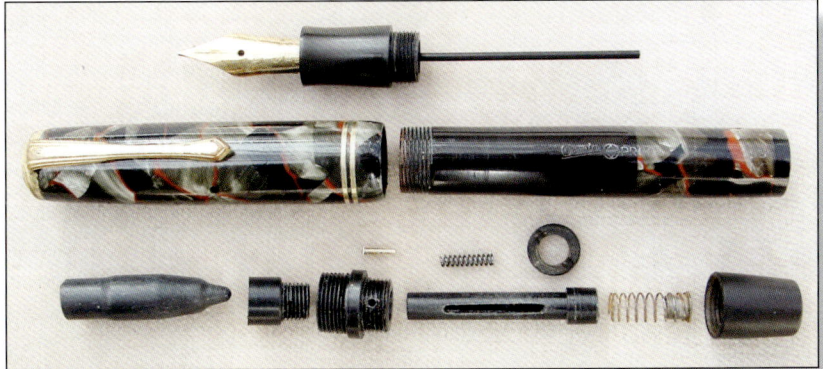

This German pen may appear out of place but Osmia was owned by Parker from 1928 to 1930 and this is truly a collector's pen. Although this was produced in the mid 1930s it bears a remarkable similarity to the Vacumatic as a result of the Parker contribution to the development of Osmia. The filler is considerably more complicated than the Vacumatic with the only obvious benefit that the blind cap is not detachable.

Servicing

Dismantling starts with unscrewing the section and breather tube, followed by unscrewing the plastic plug that holds the filler assembly. This is easier if the threaded washer that holds the spring-loaded blind cap in place can be removed by engaging it with a two-pronged tool similar to the one used in Onoto repair. The plug can then be gripped with a Vacumatic-style pump removal tool. The plug may be difficult to remove because

it was glued in place (probably by shellac). The plug contains a guide pin that runs in a slot in the pump rod; this prevents unwanted rotation of pump components. A standard Vacumatic

Filler unit fitted with a standard vac sac

diaphragm can be fitted into the socket in the end of the pump rod. The open end of the diaphragm is sandwiched between the plug and a screwed plastic bush. Unlike the Vacumatic, the attachment of the plug to the barrel must be an ink-proof seal, which explains why the originals were attached so securely.

PARKER MODERN

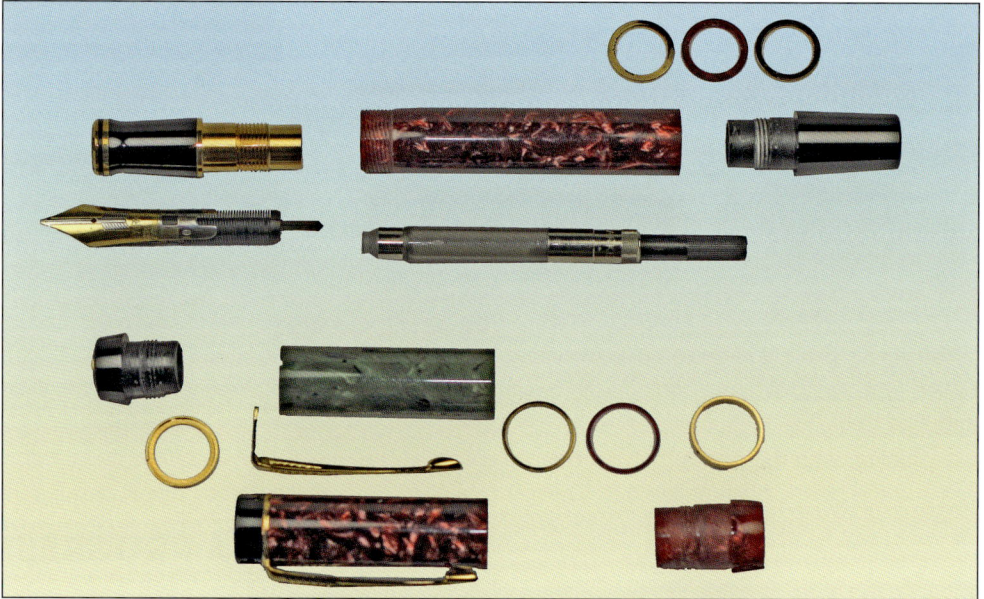

International and Centennial parts to illustrate which units can be unscrewed and salvaged.

At a pen show in the early 1990s one rarely encountered a 'new' pen unless it was a limited edition. Now more than 50% of pens on show are new or were made in the last 10 years. Couple this with the companies' disposal of parts for obsolete pens and the private repairer finds him or herself being asked to service or repair 'modern' items. The UK pen collector might also be astonished to know the official charges from the factories, which is another reason the private repairer is seeing more and more modern pens.

There is not much you can do if you don't have the replacement parts, but often a part taken from another damaged pen could be used, so it is useful to know how to disassemble new items without breaking them.

This 'modern' category includes the Centennial, International, Sonnet, Rialto, 95, Insignia and so on but we have only used the Duofold range to illustrate the basic point that parts can be dismantled and many items screw off.

Furthermore the two Duofold models are the basis of a number of very attractive modern collectors pens, such as those made by Fultz Pens, Classic Pens and Paul Rossi.

Problems with modern pens

Technology has without doubt improved fountain pens but modern items are frequently set-up with an inkflow that is below most users ideal. Simple adjustment is usually all that is required (see testing and Tuning a pen). Breakage is the most common problem and involves replacing broken parts -with Centennial and International pens there is such a paucity of spares that machining new parts may be the only solution.

Dismantling

The manufacturers manuals give clear details of how to disassemble the main units of the pen. What the manuals don't tell you is that the units themselves can be dismantled and these components used in repair jobs. This means that a 'scrapper' may provide valuable spares for other pens, pencils and ball pens. Parts frequently in demand are cap lips, clips, feeds, trim and the occasional barrel or barrel top. This is a repair topic as dismantling pens for parts has always been part of the repairer's 'supply chain'! It is important to know how they come apart and whether they are push or screw joined. In most cases glue has been used to secure assembly.

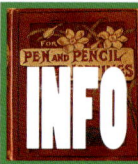

The acrylic Duofold range is screwed together and therefore can be dismantled with heat and a good pair of section pliers. It is critical to use the correct amount of heat and the part must be rotated continuously. Heating can be direct with a gun or hair dryer, but in a number of cases temperatures should be greater than 140° F so hot water measured by a thermometer is probably safer option than a heat gun; appropriate grips, squeeze clamps or rubber tube are required to pull or unscrew the parts. Tapered parts are particularly difficult and tape wrapped around the part can make the dismantling much easier and reduce any surface scratches.

Dismantling a Duofold cap and Barrel

Warm the clip end and with narrow section pliers twist the top clip screw until it moves and then unscrew it. If the clip screw has a decal, which is glued on, then it can be removed by warming and tapping it loose from the inside. Do not lose the notched trim washer!

Using a fixed heat gun and clamp to unscrew the barrel top from the metal connector

Removing the cap lip and trim rings ideally requires good curved section pliers so as not to exert too much squeezing stress, which could crack the barrel; heat is vital and a 'sensitive' gripping and twisting will ensure removal without distortion.

The barrel end is secured by a metal threaded connector; there are also metal and plastic trim rings. Usually the metal unit unscrews from the barrel first and then a Parker 51 clamp is ideal for holding the metal connector while removing the acrylic black end. Now and again there is excess glue and it requires time to soften - hence heating with a hairdryer or heat gun or immersion in hot water is advised.

Refitting a Duofold pencil or ballpen barrel

Most barrel replacements arise because of chips or cracks near the clip or from abuse. Rotary ball pens and pencils have the same plastic barrel and are interchangeable but the metal connectors at the nozzle end are different and may have to be exchanged. Dismantle by removing the nozzles and top units with heat.

Roller ball body/fountain pen

Duofold International barrel end; roller ball adjustment plug and the metal connector with trim rings

The International barrel accepts both a nib unit and roller ball unit, but to convert one barrel to suit the other, the top has to be removed and the small adjuster for the roller ball unit removed or inserted.

Take care with the Centennial as some of the connectors are plastic not metal

Most conversions are from rollerball to fountain pen and by removing the adjuster it allows a cartridge or converter to fit. If however one wishes to convert a pen barrel to roller ball then an adjusting plug has to be fitted. If one is not available then it is easily made from plastic on a lathe (3.2mm OD).

Accessing clip screws

Some models such as the Parker 95 and the Parker Arrow have the clip fixing screws hidden by trim. A small metal decal is glued over the screw, which secures the clip. The trim is difficult to remove without damage but these are easy to make from shim material.

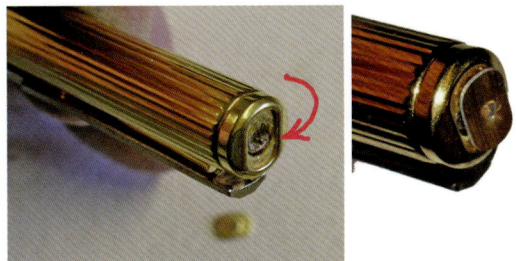

Removing trim plate to expose clipscrew

PARKER BALL PENS

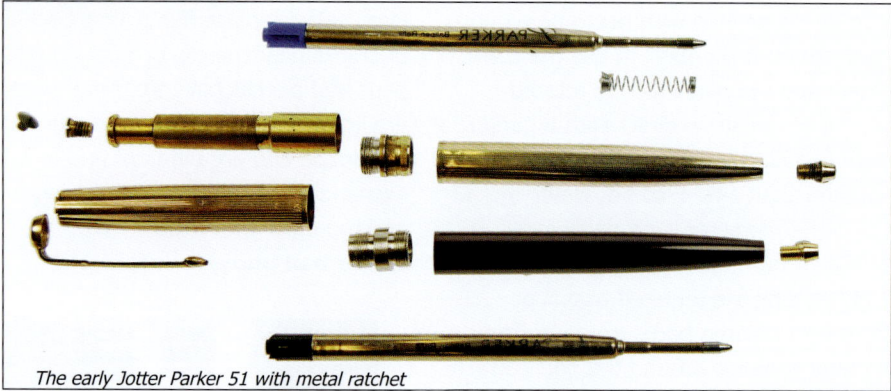

The early Jotter Parker 51 with metal ratchet

Cap actuated and button actuated ball pens are some of the most successful Parker products and consequently they are a frequent repair item. Our emphasis is on cap actuated pens but we will briefly refer to button actuated and twist pens later in this section (More detailed information is available in our web notes).

Introduced in the cap actuated Parker 51 the ratchet mechanism, evolved in slightly different forms and has been in used for over 50 years.

Problems

- Leaking refills
- Broken clips
- Broken threads
- Deformed barrel springs
- Ratchets that do not work
- Damaged nozzles
- Crossed barrel threads

Dismantling

The barrel screws off and allows access to the cap and ratchet. A ball pen arbor is used to hold the ratchet mechanism and cap, while the clip screw and bushing is removed. The ratchet can then be withdrawn. If a refill has been leaking this can be a messy job so have plenty of 'kitchen roll ' handy and clean the parts you are going to reuse with methylated spirit. Use a small box for parts - if you drop the small clip screws or tassie they are both hard to find and harder to source.

The Barrel

The barrel has a nozzle and a spring.
The nozzle on early pens screws off with warming. Later nozzles were push out. There are frequent mismatches and it pays to keep old barrels just for the nozzles.

The Connector

The early Parker ball pens had metal connectors, which screwed into plastic barrels but were a push fit into metal barrels. They can be removed by warming the barrel if necessary.

The Barrel

There are a number of threads for ball pen barrels and this means quite a proliferation of parts.
The return spring is located in the barrel and is common to all.

Diagnosis

There are few problems with barrels other than stripped plastic threads and occasionally nozzle damage. Nozzles can be reamed out and checked for clearance with a new 'refill'.

The barrel spring can be deformed; it is easily pulled out with a hook or threaded rod.

The most common ratchet damage is a split in the brass or plastic frame assembly and sheared threads; less frequently the shaft has broken or the mechanism is gummed up with a 'leaking refill'. The remedy may be to fit another ratchet if you have one. If you do not have the exact one but a spare ratchet, it may be possible to modify it for use by changing the ratchet /clipscrew bush.

The ratchet frame assembly

There is a wide variety of ratchets and over 50 years the materials used in their construction has changed. They were first made all in brass, then partly plastic but retaining a metal threaded section for attachment to the barrel and finally no metal at all other than the spring and clip screw bush. The components are - shaft, clip screw bush, spring and housing/barrel connector.

Different cap actuated pen caps and ratchets

Most of the pens can easily be repaired and include the Parker 17, 25, 45 , 51, 61, 75, Falcon and 50s Duofolds. The main differences are the way the ratchet fits into the cap.
The 50s Duofolds have prongs that line up with slots in the cap; the early 51s and 61s line up with the clip lug; the Falcon is a push fit and secured by a plastic bush; the 25 is a push fit and can be easily knocked out; the Rialto and 88 requires the trim to be removed to access the screw (see Modern Parker).

The first Duofold ball pen was cap actuated but the barrel threads sheared. It is however now a collectors item. It was replaced by a twist actuated model.

From the left-Parker75, Falcon, Imperial,17/50s Duofold, Early 51, Princess,Tiara, Minim

Different diameters and barrel connector threads mean it is not always possible to resolve a problem by simply using ratchets from other pens. Because this is probably the most important unit we have focussed most attention on the ratchet used in cap actuated pens.

Removing a cap actuated ratchet

The first step is to remove the clip screw or unit that secures the ratchet to the cap. In some cases the securing screw is hidden behind a plastic tassie, which has first to be removed without damage - try warming by inverting the cap clip end in hot water and then using friction.

Ball pen arbor makes life much easier as it fits all ratchets

Hold the cap with the Parker grooved ball pen tool fitted into the ratchet. This tool is very useful when when dismantling and reassembling a ratchet. They can easily be made by milling a steel rod but they are available on various pen tool sites (www. auspens.com, www.pentooling.com).
If the clip screw is tapered as on 45, 75 or T1 models do not use pliers as you will scratch the screw and it will become an unsightly blemish. Make a special tapered clamp from plastic tube or use rubber gas/pressure hose to make a clip screw remover.
With Parker 51, 61 and plastic capped pens - after removing the tassie use the correct size screwdriver to remove the small clip screw.

Parker screwdrivers for different size clip screws. Ensure the screw is clean and use firm pressure

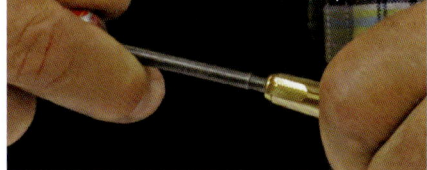

This is a critical step and why Parker made special drivers that located in the clip screw. If you damage the slot you may have to drill out the small screw. That is not an easy job without damaging the plastic or threads on the ratchet top bush.
After the clipscrew is removed the ratchet can be withdrawn.

CAUTION

Ratchet anatomy

The early ratchets were made in brass and appear to be very different from the later plastic/metal units but the components carry out equivalent functions. All cap actuating ratchets have a clip bush A, a ratchet shaft B, a ratchet housing D and a return spring C. The shaft B works against the refill E and also against the retractor spring F located in the pen barrel. The evolution of the ratchet started with brass and then because the brass housings cracked, plastic was used but the threaded sections for bush and barrel were still made in brass. Finally the brass barrel thread was eliminated for an injection moulded housing. (Innovation reduced the prices of components but introduced other problems of ratchet thread failure that was unheard of with brass thread collars). The ratchet plunger B moves in a fixed plane restricted by its shaft shape and two rectangular guides in the ratchet housing. The end of the plunger has a complex profile with 40 degree slopes which mesh with the plastic top of the refill. The clip-screw bush A allows attachment to the cap and retains the return spring C on the shaft. The ratchet housing D has two raised guide ribs which are critical for the extension and retraction and also the rotation of the refill; it is threaded to attach to the pen barrel.

The refill top E has a sloped profile which causes refill rotation but equally important is the groove that when aligned with the ridges in the housing allows the refill to retract into the housing. The force for this retraction comes from the spring F located in the lower barrel.

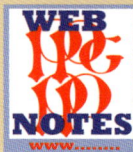

Changing the ratchet clip screw fitting

Without a ready supply of ratchets one has to adapt and modify other ratchets. The most frequent procedure used by repairers is to find a ratchet with the correct barrel threading and change the clip screw bush to fit the repair pen. The first step is to dismantle both the ratchet from the repair pen and the donor pen ratchet. Then attach the repair pen clip screw to the donor ratchet.

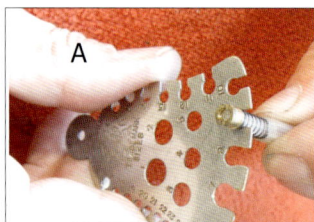

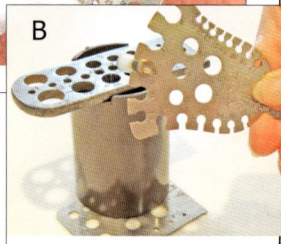

A

B

Fit into appropriate slot on Morell plate; position on knocking block; use as big a rod as possible to knock the shaft out.

C

Procedure

First knock out the shaft of the ratchet on a knocking block/sewing machine bell plate. Do the same for the other ratchet.

Clean the donor clip screw and take any plastic burrs off the repair pen ratchet shaft with a file. Reassemble the repair pen ratchet with a smear of grease on the guide ridges in the housing. You can now fit the donor bush to the ratchet shaft

Press down firmly with the Parker ratchet tool

Refitting the clip screw bush

Preheat the clip screw bush and then using a metal plate firmly press the shaft into the bush using the ball pen ratchet holder. It could be re crimped, glued or pinned but pressing on seems to be adequate.

Reassembly to cap

The ratchet is refitted into the cap and the clip and clip screw fitted. Make sure it is aligned correctly. The barrel spring can be fitted on to the 'refill' and then put into the barrel. The cap is screwed on and the mechanism tested.

The Parker 51 brass jotter

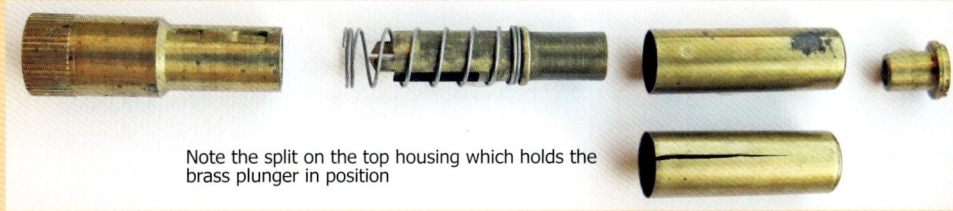

Note the split on the top housing which holds the brass plunger in position

The brass ratchet housing is frequently cracked and continues to work but sooner or later as the crack extends the pen jams or does not retract.

Repair

Remove the ratchet and take it apart to examine the spring and if there are other problems. Reassemble setting it up to the measurements on the diagram below; solder the thread skirt to the top housing.

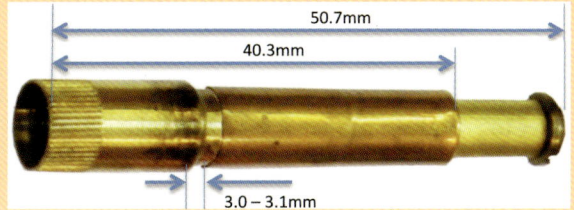

50.7mm

40.3mm

3.0 – 3.1mm

The Jotter

It would be remiss to discuss repairing Parker ball pens without referring to the button actuated jotter. However there is really little to criticise because it has to be one of the most reliable pens ever made. The ratchet system can be removed by carefully knocking out the button or using a puller but there is little point as cap/ratchet assemblies were exchange parts. The clips on the early models can be replaced by levering the broken clip off and simply pressing a new one into position. The clipless range can also be dismantled using a puller. The ladies ball pens such as the Minim and the Tiara are relatively easy to repair.

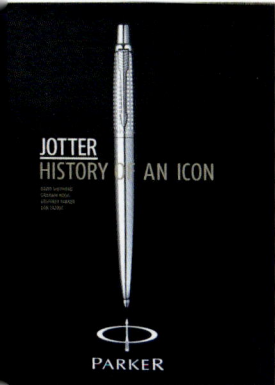

The book on Parker ball point pens

Parker 'Stick pens

The only two pocket Parker 'stick' ball pens were the Big Red and the Parker 105 but all the desk pens were 'stick pens'. In most cases these were fitted with springs.

Modern twist actuated pens

Twist actuated pens replaced cap actuated systems from the 1990s. The principle is the rotation of a cap, with a cam follower, which moves over a profiled cam. This causes the 'refill' to extend out of the nozzle. The action is against a barrel spring so when the cap is turned back it comes off the cam and the refill retreats into the barrel.

Repair is limited. If the sealed unit breaks down then another is fitted.

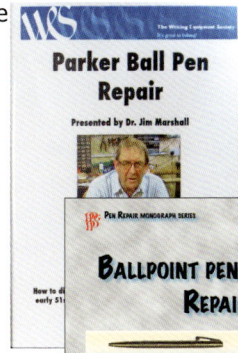

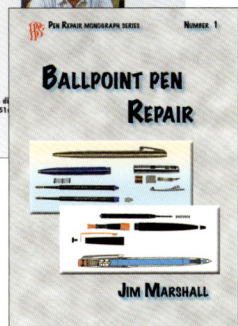

Parker Ball Pen Repair

Presented by Dr. Jim Marshall

BALLPOINT PEN REPAIR

JIM MARSHALL

The famous jotter refill

Parker stainless steel jotter robust and reliable

WES repair video and PEN REPAIR MONOGRAPH

PARKER PENCILS

Pencil appearance was at its best in the 1920s and 1930s

Parker pencils have been part of the writing business since the 1920s. They featured frequently in all the Duofold publicity and the 'Big Bro' was almost as desirable as the Big Red. They were made in a variety of colours to match the pens; the lapis, mandarin and jade are particularly sought after. In the 1930s the Vac pencils were slimmer with different stand-alone mechanisms. A continuous feed clutch pencil was introduced, which became the choice of mechanism to match the Parker 51 pen in the late 1940s. However the rotary mechanisms were still the most popular. Note that Parker used the same internal spiral mechanism but with different outer cases from about 1936 until modern times, which includes the Centennials.

Repair problems

This really depends upon the decade. The early Duofolds look good but many had split inner cases. The 1930s enclosed vac mechanisms were more reliable and did not split but they did block. Many problems with pencils are caused by over twisting or by pushing wire or needles up the nozzle to clear blockages. This invariably damages the propelling lead holder and tube. Most pencils are robust but they do not need the aggressive treatment we have often witnessed. They do need to be cleaned regularly and looked after.

The Early Duofolds

The first Duofold pencils were introduced in 1923 with an enamelled outer case. They used essentially the same mechanism for the next 10 years. The problem was that it was a complex turning unit, which was almost impossible to access. It was a propel and repel pencil and was well made but the inner support casing was too thin and tended to split. This gave rise to slackness and movement of the cap/crown; there are few 1920s inner tubes that are not cracked.

The plastic barrel of early Duofolds is easy to remove as both the crown and nozzle unscrew. This exposes the pencil mechanism which is hard to dismantle. Replacement is suggested but it can be taken apart, if necessary, by pulling off

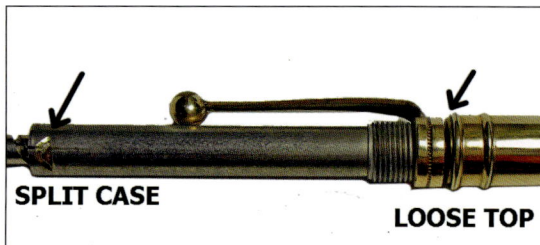

Gapping of 1920s Duofold - the tube must be soldered to stop the turning cap diplacement

the spring retaining cup and then pulling out or knocking out the spiral turning unit towards the nozzle. Spirals and springs can all be salvaged from old mechanisms. It is not a simple task to re-assemble the pencil. Most problems relate to the spiral, lead carrier and propelling pins.

The split case that causes the gapping of the crown can be repaired by filing a notch through

The internals of a 1920s Duofold

Two 1930s Vac mechanisms

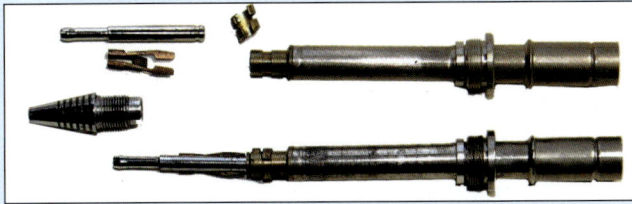

Repeater mechanisms fitted to Vacumatic and 51 pencils

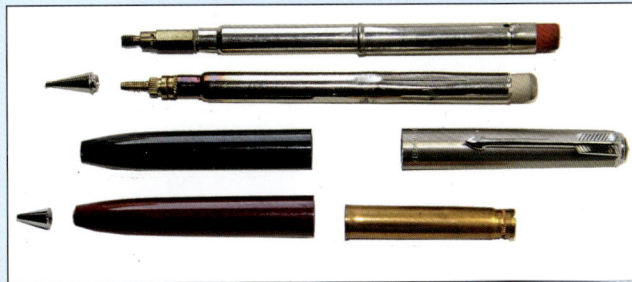

Rotary 51/61/21/45/75 with dfferent outer cases

50s Duofold above secured by a ring screw;

the split brass tube into the foundation tube; soft solder flowed into the notch is sufficient to restore the pencil to its former glory. It is rare to find undamaged crowns for the old Duofolds. They can be straightened and plated.

1930s - Streamlines and Vacumatics

All these pencils had slimmer mechanisms which were much easier to repair. There were a few variants; two that were most used had either a full length mechanism that was secured by the nozzle, or a 'half' length that screwed into the lower barrel. The streamline pencils continued with large nozzles but the Vacumatic pencils converted to small nozzles, which either screwed into the barrel or onto the mechanism. The half mechanisms knock out

Repairing these pencils involves taking off the outer case and renewing the broken or faulty part.

The 1940s and the Parker 51

A pearl Vacumatic continuous action pencil was produced in parallel with the rotary models. Not many rotary examples appear on the repair bench but continuous action 'repeater' 51 pencils are another matter. These were introduced by Parker in 1948 and apart from lead jams work very well.

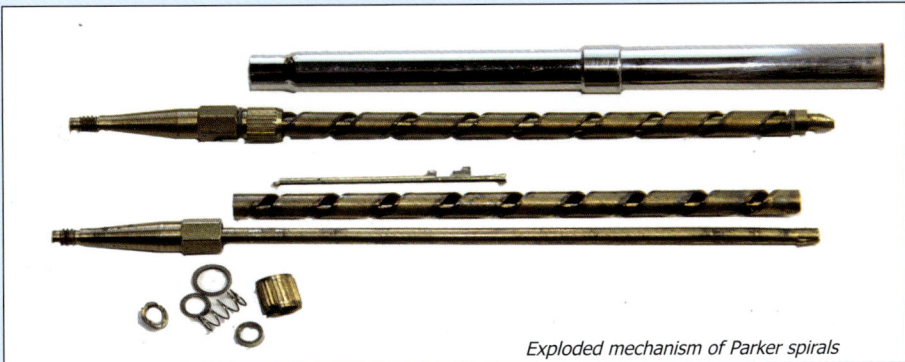

Exploded mechanism of Parker spirals

The rotary pencil replaced the repeater in the late
1950s. It was based on the older 1930s design
but with a slimmer case. The exploded mechanism
is illustrated and shows the spirals, propelling
tubes and washers. If these mechanisms fail it
is usually because something has broken or split.
Split cases make a pencil unreliable but they can
be repaired with solder in the same way as the
1920s Duofolds. The case profile changes from
model to model but the inner mechanism is usually
identical. There are some variations in length but
the cases can be interchanged.

Different cases for the various 51, 21 from parts catalogue

The 1970s and on

A slim plastic repeating pencil was designed
and used in later Parker 61s and in a number of
Parker's 1980/90 product range.
Mechanisms cannot be repaired and have to be
removed from the case by cutting off the tip.

Slim repeater mechanism and pencil cartridge for ball points

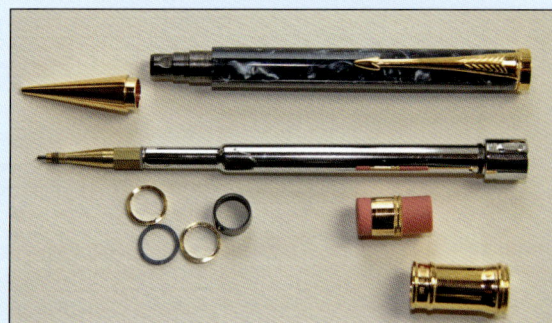

The 1990s deluxe products such as the
Centennial/International range continued with the
'trusted' spiral mechanism used in the Parker61
and Parker75 which was incoporated into a rather
more complex outer case.

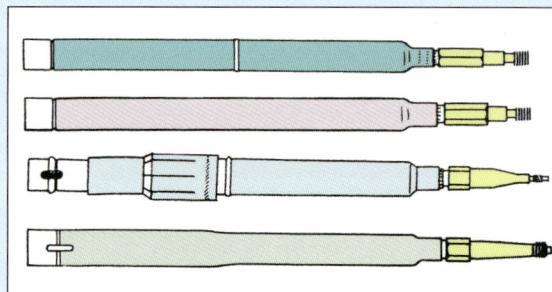

*Modern rotating mechanism with same internals buit modified
outer case*

More Parker pencils

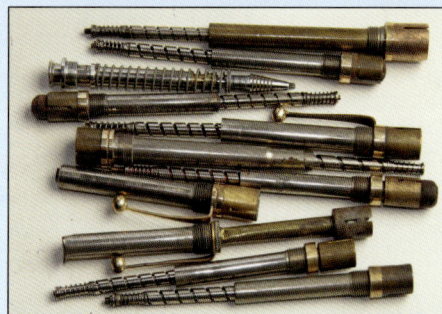

Crowns, nozzles and parts for 1920s Duofolds

WEBNOTES

This is a new feature to relieve the constraint imposed by the limitations of space in this book. It is not a major feature - it is simply adding some additional detail in a few cases, where we felt that it might be useful to some enthusiasts. We did not consider that extra pages of print were justified for all our readers so we opted for a web note as a supplement

We have no intention of adding futher information to these notes- they are what they are. It is not our wish, aim or role to have a discussion on pen repair on line - there are already very good websites that cater for this.

When you come acreoss the web note BOX there will be some specific comment on that pen or procedure and as an illustration we have included some brief notes on the items below.

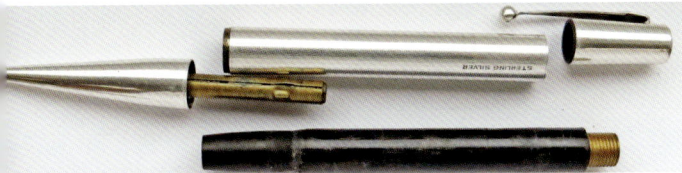

A flagship pencil to match the Swan L222. Gently warm to remove the overlay. After that you may have to use a flame on the cone.

Lamy 2000 - this piston pen is a very reliable pen that rarely requires repair. However the threaded acrylic collar can break off and may have to replaced. That necessitates removing the top end which unscrews with a suitable clamp (rh thread).

Plevonia - An Italian Vac style pen made by the same manufacturers as Stilnova. The plunger is lockable and it operates by stretching a conventional sac. There are no significant problems in servicing.

Combination pen/pencils were never popular because of low ink capacity. Repair is easy for the pen and the Sheaffer is quite collectable. The pencils often present problems but rarely as serious as this Hicks.

RECORDING YOUR WORK

Some professional repairers now have a digital camera on their workbench to record interesting pens, parts or work in progress. These repair wizards offer such images (when they have time) in their blogs or fascinating web pages or contribute quality comment to research forums. Such knowledge shared is invaluable and a privilege to read. Try the Bluefinger Blog of Ron Zorn and the Richards Blog - you may get a big surprise as to what information is freely available about puzzling pens and puzzling procedures.

SHEAFFER LEVER

1928 emerald green flat top Sheaffer.

Although Walter Sheaffer filed his lever patent in 1906, the first pens were not manufactured until 1912 when The Sheaffer Company was formed in Fort Madison. Lever pens continued to be made for the next 40 years even though Sheaffer also sold a variety of other filling systems.

Servicing

The early pens (pre-1935) were all lever fillers with slip sections, so servicing follows normal procedures (see Lever Fillers). However there are variations in the design of clips, cap threads and lever/bar. Sheaffer made small numbers of lever pens under the Kraker and Craig names.

Levers were originally pivoted on a pin located in a hole drilled across the lever slot. This pin is 0.7mm in diameter and is a push fit in the hole. The pins were not glued in and the ends of the hole do not seem to have been filled, so the pin is easily pushed out with the shank end of a fine drill after removing the accumulated dirt with a pin.

One of the features of the Sheaffer 1913 patent was a sprung pressure bar that ensured that the lever was biased in a closed position. The end of the pressure bar was formed into a collar that was forced up to the end of the barrel.

The removal of these pressure bars is almost impossible because they break away from the collar while being pulled out. However, they can be replaced with a conventional J-bar and the collar can be left in.

With the move to 'Balance' streamlined shapes in

Pressure bar with collar fitting

the late 1930s Sheaffer adopted a C-clip fixture for the lever and they also modified the lever bar unit to have a conventional hook. Nevertheless the pressure bar was quite a complicated design

Pressure bar with J-loop

with a central spring cut out and a ridge to engage with the lever fork. This gave very good extra compression. The pressure bars can be removed by compressing the end loop section with a screwdriver. If the lever bar has to be replaced it is easiest to feed the lever down the barrel with a new C-clip.

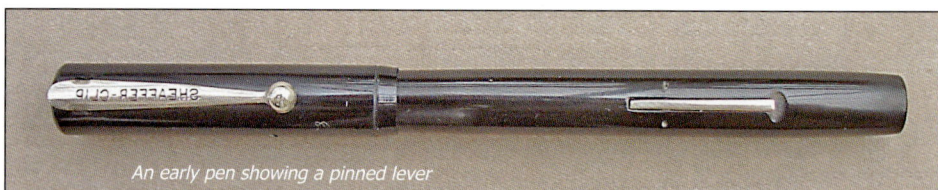
An early pen showing a pinned lever

Rare demonstrator showing clip, pressure bar and lever

Clips

Sheaffer did not follow the Swan and Parker lead in providing a screw fit inner cap to secure a washer type clip. Instead they went for a

More complex lock clip

side-mounted clip that held the pen higher in the pocket. The clip fitting varied with the flat top clips and was even more complex with balance pens.

Flat top.

One method used a nickel-silver tab that slides behind the clip lugs after they have passed through the parallel slots in the cap. Another method used the inner cap to secure a pivoted clip. The tab can only be accessed after pulling the inner cap. The hard rubber inner caps are not easy to pull even after soaking and heat, probably because of age related to plastic shrinkage.

Balance

The replacement of clips in plastic caps is a difficult task and the risk of damaging the cap must be weighed against the benefits. Access is the first challenge and there is either a disc seal inside the cap, just below the clip attachment point, which has to be removed by drilling, or an inner cap. Conventional inner caps are used with flatter intrusion clips such as the prong clip as shown right. It may be necessary to remove the broken clip by filing after the inner cap has been withdrawn. The donor clip

The prong clip and the sprung clip

prongs should be annealed and then fitted using a pair of long parallel pliers and a cap arbour. The other intrusion clip illustrated is similar to the flat top clip but it is held in place by a retaining spring that must be pulled out and reinstalled with forceps.

Prong clip with locking tab

A flat top and Balance lever pen both still working well

SHEAFFER VAC-FIL

Sheaffer Vac-Fil components with the washer and barrel seals disassembled

These pens (*US Patent 1983682, 1934*) were introduced in 1935, probably in response to a desire for a filling system that appeared more 'high tech' than the rather dated lever filling system.   Being barrel reservoir pens, they offered greater ink capacity and also had the option of an ink-visible barrel. Although these pens operate just like Onoto plunger fillers, they are significantly more difficult to service.

The basic principle of the Vac-Fil

Vac-Fil pens fill in a single down stroke, following the design principles first proposed in the Onoto patent of 1905. A sliding washer seal is pushed down the barrel by a rod that passes through a fixed seal at the end of the barrel. This creates a vacuum that is released when the moving seal enters a deep groove cut on the inside of the barrel near the nib end. Ink then flows around the washer seal into the barrel.

Seals

The filling efficiency depends upon the quality and condition of the moving washer seal and the fixed barrel seal.

The piston seal is a flat rubber washer located against a cupped backing washer held in position by a domed nut. Seal efficiency is dependent upon thickness, flexibility and friction. Seal failure is more dependant on age than overuse but with modern materials one should expect a longer life. The barrel seal is made up of two felt washers sandwiched between two rubber washers all contained within a black plastic capsule. The felt washers absorb ink and dry out when the pen has not been used for a while, so the seal hardens and contracts.

An original barrel seal with its rubber and felt washers

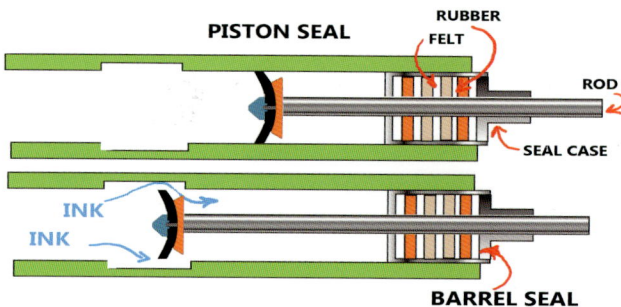

Vac-fil screw fit and crimp fit nibs, feeds and sleeves

Servicing

Essentially this involves servicing/replacement of worn seals. Before even starting on repair detail it is essential to emphasise that the repair of a Vac-Fil is not a trivial task in terms of time and technique.

Consequently it is vital to investigate whether the existing barrel seals can be rejuvenated. This is relatively new thinking in our opinion because many pens have had the barrel seals replaced without any attempt to get the old ones working again.

There is a Catch 22 situation here! One cannot do a dynamic test on a rejuvenated seal without having good piston washer seals, although a static test can be made using air pressure from a rubber bulb. So irrespective of barrel seals the repair of the washer seals must be carried out. Nevertheless we recommend that in all cases a barrel seal rejuvenation step is introduced and tested before any barrel seal surgery is embarked on. We hope that this point is clear because in our experience less than 50% actually need replacement.

If a pen has a piston rod that is rusted and split or is very slack in the top seal, then we will not be too optimistic about barrel seal rejuvenation.

Opening up the pen

Vac-Fil pens are often difficult to open. All sections unscrew on a right hand thread, but conical nib (Triumph) pens are much more difficult to open than the conventional nib types. Pens with the short section (5/16" between the base of the nib and threaded ring) unscrew at the nib joint, whereas pens with the longer section (5/8") unscrew at the ring joint.

Some of the later Vac-Fils have an ink chamber within the barrel (as illustrated). This usually unscrews from the barrel without much difficulty, but the nib unit must then be unscrewed from the chamber. Conical nibs are glued and threaded or crimped to a fragile sleeve. Do not try to remove them from the sleeve unless they must be changed (many specifications exist for the nib unit, so make sure you have a compatible replacement).

Grip the nib evenly all round to prevent distortion and apply heat to melt the rosin adhesive (a temperature of just over 60^{0}C is required). It helps to wrap the nib with masking tape so that it can be

gripped more easily. If the nib comes off without the sleeve, pull the feed out and cut shallow slots in the end to enable a wide bladed screwdriver to grip it. It may be necessary to repeat the heat treatment a few times, interspersed with ultrasound. If the sleeve breaks, you will need a lathe to remove the part within the barrel and to make a new one.

Francis Goosens has produced a very effective tool for removing conical nibs (illustrated below).

The button nut tool

Methods for threading the plunger rod through the seal; needle screwed to rod (11BA) or wire insulation sleeve (Terry Koch's method)

Accessing the rod

With the nib unit out, the barrel button must be removed to allow the plunger rod to be extracted. Buttons are held on by one of three methods. They may be simply screwed on and set with shellac, held with a locknut or screwed against a stop within the button that allows the button to rotate with respect to the rod. Except for the first type, a forked screwdriver tool is required (the one illustrated can be made from a paint can opener) to grip the holding nut recessed within the button. Heating the rod (rather than the button), a soak in water, and perhaps a little WD40, may be necessary to loosen the nut.

With the rod out, the dome nut that holds the seal washer in place must be removed. As usual, heat is needed to break the bond made by shellac or corrosion. The rod can be held in a fibre jawed vice and the nut gripped with pliers.

Piston seal replacement

After making sure that all the debris from the old piston washer is cleared away and the barrel is clean, install the new washer. The protrusion on the back of the dome nut will allow the seal to rotate on its mount when the nut is tight. The hard backing washer must be placed on the rod with the cupped side behind the sealing

washer. Replace the domed nut with shellac to prevent it coming loose during the filling operation. Lightly grease the seal and the inside of the barrel, being careful not to deposit any hairs or lint that may degrade the seal. It is very important that the correct dimensions of washer are used and that it is flexible, durable and truly circular. Some repairers discouraged the use of grease on the seal because it prevents operation according to the Sheaffer Patent, where the seal is supposed to double back on itself. We prefer to make the operation like the Onoto patent and use flat or cup shaped backing washers.

Rejuvenation of the barrel seal

This process involves immersing the end of the pen in cold water with a mild detergent for a few hours, followed by a few minutes in the ultrasonic tank. This encourages the felt washers to recover their original shape.

Assuming that the barrel seal has been undergoing this treatment while the piston seals have been replaced; the end of the plunger rod is fed through the seal with a little silicone grease after chamfering the shoulder of the rod a little to minimise possible damage to the seal. Installation of the rod is made easier using an extension needle

Washer sizes

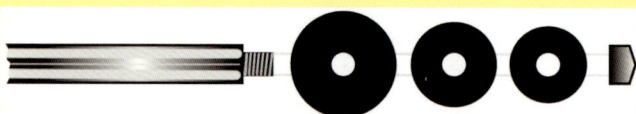

There are three sizes of seal washer, all 0.8 mm thick with internal diameter 2.0mm (some of the larger ones are 3.0mm). The external diameters are 7.14mm, 8.33mm and 9.92mm.

INFO

made from a 2.1mm rod threaded at one end with an 11BA female thread, and pointed at the other end. An even simpler tool is a short length of 2mm diameter tubular plastic insulation; this can be threaded through the barrel seal first and then screwed on to the end of the plunger rod so that the rod can be pulled/pushed through.

Testing

Now for the barrel seal test, but first apply a little silicone grease to the protruding end of the plunger rod and ease the plunger down. This will recharge the seal with new grease.

You should hear a clear 'pop' as the barrel seal falls into the groove at the bottom. Do this a few times and then screw the section on lightly after it has been cleaned and flushed in the ultrasonic tank. Try filling and observe the barrel seal as you withdraw the piston to empty it again. Remember that the water must now bypass the piston seal, so do it slowly or you may rip the seal off its mount. If the barrel seal is good there should be no sign of fluid leaking out of the back of the barrel, but remember that this is a severe test and that the pen does not have to suffer such stress in normal operation, a trace of fluid on the rod is quite acceptable. If the pen fails, the barrel seal will have to be replaced.

Refer to the table of ink capacities to see how much ink the pen should hold, and do not expect the barrel to be full, (see Filling a pen).

If the filling seems OK, then the section can be screwed in fully, but remember to heat the barrel end to avoid cracking and to ensure that the old adhesive can reseal the joint. If the joint seems to be lacking tightness, use shellac or silicone grease. There are two sorts of rod ; the plastic coated mild steel rod, which usually rusts and splits or bulges, and those made of stainless steel. In general the plastic rods are rubbish and should be replaced with stainless steel. Of course this is not always possible bearing in mind that at least eight different rod lengths were in common use by Sheaffer. However it is not a difficult task to use a stainless rod and thread it with an 11BA die. If supplies are hard to find, size 13 knitting needles (US size1) can provide a suitable option in laquered brass or alloy. It is essential to use the correct length rod because the seal must finish its motion in the centre of the barrel groove.

Barrel seal solutions

On early models the capsule is left hand threaded to the barrel, but all others are glued in and are usually very difficult to remove. Sheaffer repairmen were advised to drill them out. Original replacement seals are extinct.

If you have a pen with an unrecoverable barrel seal, there a number of options open depending on your repair skill and your workshop equipment:-

Rammed rubber washer

Make or find a rubber washer that is slightly larger than the internal diameter of the barrel (like a PFM point washer) and ram it as far as possible down the barrel. This is a poor option, but it may be all you can do. It has the merit that no permanent changes have been made to the pen, but it makes the plunger stiff, it reduces ink capacity and there is no guarantee that the washer will stay in position against the considerable forces that act against it during filling.

New O-seal and spacer for the old capsule (David Nishimura method)

Oldfield seal capsule, the seal it contains and the tool used to put it in place without depositing glue in the barrel

Changing the rod diameter

Make a slightly larger diameter rod, say 2.25mm rather than the original 2.1mm. This will have to be threaded 11BA at each end. If you can obtain the right material (size 13 needles are 2.25mm) this is a good option, but you might have to ease the seal capsule apertures at each end.

Rebuild the original capsule (O-ring)

First try to press the old capsule out after heating the barrel end. If this does not work, drill the contents out from the inside. You will then need to make a new closure washer. Make sure that the capsule is thoroughly cleaned out so that the O-ring can seal properly all around. If the capsule was not removed from the pen, it can be tricky to glue the end back on without contaminating the inside of the barrel or the seal itself. This method is good because it leaves the pen in a better technical condition than it ever could have been, and it preserves original structures. The only problem is that it requires a specially made O-ring to fit the capsule (available from David Nishimura)

Replace the seal capsule with a new unit This can be done either by removing the entire capsule and replacing it with a new one complete with button cap threads, or by drilling out about ¾ of the capsule from the inside so that the original barrel threads are retained, and gluing in a new unit.

This is a good method, because the capsule contains a standard O-ring. The main problem is making the capsule and gluing it into place without

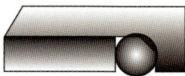

New capsule insert

contaminating the inside of the barrel. Epoxy spread only on the chamfered area gives a secure bond without air leakage, and a pusher tool guides the seal into place and holds it firmly while the glue cures.

There are other designs of capsule in use available from Francis Goosens. Plastic versions might

be favoured because heavier materials could endanger the balance of your Balance.

All the O-ring methods enable the pen to work better than it could ever have done, but some are more intrusive on the original structure than others – your choice depends upon how much of a purist you are.

Cap, clip and trim

Sectioned plastic cap

Not usually a problem area, but if work needs to be done on the clip, the inner cap will have to be pulled. Metal caps are more of a problem because even specially designed tools sometimes struggle to remove the glued metal inner cap (see Dismantling metal caps).

The clip is secured by the folded metal spring A which is held in position by the top of the metal inner cap B.

Cosmetic repair to caps such as dents near the top can only be removed after completely dismantling the cap.

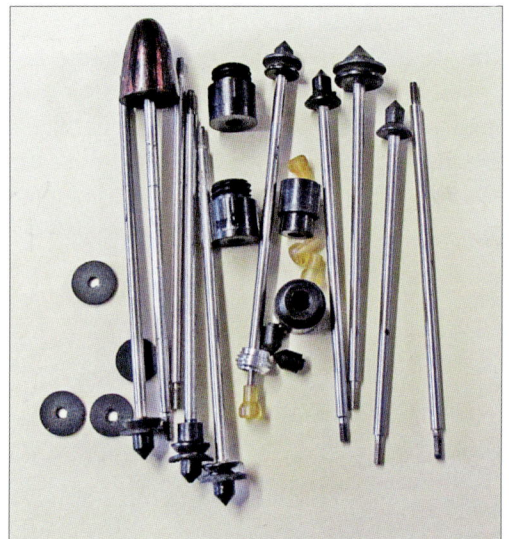

A collection of new old stock parts from the 1930s illustrating seal units, rods, piston heads and button attachment fittings

The Vac-Fil patent

There is much debate on the design of the piston washer and it's mode of operation in the barrel. Is a more rigid washer as effective as a thinner flexible washer that 'flips', as indicated in the Sheaffer patent ? That is if in fact the washer does 'flip' at all. Gerry Berg informs us that he has been able to reproduce a 'flip' but never in a situation with liquid present. The efficiency of filling is an important issue but it would appear that good filling results can fortunately be obtained with less flexible washers as used for Onoto repairs for the last 15 years.

Does it matter? Yes we think so because a true appreciation of what is actually happening within the pen will help to get better materials and parts made.

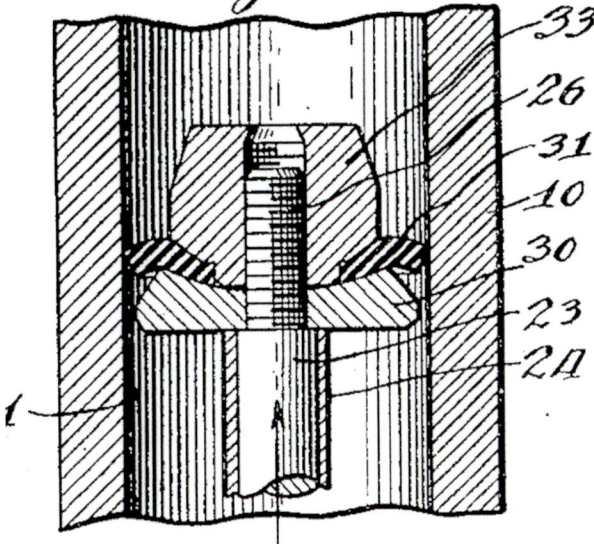

Extracted diagram from Sheaffer patent US 1983682, showing:

-seal 31
-dished backing washer 30
-piston nose 33
-rod 23

Early Balance Vac-Fil pens with open nibs.   There is no inner ink chamber like the pen at the head of the article. These are the easiest of the Vac-Fils to repair. Note the stainless and plastic coated rods)

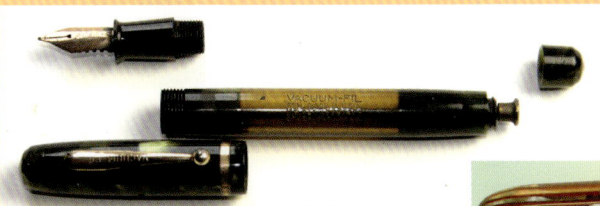

Two interesting pens; above a Fort Madison Vac-fil which is engraved on barrel, clip and nib; right a rare Conklin 'Vac-fil ';

SHEAFFER TOUCHDOWN

Exploded components of the Sheaffer Touchdown

The Touchdown pen was introduced in 1950. The early pens inherited from the Vac-fils the same form of conical nib. In common with other manufacturers, Sheaffer adopted a new injection moulded plastic and thus departed from the barrel reservoir inkview pens that were so popular in the late 1930s and early 1940s.

The principles

The illusion of technical progress in the face of a reversion to sac pens was preserved by the introduction of an air pressure method for compressing the sac rather than the traditional lever or button.

This was also hardly new because Crocker and

Old style Touchdown (with Vac-fil front end)

New (slimmer style) conical nib unit

Chilton pens had used such a principle in the 1920s. Compressed air is produced by the depression of a piston sealed to the end of the barrel by an O-ring seal.

Release of the pressure at the end of the stroke is achieved as the seal passes over a short longitudinal groove, allowing the sac to expand and draw in ink. The sacs in these pens are thin in order to respond properly to the air pressure, so they are contained within a metal sac protector. There is no breather tube (fitted to other pens of the period to allow greater use of the sac volume) because the pen was intended to be a single-stroke filler.

Problems

- barrel cracks
- dented cap
- missing white dot
- clip loose

Dismantling

Touchdown sections unscrew, but remember to use some heat to release any adhesive. Look out for the rubber seal between the back of the feed and the connector; it should not need replacement. Often the sacs are found to be serviceable, but to check this prod through the holes in the sac protector with a blunted toothpick to check flexibility. If the sac needs replacement, the sac protector must be pulled off. They are a tightish fit reinforced by several punch dimples, but with the help of a little heat, they will come off. The sac protector tube will probably contain deposits from the old sac, so it must be scraped clean. Make sure that the new sac fills the sac protector, but is not compressed. Fit it to the nipple with shellac. It is usually necessary to talc the outside of the sac at the top so that the sac protector can be fitted easily. Lightly crimp or punch the top of the sac protector to ensure that it stays in place.

Replacement of barrel seal (O-ring)

To renew the barrel seal, a long thin screwdriver is required to reach the slot headed screw that secures the plunger knob to the piston. If the screwdriver is equipped with a sleeve that is just able to enter the piston, it will be easier to engage the screw slot, particularly when the screw is corroded, as they often are.

With the button removed, the piston can be extracted through the barrel. The O-ring seal in the end of the barrel is contained in a deep groove, and it is often difficult to remove the old hard seal. If a pointed or hard instrument has to be used, be careful not to damage any part of the groove. With the old seal removed it is an opportune time to clean and inspect the barrel. Cracks are fairly common with these pens, especially at the button end; they prevent the pen from filling properly and are difficult to seal adequately, so a replacement barrel will be necessary.

Insertion of the new seal can be tricky, especially if it is coated (as it should be) with silicone grease. The process is made easier with the help of a flat-ended pencil pushed down the barrel to prevent the seal falling past the groove.

Final touches

Before refitting the piston be sure to clear the small air hole near the end of the barrel. Refitting the barrel button screw is made easier if it is attached to the end of the screwdriver with a little 'Blu Tack', but first inspect the small rubber washer that provides an airtight seal between the piston and the button. This seal is rarely damaged, but if you have a new one fit it with a smear of silicone grease. Add a trace of grease to

Screwdriver with a sleeve on the blade

Inserting the barrel seal

Using section pliers to hold the plunger knob

the piston and reassemble the pen, remembering to add a little grease or mild thread sealant to the barrel threads. It should now operate with a satisfying 'hiss' as the air pressure is released at the end of the filling stroke.

Cap clip and trim

Make sure you get a good cap with a tight clip as access to the clip spring requires removal of the metal inner cap. This is glued in and is a major removal task.

Testing

Touchdowns do not hold much ink especially when sacs become tired and lack flexibility.

SHEAFFER SNORKEL

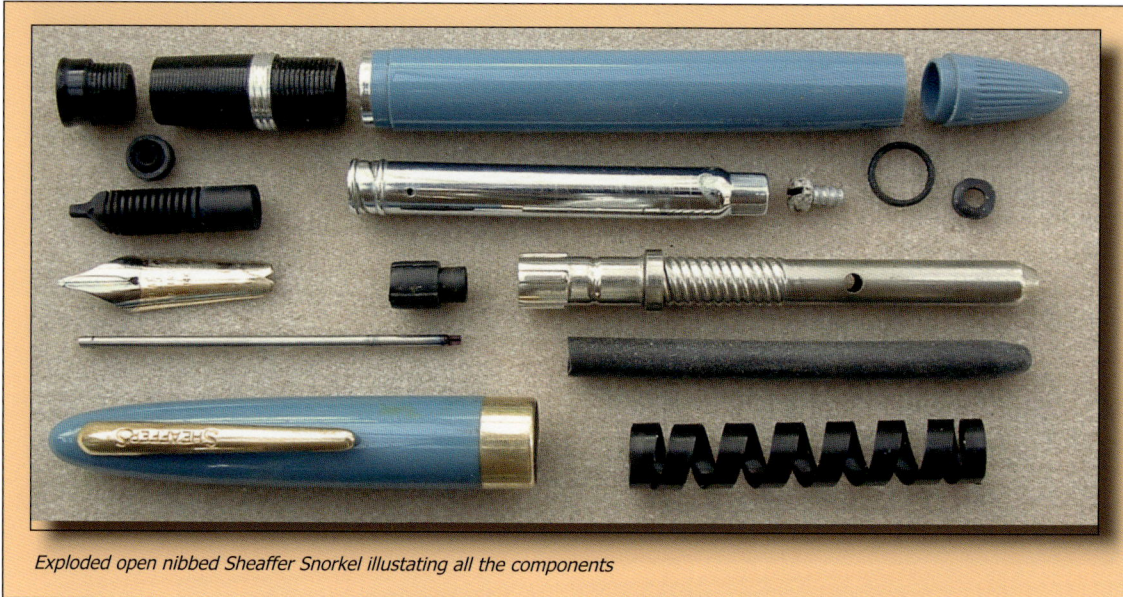

Exploded open nibbed Sheaffer Snorkel illustating all the components

The Snorkel was introduced in 1952. It is a refinement of the Touchdown, its specific virtue being that it allows filling without the need for deep immersion in the ink and the need for a tissue to clean the pen tip. The snorkel tube extends beyond the nib point by about 10mm by spring action when the barrel button is unscrewed. The open nib and the Triumph nib were introduced together, offering the customer a choice of styles.

The servicing of these pens is similar to the Touchdown, but an extra seal is involved to prevent the escape of air from the barrel due to the introduction of the snorkel tube.

Main Problems

- pen does not fill
- snorkel tube damaged; does not retract
- cap problems (see Touchdown)

Following dismantling of the pen, a number of faults may be observed.

- corrosion of the spring and sac protector
- damage to the filler tube insert
- cracked barrel

Servicing

A factory service involved the replacement of sac, all seals and the cleaning of the filler tube plus testing the snorkel orifice. The price for that in 1994 was £28 plus postage.

Most of the problems result from the deterioration of renewable parts. A corroded spring may be difficult to remove. If it comes out in pieces, be sure to clean the inside of the barrel. The clearances are very fine and the new spring needs to move without becoming stuck as it is compressed. Silicone grease will help; be sure to engage the end of the spring in the socket in the sac protector before re-assembly.

Changing the sac

On most old pens it pays to change the sac, this involves three steps

Opening the crimping of the sac protector

This makes it easier to remove the sac protector bushing (the nippled unit to which the sac is glued). A tool can be made to gently prise the crimps back.

Note whether the sac protector has all the ridges the same width or is the earlier style with one broad and three narrow locating ridges. All the gripping sections have three narrow and one broad groove (the sac bush should go back into the same slots!).

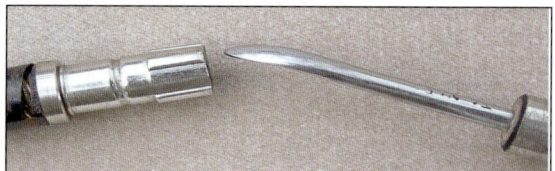

Tool for opening the crimps

Removal of Snorkel tube and bush

If you are lucky the sac bush may pull out with the snorkel tube following some hot air treatment, but in some cases, where the sac has deteriorated or the sac protector has corroded, it has to be knocked out. It is a good idea to remove the snorkel tube first for fear of damaging the tube and its delicate feed. Normal pliers must never be used to pull snorkel tubes. The factory procedure used small Bernard pliers with narrow grooves on each jaw and a piece of fine emery paper to provide sufficient friction and non-destructive grip to withdraw the tube without damage; a 3-jaw pin chuck also works well. It is essential to apply heat to the end of the sac protector.

With the tube removed, the bush can be knocked out safely using a rod inserted through the end hole. It is useful to screw on the plunger tube first so that a knocking block may be used to support the sac protector during this operation.

Resaccing the bush

The nipple should be cleaned and fitted with a No.14 or No.15 sac and left to dry before refitting the sac into the sac protector and remaking the crimps.

Reassembly

Insertion of the snorkel tube completes the filler unit. The tube with the tip slot uppermost to the nib is positioned and also fitted in correct orientation to the guide ribs on the sac protector. It is pushed in to the correct depth (normally 38mm for open nibs and 40mm for conical nibs) with the help of warm air and sealed with a blob of shellac around the root to ensure that it does not move or leak in use. Alternatively, it can be fitted after the pen has been assembled.

The point holder gasket or snorkel seal

The snorkel seal should always be replaced. It is easy to make the special tool required for separating the gripping section from the point unit. All that is required is a piece of 1mm thick steel filed to a width of 7.5mm so that it fits into and between the grooves. Alternatively, two pairs of section pliers and a piece of spongy tube also work if a plug is placed in the open end to prevent it being crushed. The original snorkel seals were moulded specially to allow the best possible freedom for longitudinal motion of the snorkel

The two styles of point unit that were offered as an option

Knocking out a sac bush from the protector

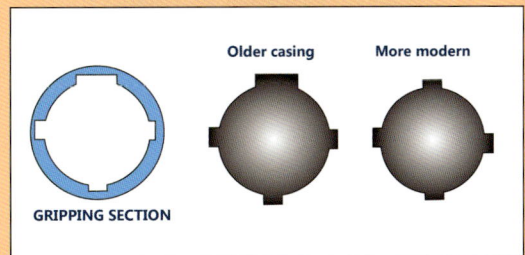

GRIPPING SECTION   Older casing   More modern

Illustration of the gripping section grooves and the two protectors used.

The factory pliers used for removing snorkel tubes
Using emery paper to enhance the grip

Point   Point end   Point gasket   Gripping section

Tool for holding griping section

tube whilst maintaining air pressure in the barrel. This design has recently been reproduced, but most repairers use simple flat rubber seals; these do a satisfactory job, but they do tend to provide more friction to movement of the snorkel tube so that the return-spring appears weak. The old seal will come out easily and the new one can be pressed into the recess.

A trace of silicone grease is good for lubricating the snorkel tube, but it must be used sparingly otherwise it can block the ink channel within the tube. The best way is to lightly grease the outside of an old snorkel tube and use this to prepare the way through the seal by leaving a light coating of grease on it.

Pens with the conical nib have a pointed snorkel tube, so the correct orientation is obvious, but for both styles of tubes it is important that the fine longitudinal slot near the tip rests against the under-side of the feed. If the sac protector has one large and three small ribs the orientation is fixed. If it is the later sac protector with equal ribs, then choose the nearest of the four available slots in the gripping section. Rotate the tube in its rubber nipple to achieve exact rotational and longitudinal alignment when the button is screwed in fully. Make sure that the sac holder slides smoothly in the slots and use a fine file to relieve any tight spots. Complete the assembly of the pen by screwing the barrel on with the piston withdrawn. Grease or lightly seal the threads.

Some repairers fit the snorkel tube after assembly by pushing it in with a thumbnail until it is flush with the feed. However, this is not recommended because of the risk of movement and ink leakage unless the joint with the rubber nipple is subsequently sealed.

Testing

When pressing the plunger down there should be a 'hiss' at the end of the stroke, as the high pressure in the pen relieves itself through the small hole at the end of the barrel. If this does not happen, check the vent hole, the barrel seal, and make sure that the plunger is free to go down fully. Correct filling, as demonstrated by two or three healthy squirts of ink do not mean that the pen will write properly. Dipping the pen is not adequate for the writing test because it must be ascertained that the ink is able to reach the tines via the snorkel tube. The pen must be filled, and if it is working properly, it should continue to write after the nib and collector has been dried off with a tissue.

If the pen does not write, or quits after a few lines, it will be for one of three reasonsa; there is a blockage in the fine slot near the snorkel tip; the orientation of the tube is incorrect or because of grease at the end of the collector. The aperture in the snorkel tube feeds the collector, so it must be greaseless. By probing with a very fine wire and washing in detergent, (preferably in an ultrasonic tank) the pen should work properly.

SHEAFFER PFM

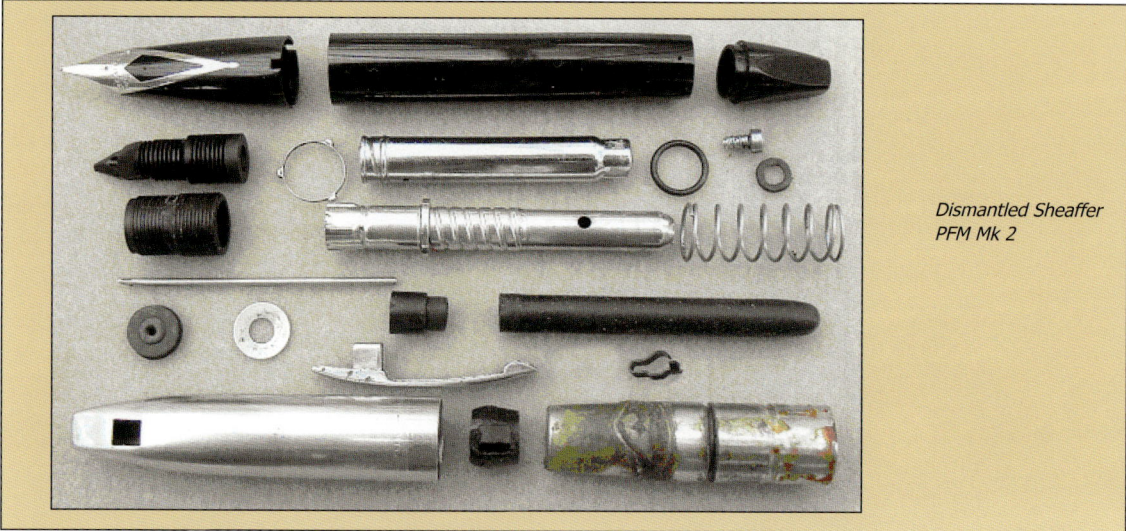

Dismantled Sheaffer PFM Mk 2

The PFM was introduced in 1959 as a development of the Snorkel. It was probably intended as an answer to Parker's 51, with which it competes admirably in terms of style and reliability, but perhaps not in ink capacity.

The parts are larger, but similar in design to the Snorkel (refer to the previous articles for more detail). The main improvement offered by the PFM is the larger sac (actually the same size as the earliest Touchdowns) and the nib unit.

Problems

See Snorkel

PFM's contain four perishable parts – three seals and a sac. The main reason why pens cease to fill is that the O-ring barrel seal has hardened. The snorkel seal is also prone to failure; this must be in good condition to maintain pressure in the pen during the (single) filling stroke. Sacs are bad on about 50% of the pens seen. The knob seal is static so it does not fail in use, but it should be replaced when the pen is serviced.

Servicing

Before starting a PFM repair, inspect the barrel for cracks as these are often difficult to see, difficult to mend, and disastrous for filling. This pen relies upon generating high pressure in the barrel during the plunge part of the filling cycle.

Dismantling

First unscrew the plunger knob and pull up about 20mm before unscrewing the barrel. The barrel is

not normally screwed on very tightly. Be careful not to lose the spring, the three point clutch ring and the thin trim washer if it is present (not all models had one).

Pull the sac-unit out of the section and assess the condition of the sac by gently probing it through the vent holes. If a replacement is necessary, be sure to fit a 15 or 16 sac (sacs vary a little in size!). Unfortunately many sac protectors suffer from serious corrosion. If a sac has to be changed and the protector is 'peppered' then attempt to get a replacement. It should be possible to get replacement sac protectors as they were remade by Jim Beattie a few years ago. If the protector is thin take great care cleaning it.

Replacing the sac is an identical procedure to the Snorkel, but there is only one sac protector design.

The writing unit

Factory tool for removing threaded bushing

The snorkel seal (point holder gasket) is buried within the section and is accessed by unscrewing the black plastic bush. The Factory tool is a square

Exploded point and gripping section, feed, gasket, washer trim ring and bush

cross section key but you can easily make one or even simpler, a flat key, similar to the one used for the Slim Snorkel, but 8.5mm wide. Most shell/nib units require a little heat to release the threaded bushing.

Components

A metal washer is located under the bushing above the seal gasket, which may be lightly stuck to the back of the feed/collector. A new seal should be fitted and can be lubricated but keep the hole clear. Replace the bush but do not over tighten it.   The snorkel tube may now have to be adjusted so that the tip appears through the feed at the correct orientation. It should project 40mm from the end of the sac protector. If the snorkel tube does need to be removed, refer to the previous article. After final assembly, a trace of silicone grease can be put on the tube to ease its movement through the new seal.

Testing

If the mechanism is working properly, the pen should produce at least two squirts of ink when it is emptied. The writing tests should be done with a full pen as at least a half page of rapid writing is required to be sure that all the ink channels are open (see Snorkels).

Caps, clips and trim

These caps are not easy to work on because the inner cap is closed at the end and glued in so that the clip mechanism is concealed. Sheaffer repairmen were advised to drill out the end of the inner cap to gain access to the clip spring if it needed tightening or replacing.

The metal caps can be heated and a puller used to extract the inner cap, but the plastic caps are more difficult because they need to be heated on the inside without damaging the plastic. This may be achieved with a hot air gun and a shaped nozzle or even a flame. The wide trim band is glued to the inner cap so it may or may not remain attached when the inner cap is withdrawn from

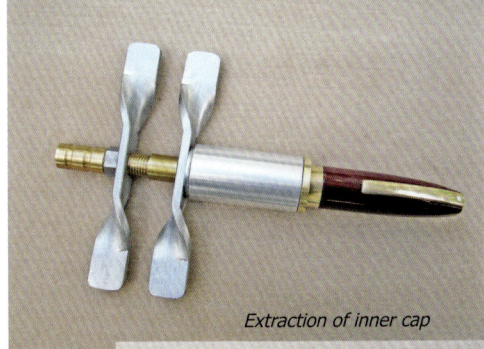

Extraction of inner cap

the plastic sleeve.

The clip is secured by a spring that was pushed into the space between the clip lugs. Forceps or a hooked tool are therefore required to lift it out so that the clip and the black plastic spacer are released.

With the cap tube empty, there is an opportunity to remove any dents in metal caps.

A PFM demonstrator illustrates the tension on the spring and the position of the O-ring (barrel compression gasket)

SHEAFFER IMPERIAL I

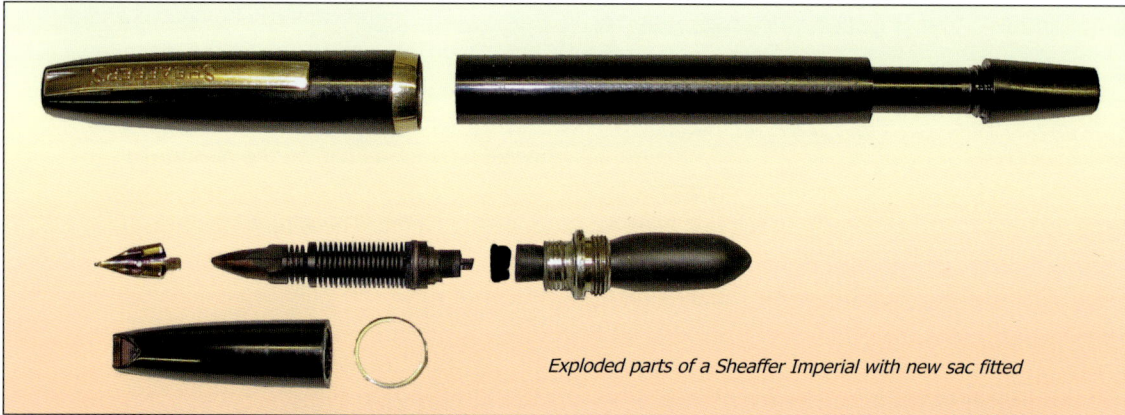

Exploded parts of a Sheaffer Imperial with new sac fitted

The Imperial I was a novel 'short stroke Touchdown' with a plated nib and a 'throw away' plunger/barrel. It was made in Australia and Canada and shipped around the world; an economic pen at $3.80 in 1966 compared to $19.50 for a PFM MkV.

Problems
- filling
- shrinkage of plastic
- small ink capacity

Servicing
The major repair was replacing the sac but with the non availability of barrel units it may be necessary to refurbish these.

Dismantling
The writing unit
Unscrew the barrel unit and then with a suitable clamp unscrew the connector unit, which is also the sac seal. The sac nipple unit and deteriorated sac can be withdrawn from the connector. The feed and nib are easily pushed out of the shell.

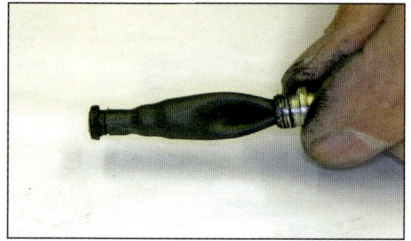

Fit the sac to the peg before pulling through the connector ring.

Changing the sac
A short necked sac is fitted onto the nipple unit with rubber solution and allowed to dry. The sac is then fed through the connector ring and gently pushed into position (liberal use of talc helps). The nipple unit fits into the connector ring. Replace the nib and feed back into the shell and then screw the connector into the shell so it seals onto the feed
Test and move on!

Refurbishing the plunger
The plastic plunger can be serviced. The plunger knob is heated and when the adhesive has softened it can be pulled off the shaft. It can be stubborn but keep warming and pulling until it realises who is the master!

The shaft is then pushed out and the O-ring can be removed and a new one refitted. It is the same O-ring size as the Snorkel and Touchdown.

The shaft is then lubricated with silicone grease, refitted and then the knob is reglued to the shaft.

SHEAFFER IMPERIAL RANGE -II,III,IV,V,VI,VIII

Sheaffer used the word 'Imperial' with abandon in their product names. Initially the Imperial was used for the square shaped Touchdowns with various nibs and caps. However it was obviously too good a name to waste so there are Imperial Sovereigns, Silver Imperials, Imperial 700s, 800s as well as the 1950s I,II,III, IV, V, VI, VIII and an Imperial Silver and Imperial Triumph. The Letter C denotes cartridge pen.

Problems

See Touchdown and Snorkel

Servicing

Apart from sac replacement, which is dealt with in the Touchdown section the other activities are:

- cleaning, and with the cartridge pens removing converters, which are sometimes 'glued' in with dried out ink.

- nib replacement

Nib removal

-conical nib (II,III) removal is simply by warming and screwing off the shell. If stubborn dip in hot water.

- inlaid nibs; there are two styles with a long diamond and a short diamond both of which were used on touchdown and cartridge pens.

The nib unit is gently warmed either with a hair dryer or by putting in water at about 140 degrees F. Use a clamp to hold the Touchdown foundation unit or the cartridge support tube. Unscrew the shell from the connector using a piece of hose. Soak the nib units and tap out the collectors. Shells are interchangeable and this applies to both inlaid and conical nibs.

Collectors , connectors and shells of Cartridge and Touchdown

Inlaid -large and small diamond and conical nibs

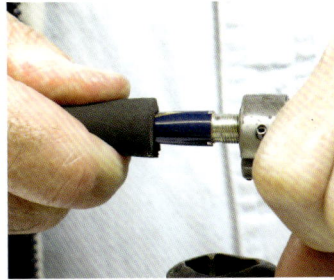

IMPERIAL MODELS FROM 1960s to late 1970s

II
III
IV
VI
TRIUMPH
VIII

Note the white dot is only on the expensive models

SHEAFFER 444 and 506

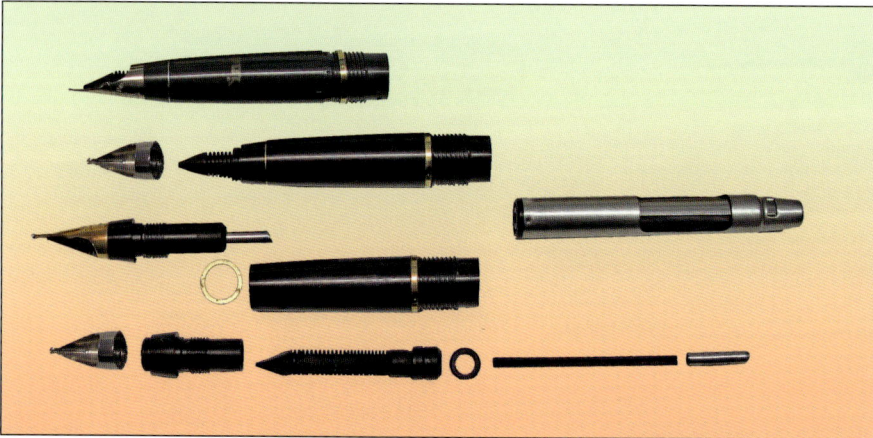

*Point end unit complete
and dismantled
illustrating components*

From the mid 1970s, these were the perpetuation of Sheaffer's tubular nibbed pens, when the Imperial range was moving to inlaid nibs. In the 1980s, the Crest pens reintroduced tubular nibs and both these models are still regular repair items.

Problems

- point holder threads strip.
- ink flow

Dismantling

The writing unit is soaked or given a short ultrasonic treatment. It can also be warmed or dipped in hot water(66°C/150°F) for 5 seconds.

If the point threads have stripped then the point holder and feed must be screwed out of the gripping section. Use section pliers and withdraw the unit. Take care not to lose the thin trim washer and the rubber O-ring gasket.

The nib may have remnants of the threads in it so it should be checked. Look for cracks in the tubular nib because this can also cause bad fitting.

The holder can now be removed from the feed, and if required, the cartridge pierce unit and the capillary feed can also be removed and cleaned in an ultrasonic bath. These pens can be quite temperamental to tune so it is advisable to clean thoroughly.

Re-assembly

Prefit the short cartridge feed and then push the piercing tube back into position. There is a special tool for this, but small grips are effective.

The nib is screwed onto a new point holder and then the complete feed is aligned correctly with the nib. Prior to fitting the feed into the point holder clean the channels with a thin scalpel, feeler gauge or nib wedge.

Push in the feed until it is firmly in position and check the gap between the nib and feed (there are two slightly different designs of feed but both are interchangeable).

Replace the gasket and trim washer and screw the refurbished unit into the gripping section. Make sure the feed does not twist and that the pierce unit locates through the orifice in the gripping section.

Testing

All pens must be tested but these pens can be particularly fickle after a repair. Perhaps it is the fine channels or some residues or the tubular nib but often the unit requires extra tuning. A good wash in detergent in the ultrasonic and a flush through with a bulb can often work wonders.

TIP As a last resort if you cannot acquire a new or good point holder - an epoxy mix will work for a while, provided the unit is dismantled as described and the nib and stripped holder scrupulously cleaned.

LADY SHEAFFER

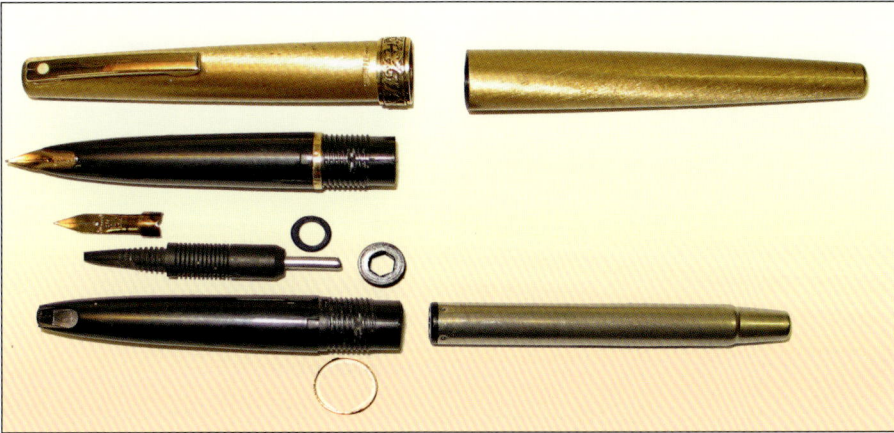

Sheaffer started the sex pen wars with the Skripsert Lady Sheaffer and the Pen for Men. The Lady Sheaffer range were not dinky pens but quite substantial and often accompanied by pencils and ball pens. Decorative trim was usually a cast band on the cap and the nib had the appearance of a fingernail.

Problems
- shell cracks or shrinks under the nib/feed
- converter leaks (poor sealing)
- barrel liner threads split
- nib diplaces sideways.

The main repair activity is servicing the nib unit

Dismantling
Unscrew the barrel and pull out the converter. In order to access the nib the retaining plug inside the writing unit must be unscrewed without disturbing the pierce tube; this can be done in two ways.

Feed, seal plug and Allan key tool

A 'spiked' tube can be made to grip the plastic threaded plug seal and this can be unscrewed. This is similar to the seal removers for Onoto seals. The disadvantage is that such a tool can chew up the plug seal and may damage the protruding cartridge pierce tube.

A better way is to adapt a 4mm Allan key to engage the hexagonal orifice in the plug seal. The Allan key has to be drilled to allow the pierce tube to fit inside without damage.
It is a remarkably efficient tool for both removal and assembly.

After the seal plug is unscrewed it can be pulled out. Sometimes the shell has shrunk a little, so a bent dental tool can be used to pull the plug/seal out of the gripping section.

With luck the nib and feed will push back easily but sometimes luck stays in bed. If removing the nib and feed is difficult, then after soaking and mild warming tap the feed out with a flat ended small drift rod.

Reassembly
Make sure that the nib is fitted on the correct side of the feed. Line up the feed and nib and push into the gripping section with the Allan key. Place the plastic seal plug on the Allan key followed by the gasket and then invert the gripping section onto the Allan key and screw the seal up tight. This procedure ensures that the gasket is correctly positioned.
Always check that the nib is correctly positioned and it has not moved 'off centre'.

SHEAFFER REMINDER BALL PEN

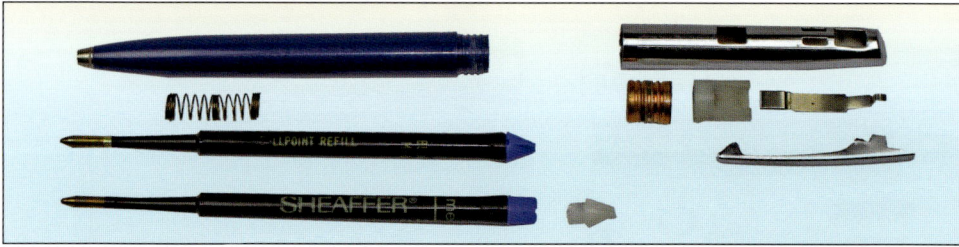

The ball pen was first introduced to accompany the PFM. The novel mechanism was promoted as a safeguard or reminder to retract the refill. There were two sizes of barrel and innards

Problems
- leaf springs break
- clip jams
- cap splits at slots
- refill does not stay out

How it works - the clip is designed to pivot and when the clip base is pressed into the cap body it acts on a pressure bar which moves a cam down the cap. This causes the writing unit (refill) to propel out. The refill stays out because the pressure bar is finely balanced to hold the cam in position. When the top of the clip is pressed it allows the cam to move back under pressure from the refill spring.

Dismantling
Before any internal parts can be examined the threaded bush must be pulled out of the cap. This can be done in a number of ways but in all cases it requires a threaded 'puller' (an old barrel) and a shoulder plate/holder for the cap.
The factory method uses a lever press 'backwards' to pull the bush out; a colleague uses his lathe and tail stock; we use The Universal puller with a ball pen fitting (see Pullers).

The thread bush is a good fit but it is not a major task to remove it. However, do not use excessive heat otherwise it will deform the plastic cam, which has a very thin skirt. With the bush out the cam falls out and the spring can be unhooked to release the clip.

Clean all the parts - if the cam and cap are covered with ink, wash well with methylated spirit.

Reassembly
The clip is placed in the cap slots; the pressure bar clip spring is fitted to the insertion tool and it is gently fed in until it engages the clip. The cam is inserted and the bush replaced.

The end of the refill can be pulled out and the tapered unit from an old refill fitted if required. The problem is the dearth of parts so save old Sheaffer ball pens for parts.

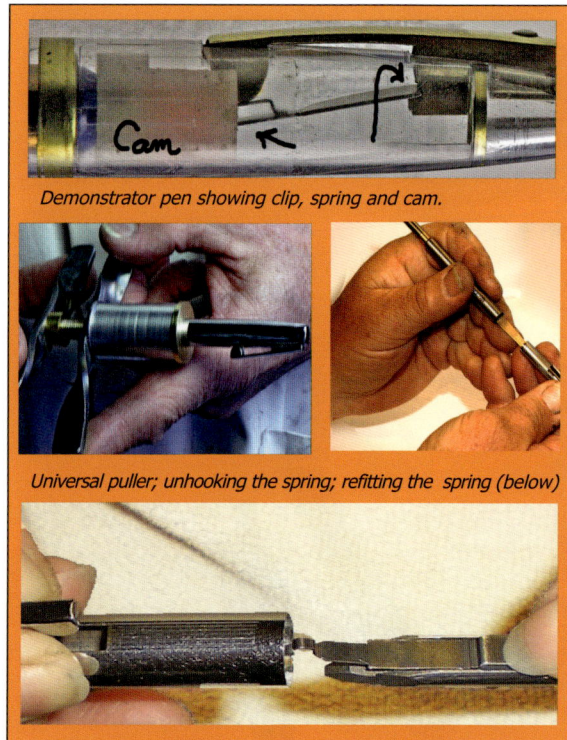

Demonstrator pen showing clip, spring and cam.

Universal puller; unhooking the spring; refitting the spring (below)

Repair tool for installing the spring

SHEAFFER TARGA

Two attractive laque Targas

When the Targa was withdrawn, most pen shops could not understand why this functional pen was being phased out. It had a simple construction and was truly robust. For that reason it has only a short mention in this book. Apart from damage to nibs and clips this pen rarely needs anything other than cleaning. There are two sizes the slim and the standard.

Clips and caps
Dismantling The spring clutch must first be pulled out -a Parker 51 cap spring puller works. Then the polythene inner cap has to be removed to access the 'Phillips' clip screw.
It is possible to pierce this plastic insert without removing the cap and unscrew and access the screw but it is always difficult to refit a new inner cap so we prefer to pull the cap spring.

The ornament (external decoration on cap) screws off and can be replaced.
Frequently a well used Targa has damaged metal flanges on the ornament and the barrel end and replacement is the only solution.

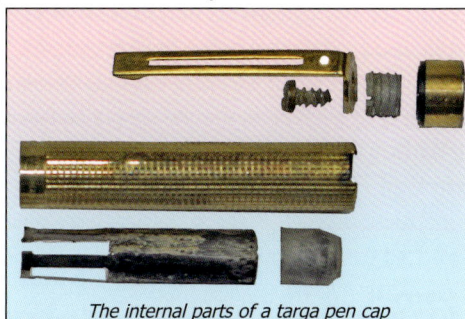

The internal parts of a targa pen cap

Note that ball pen and pencil clips have different bracket lengths and cannot be inter-exchanged

OTHER MODERN SHEAFFERS

- The Connaisseur is one of those Classics that should have been more successful than it was.
- The Nostalgia is a pen that somehow never had the gravitas of the quality pen that it was.
- The Legacy is a 'reborn PFM' shape and has recently been made with very desirable exotic silver decoration.

Nibs
Most Sheaffer nibs are sold as 'units that cannot be dismantled'. This is the case with inlaid nibs but some open nibs such as the Nostalgia and Connaisseur can be dismantled. This is important because a complete new nib unit can be very expensive.

Three unusual modern Sheaffers; Japanese lacquered Connaisseur; a vermeille Nostalgia; 1990's Balance demonstrator.

One might consider that the pens on the last few pages are modern but most of them are more than 40 years old and beyond any 'lifetime' servicing. With the demise of Sheaffer (and other major manufacturers) even 'modern parts' are now unavailable from the companies.
There are shops that deal primarily with Sheaffer and they might be able to help but most Sheaffer spares have 'vaporized'.
In such circumstances purchasing old and damaged models at Pen shows or on the internet is the only solution to repair.

WATERMANS EYEDROPPERS

(Circular No. 29.2)

A. Gold Pen. B Feed Bar. C. Point Section (or Neck). D. Barrel. E. Cap.

The most perfect piece of mechanism can be made to work badly by careless handling. Following are a few suggestions which should be of value to those who wish to get good service from our pens:

Pens which were filled with a dropper or a special adaptor for ink bottles dominated the market for almost 25 years. These so called 'eyedroppers' continued to be made well after Watermans had introduced self filling systems. Although such pens are rarely used today, they often have wonderful nibs, which makes them excellent calligraphic pens. The anatomy of such pens is quite simple consisting of five parts.

Instruction

Such instruction brochures are fascinating - where else are told to wax up vent holes!

Carry it with the pen point up.
Lay it down so that the pen point will be raised an inch or more.
Open the vent holes in the cap if the pen is to be carried in the pocket; otherwise, the warmth of the body will cause it to sweat inside the cap.
Close the vent holes with wax if the pen is to be left lying on the desk; otherwise the ink in the feed will dry up and the pen will not write readily.
The cap may best be removed or put in place with a slight twist from left to right which will cause it to move easily without suction or jarring. This should be done with the pen point up. If the inside of the cap becomes soiled, clean it; otherwise, it will soil the neck of the pen and then your fingers.

Servicing and storage

Part of a service is cleaning and that involves dismantling the pen and rinsing and flushing.

If the pen has not been opened for 50 years, then take care trying to dismantle it. They do break off at the threads if handled roughly. Dried ink can set like glue and removing the section can be very difficult. Soaking is unlikely to penetrate the screw threads from the outside so it often requires a

considerable time to access the joint from inside by soaking up the ink channel in the feed. An ultrasonic bath will definitely help.

If you have a valuable treasure that is rarely used, it is necessary to store it correctly. A good example will quickly become a bad example in direct sunlight and an acid atmosphere so these must be avoided. Store in clean cotton in a closed pen box.

Feeds, nibs and sections: Watermans feeds are robust without delicate fins and rarely require attention. Replacement nibs may crack if incorrectly fitted into small sections (this sounds obvious but match the pen number with the correct Watermans nib number- e.g a 52 pen with a no2 nib). Section threads are well cut and a little silicone grease will keep these joints in good condition. Chipped sections can be re-made.

Barrels: few problems but always keep old barrels as they will become most valuable if one requires a replacement for an overlay (particularly Waterman 1/2 and V sizes). Overlays are much easier to remove than from self-fillers. The Cardinal red hard rubber pens are rare and any parts should be kept. Take care with polishing Cardinal barrels, particularly with buffing as darkening/discolouration will most probably occur.

Caps & Clips: Slip caps do crack but not as easily as Swan or Onoto; taper caps are more delicate. Some eyedroppers were produced with screw caps and these are hard to find as spares. Clip caps and accommodation clips were options for Waterman pens from 1905; they were designed to encourage the carriage of eyedroppers in an upright position.

No.12 with early threaded cap and No24 taper cap

WATERMANS PUMP

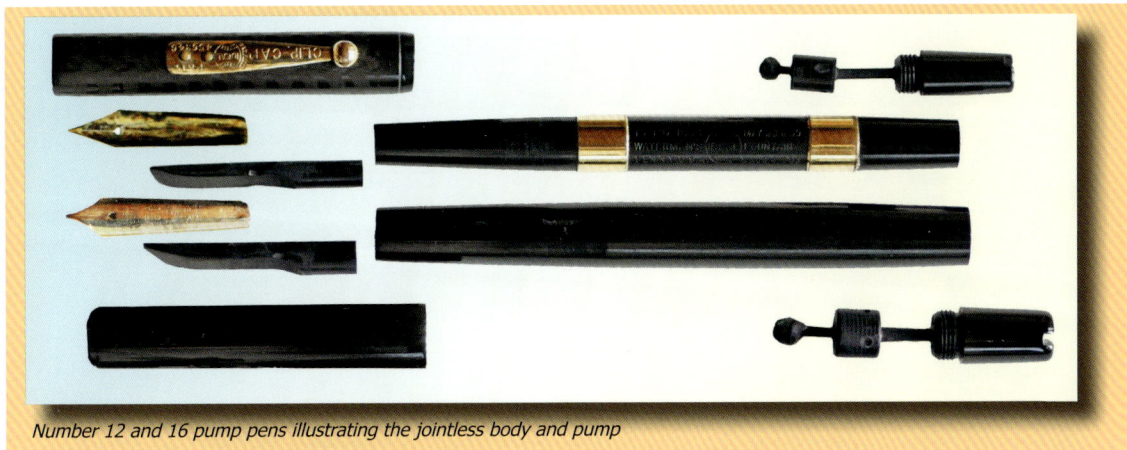

Number 12 and 16 pump pens illustrating the jointless body and pump

The pump filler was a great idea but not a commercial success possibly because the materials and manufacturing process was inadequate to make a good seal and a valve that did not stick. The barrel is a 'jointless' tube with the gripping end turned to accept the nib and feed while the pump screws into the opposite end of the barrel. Reduced pressure is created within the barrel by pulling air out with a small valved piston. On the downstroke the valve opens as the piston moves and air pressure lifts the valve. On the upstroke the valve closes and the air above the valve is extracted. The operation is repeated until the pen is full and then the pump button is tightly screwed to seal the pen. (If you carry on pumping the ink comes out of the end of the barrel - which was another reason it was not a commercial success).

Problems
- The valve sticks
- The piston wears and does not seal effectively
- The barrel wears

Dismantling
Soak the nib/feed and remove the nib by rocking. Fill the barrel with a mild alkaline solution using a syringe and leave for a few hours. Decant the liquid and unscrew the pump system.

Examination
Treat the pump with ultrasonics and if necessary it can be dismantled by removing the retaining pins. First check for damage and then check the fit in a cleaned barrel with a smear of silicone grease. If there is no suction at all then it may be

necessary to refurbish or even remake the pump system. If the cylinder has to be remade then the design can be improved by adding an O-ring.

Making a Replacement pump
The two weakness are that the valve does not work or the pump cylinder is a poor fit in the barrel.

The cylinder can be made from plastic or hard rubber rod. Fitting an O-ring, involves machining a groove into the piston. It should not be a very tight fit in the barrel but should seal loosely like a Sheaffer Touchdown.

The valve is simply a thin disk with a thin shaft and counter weight. The shaft length is not important as long as the valve can lift. Make a new valve by cutting a very thin hard rubber disk with a parting tool, Fix a 0.5mm carbon fibre rod and make a balance weight from a blob of supersteel. Alternatively the disc and rod can be made from PTFE to minimise the risk of sticking. One can also fit a stronger metal pin/pulling rod if one wishes. Use a small amount of silicone grease to lubricate the piston.

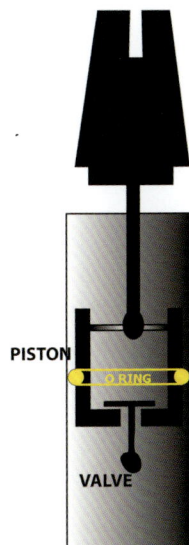

Pump components and position of additional O-ring

WATERMANS 1920s - 40s

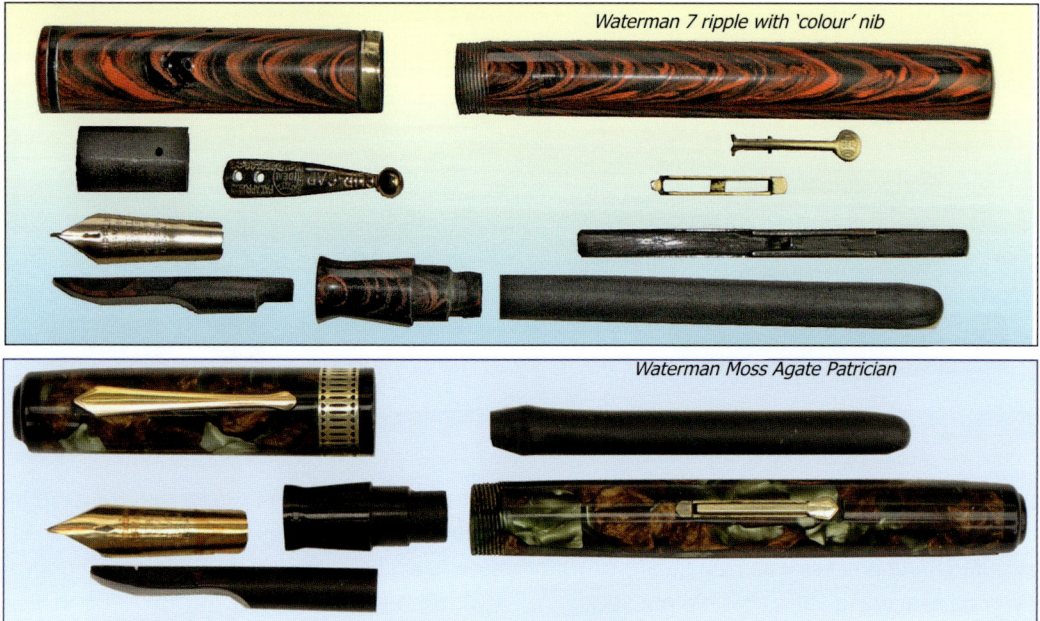

Waterman 7 ripple with 'colour' nib

Waterman Moss Agate Patrician

General characteristics

The common features of the early Watermans pens during this period were a screw-on cap with a riveted clip and a boxed lever/slide bar filling system. These pens are robust with thick hard rubber barrels and caps and few body problems. The clip and lever box are the weak points. Although they made eyedroppers, pump fillers, sleeve fillers and safety pens the majority were the traditional lever fill. The Waterman 52 is probably the most common of all 1920's pens and was made from black and red mottled vulcanite.

From the end of the 1920s Watermans made some exceptional pens in moss agate, turquoise and Persian plastics. These are amongst the most desirable of collector pens particularly the 94 ripples and the famous Patrician. In the 1930s intrusion clips became more common than riveted clips and the lever box was redesigned; the 'Ideal' logo lever was displaced by a rather boring but stronger plain slim lever.

The 1930s depression pens include attractive translucent and ray patterned plastics.
Of all the manufacturers Watrermans were probably the most prolific in using metal overlays for decoration. The most well known filigrees date from the 1920s but a stunning 'bay leaf' design was made in the 1930s.

Problems

Until 1929 *(includes eye droppers, safeties, the 52, 5 and 7 range with slip and screw caps.)*
- clips break or rivets pull out
- damaged nibs
- lever boxes break at the pivot point
- Vulcanite discolouration
- coloured trim 'plastic ' bands shrink

Models after 1930

(Patrician, depression pens, number 7, 92, 94, 32, Emblem and One Hundred year)
Problems in this era are often due to quality problems with plastic materials.
- clips pull out of the caps
- some Patricians discolour and caps shrink,
- some Persians are stained.
- some Hundred Year pens are crystallised at the clip and barrel ends.

Servicing

From a repair standpoint Watermans produced pens with good nibs and a reliable filling system. However most of the pens of different designs produced in these two decades suffered from clip and lever box problems.

Dismantling

The barrel and nib unit

As with any old pen the preliminary examination will direct you to the areas that must be repaired.

First soak and warm and then remove the section. All lever pens have push in sections, which are easily removed. Black hard rubber sections rarely shrink or crack but the nibs are a tight fit and soaking is essential before knocking out the nib. More care must always be taken with the cardinal red pens as red hard rubber is much more brittle than black or mottled.The best way to clean the inside of a barrel is with the slide bar removed. Press down on the retaining lug through the lever slot with a dental pick or flat file. The slide bar will drop out. Early barrels rarely present problems as they were turned from hard rubber rods. 1920-40s Waterman nib shape is squat often with a pierce hole as a keyhole or diamond shape. Older nibs were sturdy but some larger sizes had a tendency to crack; the radius of the feed and section often appear too curved for the larger nibs. The nibs had to be a tight fit as there was less length to hold them in place compared to other makes of Senior Pens. The Patrician and Emblem feed radii were 7.3mm compared to a No 52 of 4.8mm.

The cap and clip

Flat top caps are robust with strong support from an inner cap. Cracked caps are rare including streamlined pens made from mottled plastic. The clip is the weakest point and all Waterman clips, from riveted to top button have problems. Repeated flexing causes clips to snap off below the rivets or pull out of the insertion slots. Riveted clip repair is not difficult but is time consuming (see page 130 - Repairing a riveted clip). Pronged clips and military clips have their own problems, but they can be repaired and we have given more details in the following pages but it is impractical to cover every example. We acknowledge that one of the challenging repairs is the replacement of a Patrician clip but we have relegated this to our websites for those who have the luxury of having a spare Patrician clip. You can follow the procedure in our web notes.

WEB
pg
NOTES
WWW.........

Watermans pens are without doubt excellent pens to use. They are easily serviced and there are plenty of parts for the most common, which is an important factor today. The more exotic are very desireable but sadly have become almost too expensive to use on a regular basis.

WATERMANS SLEEVE FILLER

The sleeve filler is a classic pen. Waterman refused to licence the lever from Sheaffer and consequently developed their manual press system similar to the later Parker aerometric system. The sac could be depressed to fill the pen by pressing down a pressure bar, accessible through a cut out section in the barrel. The cut out section was covered by a hard rubber sleeve when the pen was in use and which slid back to expose the aerometric system for filling. The pressure bar is secured in position by a spring clip and can be pulled out with a pair of pointed nose pliers and refitted. There are internal grooves in the barrel to ensure it is refitted in the correct position.

If the sac is badly polymerised, the barrel is best cleaned with the pressure bar removed.

A similar system was used by Le Beouf, Latremore and other makers, some of whom simply glued a piece of metal onto the sac.

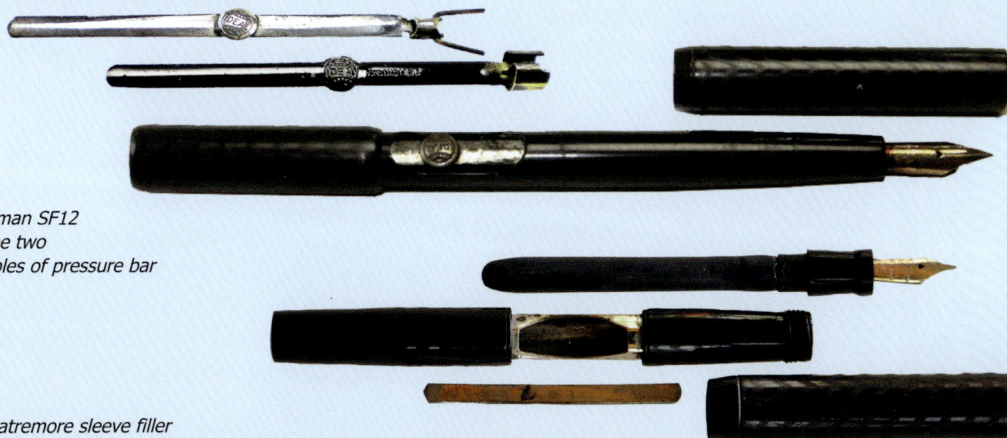

Waterman SF12 and the two examples of pressure bar

Latremore sleeve filler

WATERMANS INK VUE Mk1

Dismantled Ray Ink-Vue

The Watermans Ink Vue is a bulb filler and was introduced in 1935 as a competitor to the Parker Vacumatic. With this model, the pen barrel can be separated into two sections; the lower ink reservoir; and the top pump system. Air is expelled from the body of the pen by compressing the top sac with the small hinged lever. Upon release this allows ink to flow into the area of reduced pressure through the ink channels.

Problems with the Ink Vue
- blockage of the breather tube
 - deterioration of the pump diaphragm
 - dislodged pressure bar

Dismantling
Remove the section; most Ink Vues have a thin walled section, so do not remove without the feed in position (otherwise there can be distortion). Soaking and warming as usual! The next task is to separate the two parts of the barrel. Immerse the pen in an ultrasonic bath for at least 30 minutes. Gently warm the barrel above the joint line and unscrew the top.

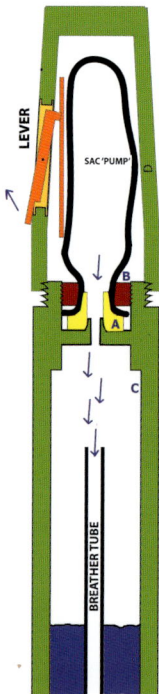

Illustration of the mechanism
The sac is secured in position by a screw ring (B) which seals the sac against a tapered plug. This plug fits over the raised nipple as illustrated. When the lever is raised air is forced from the barrel (C) down the breather tube and ink is pulled into the reduced pressured reservoir, when the lever is lowered.

Most repairs are on pens where it is only necessary to replace the pump diaphragm. However, proceed carefully when unscrewing and ensure the lever/bar unit does not get entangled. Section pliers and a piece of rubber are required.

The top section
This must be cleaned by removing the sac debris and the small pressure bar. Depress the single prong on the bar through the lever box (the end of a flat needle file works well). Check the lever box lugs, clean the pressure bar and replace it straight away. These bars are impossible to find and you will have a tedious job making another one if you lose it. It is not necessary to remove the lever box but this can be done if there is damage (see Waterman levers)

The lower section
Clean the sac debris from the retaining plug and unscrew it with a spanning screwdriver or equivalent. (A simple removal tool can be made from steel tube see image). Do not rush otherwise you can damage the slots and if the slots are already damaged the plug will have to be removed with a spiked lever similar to Onoto/Ford seal plug tools.

The joint cavity must be cleaned and this reveals the short tube, which fits into the diaphragm 'neck'. Clean all the parts well including the seal plug in anticipation of re-assembly.

Fitting the rubber sac diaphragm

The first stage is to resac the 'pump' unit. This is the fiddliest part of the operation.

The open end of the sac is folded and fed through the hole in the retaining ring. The sac is pulled into position (see picture). Do not cut the sac until it is fitted to the retaining ring! There should be enough rubber left to make a good seal but it should not extend beyond the outside diameter. The diaphragm/ring is now ready to be fitted. Screw the sac assembly into the barrel using a specially made spanner or tubular tool. Exert a firm downward pressure. It is important that there is an airtight seal between the ring, the sac and the plug. Sometimes there is resistance or the sac can twist out of position but water or silicone grease on the inside of the diaphragm can help.

Reassembly

To be completely sure of a good seal, the sac end can be immersed in water and pressure applied to the barrel (blow through the barrel or use a squeeze bulb).

Liberally talc the diaphragm and carefully screw on the top section, checking the pressure bar does not snag on the sac.

Now screw in the section and fit the nib so it lines up with the lever. Fill the pen by the normal operation of pumping the lever 6 or 7 times.

These pens are unusual in that they use a lever to compress a sac, which is usually associated with being filled with ink. In this case the lever and sac are a pump (see pumps and filling systems).

Removing the plug seal

The barrel reservoir with the seal ring ready for removal and then without the ring showing the 'top of the plug

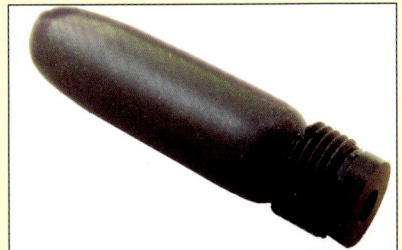

Special spanner for two sizes of ink-vue.

The tubular tool and with the trimmed sac ready for reassembly

The sac first with ring, then trimmed sac and finally with plug

WATERMANS INKVUE Mk2

The Mk 2 pen differs in four important respects from the Mk 1.

- the barrel is a one-piece item with no demountable joints.

- there is no structure in the barrel that can be tightened to grip the sac/diaphragm.

- access to the mechanism is through the threaded end button.

- the sac has a moulded lip.

These pens tend to be avoided by many repairers, but they are not a big problem when the construction is understood. Waterman designed the pen this way to achieve rapid assembly.

Dismantling

First remove the nib and feed by easing and pulling them out after soaking and heat. Few nibs will give problems. The breather tube must be clear for the pen to fill properly, so check it with a fine wire and by blowing through it.

Removal of the end button

This can be difficult; it will have been attached with shellac, so heat is essential. A thin rubber sheet or a piece of adhesive tape is required to grip and unscrew the button. If conventional methods fail, it is best to glue the button to the hollowed end of a wooden stick with super glue. The button will be slightly damaged, but with care

it can be cleaned up after cutting or breaking off the stick. Waterman used to cut a screwdriver slot in the button and then replace it later with a new one.

Removal of lever box and pressure bar

The next step is to remove the pressure bar with long nosed pliers and then the lever box that is held in by a tab on the inside. Bend the tab carefully and only sufficiently to allow the box to be raised. Once the tab is clear of the barrel, pull the box out along the axis of the pen.

The internal unit

With the box out, insert a rod from the nib end to push out the contents of the barrel. Carefully preserve the nipple and clean off residues. Make sure that the inside of the barrel is clear and clean. The inside of the barrel near the centre of the pen is a sealing surface, so be careful not to score or damage it.

Reassembly

The correct sac is no longer available, but a good alternative can be made. Use a standard No 20 sac and cut it to 35mm length. Attach it to the nipple with shellac. Now fit an O-ring over the nipple (the O-ring designed for the barrel seal of a Sheaffer PFM works well, but a slightly thicker one with 7mm internal diameter is better).

The sac with O-ring will resemble the original Watermans design that used a sac with a thick collar. This collar is important because it makes a seal between the outside of the sac and the inside of the barrel. Originally it would have nestled in a groove cut into the barrel and the nipple would have been pushed from the section end to complete the seal. To fit the modified sac you need to find or make a thin walled tube that will just fit in the barrel end.

The O-ring is placed over the sac, but not pushed up onto the nipple. It is important to use silicone grease on the inside of the barrel and on the nipple end of the sac and O-ring. The assembly is then pushed into the barrel up against a stop provided by a rod inserted into the section end to a depth of 59mm. It is important that this stop is at a point that locates the nipple about 2mm nearer the end of the barrel than it's original position. Assembly is complete when the O-ring is pushed over the nipple to the point where it rests against the outside of the groove that formerly held the sac collar. It would be better if the O-ring sat in the groove, but this would require it to be fitted first. As the O-ring is not attached to the sac, it would not be possible to fit the nipple without pushing the sac out.

Final position of the modified sac before tool removal

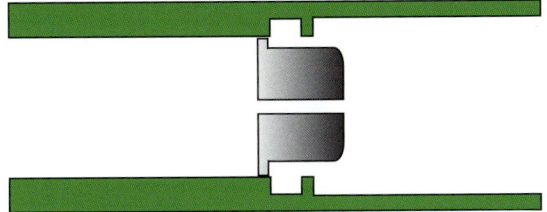

Position of the nipple in the barrel as originally designed for the collared sac

Test the seal by placing tape over the lever slot and blow into the barrel with the other end in a glass of water. No bubbles? – Success!!
When you are satisfied, anneal the lever box tab and fit the lever box and pressure bar. The box tab may break off even if annealed, and if this occurs you will need to glue the rear end of the box into the barrel. Fit the nib and feed in line with the lever and check the filling. The pen should hold about 2.3 ml of ink (similar to other 'vacumatic' pens) after about 10 cycles of pulling the lever fully back.

Cap, clip and trim
For work on the clip, the inner cap must be pulled to obtain access to the large headed screw in the cap top. This screw passes through a hole in the clip and into the brass insert in the head of the cap.

New sac and the remains of the old one

Tools used to position sac

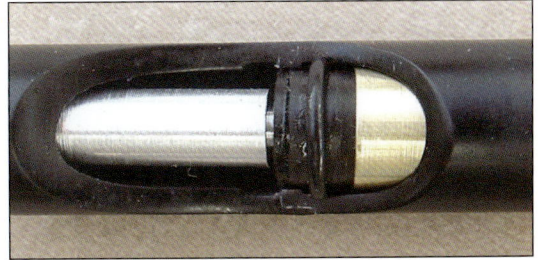

Remember that the section does not detach from the barrel and under no circumstances heat and twist the nib end.

CAUTION

WATERMANS CF

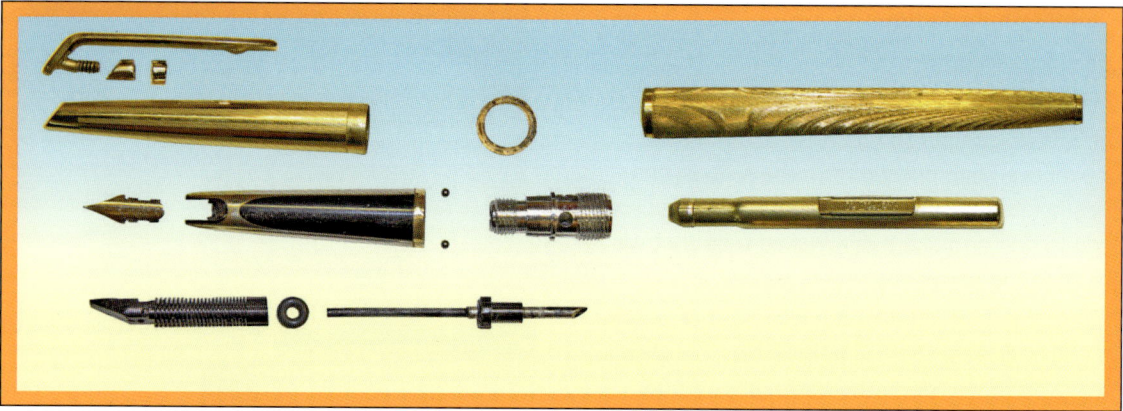

Components of the Waterman CF; note the long pierce tube

The Watermans CF deserves a mention not only because of its iconic status as the first cartridge fill pen in 1954 (CF= cartridge fill), but it demonstrates Watermans new direction in the 1950s of 'style' and design. It was a well made pen inside but lacked quality in its section trim.

Problems

- the gripping section trim corrodes and breaks off which makes it look unsightly.
- current shortage of cartridges and the almost total absence of convertors.

Disassembly

The connector unscrews with section pliers but this can be facilitated by using an old CF barrel (see Parker 51 Aero). The removal exposes two very small ball bearings in recesses below the trim ring. Do not lose them! The feed and pierce tube can be withdrawn leaving the nib in place. This can then be removed by lowering the end slightly and pulling. The nib cleats fit into slots inside the section.

Servicing

The main service is replacing the point end (section) shell and the nib; occasionally one encounters a blocked cartridge feed.

Re-assembly

Slide the nib into position and refit the feed and pierce tube. This is pushed into position with a small diameter metal tube. The trim ring is fitted onto the ball bearings which are kept in position with a dab of silicone grease and the connector is screwed in and tightened.

Test the pen first with a converter and then with a cartridge. As these are hard to find, simply refill an old CF cartridge with a hypodermic syringe. (see the section on converters and refurbishing a CF converter).

The clip and cap

The clips are not the easiest to replace because although one can access the nut with a spanning screwdriver , the threaded peg is bent and we have found a number cross threaded. Hold the clip in position until the nut is released.

The classic CF crocodile with heavy indented pattern

During the last year we have converted a number of cf pens by boring out the connector to accept a larger diameter converter. This has been done on the lathe and we have fitted various Waterman, Italian and Sheaffer converters. In some cases the piercing tube has to be changed. It can be quite involved but it is a permanent resolution.

WATERMANS MODERN

Three modern Watermans Rhapsody, Fontainbleu and silver Man100

Modern pens have become repair items for the private repairer because there are few parts left in the factory and it might appear that 'secular' repairers are more ingenious?

There is little that one can really discuss other than creative repair of modern Watermans. Either you have the parts or you don't. If you don't it is unlikely that you can repair the pen, pencil or ball pen. Parts if they are available, cost a fortune. An Edson stub nib would buy a flight across the Atlantic!

Nevertheless there are possibilities - this is a 'scavenger' page, imploring repairers to bear in mind that new spares have a value as well as old, and broken new pens may be more valuable as parts.

The Watermans Manual

This is not the most helpful workshop offering but it illustrate the range of Watermans styles, designs made from the 1970s.

It is interesting to quote the Watermans company big repair manual for the Edson.

Tools required - None

Recommended operations - replace complete units!

As a professional one keeps an eye open for good nib units, ball pen and pencil mechanisms and caps in good condition. Unfortunately it is rarely the case that one can adapt complete units from one model to another, but one can disassemble items and often use the parts to advantage.

Dismantling items
Caps

These are sometimes threaded and assembled with screws so they can be a supply of inner-caps, clips and trim. The cheaper pens are usually glued together but parts can be obtained by selectively destroying an older cap. Inner caps are particularly useful because they are part of the push fit of cap to barrel fitting.

Nibs and Gripping units

This is perhaps the most productive area and although there is a wide range on premium gripping units (sections in old 'penspeak'), many are assembled with threaded parts but glued so warm before attacking. Watermans did supply both tools and instruction (surprisingly not in the manual?).

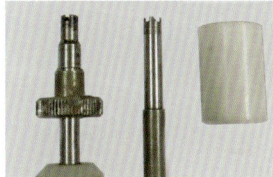

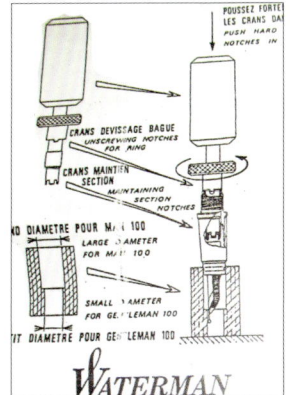

Using Waterman tools to dismantle man100 nib unit

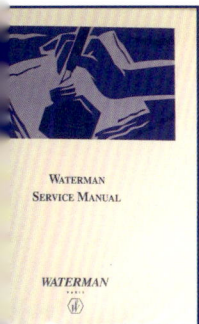

Variety of Waterman modern nib units -some parts are interchangeable.   RHS parts from dismantled gripping sections

WATERMANS CLIPS

Riveted clips

There are a number of different designs of clip made from a variety of materials such as silver, yellow metal and white metal alloys. Replacing a clip is straightforward but you do require the right tools, patience and a little riveting practice. It is also necessary to have an appropriate replacement clip.

There are two options ; to make a 'U' double rivet or a back plate with single rivets.

Tools and Materials required

Silver, silver solder, annealed white metal, brass, copper or yellow metal wire; brass rivets, brass sheet, cutters, files, 'U' bar template, small drills, small hammer, vice, dental clamp, riveting liner and optional buff, Dremel and inner cap puller.

Preparation of the cap

The first step is to pull the inner cap (see Pullers)

Carefully remove the heads of the rivets with a file or Dremel fitted with a disc (in our experience dental burrs are effective but can run off and damage the cap). Push out the rivets with a small pin punch. In a few rare cases the holes are not in line and if this is not corrected any new clip fitted will be skewed. At this stage it is very important to assess the holes in the cap and measure the sizes so that the rivets will be a good fit. There are different sized holes in Waterman clips. One

has to decide which size rivets to use. The holes in the cap and clip should be the same but this is often not the case so some enlargement may be necessary to achieve a match.

Making the rivet unit

The most simple unit is made as a 'u' clip from wire. Silver solder, silver, brass or copper alloy wire can be used and the wire is pushed through the holes in the steel plate (see picture) and hammered to give a flat bottomed 'u'. Note the two sizes in the plate which should cater for most clips.

In some cases, where the cap may appear rather fragile, we prefer a rivet unit with a flat plate, which gives a larger bearing surface inside the cap. The plate is made as follows: mark two holes on a brass sheet (thickness 0.3mm) using the clip to be fitted; punch small holes through the sheet. The brass or silver rivets (we use mainly 3/64"

domed rivets) can be purchased or made; if they have been filed to a point they will easily push through the punctured brass sheet. The sheet is then cut to form a small 'back plate' (about 8mm x 6mm).

Rivet plates and 'u-clips' must fit into the clip and cap holes perfectly. Referring to the illustration only condition C is acceptable. If this is not the case, you must make a new plate or 'u-clip' otherwise the clip will not be firm or will become loose with use in a short time. Do not try and make a wrong sized rivet fit; it may crack the cap.

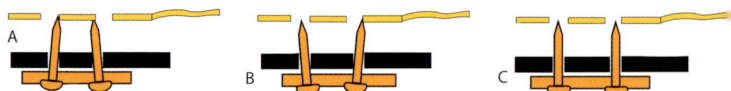

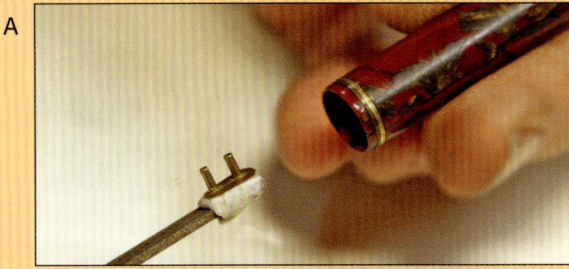

A - Position rivet unit on a spatula and fit into cap, B - Secure rivet in position with anvil and fit on clip. C - Secure the clip with a band clamp and then after riveting and checking, D - Re-insert the inner cap.

Fitting the rivet unit

The unit is fixed onto a spatula with 'Blu-Tack'. It is a good idea to pre-mark the spatula to make it easier to line the rivets up with the cap holes. Once these have been fed through the cap holes, they can be pulled gently into position and the cap is rotated so that the 'u-clip' or rivet/plate is pointing downwards. The riveting anvil is gently pushed into the cap and the tapered shape ensures that the plate is fixed firmly into position (see Tip). The clip is placed over the exposed rivets, pressed down onto the cap and secured with a clamp. The rivets must be trimmed to the correct height with a file or a Dremel. (A metal sheet may be placed over the rivets to protect the cap and ensure the rivet height is correct). Not more than 1mm is required to give a nicely shaped domed rivet and slight countersinking of the clip will give a stronger fixing. Both brass rivets and the silver wire rivet easily, but it is vital that the cap and riveting anvil are firmly fixed. A recent procedure, which works well, involves the use of a band clamp, as illustrated, to keep the clip straight and in tight contact with the cap.

Riveting

Practice using a light hammer by tapping around the rivet. Many light blows are preferable to a few heavy blows and your aim is to get a firm clip that does not move.

The final stage is tidying the rivet appearance with a gentle polish or buff. It is more pleasing if the rivets have a domed appearance and that is achieved with practise. Be careful that the clip you have is not a plated clip, because buffing may well remove the plate.

When refitting inner cap, file a flat to ensure that it clears the plate.

The riveting anvil can be made from some 10mm bar, which suits the most common Watermans 52 . There are two options to help secure the rivet firm against the inner surface of the cap. Make an anvil with a tapered flat by filing off enough material to allow clearance for the rivet. The second option is to make an anvil with an offset cam which, when rotated, will push the rivet firmly through the holes and against the inside of the cap. In both cases it is important that the anvil should be firmly held in a vice when riveting.

TIP

riveting anvil profile

WATERMANS PRONGED & RING CLIPS

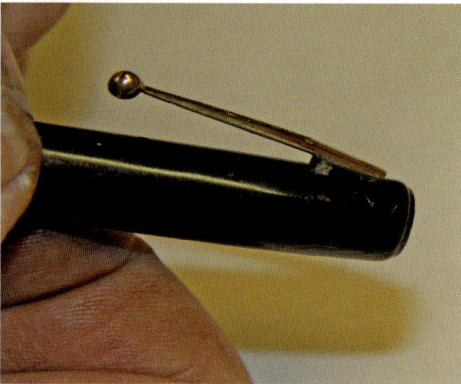

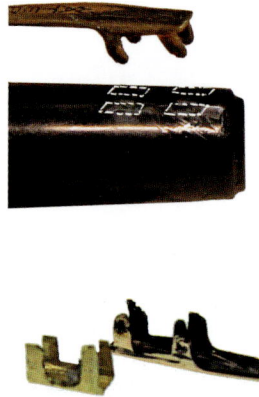

Pronged clips

Watermans moved away from double riveted clips in the 1930s to an inefficient single rivet clip and the pronged clip. The Patrician clip is an intrusive clip, which has a bifurcated prong held in place by the inner cap. The main problem with such pens is to remove the inner cap without damaging a valuable pen. It is not correct to fit the clip without removing the inner cap. If the inner cap will not budge, then although tedious, it is better to bore out the inner cap and make a new one before fitting the clip.

The Ink Vue and others had a four pronged intrusive clip, which frequently tears out. Replacing these is not a problem if you can source a replacement clip and the cap has not been damaged. After removing the inner cap the clip must be firmly tapped into place against an arbour thereby bending the prongs over towards each other. Warming the plastic helps to get the prongs well seated. In general annealing pronged clips in the same way as lever boxes is never a guarantee that the prongs will not snap off but it must help!

Four pronged clips can be restored with an insert. Prongs are secured by inserting a cap arbor and tapping the clip with a mallet.

If the prongs are broken all is not lost because the clips can be restored by fitting replacement prongs. A four pronged small box made from brass sheet can be soldered into the clip and the original clip can be replated if necessary before refitting. Spare top pronged clips are harder to find but if the inner cap is removed the donor clip can be clamped in position and the lugs bent over with a modified G clamp.

Ring clips

The small ring clips of Taperites and 1950s models are secured with an hexagonal nut and a threaded stud. These are often corroded but with patience many of them can be undone. Another variant has a threaded nipple joined to the clip and this is secured by a screw from the inside.

Spare top mounted prong clips are hard to find .

Ring top clips with screw and stud

WATERMANS LEVER BOXES

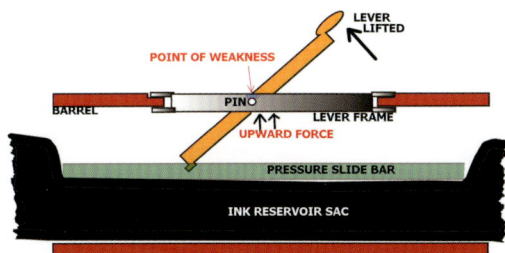

Sketch of the lever box in use, illustrating the forces and the fragility of the lever frame

Actual failed lever with the crack at the pivot hole, causing the whole frame to become displaced.

The lever box is both an eyecatcher with the Ideal globe and an eyesore when it has a broken frame. It is a frequent problem that dramatically reduces the value of a pen but it is a very easy repair, providing the pen does not have an overlay.

Why they fail

First the lever boxes were cast and in general while cast metals resist deformation they are brittle and on a micro level they are likely to be porous. Second, when the lever is used the forces on a thin section above the pivot hole are sometimes too great and the frame cracks causing the pivot and lever to be pulled out. Few levers break as it is predominantly a frame problem. Consequently there are many spare levers looking for boxes! What is so surprising is that the solution was so simple by putting side central gripping lugs onto the box, but Watermans presumably disregarded any criticism that the design of their boxes was flawed!

Note that the pivot hole position varies; it is nearer the thumb tab for larger barrels.

Replacement

The old box has to come out without damaging the barrel. First of all detach the slide bar by depressing the bar tab. If the frame is completely cracked then no problem, but if not bear in mind that the top lugs are recessed into the barrel. Work from the inside and prise the nearest lug to a 90⁰ angle; you may be able to lift and withdraw the box but take care not to crack the barrel. It may be necessary to ease the back lug with dental pick/hook.
Check the donor box well especially tabs and frame for cracks. Presuming it is OK and has been cut out of another pen then the bottom lugs will have to be bent down in order to fit the box. Use a flame to anneal the lugs by heating until cherry red and then leave to cool. As this is a cast item it may still fail. Gently bend the two bottom lugs down and test fit into the box. It should be a good fit.
The lugs are then bent back. If you are lucky enough to have some Waterman box pliers then life is easy. If not then a rod inside the barrel and a shaped notched probe will do a very good job.

Replacing a lever in a good box

This is worthwhile bearing in mind the prices of good boxes. First examine the box and lever carefully. If the lever still has a pivot in it, then it must be pulled or knocked out. Check with a pin that the holes of lever and box line up and check the closing 'click'. Anneal the lugs first and bend them down. You must make a pivot and there are two options for fixing it; riveting or threading. Most will rivet so use a steel pin and make sure it is the correct diameter. Peen over/ flatten one end in a drill plate and then fit and cut the protruding end to size and rivet on a firm block. You just have to ensure the pivot is long enough and gentle riveting is adequate. The threading option is easy if you have small jewellers taps; simply tap the box and rough die the

Three different lug crimping tools

pivot; it simply screws in and can be ground flush to the box with complete confidence.

Boxes may require plating, so if you are repairing Watermans regularly, then make a few restored boxes up and get them plated and ready to add value to that 'dog in the drawer'.

WATERMANS OVERLAYS

Removed Sterling Vine overlay, which will provide a rewarding task after fitting on to an old 52.

A
B
C
D

Sequence of removing a gf overlay from a 52V. Note the gold filled tab D, which is often missing.

Removing Watermans overlays

Make absolutely certain that it is necessary to remove the overlay. This can be a difficult task not without risk to the overlay and should not be embarked upon without careful thought.

Overlays are usually made from tube which has either been patterned or pierced and they are usually silver or gold-filled (gold overlays are quite rare).

A full overlay has metal covering the section, cap and barrel. A part - overlay is usually barrel and cap. A half overlay is barrel only. The most frequent repair request is when a lever box has to be replaced, although this can be done without removing the overlay (see Penpractice and Penpencilgallery websites).

Removing a barrel overlay

The first thing to look for are any pins that are in place to stop the overlay moving. Not all overlays were pinned but look on the lower part of the overlay.

Watermans overlays usually come off over the end of the pen barrel, not the nib end; heating and manipulating is required. Sometimes the overlay has been shellacced and heating or soaking in methylated spirits is essential. Unfortunately some overlays which have been moving may have been superglued or even epoxyed and that will present a challenge but with patience even those overlays can be removed.

It is a gradual process of moving forward over the lever box and then back repeatedly. The overlay deforms slightly but this is unavoidable and not a problem but disconcerting for the first time. In extreme cases it may be necessary to sacrifice the barrel in order to preserve the overlay but this means the end imprint will be lost.

Take care not to lose the small lever plate cover D.

Most non-filigree overlays have the barrel reduced in diameter to make the original fitting easier. It is always easier to remove a solid overlay. Filigree overlays can be fragile so use a wood dowel the same diameter as the barrel to support the overlay when it is partly off.

Sometimes it is possible to push off an overlay with a metal tube with the same internal diameter as the barrel outer diameter. This can be done using a lathe.

Refitting

The reverse of removing but easier with solid overlays as the barrel can be pared to fit. The problem is going over the lever box. Take your time!

Removing a cap overlay

If the cap crown is split it may appear desirable to remove the overlay but this can be a complex process if the cap has a clip as it will have to be removed. It really is only justified on a very valuable pen.

One of the practical problems with a cap is holding it firmly when attempting to slide off the overlay. We have used a Universal puller to hold the cap securely, and it is important, because cap overlays are usually reluctant to move.

Make sure that the overlay has not been swaged round the cap lip first!

Not for the purists but we have repairied a lever without taking the overlay off. This involes cutting a channel in the inside of the barrel, removing the bridge on the lever box and fitting a C clipped lever from the inside.

WATERMANS EMBLEM & HUNDRED YEAR

The starting situation of a Hundred year pen in need of care

Modern coloured Lucite-
An original blue end from a new old stock 100 year pen and the restored black pen with a clear end.

Exploding Pens was a term coined to describe the ends of Eversharp Doric and Waterman 100 year pens. The barrel ends develop a discoloured cloudiness, then small cracks and finally they disintegrate leaving a crystalline stub. The situation can only be remedied by major surgery and this can be very successful with the Watermans Hundred Year range.

Restoration

If one has a good example, this should be used as a model. First measure the pen and then using transparent coloured Lucite, turn an end for the pen with a suitable taper. The end should be turned to near final dimensions before being glued to the pen and it should have a small recessed step to fit into the barrel.

Barrel Preparation

The barrel end must be prepared by removing all the offending material completely and then boring the pen barrel to accept the replacement end. After checking the fit, this can be glued in place with clear epoxy or superglue. (If during checking there are internal reflections, then the base of the replacement barrel tip can be painted black before inserting.)

Lucite is harder than celluloid, and this can lead to problems on the lathe if the end is turned to its final shape after gluing to the pen. Only very light cuts can be taken or the celluloid will deform slightly and the tool will catch in the Lucite. The safest way to clean and smooth the joint is by the use of files and increasingly fine abrasives. Judging from pens seen with good ends, there was some variation in the shape of the originals, possibly as a result of hand finishing techniques. Colours were also not always consistent. The oversize 100 Year and Emblem pens had flat ends, whereas other models had bullet shape ends.

An original yellow end on a brown oversize pen.

If appropriately coloured Lucite is not available, a good alternative can be found in cheap tool stores in the form of screwdriver or chisel handles. This material is softer than Lucite and comes in a range of colours including amber, red and blue.
For the repairer without a lathe, the job is possible using coloured epoxy to cast a pen end in place. However, it is difficult to avoid air bubbles and it may be necessary to use vibration in reduced air pressure – in practice a vacuum cleaner attached to the component whilst it is being agitated in an ultrasonic cleaner.

MABIE TODD EYEDROPPER PENS

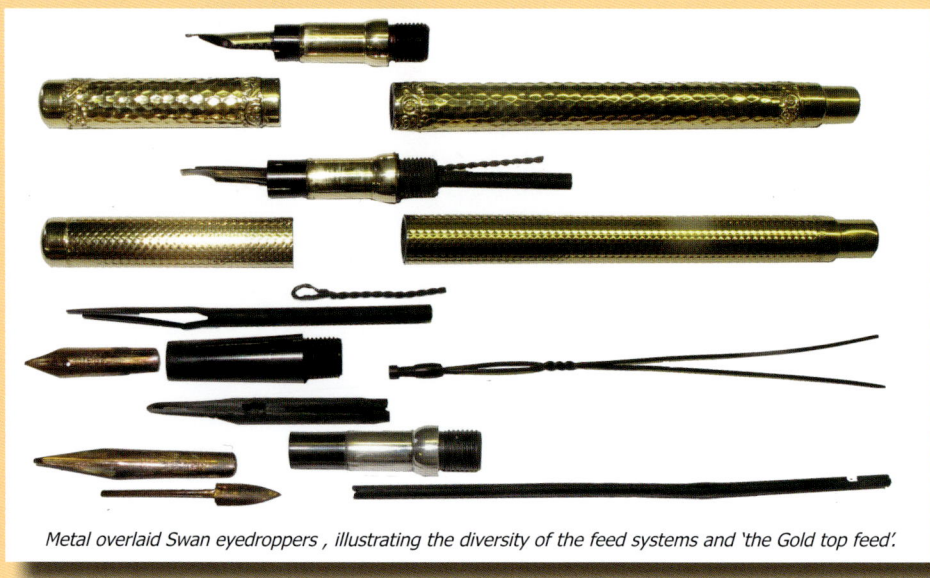

Metal overlaid Swan eyedroppers , illustrating the diversity of the feed systems and 'the Gold top feed'.

Mabie Todd and Bard made stylos and eyedropper pens in the USA from the 1890s and were prolific advertisers in the UK. Bard was dropped in 1907 although catalogues of 1908/9 continued to advertise Mabie Todd and Bard. After 1910 probably all pens made were stamped Mabie Todd & Co. Some pens were as much men's jewellery as writing instruments with stunning high quality overlays. All metal overlays and chatelaines were manufactured in the USA. It is not certain when UK manufacture of nibbed pens started but probably after 1919 when the Company was sold to UK investors. 'Swan' was the traditional brand name used, but 'Blackbird' eyedroppers were also made. Eyedroppers continued to be made until the 1920s although lever fill models were introduced about 1918.

Problems
- cracked caps
- chipped section
- brassed/corroded metal,e.g. section overlays
- pins missing on chatelaine
- shut-off plug missing

Dismantling and repair
Unscrewing the gripping section can reveal a variety of designs. Early models had an under-over feed with a twisted wire pushed into the section/feed. On larger models there was a unique 'onion' shaped end to the feed.

Swan No.8 nib unit

Some pens had a cylindrical perforated tube to support the nib and a 'valve' attached to two long wires allowed the flow to be adjusted. Other examples have the valve and wires replaced with a long tube with two lateral holes.
After soaking, carefully remove these feed parts by working out the nib and withdrawing the under over feed from the threaded end, and the tubular feed and plug from the open end.

Sometimes there is a 'Gold top feed' as well as the nib. This is a thin gold channel located on the top of the nib, which was supposed to guarantee good ink flow as the pressure on the nib varied.

GF engraved barrel overlay on a Mabie Todd and Bard pen with under over feed.

"The 'Gold top feed' carries ink to the very point of the pen which, acting in conjunction with the under feed, supplies ink in exact relation to the pressure put on the pen. No skipping, no blotting". Optimistic? Feed or wire parts are often missing and if one cannot acquire a replacement it is not too difficult to make them.

Nibs. Swan produced three categories of nibs:
Posting for bookkeepers giving fine lines which dry very quickly and do not require blotting;
Manifold for duplicating work with stiffness to make several copies at one time;
Stenograph where reliability and shading of characters is necessary (usually with a 'Gold top feed).
From 1914 most of the pens had ladder feeds.

Take special care with feeds because they can easily snap

A corroded metal section is possibly the most serious defect of overlaid Swans. Restoration is a major task as it may involve the fabrication of both a new hard rubber section and the overlay.
To dismantle, warm the section and pull out the hard rubber part. If this proves unsuccessful and the overlay is good, burn it out! If the overlay is bad, file it off and preserve the hard rubber foundation. If the metal part is only brassed it may be reusable after plating. However, a new metal overlay will be a job for a silversmith or some very delicate lathe work.
A black hard rubber section can be used to replace an ugly corroded example and this is not too challenging for a repairer with a lathe (see Machining practice-making a section)

Chatelaine Swans

Chatelaine Swans are conventional eyedroppers suspended by a chain attached to the cap. The

Three chatelaines with three different pin securing methods.

cap is secured to the pen by one of three designs; an open bayonet catch similar to a light bulb fitting; a closed bayonet catch where a rotating band locks the cap; a channel and pin (no bayonet design) with a rotating locking band.
Ignorance of these securing systems is, sadly, often the cause of major damage to cap or pin by an enthusiastic customer trying to open the pen. It can be difficult to remove the cap due to the bayonet or rotating band being 'gummed' up. It is important to take your time otherwise the locating pin can break off or crack the section. Warm the joint or soak with WD40, gently twist and pull...repeat and repeat until it moves.

Refitting a chatelaine pin

It is not necessary to remove the old broken pin, which may often leave an unsightly hole.

Location of pin for an open bayonet catch..

File it level and position the new pin at 90 degrees to the old location. Make the pin from 1.2mm stainless steel or brass and die the end with a coarse thread. Drill and tap the section. Make sure the pin length is flush with the inside and protrudes 1mm. Check it works before sealing it in position with supersteel or shellac.

Two chatelaine eyedroppers with different cap securing systems. The top pen has a bigger diameter barrel and cap (9.8mm).

MABIE TODD LEVER PENS

Mabie Todd & Bard grew faster in the UK following the establishment of a branch in 1884. The conservative design seemed to appeal more in the UK, and the name 'Swan' was a good choice. Mabie Todd's success with eyedropper pens was enhanced when lever filling systems were introduced around 1915.

The Swan pens had a very efficient and simple mechanism. Catalogues of the 1920's make a virtue of the simplicity of the pen as '*easy to use and easy to fill by simply lifting and closing a lever, which is flush with the holder*'.

One significant innovation by Swan was the introduction in 1911 of a 'two part cap' to prevent leaking – now known as an inner cap.

Mabie Todd continued to make lever pens in a similar style until 1954 and they were frequently promoted with a calligraphic style of advertising.

Problems

- the lever becomes pitted and brassed
- deformation at the lever slot
- some designs of feed are fragile and can snap
- clips can tear out of the cap
- later clips snap off
- metal covered sections corrode

Servicing Swan/Blackbird/Jackdaw lever pens

The sections, made from hard rubber, are a push fit into the barrel and easily removed if resacing is required. One solution to barrel distortion is possible by removing the lever and C-clip and restoring the original barrel shape with heat and a mandrel.

The Jackdaw has a short lever with a J-bar. Lever Blackbirds also used J-bars, but Swan had a more sophisticated pressure bar with the lever directly attached. Refitting such a bar requires manipulation with long nosed slim pliers and a dental probe. Once 'threaded through the slot the lever is positioned by a 'C' ring that engages with a groove inside the barrel.

Refitting a lever can only be done through the barrel

Removing and refitting an intrusion clip

Variety of Swan and Blackbird caps/clips

Replacing the clip - early pens

The clip fitting is by a brass tab that slides behind the clip lugs after they have passed through the two parallel slots in the cap. The tab can only be accessed after pulling the inner cap if the pen does not have a screw fitting inner cap like the one illustrated. If the tab has corroded, it is easy to make another from thin brass sheet. Clip exchanges are most problematical when the cap slots are damaged. If the material between the slots is cracked at the top end, a glued repair will be satisfactory. If the material is missing or cracked at the bottom end, then a longer tab with a wider top should be used. Resist the temptation to glue the clip in place and thereby prevent the inner cap from being removed in the future.

Fitting a clip to a clipless Swan

Not all Swans had clips because this was an optional extra. Swan charged 2/6 for fitting a gold filled clip, 10/6 for a 9ct one and 20/- for a 18ct one, so clearly Swan did not regard this as a labour intensive activity.

Collectors often ask for a clip to be fitted to a pen that never had one previously, so new slots have to be cut.

Slots are 9mm long and 1mm wide. They start 9mm from the end of the cap tube and the material between the slots is 2.5mm wide.

One easy way to cut the slots is to use a 1mm drill in a pin vice to make a closely spaced series of straight through and angled holes, and then to use a needle file to finish to the exact clip dimensions. The success of this fitting is dependent on accurate marking out, so make sure that the slot centre lines are scribed and parallel to the axis of the cap.

Replacing a clip - later pens

Lever pens from the late 30s and post war had an intrusive clip which can be prised out by using a screwdriver. Versions of these clips are with two prongs or as a bar with serration. If the clip breaks off at the cap surface, the tag cannot be pulled out so the inner cap must be removed and the tag worked out from the inside using a sharp awl.

Swan clips - both washer and intrusive design.

Caution: Not all levers have the pivot point at the same place because different barrel diameters require different penetrations of the pressure bar.

MABIE TODD (SWAN) LEVERLESS

Large Swan leverless with a no4 nib

These pens appeared in about 1934 following the publication of a patent in 1932 for a leverless sac pen. Other leverless mechanisms existed at this time, but the Swan Leverless used a sac twisting approach. A pressure bar with the end connected eccentrically to a button on the end of the barrel compresses the sac when the button is rotated ½ turn, and ink is taken up when the button is returned to its original position. Despite the filling system being less efficient than lever fillers, the Swan Leverless was on sale for at least 11 years. They came in three sizes appropriate to size 2, 4 and 6 nibs.

Servicing

The sections are a push fit, and are responsive to the usual hot air treatment. Sac replacement is a little unusual because the twist filler performs at its best with a sac that fills the barrel space. Fitting a sac that is larger than we would fit to a conventional lever filler demands the use of a pusher to make sure the end of the sac reaches the end of the barrel without being crumpled.

The pusher is operated through the section, so the nib and feed cannot be fitted until the sac is in place. The use of a large sac will mean that it also has to be a necked sac, or it will not fit tightly onto the section nipple.

The pusher is a piece of 3mm dowel with a knob on the end to prevent it from being pushed too far. The sac should be well covered in talc.

The sac about to be fitted using the pusher

The sac is fitted and the pusher is about to be removed

If the pressure bar is snapped off or missing, and a spare is available, the remains of the old bar will have to be removed. Bars are usually welded to the head of a left hand threaded bolt that screws into the knob and a special tool is required to remove it. Rarely a left hand threaded brass slot-headed screw holds the assembly in place and a long handled fine screwdriver is all that is required (see the examples at the top of the next page).

Original Mabie Todd tool for removal of the twist fill mechanism. They were made in three sizes

Pressure bars with alternative mounting styles and differing left handed threads

Cap, clip and trim

The gold plating on Swan Leverless pens was usually good quality and it rarely need replating. If however the clip needs to be replaced the cap top button must be removed; on the earlier pens it should unscrew after the application of some heat. The later pens are more of a problem because the gold Swan emblem in the cap top needs to be removed to gain access to the brass screw that holds everything in place. The emblem was glued in, but most come out easily with a little persuasion from a sharp blade.

If the clip just needs retightening, the clip unit as a whole can be unscrewed from the cap providing the blind cap is prevented from rotating.

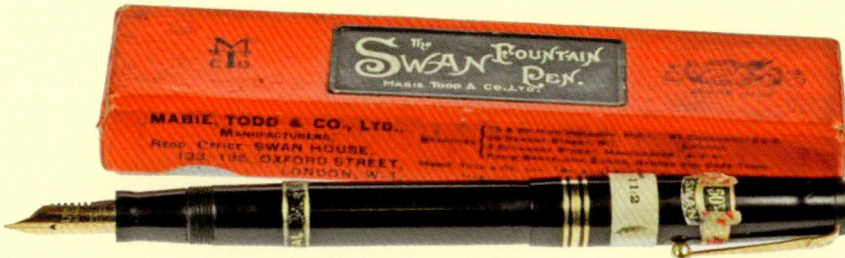

Four very desirable leverless pens; from the top; mint black model with No 4 nib; silver slim with stepped clip; hallmarked silver and gf larger diameter later models.

MABIE TODD BUTTON BAR

These pens are easily confused with the earlier Leverless pens, but the mechanism is quite different. Like the Leverless, the button unscrews and then screws up again to fill, but the bar is a pressure bar, not a rotating bar. Externally, the main distinguishing feature is the aluminium thread on the button. The Blackbird version had a knob which screws a small cam down and compresses the button bar, whereas the Swan version illustrated has a square tube, which fits into a hard rubber washer in the barrel and also engages with the 70mm button bar. In both cases the other end of the bar fits into a recess in the threads of the section.

It is often a mystery why unscrewing the button compresses the bar. The answer lies in the three-start thread on the end of the square tube part that is threaded into the button. The external thread on the button is a single start thread. Both threads are 36 turns per inch and both are right handed. If the button is unscrewed one turn, the inner part is prevented from rotating by the square washer, so it unscrews from the button by three thread intervals. The **nett movement down the barrel is therefore two thread intervals.**

Servicing

These pens are simple to restore provided the button does not need to be replaced. When the sac has been fitted, insert the pressure bar (with

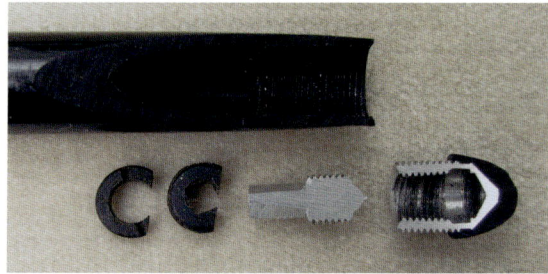

Demonstration of the button mechanism

the button screwed in) and make sure it is located properly and responsive to button movement. It is important that the bar is exactly the right length – the top must be flush with the end of the barrel. Now screw the button out to the stop (about a half turn) and locate the end of the bar into the slot in the side of the section. Now screw the section on a bit, and then screw the button in a bit. Repeat until the button is all the way in and the section is all the way on.

Button replacement is not a simple task, and it is almost essential to make a set of special tools. The main problem is setting the button stop so that the full compression of the bar is achieved. Assembly starts with the square washer screwed into the barrel so its top face is about 1mm inside the barrel. The square tube is screwed all the way into the button and the

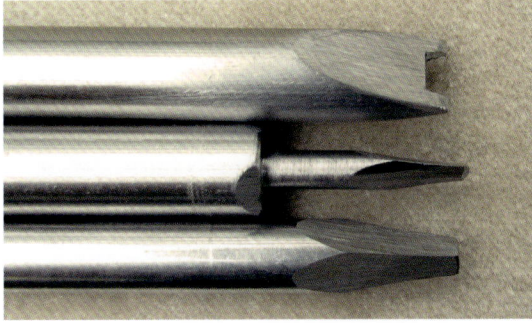

Spanning screwdriver for adjusting the lock washer, triangular tool for turning the square tube and the square tool (not essential) for inserting the square centred washer.

Correct assembly. Note that the square washer provides the stop to further movement

The button screwed fully home

The lock washer is tightened

button is screwed into the barrel as far as it will go (about a half turn). The square tube is then rotated 1 turn anticlockwise from the inside using the tapered triangular tool pressed into the circular bore.

The button is then screwed in as far as it will go and the previous step is repeated approximately four times until the knob is all the way in. The square tube is then moved a little further anticlockwise until a position is found where the button will only unscrew to about two and a quarter turns. The locknut is then tightened against the square nut to prevent any further movement.

The lock nut has to be inserted from the barrel mouth (the section threads are the same, so it has to be screwed in to start) keeping the barrel vertical so that the washer does not turn over when it clears the barrel threads.

For dismantling it is essential to heat the barrel because shellac may have been used in the original assembly. A warm barrel aids assembly.

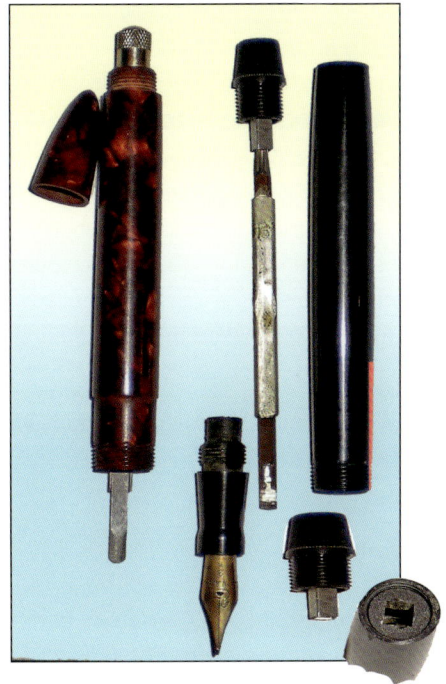

Flat top button on later 1950s model and marbled model from same era

Button bar demonstrator indicating efficient compression

SWAN VISOFIL V

Components of the Senior size Swan Visofil V

The Visofil V was patented in 1934 as an ink-visible sac pen with increased ink capacity. The transparent ink reservoir is an extension of the rubber sac and acts as a push button to compress the sac longitudinally against the action of a surrounding spring. The filler is prevented from rotating by an octagonally bored brass bush fixed to the end of the barrel; this also provides attachment for the blind cap.

Visofils came with a long breather tube. This enables almost complete filling of the reservoir following about five pushes on the button. There is a large range of stunning colours and there are three sizes of Visofil V. The lady and some mid size pens were made without clips.

Problems
- crazing and cracking of plunger chamber unit
- cracked barrel threads
- corrosion of spring

Dismantling
The pens are dismantled by removing the section and then by pushing the filler down through the barrel. The sections are slip fit and although much easier to remove than those in the Visofil VT, care must be taken otherwise a cracked barrel is the result.

In some cases the spring is broken or missing

as well as the breather tube and the small hard rubber washer that sits between the sac and the transparent ink chamber. The washer will need cleaning out because the sac rubber tends to stick to it.

The transparent chamber is a frequent source of problems as it is often laced with fine cracks, crystallised and friable. Making the chambers requires a lathe, milling machine and expertise. Spare parts can only be obtained from cannibalising another pen, so beware of buying any damaged ones if you want to use the pen. The chamber will need a good clean to remove hardened ink residues. Soak it in cold water followed by vinegar applied with a makeup brush. Ultrasound will help.

Reassembly
If the hard rubber washer is missing, a replacement can be made from a plastic tube. If you leave it out there is a danger that the spring end will cut the sac. If the breather tube is broken or missing it can be replaced with a piece of plastic covered wiring, from which the core has been withdrawn (about 1.5mm diameter and extending to within about 10mm of the end of the chamber).

The length of the sac (30mm for the Senior pen) should be such that it is not under compression

Three bent paperclips holding the spring back to allow attachment of the reservoir

when the filler is inserted into the pen. This means that it will be under a small amount of tension from the spring before insertion. It is difficult to attach the sac at both ends unless the spring is held in compression, but with practice it can be done. The best solution is three paper clips bent with hooks on each end; these will hold the spring during attachment of the sac and also while you wait for the shellac (or other sac adhesive) to cure.

When the clips are removed, the spring will push the washer down onto the mouth of the chamber and it should stay attached. Now fit the nib and feed, making sure that the breather tube is securely attached and that the airway is clear. Remember to heat the mouth of the barrel a little before pushing the filler unit in.

Filling

The pen is filled by the depression and release of the filler until no more air can be expelled. The top of the breather tube extends well into the clear reservoir, so the pen will fill to this level. It will contain some 1.6ml of ink (a modern converter holds about 0.75ml).

Cap, clip and trim

If you need to remove the clip, you will almost certainly find that the button threads are

extremely tight as these plastics usually shrink. A cold water soak and then hot air will be required. Be careful not to rotate the clip on the cap top – clips are held in a shallow recess to hide the clip washer, and if you allow the clip to rotate, it will take the plastic wall with it. Many pens have damaged cap tops due to previous owners rotating the clip. If only part of the wall is damaged, it might be possible to fill it with coloured epoxy. If it has all been scored away, a lathe will be needed to cut a new recess. The cap will then be 1mm shorter and the nib may have to be pushed a little further into the section to save it from damage when the cap is screwed on. The model V212 illustrated has a two banded cap and a small ball clip; other models have a decorative band and a clip ball of normal size.

Different cap/clips illustrated.

WEB
PAGE
100
NOTES
WWW..........

The filler unit ready to go back in the barrel

> **Be sure to fit the sac and chamber together before fitting the nib and feed – otherwise you are very likely to break the delicate hard rubber breather tube**

CAUTION

SWAN VISOFIL VT

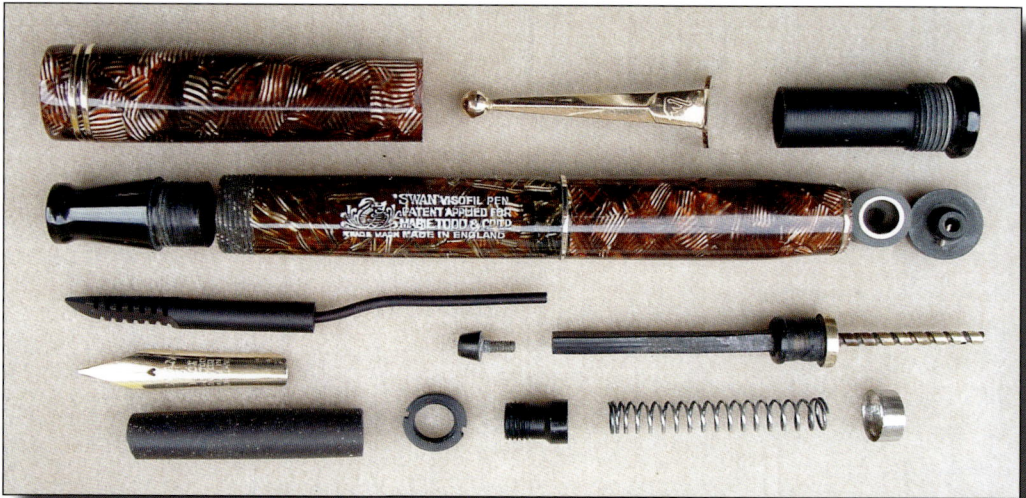

Components of the more complicated Swan Visofil VT

The Swan Visofil VT was introduced in 1937 and colours were limited to red, green, grey and black. The filling system works on the same principle as the Parker Vacumatic, but it is more difficult to service and requires special tools.

Working principle

It has a diaphragm that is a straight section of tube rather than a tube folded back on itself like the Vac. The anchor points for the diaphragm are therefore at the end and centre of the barrel. There is no blind cap because the plunger knob is designed to extend from the end of the barrel on a coarse thread.

The pen fills like the Vac Standard; it has a similar ink capacity and the front section of the barrel is ink visible. The servicing difficulty arises mostly because the end bush cannot be unscrewed like the Vac; it is glued into the end of the barrel and finished flush. It's removal is a sacrificial job and a replacement must be made.

The barrel is made in two parts glued together over a hard rubber sleeve that also acts as the anchor for one end of the diaphragm. Occasionally a threaded joint is found. It is not usually possible to open this joint, but if it does come undone, the servicing is slightly easier.

Problems

- filler knob broken off or missing
- knob jammed
- knob rotates but the filler does not extend
- broken spring
- twisted or broken internal components
- loose or missing barrel trim
- broken recess for the clip washer
- glued in mechanism
- other problems and solutions are detailed under Blackbird Top Filler (page 154)

Repair procedure

The dismantling stages include section, barrel nut, end plug, extraction and repair of the mechanism and repair of the cap clip.

Removing the section

Sections make a ridged joint with the barrel (not threaded) and are sealed firmly in place. To reduce the risk of cracking the barrel, hot air must be used around the threads. Take care not to let the pliers slip over the end of the section. Try rotating the section, and when the bond is released - pull it straight out.

The view down the barrel should now reveal the plunger nose and the hard rubber nut that holds the diaphragm mount against the barrel-jointing sleeve. A special spanning screwdriver is needed to move the nut. The nut should unscrew easily,

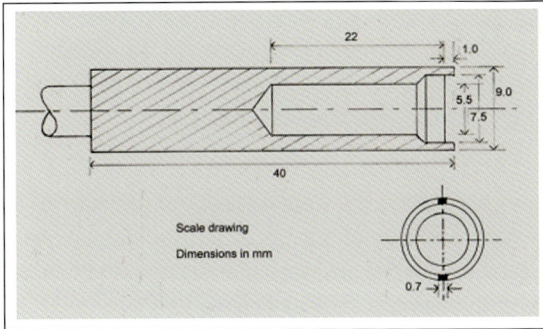

Dimensions of the nut removal tool

but do not remove it completely at this stage. After 1.5 turns, push the tool firmly into the barrel; if the old diaphragm is stuck to its seat, it will then be released. The nut can now be unscrewed completely, but if it does not fall out, it can be left in the barrel at this stage - but cover the opening to prevent loss. Now hold a small box spanner against the plunger nose to stop it rotating, and unscrew the button on its scroll threaded rod. If it is very stiff a little WD40 may help, but do not heat the mechanism because the square plastic tube that contains the rod goes soft at quite low temperatures.

Removing the plug

The black plastic plug in the end of the barrel must now be removed. The plug with its brass insert is there only to align the filler rod and button – it does not contain any seals. It was originally fitted with glue so its removal is normally by reaming or drilling. It is worthwhile to try pulling it out with the assistance of some heat, but do be aware of the fragility of the brass rod as this component is not easily remade. Your chance of success in removing the plug intact is less than 5%.

Do not pull on the button-it will break off and do resist the temptation to push the mechanism out because the filler nose will buckle very easily. The button must now be removed by knocking out the brass locking pin that secures it to the rod. A 0.75mm pin tool is handy for this, but make sure that the button is is fully supported or the rod may be bent. A 1mm drill held in a pin vice can be used to remove the plug by drilling an array of holes, but a far better method is to use

a hole saw reamer that you can make from silver steel if you have a lathe. The reamer can be held in correct alignment through the use of a plastic sleeve that fits over the end of the barrel. Try to prevent the plug from being pushed into the barrel by exerting gentle pressure on the plunger nose. The filler may still resist removal due to sac debris, broken spring or residuals from the plug, but a little heat will help. Some pressure from the front may be essential, but make sure the rod is screwed fully in to minimise the risk of damage to the square plastic tube.

The spring

After pulling out the old filler, the condition of the spring needs to be assessed. In about 50% of pens the spring will be good, but in others

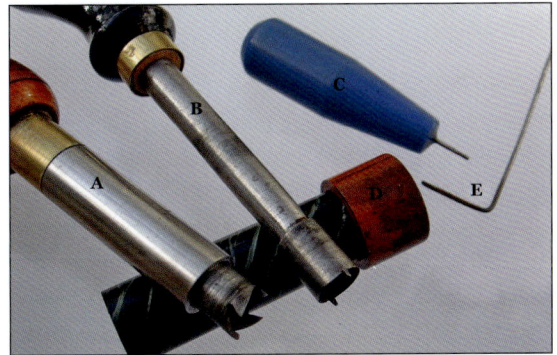

The repair tools A Barrel plug reamer; B Nut removal tool; C Button pin remover; D Sleeve for guidance of the plug reamer; E Tool to prevent rotation of the mechanism as the nut is tightened

it may have broken or become very weak. Replacement of the spring requires the removal of the plunger nose. It was originally glued in, so it will need to be cut off. It can be reattached with metal or plastic dowel or, better still, by 8BA hard rubber or brass studding. The stainless spring is 1.25 inches long and 0.2 inches external diameter. Make sure that the mechanism runs smoothly on the square tube and adjust with a file if necessary. It does not matter if the tube

Removal of barrel plug with reamer and guide sleeve

Extended plunger filler button

Filler ready for fitting into the pen

is slightly twisted - they usually are. Following a good clean of the filler, the brass retaining ring at the top of the filler must be removed. It will not be needed for the repair, so it is best to break it off by filing through on one side.

Reassembly

The new diaphragm may be obtained by cutting the end off a conventional number 18 ink sac to give a tube of length 31mm, and internal diameter just greater than the spring diameter. A Parker pli-glass sac is recommended because it will ensure a much longer life for the filler. Before fitting the sac, float a little superglue around the root of the square tube. This is an important joint that must be air tight. The easiest way to fix the sac is to silicone grease it on the inside and compress the spring so that the sac slides over the nose on to the mount without becoming trapped in the spring. When the sac is in place, bind it tightly with fine thread around the mount at the button end and superglue the thread ends (there will be no room for knots). This technique is just as effective as the original technique that used a brass ring and it is independent of the thickness of the sac. Note that no adhesives are required to attach the sac. The filler assembly should now look like the example shown.

If a new plug is required, it can be turned and fitted with the brass insert like the original, or it might be made using scrap pen parts, for example the end of a barrel. A little careful filing may be required to ensure a comfortable fit. An alternative technique is to cast the plug from epoxy resin, using a thin card tube as the mould.

A simple cylinder will be adequate, because the hole for the shaft and the recess for the button can be drilled out later. Remember not to fit the plug until the seal has been tested.

Before inserting the filler, ensure the pen barrel is clean and free of any hardened sac debris. An old triangular file ground square at the end can be used to clear the internal sealing flange.

The filler should be pushed into the barrel against the spring. It is better not to use silicone grease because this may allow the assembly to rotate and thereby prevent the nut from being tightened properly. Rotation can be prevented by using a bent wire (tool E) or jewller's screwdriver to wedge the end of the filler unit against the inside of the barrel.

To check the installation, blow into the front of the barrel; there should be no bubbles when the back is immersed in water. The plug and button can now be refitted, but make sure that the holes for the locking pin are properly aligned so that the rod is not stressed at its weakest point.

When fitting the nib unit, remember that the breather tube is designed to have a bend to allow the tip to remain clear of the filler nose. If the nib/feed needs to be reset, the breather tube will have to be removed or straightened (using hot air) so that the feed can be knocked out. Ensure the breather is clear and re-profiled before assembly.

The section needs a sealant such as rubber cement or shellac to make a good seal to the barrel. Following the application of some heat to

Typical damage to the plunger tube and rod, broken where the button is normally mounted. A repair challenge!

The clip washer is hidden within the cap top

The cap components, showing the recess in the top and the groove in the inner cap for holding the clip

the end of the barrel to help prevent cracking, the section is pushed firmly home. A nib knock-out block provides a convenient support.

What can go wrong

The Visofil VT is often found with broken parts, and many show evidence of previous abortive repairs that have caused near irreparable damage.

Cap & clip

It is frequently necessary to remove the cap button in order to replace a clip or renew the recess in which the clip is seated. The walls of the recess are extremely thin and have been damaged on many pens due to clip rotation, so be sure not to let the clip rotate when attempting to unscrew the button. On most pens, plastic shrinkage has made the button threads extremely tight, so soaking and heating will be required, and it may be necessary to wrap gripping material such as a rubber or leather sheet, around the top before it will move. Loggerhead pliers with a rubber tube are ideal for this. The clip can be levered out of the groove in the button with a screwdriver blade.

If the cap recess is damaged it can be recut on a lathe, but the cap length will be shortened by about 1mm; this could affect the cap threading and that should be checked and if necessary adjusted by shortening the inner cap. When the recess has been cut, the gap for the clip should be cut with a fine file.

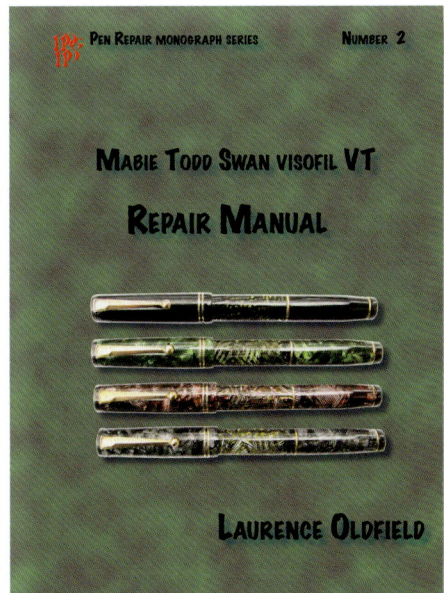

Filling instructions and repair booklet with additional practical detail on the repair of Visofil VT.

SWAN VISOFIL NEW YORK

The complex mechanism of the US Visofil

This pen was introduced about 1938, towards the end of the Mabie Todd production in the USA. According to the book 'Mabie in America' by David Moak, there is no patent information and no barrel imprint. The dismantled pen is the very same pen illustrated in his book, and it shows that the pen is not a button-filler as previously believed; it is another type of diaphragm bulb-filler.

The bulb/diaphragm is formed from a length of sac. Instead of being folded back like the Vacumatic or compressed with a lever like the Ink Vue, it is twisted by means of a push button and a short length of coarse threaded rod. Like all pens that use this filling method, several operations of the button are required to fill the pen. The ink level can be clearly seen through the highly transparent one-piece barrel. We do not know the reason for the breather tube being curled.

Servicing

The section unscrews on a right-handed thread, and the breather tube is a push fit into the back of the feed. The filler unit/cartridge is not so easy to remove. The main problem is gripping the end without damaging the button threads.
A C-ring threaded 8mm diameter by 1mm pitch can be used to grip the external thread. The cartridge is threaded left-handed to the barrel; be sure not to forget because the barrel is fragile! The joint is made with shellac, so it will be

necessary to use hot air for its release.
The closure plug on the cartridge is threaded right-handed; a three-pin wrench matched to the three holes provided is the best way to remove it. The filler button can be pulled out to release the nickel rod that carries the mount for one end of the diaphragm. The rod is covered with hard rubber tubes that act as spacers. Note that the shaft of the button carries four external grooves, one of which engages a small pin fixed through the button threads to stop rotation of the button. The other grooves allow air to enter the pen during the filling cycle.

Cartridge with diaphragm unit before fitting

Assembly commences with fixing a length of No 17 sac to the rod washers at one end, and the cartridge closure plug at the other. The sac needs to be glued to the rod washers, and binding with fine thread will make it secure. Originally, it may have been intended to trap the end of the sac between the two washers, but no evidence of this was found on the three pens we have repaired.

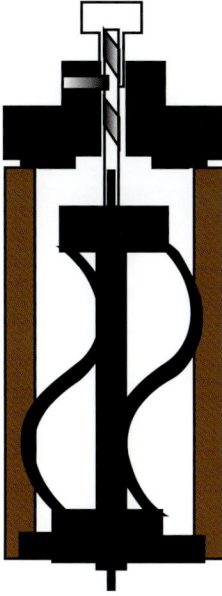

Diagram of cartridge with sac plunger

The filler cartridge assembled. Note the twist in the sac when the button is depressed and the locking pin on the shaft to prevent rotation of the button

The sac assembly is then screwed (by means of a special three pin tool) into the cartridge until the end of the brass rod is observed to stop rotating – we then know that any further tightening will be twisting the sac. The joint needs to be airtight, so it should be sealed with shellac.

The button is then placed on the end of the brass rod and turned a little anticlockwise (it is left hand threaded) until the guide pin in the end of the cartridge engages with one of the grooves in the button. The sac unit is then unscrewed a little and this pulls the button into the pen. Stop when about 5mm of the button shaft is visible.

For filling, this pen requires a large number of operations of the button (more than the Vacumatic). There is no return spring, so it is a push-pull action.

The filler cartridge and the mounted sac

Check that the vent holes in the end of the plug are clear.

The assembly of this pen is a little tricky because it is most important that the sac should not be twisted when the button is in the relaxed position. We have developed a method that works, but it is not known whether this was the method originally used.

First, the threaded brass rod is pushed firmly onto the pin where it grips like a Morse taper fitting.

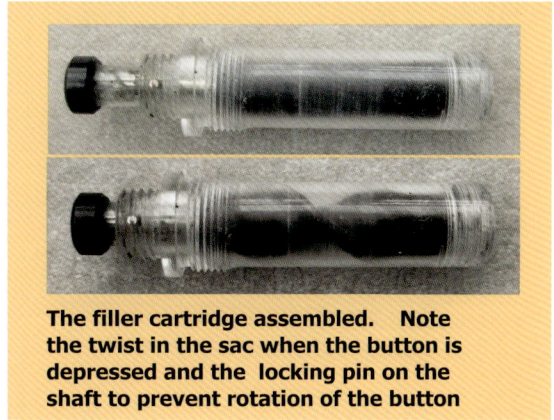

Completed demonstrator

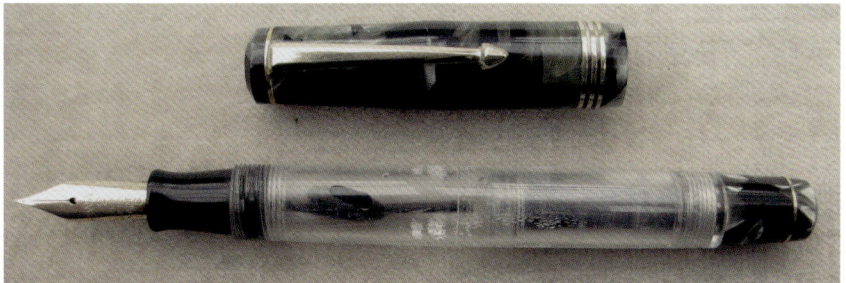

This is a handsome pen and a rare one because it was in production for only a short time

BLACKBIRD TOPFILLER BT

Topfiller with original mechanism

The Blackbird Topfiller BT200 pen was developed in the 1930s to meet a growing requirement for a 'high-tech', classy looking ink-visible fountain pen at a very affordable price. The filler works on the same principles as the Visofil VT and is generally described by the same patents. A large blind cap covers the filling system that is open to view, rather than hidden within the barrel like the Visofil. There are three types of Topfillers: all use the same principle, but they differ in their construction.

The pens use the bulb filler principle, where ink is drawn directly into the barrel by the flexing of a diaphragm to create the required pressure difference.

Dismantling

The first step is to extract the section. Like the Visofil, the fit is usually very tight as a result of the ridged surfaces (not threaded) and the sealant used to prevent leakage. Careful use of hot air will reduce the risk of cracking the barrel. Rotate the section to release the seal, and then pull it out making sure to keep the force parallel to the axis of the pen. The next step depends on the version of the pen (not identifiable by the type number).

The simplest version is a direct bulbfiller where the bulb is squeezed with the fingers five or six

Split nut for removal of the bush

times to fill the pen. This type is easily repaired with a short length of conventional sac, so there is no need to comment further.

The other two versions are constructed as illustrated. Externally, they appear the same, but one has a hard rubber bush threaded into the barrel, whereas the other has threads as part of the barrel.

The original and modified mechanisms

Original mechanism

The early pens are dismantled in the same way as the Parker Vacumatic, where a threaded split nut is required to grip the protruding part of the bush. The thread is an unusual one (13/32", 36tpi). Assuming that the correct tap is unobtainable, the 0.75mm pitch M10 is a good approximation.

First unscrew the plunger button from the square rod so that the plunger can be pushed out through the mouth of the barrel. The bush can then be unscrewed; two washers and the remains of the old sac will be found beneath it. The hard rubber domed washer is the seat for the diaphragm, and the thin washer allows the bush to be tightened down to make the seal. They are best knocked out from the front of the barrel.

It may be difficult to remove the brass ring that holds the other end of the diaphragm in place on the button. This ring may have to be filed off and replaced with a new one.

Once disassembled, it is very important to clean all components and to ensure that all sealing surfaces are undamaged. With all ink-view pens it is important to clean the inside of the barrel (a suitably sized bottle brush is useful for this)

Reassembly

The mechanism can be assembled as a complete unit and fitted into the pen in the same way as a Vacumatic.

First make the diaphragm from a 31mm length of 17/64" sac, and then assemble the components onto the square plunger tube. A trace of silicone

An unserviced modified mechanism

New barrel plug ready for attachment of the mechanism

to ensure a good seal. When refitting the section, remember that the breather tube must lie within the small slot in the plunger nose so that it will not be fouled when the filler is operated. Hot air applied to the barrel end will help the section to fit and it will minimise the risk of cracking.

Modified mechanism

These pens have the blind cap threads as part of the barrel. They present a challenge because there appears to be no method to remove intact the glued plug that acts as an end seal and mount for the mechanism.

First, the plunger button must be unscrewed to allow removal of the plunger and spring. Just beneath the threads, lies a brass ring that secures the end of the diaphragm to the barrel plug. The end of this lies flush with the end of the barrel threads, so there is no accessible gripping surface. The only practical solution is to bore it out on the

The unmodified restored filler

The modified restored filler

grease will enable the metal retaining ring to be fitted over the button end of the diaphragm. Any excess rubber at the button end should be removed with a sharp blade. The assembly is completed by screwing on the plunger nose against the pressure of the spring. The bush can then be screwed home, but only sufficiently tightly

lathe and make a replacement plug with a nipple to which the new diaphragm can be attached. The new plug must contain a square hole to guide the plunger rod.

The diaphragm is made from a 23mm length of sac, notably shorter than that used in the earlier mechanism. The complete mechanism

Topfiller with modified mechanism

is assembled as a separate unit and then glued into the pen. However, spare a thought for the next time the pen will need repair, and do not use anything stronger than the traditional shellac.

The modified pens have a smaller plunger nose without the groove for the breather tube, so it does not matter about the orientation of the section with respect to the barrel, only that the end of the breather tube lies on the inside wall away from the plunger.

Filling instructions
The original wording of the instructions:-
"Having removed the cap covering the nib, also unscrew the one from the other end of the pen thus exposing the depressor. With the nib completely immersed in the ink, fully press down and release the depressor several times until the pen is seen to be full. A lesser number of pumps will be required if a slight pause is made after each release, so that the ink can fully fill the vacuum created. Remember to replace the small cap when the pen is full."

Problems with the Visofil VT and the Blackbird BT

Section cannot be removed
It is never worth risking cracking the barrel. The last resort method is to heat the section so that the nib and feed can be removed from the front, and then saw the section off with a razor saw and ream/drill/turn out the part stuck in the barrel. This way you only have to find a new section.

Button will not turn or extend (VT)
This means that the square tube is damaged (see picture) or the rod is corroded within the tube. Either way, the button must be removed before progress can be made, so it will have to be sawn off unless it can be moved back to the position where access can be gained to the locking pin. This is a pen where you will probably have to make a new square tube from plastic or metal tubing, and you might have to rebuild the button.

Brass Rod broken off at button (VT)
They only break where the button pinhole is – about 4mm from the end. A new pinhole must be drilled (#64) as near to the end as possible. The stroke will be shorter but this will not prevent the pen from filling.

Blind cap does not grip on the threads (BT)
This is a common fault on the modified pen and is due to shrinkage of the barrel end. The problem can be cured by fixing a sleeve inside the blind cap and cutting new threads

Broken or twisted square tube
These can be made from square section brass tube available from model engineer suppliers or by drilling plastic rod and filing it to the correct cross-section

STYLOMINE 303V

This pen was introduced by Stylomine in France c.1938. It fills by longitudinal compression of a concertina shaped sac. Ink visibility is achieved through a glass chamber incorporated in the top of the sac, and this acts as the filler button. It is similar to the Swan Visofil V.

Servicing

This is not a difficult pen to service provided the sac and chamber are intact. If the sac is perished, the answer is to use a plain sac inside a compression spring, just like the Visofil.

The problem with the pen illustrated was a missing visible chamber. In this case a new one was made from Perspex (Lucite). A good alternative would be provided by a cut down glass tube – possibly from a perfume sample bottle. To attach the sac, glue would most likely have to be used instead of the original aluminium ring.

Work on the cap and clip is simplified by the simple and effective design that uses a slot with an internal screw to keep the clip in place.

GOLD STARRY

Repair

The pen is dismantled and the residual crystallised rubber sac removed. As concertina sacs cannot be obtained a straight size 16 sac will work well enough to fill the pen. However, as above, it is improved by having a spring to aid the top plunger return; the spring also serves to fix the sacs more securely to the peg. This can be rather tricky to fit so use a wooden rod as a sac supporter and fit the sac to the plunger first.

It is important to ensure that the breather tube extends as far as possible into the plunger.

Thick shellac or rubber solution is very effective to fix the sac on to the pegs. It is an adaptation so testing is essential.

The small post war French pen was identical in design to the Stylomine but used acrylic or metal parts. They had good quality Inox nibs and worked well as long as the concertina sacs were in good condition.

WAHL EVERSHARP

After The Wahl Adding Machine Company of Chicago purchased the Japanese Ever-Sharp Pencil Company in 1914, they broadened their business activity in writing equipment by purchasing the Boston Fountain Pen Company (1917). The first Wahl lever pen produced was the same design as the original Boston pen. Metal pens were introduced in 1921 to match the metal pencils, but they were slow to adopt the modern plastics compared to Sheaffer and Parker. The pens were produced by the Wahl Division of the company, but frequently branded Eversharp with 'Eversharp' stamped on the clip. In 1940 the Wahl (pen) and Eversharp (pencil) combined to form the Eversharp Pen Company. In 1957 they were purchased by Parker.

Before the war they produced some quality collectors pens such as the Equipose, Doric, Decoband, Gold Seal and Personal point most of which were lever fill. Innovations included screw-in nib units, roller clips and from 1935 piston pens. Their wartime and pre-war record was clouded by the disastrous ball pen fiasco in 1947, which in effect destroyed the company. Some materials were suspect, such as the Kashmir plastic, but in general many of their products are still being used.

WAHL EVERSHARP PISTON

Eversharp piston filler with shut-off feed

The Wahl Eversharp Doric range was upgraded in 1935 to include a plunger filler with ink visible barrel. As the mechanism is similar to that used in the Sheaffer Vac-Fil pens, much of the servicing information is common; consequently our emphasis is on some of the differences.

Problems

- fragile section
- nib adjustor
- filling problems
- ink cut-off mechanism

Section and nib unit

The section should unscrew without too much difficulty, but it must be done with the nib unit in place because the section is a fairly thin shell into which the nib unit is threaded. It is a good feature of many Eversharp pens that the nib can be changed without having to remove the section.

If work is to be done on the nib, it can be knocked out of the inner sleeve along with the spring loaded ink cut-off valve, but be careful not to damage or lose the small spring. The ink cut-off valve never worked very well and is not worth spending time on to improve it. If the shaft is straight and the spring is OK and free to move, then that is all the servicing that can be done. The nib adjuster was also more of a novelty than a useful facility and again there is not very much that can be done in servicing, particularly if one of the clips on the adjustor is broken.

Barrel and piston unit

Barrel seal capsule and end trim can be removed

The plunger knob is held on with an 11BA locknut. When it is unscrewed, the rod can be taken out and the plunger seal can be replaced. The smaller pen (barrel ID 7.6mm) uses an 8.0mm flat seal and the larger pen (barrel ID 8.8mm) uses a 9.2mm flat seal (not compatible with Sheaffer).

The barrel seal on these pens is very similar to the Sheaffer one, so all the same hints apply. The unit is l/h threaded in and glued. It is not easy to extract because there is nothing to grip on without risk to the thin gold plated trim at the end of the pen. The trim does come off with a little care and luck, but not easily, so it is better to service the seal from inside if it needs to be replaced. Before contemplating drilling out and replacing, try the ultrasonic regeneration of the seal as described for the Vac-Fil.

The rods in these pens are stainless steel covered with a vulcanite sleeve and are 2.18 mm in diameter. Examine the rod carefully for damage. Cracks must be repaired because they could cause a leak past the seal. Epoxy is good for this. Vac-Fil rods are 2.12 mm in diameter, but they can be used as replacements if the barrel seal is updated to an O-ring.

Caution: The vacuum release groove in these pens is cut deeply into the wall, making them very fragile at the base of the threads. Be very careful not to overstress the barrel when removing the section.

CAUTION

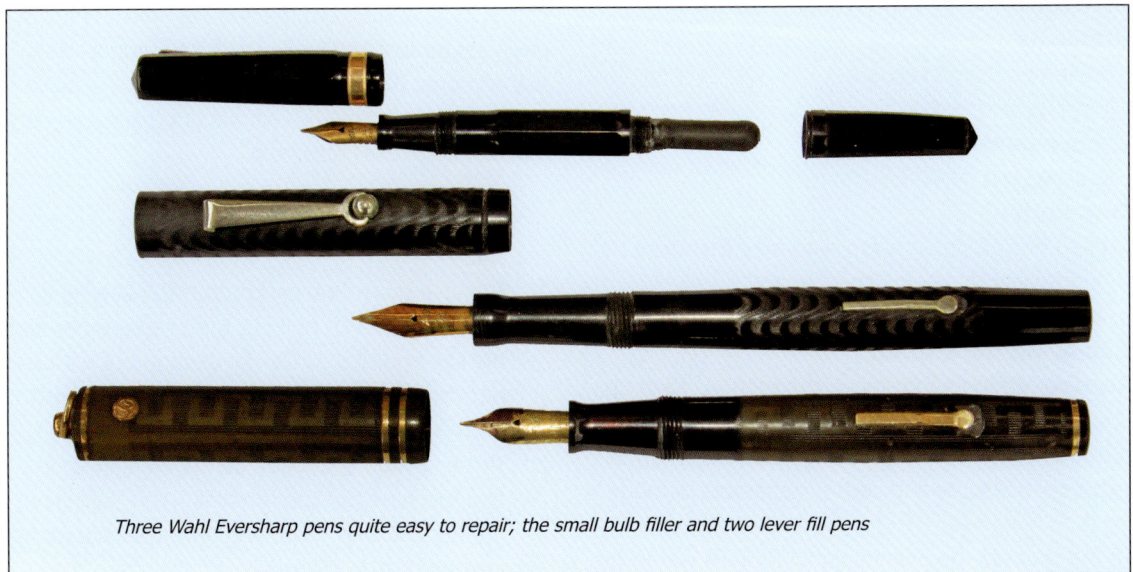

Three Wahl Eversharp pens quite easy to repair; the small bulb filler and two lever fill pens

Eversharp pen repair is facilitated by the availability of original company repair manuals. However even armed with such information it may still be necessary to make special tools as frequently described procedures require 'tool L4373A to withdraw the bush'. Such manuals can be obtained from the archives of PCA, WES or commercial companies specialising in old manuals. (See Information)

INFO

WAHL EVERSHARP DECOBAND

The dismantled pen

These pens are arguably the most glamorous of the art deco era and their design and manufacture is of the highest quality. Following their success in black hard rubber, a range of colourful plastic pens was introduced in 1928/9. They were perhaps the first to offer a range of screw-in interchangeable nib units. Nibs stamped 'Flexible' and 'Signature' were obtainable in a wide range of widths.

Problems
- broken or scored section
- loose lever
- broken pressure bar retainer
- stressed clip

Dismantling
These pens are lever fillers, and may therefore be thought easy to repair. Think again!

Removing the section
Abortive attempts to remove the section make up the majority of problems. Sections are often so hard to remove that 'would-be' repairers resort to extreme measures and cause irreparable damage.

In many cases the aluminium liner fitted within the barrel has corroded and fused with the metal col-lar fitted to the section. The collar is crimped and punched onto the section, so it is rarely possible to pull the section out of it. The liner was fitted to reduce the risk of barrel cracking and perhaps to isolate the plastic from contamination by the ink sac and its contents.

Removal of the section is compounded by its fragility. The screw-in nib unit has resulted in the section wall being very thin, so no attempt must be made to remove it without the nib unit or a plug to support it. The section must be pulled straight out because it will not rotate. In most cases conventional section pliers will not do the job and may slip off, possibly causing damage to the nib or the end of the section. Additional grip can be achieved by wrapping the section with a strip of medium grade sandpaper before using the section pliers. This will cause some damage to the surface finish, but it is easily restorable and well worth it to reduce the risk of worse damage. If you are lucky, a soak in cold water and some hot air will bring success - the ultrasonic bath will also help.

If the section remains firmly stuck, two options remain:
1. Remove the barrel end button (by sawing it off if necessary), pull out the pressure bar and old sac and then drive the section out with a punch. A replacement button can be turned on the lathe or adapted from an old cap top.
2. If the section is already damaged, saw it off and machine out the remains. You then have the difficult task of finding a new section or making one, but you haven't damaged the barrel or nib!

> **The later models (with the longer clip) may not have the metal collar so the section will come out much easier.**

Section and nib unit

This contains nothing that will be harmed by hot water. Boiling water will raise depressions caused by plier misuse, but it will also cause any oxidisation to turn an objectionable colour. However, the section will have to be treated with abrasives to remove residual marks, so it will then become black again. The nib unit, if not already out, should unscrew easily after the hot water soak.

Lever and pressure bar

The lever filling design has some novel features. The mid point of the pressure bar is held conventionally by forks on the lever, but the end of the bar is formed into a 'T' shape that moves within a slot provided by a metal retainer sprung into the barrel end. This forces the bar to remain in position longitudally and thereby prevent contact with the section sac joint. If the bar is broken or missing, a J-bar may be used instead. The easiest way to service the pressure bar and its retainer is through the end of the barrel. If the job is being done from the barrel mouth and the retainer cannot be rotated, the lever will need to be removed before the pressure bar can be disengaged and pulled out.

The lever is pivoted on a straight pin that crosses the barrel slot. The pin can be pushed out with a fine drill despite the accumulation of filler/dirt that may be in the holes. The lever contains a spring clip that is intended to retain the lever in the closed position; it protrudes slightly through slots in the sides of the lever to press against the inside of the barrel slot. A replacement spring can be made from 28 SWG piano wire (available from model shops) if required, but it is not essential because the lever tends to stay closed if a sufficiently large sac is used.

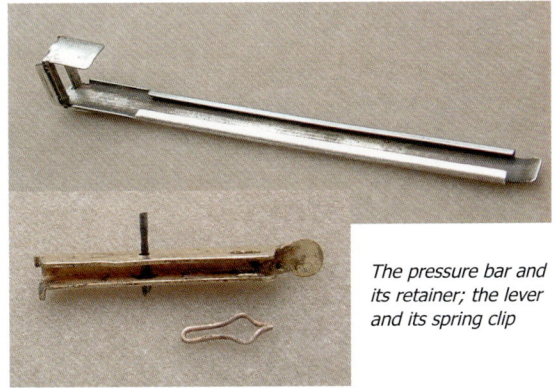

The pressure bar and its retainer; the lever and its spring clip

If the lever is already in place and the original pressure bar is to be refitted, it will be easier to do it after removing the barrel end button. The retainer is pushed in with the lugs directed towards the mouth of the barrel. When the end of the pressure bar is through the slot in the retainer, the retainer must be rotated 90 degrees to lock the bar in place. If assembly is from the front of the barrel, the lever must be removed and refitted after the pressure bar is properly located. The lever forks need to pick up the groove in the pressure bar as it is rotated into position for refitting the pivot pin.

Cap and clip

The clip is held in place by the inner cap, but unfortunately the inner caps are fitted extremely tightly. Even after the usual soak and hot air it may not be possible to extract the inner cap without risk of damage to the cap lip. Rather than risk such damage it is better to drill or turn out the inner cap; a lathe will be required to make a new one. With the inner cap removed, the clip can be rotated up and lifted out through the slot.

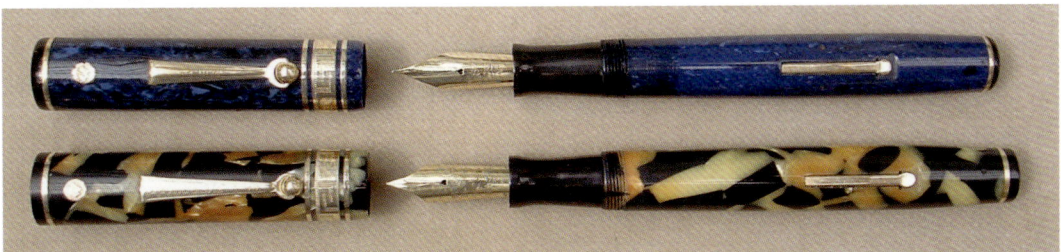

Pens with the short clip and the long clip

WAHL EVERSHARP OXFORD TWIST FILL

These early 1930s pens work on the same principle as the Parker Vacumatic and the Swan Visofil VT. In this case a knob at the end of the pen is repeatedly rotated a half turn to twist the diaphragm/bulb rather than compress it end-on as in the Vac and the Visofil. Oxfords were made in three sizes. The design and construction principles were common although there may be some minor variations. The Oxford is a quality pen, and despite the fact that the special diaphragm is no longer available, there is no good reason why it cannot be successfully restored in its original configuration.

Dismantling

The first step is to remove the section; this is attached on a right handed thread and usually presents few problems. Through the barrel mouth will be seen about half way down a hard rubber nut that should be undone with a spanning screwdriver, (the Parker65 Mk1 tool is ideal). The nut is the means for securing the open end of the diaphragm to a gasket held permanently in place by spring washers. This gasket will not need attention and great care must be taken not to move it while cleaning out the barrel.

The pump unit is mounted on a fine thread rather like the Vac. It can usually be removed using rubber or leather covered pliers. Examine the red plastic filler button to see whether it has a locking pin. Be sure to remove the pin before trying to unscrew the button. With

the button off, the diaphragm mount will be free, but be careful not to lose the tiny eared washer that lies beneath the button. The purpose of this washer is to limit the button rotation to a half turn so that the diaphragm is not torn off its mount. When the diaphragm mount is cleaned up it will be found to have a square recess into which fits a square rubber plug that locks the diaphragm in place.

As the correct diaphragm and plug are no longer available, and as the original design was probably not the best, Vacumatic parts are recommended for the repair. Use a Debutante Vac diaphragm and the black plastic ball socket holder fitted to later Vacs. The square hole in the Oxford holder can be drilled out to take the Vac holder, and it can be attached with epoxy or superglue gel. The old diaphragm and its mounting nipple can be pushed out and the barrel cleaned. If you are very unlucky and the central gasket comes out, the diaphragm should be fitted to the gasket assembly outside the pen with a new rubber gasket) 2mm thick, 9mm OD, 5mm ID for the pen illustrated) The whole assembly can

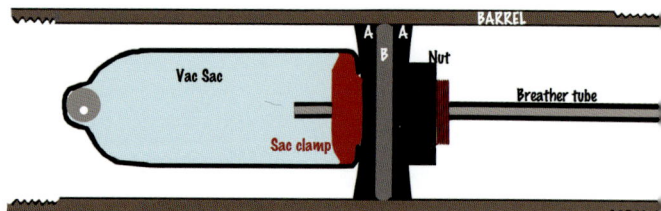

Diagram of diaphragm filling unit - A A are two plastic washers; B is a 2mm soft rubber gasket

be pushed in through the button end with a thin walled metal tube. Silicone grease will be required and the nut may have to be tightened further to get a good seal.

Assembly

The length of the diaphragm must be such that it is not compressed when the pen is assembled, but a little stretch will do no harm. Cut the diaphragm so that when the nipple is in place and the assembly is on its seat within the barrel the ball end is about 4mm below the end of the barrel. Make sure that the diaphragm folds over the end of the nipple slightly so that it will be gripped when the nut is tightened. Push down on the ball end of the diaphragm with a rod so that the nut can be tightened with the spanning screwdriver. Pull the diaphragm back up to its proper shape and try blowing through the barrel with the button end submerged in water. We pray that there will be no bubbles!

The attachment of the ball end of the diaphragm to its holder requires a long pellet pusher acting through the mouth of the barrel (2mm diameter countersunk rod is ideal). The pump holder can now be screwed tightly into the barrel and sealed with shellac to prevent it coming loose when the button is turned. The diaphragm holder must be depressed to prevent it being rotated. When the pump holder is firmly seated, raise the diaphragm holder into its location, The eared washer can be fitted in six possible positions on the spindle. It is important to choose the one that allows a half turn while ensuring that the diaphragm is not twisted in the rest position. The button is then screwed on as tightly as necessary.

Testing

If the job has been done properly, the pen should expel air for at least five operations of the filler button, but in practice it may be a few more before the pen is full. If you are selling the pen or repairing it for someone else, be sure to tell them not to try turning the button through five complete rotations as the inscription on it appears to invite you to do!

A well restored Oxford

NIB ADJUSTMENT BY EVERSHARP

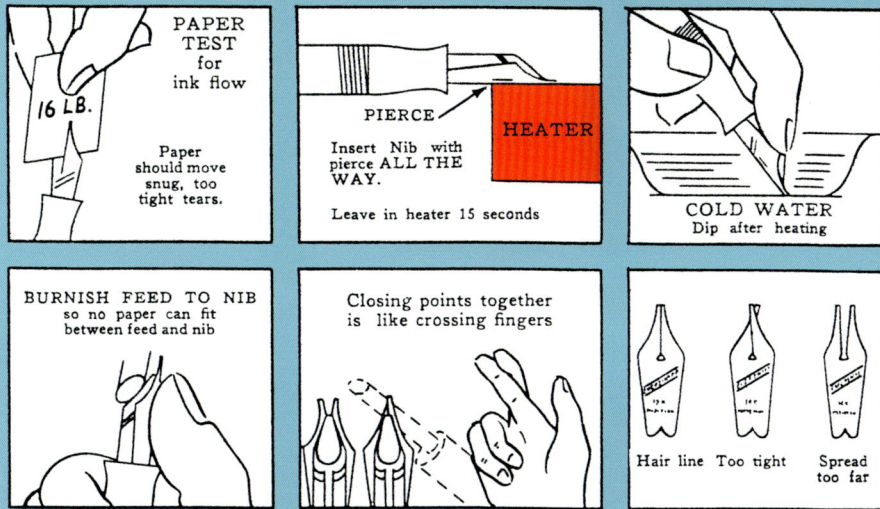

PAPER TEST for ink flow

16 LB.

Paper should move snug, too tight tears.

PIERCE

HEATER

Insert Nib with pierce ALL THE WAY.

Leave in heater 15 seconds

COLD WATER
Dip after heating

BURNISH FEED TO NIB
so no paper can fit between feed and nib

Closing points together is like crossing fingers

Hair line   Too tight   Spread too far

Eversharp produced repair manuals but we felt their nib guide 'hits the spot'!

EVERSHARP SKYLINE

The Eversharp Skyline, introduced in 1941, looked as if the cap was too large for the pen. However, with the cap posted, it became a balanced writing instrument and is an icon with it's unique 'warrior helmet' clip. (It was reproduced for Eversharp in 1997 by Nicholas and Emanuel Caltagirone as a demonstrator and 'yellow cab'). The vintage

models were produced in a range of sizes and rather sombre colours. A rare streamlined version was made but the most desirable is probably the all metal Skyline.

Problems
- lever can be displaced
- pressure bar loses spring
- clip becomes loose

Dismantling and repair

There are three sizes of pen. Minor modifications were made over the 10 year life. The section unscrews revealing a breather tube, which is usually broken and has to be replaced.

Barrel/lever system

The plastic barrels are thick and robust and the main repair is replacing the lever or pressure bar. Metal barrels have inserted metal threads.

The early bar/lever system was in two parts with a copper V pressure bar, which lost its spring quickly and a lever with a C-ring attached to a small slotted plate. (Note that this bar extends right to the end of the barrel). The later design was a complete unit which was held together by a band. This lever system was also secured in the barrel with a C-clip.

Removal of both variants involves pushing the lever towards the section end, after cleaning out the sac debris. This pulls the C-clip from the positioning groove inside the barrel and the lever with its pressing plate can be pulled out with a pair of long nosed pliers. In the early example the V pressure bar can then be pulled out after compressing the securing end with a screwdriver.

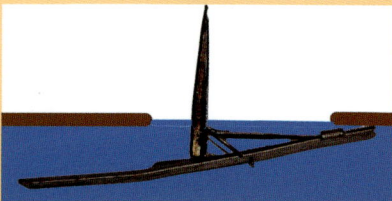

Two lever/bar systems. The early model sectioned with a separate V bar and plate/lever; the second model is an integral unit. Both systems used a C-clip to locate in the barrel. Note the open lever acts against a raised ridge on the bar to get a more efficient bar movement.

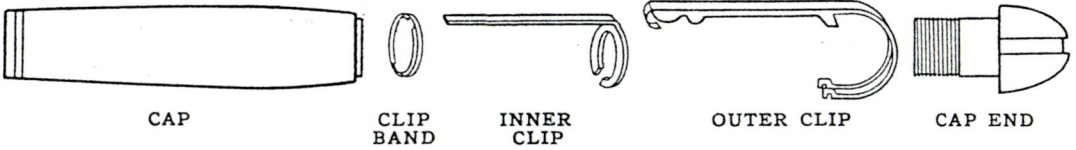

CAP CLIP BAND INNER CLIP OUTER CLIP CAP END

Helmet clip with short clip screw

Later cap with long clipscrew; unsprung clip without top band.

Reassembly is the reverse. A new C-clip may have to be used; the lever is always refitted through the barrel.

Section/nib/sac

The breather tube can be replaced with fine plastic tube and one option is plastic covered electrical wire with the wire removed. The nib is easily removed. The sac should be replaced with a tapered sac (full size $16^{1/2}$, smaller size 16).

Clip

The original 'helmet' clip has an inner clip crimped to a sprung metal outer clip and it hooks on to the clip band. The plastic dome unscrews and the clip hooks can be pulled away allowing removal from the cap. There are three different 'domed' clip screw designs. Refitting must ensure all the plates and hooks are in position as one tightens the screw cap.

Later models were much easier to dismantle with a ring clip, with no over band.

Demonstrator Skyline made in the 1990's in France for Eversharp

WAHL (EVERSHARP) METAL PENS

Wahl made
quite a range of metal pens, originally to match metal pencils. They had threaded metal inserts and no hard rubber other than the section. Gold filled pens seem more robust than the silver pens which often crack at the barrel end seam. Some

streamlined sterling Eversharp pens were made in the 1950s in the UK.

Sac replacement is straight forward. Sections are serrated, not threaded, and are pushed into the metal barrel. The most taxing repair is re-fitting a lever on the small models.

EVERSHARP FIFTH AVENUE

14ct gold capped model with '6?4' engraved on cap

This hooded nib pen was planned to compete against the Parker 51 and was made from 1943-6. It was not a popular pen, with a reputation for poor ink capacity and an old fashioned truncated shape. The cap had a sprung clip. Solid 14ct gold caps can be distinguished by the engraved '6?4', taken from a popular New York Quiz Show of the time, sponsored by Eversharp. The fountain pen was phased out but the barrel and cap design were used for ball point pens.

Problems
- ink capacity
- nibs

Dismantling
The section screws out and the repairs are similar to the Skyline except for the nib unit
Soak the unit well in an ultrasonic bath and after drying check the alignment of the nib position with the shell ridges before pushing the nib and feed out, by hand, in the conventional direction. If it requires tapping out then make a shaped wooden clamp (see page 35) to avoid damage to the shell. The 1947 repair manual illustrates a nib bushing, which is fitted into the shell ('sheath' is the Eversharp term).

They recommended that this is driven out, however in most cases the feed knocks out leaving the bush in situ. We see little to be gained by removing the bush unless it is damaged. It would appear that the purpose of the bush is to accommodate the small feed, required for the narrow nib.

Reassembly
The nib and feed are pushed into the section with

care to ensure that the nib and feed line up with the ridge and 'beak' of the shell; warm the shell if it is difficult to fit. The pen can then be resacced. The pressure bar assembly is the same as the Skyline.
We cannot understand the reputation for poor ink capacity because the pen has an adequate reservoir and fills well but it may have been the fault of a broken breather tube. The appeal of the stylish Parker 51 was perhaps too much for the Fifth Avenue.

DIS-ASSEMBLY OF SHEATH AND NIB UNIT

1. Unscrew sheath assembly No. 21. Remove sac No. 20. Remove nib assembly No. 15 by fitting prongs of bushing adjusting tool No. L-102 into slots of bushing and pushing through point of sheath No. 16. (See illustration A.)

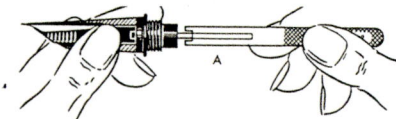

2. To remove nib and feed from bushing—insert nib assembly No. 15 into anvil tool No. 47. Then insert feed tool No. L-100 into bushing. Tap tool No. L-100 lightly with mallet. (See illustration B.)

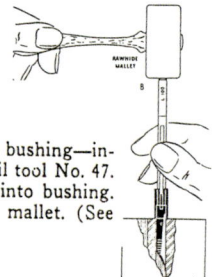

EVERSHARP PENCILS

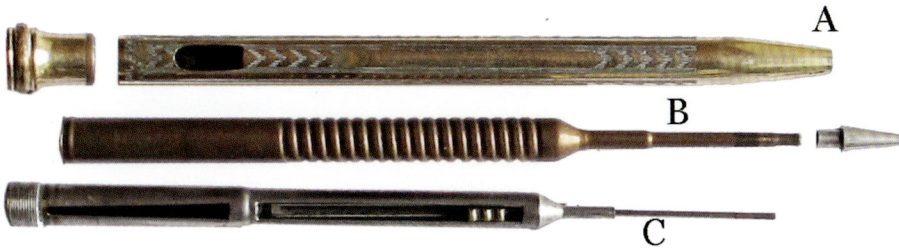

Components of the propel only Eversharp pencil A Outer case; B Spiral drive tube C Guide tube/propelling unit

In 1912 Tokyi Hayakawa founded the Ever-Sharp Pencil Company and patented the simple propel only pencil. He sold his interest to Wahl in 1915 and the operation moved to Chicago. The pencil design stayed the same from 1915 to the 1950s and they are probably the simplest and cheapest pencils to repair.

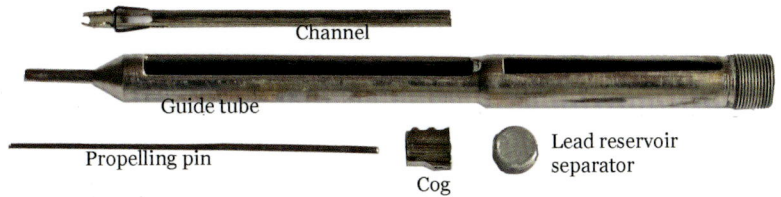

Components of the guide tube/propelling unit

However the low price does not mean they are poor quality and in fact some of the examples are superb. There were probably more Eversharp pencils made than all the others put together so the variety of design and size is extensive.

In the 1930s Eversharp broadened their mechanism design by introducing a repeater (continuous action or clutch) pencil and a variety of Coronet, Doric and Skyline pencils to match the pen range.

Problems

Propel only
- clips break off
- drive cogs wear
- metal bodies corrode and outer plastic shrinks

Repeater
- lead blockage

Dismantle and service

As with all pencils, at least 50% of problems are due to broken leads. A pin vice and 1mm drill are essential.

In all pencils the first stage is to remove the nozzle; then if the cogs are good use the propelling unit to pull the inner tubular spiral from the outer case. This will allow access to the clip.

If there is a problem with the lead propelling pin it is easiest to replace the whole drive unit, however the drive unit can be dismantled. First pull out the propelling pin from the cog and then pull the drive cog out through the guide tube slot. It is not necessary to remove the guide channel. Replace the appropriate items (it is suggested to tap and die the cog and propelling pin, to make it easier to assemble).

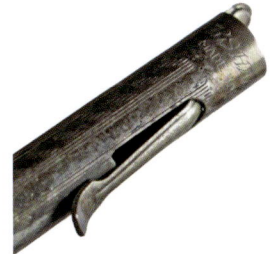

Clip is fed into the outer case and fixed with drive spiral tube.

If a new clip is required, fit one and then replace the spiral tube.

The repeating pencil mechanism can be removed as illustrated and replaced.

Repeater pencil mechanism exposed by removing nozzle

CONWAY STEWART

Conway Stewart pens originated in 1906 as eyedroppers. Lever operated sac pens were introduced in 1919. 1920's pens used red, black and ripple hard rubber and shared the style of the American Parkers. Conway Stewart was quick to recognise the potential of the new cellulose acetate materials that could be marbled and patterned so extravagantly, and during the 1940's they became very successful on account of the good value for money that they offered.

Most pens were lever fillers, but some button fillers (CS20) and some syringe fillers (CS700) were produced. Some of the early lever fillers used lever boxes, but later ones used the ring method of lever attachment.

CS gave priority to simplicity, presumably to keep prices low, so generally these pens are easy to restore; an exception being the 'Speedy Phil' pen (CS74) introduced in 1956.

Problems

- crazing of casein pens
- broken lever tabs
- plastic distortion
- unwinding of the spiral plastic

Although stable cellulose materials were used for most pens, some were made from casein because this material offered other options for extravagant design and colour. Many of the casein pens have distorted, crazed and cracked, so they must be treated with great caution.

Servicing

The sections are all push fit (except CS700, 800 and Speedy Phil) and rarely give much resistance to being pulled out. The general articles give all the information required for servicing these pens, which are among the easiest to work on. The more difficult aspects such as changing a lever, adjusting threading and cosmetic work are also covered in other articles. The CS approach to locking the lever, in the closed position, was to fold a gold plated brass tag around the end of the slot to engage with the underside of the lever end. The tag is only crimped in place so it is often missing. Replacements can be made from brass shim if no spares are available.

The Speedy Phil (CS74)

This pen has a conventional sac and compression is achieved with a pressure bar operated by a button mounted on a sac protector tube. The end of the pressure bar is located through a small slot in the base of the sac protector onto a plate with a ramped profile. When the button is rotated, the end of the pressure bar rides up the ramp and the sac is compressed. When it falls off the top of the ramp the sac relaxes and the pen fills. The button is therefore turned one way, and only as far as the first 'click'.

Casein pens must not be soaked in water for more than about 10 minutes because the material is hygroscopic. Be cautious with any plastic that you do not recognise.

The button moves in a crimped groove so it cannot be detached from the sac protector. The sac protector tube can be pulled off the section with the help of a little heat; it is just a tight push fit. Around the top of the tube on the inside is a length of spring steel shim that keeps the top of the pressure bar against the inside wall of the tube. When this is pulled out, the pressure bar and the remains of the old sac can be removed. If the pressure bar is in good condition, reassembly should be straightforward. If it is corroded, the replacement must be the correct length and it should have a tab crimped on the end to enable it to ride smoothly on the end plate.

When refitting the sac protector to the section, a spot of shellac is a good idea to prevent movement at the joint when the pen is being filled; filling does require more turning force on the knob than one might expect in order to achieve the 'click'.

Cap, clip and trim

The weakest part of CS pens is the gold trim. The original was poor quality and in many cases the trim will benefit from replating using light colour gold.

Until about 1938, washer-type clips were used, held in place by a combined button/inner cap. Later pens used a slimmer button and a separate inner cap.

Of these pens, some had a flat clip washer and others had a dished top to the clip into which the

Types of clip fastening and spanning screwdriver

button was recessed. The recessed-type clips are liable to breakage, so they are now very scarce. They can also be quite difficult to replace because the cap buttons have become tight in their threads and there is little surface area to grip. Most were fitted with an aluminium button that was usually anodised black. They were screwed into the cap top, or held by a small slot headed brass nut for which a special spanning screwdriver is required.

Soaking and heating will almost certainly be required to loosen the corrosion that often holds the brass nut. It may be necessary to superglue a wooden or plastic tube to the head of the button to obtain a grip on it.

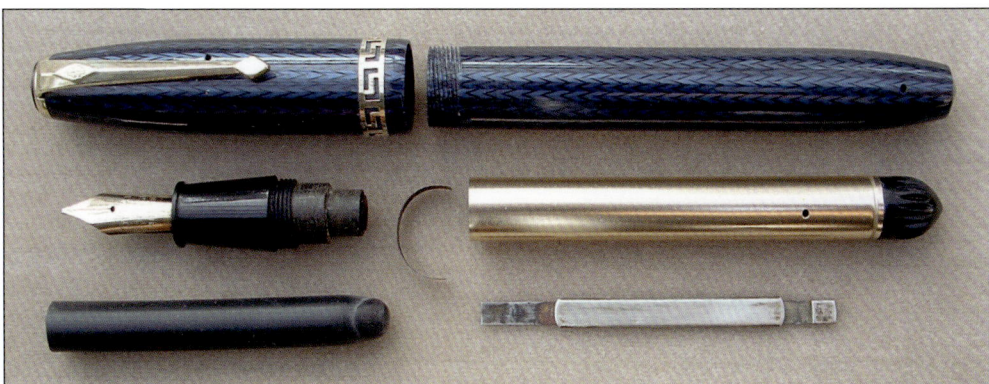

Speedy Phil pen

CONWAY STEWART 700/800

Exploded view of a conway Stewart 700

The piston Conway Stewart was introduced in 1937 as two models, the bandless 700, and the 800, which is often in 'cracked ice' pattern and has a transparent ink view 'window'.

This is quite a rare piston upfiller (syringe), that works by rotating the end cap to lower the plunger and by reversing the action to raise the piston and draw ink into the barrel.

Problems
- cork seals deteriorate and pen does not fill
- plastic shrinks (cap near clip)

Dismantling
The section is sometimes very difficult to move and cannot be taken off without risking damage to a rare and valuable pen. Do not worry because the filling system can be restored without removing it.

With the section removed or alternatively the nib and feed, invert the barrel and fill it with a detergent mild alkaline soaking solution. Keep the barrel upright and leave for a few hours. Apart from dried ink residue and cork there may be some corrosion of the metal spiral so soak, try, soak, try and soak again!

Ultrasonic agitation and heating the outside may help. The main aim is to release the 'frozen' internal parts without breaking them so do not exert too much pressure and always stop if there is resistance to twisting the end cap.

Once slight movement starts then you are almost there but do be patient as parts for these pens are scarce.

Once the piston is moving you are now ready to remove the unit.

Position the piston at the bottom of the barrel, (full clockwise rotation of the knob), where it is visible in the transparent ink view section. The 'collar' unit screws into the barrel end and must be removed to gain access to the piston; grip and unscrew the collar with some narrow section pliers. Do not also grip the end cap as you may shear off the peg on the piston holder or crack the barrel.

This is a gradual process of about half a thread at a time; as the connector is unscrewed, the piston moves up the barrel and it must be moved down again before any further collar removal is attempted. This is done by twisting the end cap to get the piston back down to its lowest position. The collar is unscrewed a little more, and the process is repeated until the spiral can be withdrawn.

Those familiar with safety pen repair will have little difficulty with this principle of unscrewing and repositioning repeatedly. This normally leaves the piston in the barrel and it can be gently tapped out.

Comparison of the Conway Stewart models 800 and 700 with ink view plastic; note the bandless cap of the 700.

Restoring the piston

The barrel must be cleaned and the piston unit soaked again. The plastic seal retaining bolt, which has a right hand thread, is easily removed together with the old cork remnants. The metal spiral can be removed from the blind cap, but this is not always necessary.

Cork seal

The parts are now ready for re-assembly and a suitable cork seal must be made (8.3mm OD, 6.2mm ID by 7.2mm). Use good quality cork (expensive wine!) with either a mandrel in an electric drill/small lathe or by making a special cutter (see Seals).

The cork is fitted on to the stud which is screwed into position and the seal can then be 'fine fitted' to the barrel using abrasive paper to give a neat fit. The cork should be brushed or blown to remove residual traces of abrasive and then impregnated with wax and silicone grease applied as a lubricant.

Fitting the piston

The piston plus seal must fit into the barrel easily, moving over the internal end threads with the peg and aligned to the barrel groove.

The spiral can now be replaced with the collar in position and refitting is the same gradual process of screw down, move the piston, screw down and so on. The effectiveness of the filling system seal can be checked by drawing up water and checking for end leakage.

Final assembly

The section or nib and feed is now replaced and the pen is filled with ink. A quick test of the effectiveness of this repair can be done by suspending the pen over some tissue and checking if there is the repeated development of drops on the nib. If this happens, the seal is not making sufficient uniform contact with the barrel and you will have to start all over again!

The propelling unit with metal spiral, which can corrode, and refitted new cork seal,

Cork cutter made specially for the Conway 700/800

ONOTO PISTON

Top
An older vulcanite long piston Onoto illustrating the cone shaped plunger body compared with a parallel plunger, which has a hard washer and a cup washer. Note the under - over feed.

Left
A 'modern' post war Onoto with a marbled cellulose body and screw cap with a parallel plunger, which is ready for refitting a flat hard and flexible replacement washer.

Dating from the turn of the century De La Rue's Onoto Pen Company was probably the first to use a piston down filling system. It was very successful and continued to be used with few modifications until the 1950s. The principle is to evacuate a reservoir barrel and then break the seal, which then allows ink to flow into the barrel*. Onotos, were for one year in the 1930s, the company with the largest UK pen sales and always had a reputation for quality.

The anatomy of the Onoto is clearly explained in their advertisements and it gives the terminology for their shut off and self filler parts.

Problems

- damaged nibs
- dried out seals and leaks
- stripped threads
- snapped shafts

Dismantling (see also Onoto Magna)

The first step is to unscrew the section, (pen carrier) which has a normal right hand thread. The cone/plug/piston assembly is exposed, which is secured to the rod.

It is now necessary to remove the rod assembly. This is best done before unscrewing the plunger body (left hand thread), because it is so easy to break the rod.

The filler knob has to be removed and the first step is to carefully knock out the hard rubber retaining pin to allow it to be unscrewed (left hand thread). If the ends of the pin cannot be seen try dipping it in boiling water; this usually reveals the pin. There are various ways of removing the pin but our preference is to use a staking punch. These are quite rare items so a shaped wooden block and a good flat ended punch is a practical alternative.

Onoto components

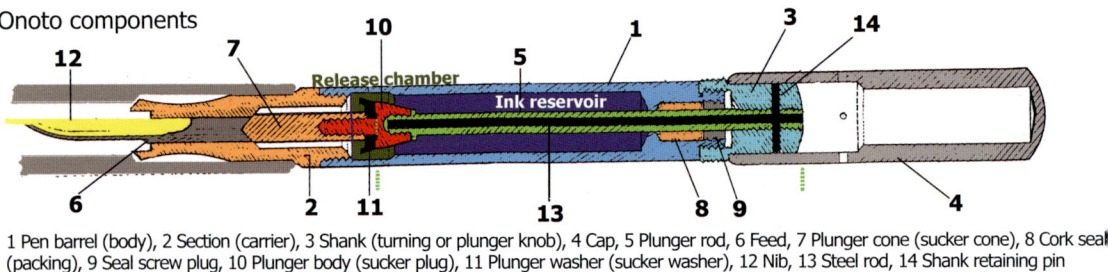

1 Pen barrel (body), 2 Section (carrier), 3 Shank (turning or plunger knob), 4 Cap, 5 Plunger rod, 6 Feed, 7 Plunger cone (sucker cone), 8 Cork seal (packing), 9 Seal screw plug, 10 Plunger body (sucker plug), 11 Plunger washer (sucker washer), 12 Nib, 13 Steel rod, 14 Shank retaining pin

* See Japanese Piston (page ...) for alternative filling method

In order to punch out the pin cleanly, its position is marked in the centre, with a small scriber or a dot of white or silver marker. The knob, which has a left hand thread, can be unscrewed from the rod and then the whole rod and piston unit can be removed through the open end of the barrel. If parts are broken, the part in need of replacement can now be removed from the rod; soaking and gentle warming will facilitate removal without stressing the rod. Remember that this is also a left hand thread.

You now have the rod, the barrel, the piston assembly and the knob as separate parts.

The rod is made from hard rubber with a central reinforcing wire. It should be carefully examined for unevenness or cracks and if damaged it should be replaced.

The knob should be checked for splits and cracks The barrel should be cleaned thoroughly with water and then the cork seals replaced.

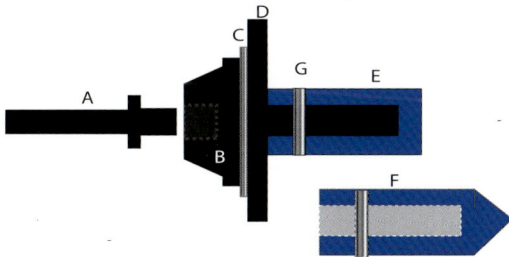

Piston unit shaft A, piston B, hard washer C, flexible washer D, Non shut off plug E, Shut off plug F, Plug retaining pin G

Servicing the piston unit

The unit should be well soaked before any attempt to dismantle as the thin male piston can easily snap inside the female plug unit. Before rushing to knock the pin out it is helpful to mark its location. The pin is knocked out with a fine steel punch (over a hole!) and the two parts are separated. Make a grooved wooden block with holes and use a staking punch. Keep the pin if you wish but we usually replace the pin with a brass pin or carbon fibre rod, which we find easier to fit.

Factory clamps and a staking punch

Replacing the piston washer

Remove the old gasket which will be hard and fossilised and may disintegrate between finger and thumb, also remove old backing washer if fitted. It may be necessary to use a probe to break the gasket.

Fit a new hard washer onto the peg, then soft washer (8mm OD, 2.7mm ID, 0.8mm thickness). Replace the plug to make a tight fit, line up the hole and fit the pin. It is easier using a pair of surgical forceps for small pins the end of which can be rounded. With carbon fibre - use a slight taper and cut the excess after fitting. Sometimes the thickness of the backing hard washer or length of the plug may have to be reduced to get the pin holes to line up.

The washer should have adopted a slightly curved shape. Smear the soft washer with a small amount of silicone grease, which will also grease the internal barrel wall. The refurbished piston unit is now screwed back onto the rod (anticlockwise).

Plungers illustrating flat washer and flat backing washer with no pressure (A); with clamping pressure to create curvature (B); with pressure and curved backing washer (C).

Using the Onoto tool to remove the cork seal disc

Replacing cork seals

As the rod has been removed, an old rod is inserted to give support when unscrewing the hard rubber threaded seal retainer. The factory tool to remove this retaining ring is a two pronged unit which fits round the rod and engages the ring. Firm pressure is necessary but not too much as the rod can easily break or get chewed up. The seal cover retainer is small and easily lost so make sure you either leave it on the old rod or put it somewhere safe because without it your new seal may not stay in the pen.

The old cork seal is then removed with a dental pick. Two new corks are fitted with the actual rod in position. Silicon grease can be packed in with the corks and the retaining ring is then refitted and screwed down.

Tool is used to compress the cork seal

It is possible to replace the cork seals without the complication of removing the rod, by unscrewing the seal cover and fitting split corks but this is no longer a recommended procedure and should only be carried out if the head cannot be removed (for example where a metal overlay covers the pin).

O rings can be used to replace the cork seals but we favour corks. The seal chamber is often roughly formed and although the seal is good on the rod it is not always the same with the pen barrel. If an O ring is used spacers must be fitted to stop the movement of the seal in the chamber.

Variety of end buttons. Shapes are different and older pens may have two start threads.

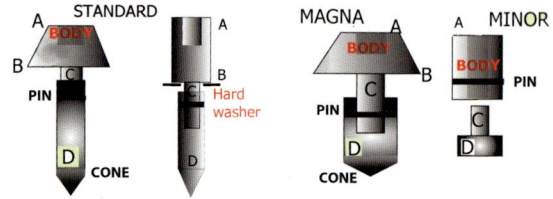
Two designs of Onoto pistons used in standard pens. Minor and Magna are different.

Rods

Different models have different length rods and different piston plug diameters, e.g. the Magna; the Mammoth; the Minor, but the diameters of the rods are the same. If a rod is broken it can often be interchanged or an old longer rod threaded down (5BA l/h). There are 6 different lengths of rod from 56mm to 82mm.and a variety of end buttons.

Plunger/piston

The plunger in most pens has a pointed end, which fits into the concave top of the feed. This is a shut off valve, so to allow the pen to write the knob has to be unscrewed half a turn. For safety the top is screwed tight when not in use. Later models such as the Onoto Minor have a truncated plunger, consequently there is no shut off. When working on the nib/feed with a shut off, remember to use a cone ended drift rod to avoid damaging the end of the feed.

Pins

The knob and the piston are secured by small hard rubber pins. The piston pin is 5mm x 1mm and the top is 9-12mm depending on the model.

Pin removed from top button. 1.2mm carbon fibre rod available from model shops is an excellent replacement

The pins in the knob are notoriously difficult to find and many hours of searching with an eyeglass awaits the diligent Onoto repairer. If the pin is lost or broken do not be tempted to use pencil lead. Replacement carbon fibre (1mm and 1.2mm from fishing or model suppliers) is very effective and copper wire or brass wire can also be used. If you use metal cut the wire shorter and then fill the hole with black wax (crayon).

The parts of the Onoto Magna flagship pen

The Magna was a development of the Mammoth, the largest Onoto. It first appeared in 1937. Production stopped during the war and it did not start again until 1946. Pre-war pens followed the fashion of the period for ink visible barrels, but this was dropped in favour of opaque black plastic for post-war production, so the lovely gold and silver transparent plastics only appeared on pre-war and early war pens.

Problems

- clips break at washer
- nobs break off rod
- see general Onoto

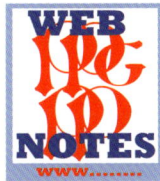

Dismantling

Servicing is broadly the same as other piston Onotos but they have some unexpected problems. First read the article on Onoto Piston.

Unscrew the section followed by the filler knob. If the knob cannot be withdrawn, do not force it because you will have a serious problem if it breaks away from the rod. The rod may have to be released by gently tapping the plunger nose to break the hardened plunger seal. The knob may now be released by removal of the pin that locks it to the rod, but first make sure that it is screwed to the barrel and is properly supported before knocking the pin, or you risk breaking the rod. On some Magnas the rod was provided with an

8BA brass threaded inner rather than the more common steel wire inner. The brass inner carried a nut at the end that could be locked against a nut inside the knob, allowing small adjustments to be made in rod length. A short slotted box spanner is required to loosen the lock nut so that the knob can be taken off. Pens with this type of rod will have a knob made of plastic rather than hard rubber.

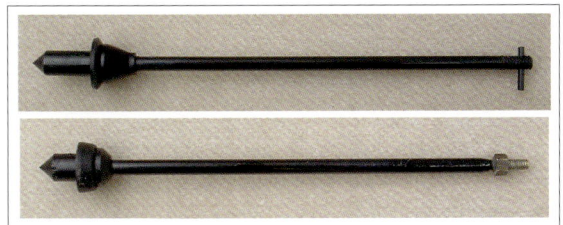

Steel reinforced rod with flat seal and brass reinforced rod with original moulded seal

Novel tool for removing Onoto seal washer made from a staple

Servicing

The retaining ring for the cork barrel seals can be removed using the Onoto tool (or even a fencing staple with the points ground to a chisel profile so that they can grip both sides of the washer). Having removed the old corks there is a good opportunity to clean out the barrel and examine it. A variation found occasionally is an off-centre vacuum release groove, presumably designed to ease the flow of ink into the pen after the vacuum is released. This has no effect on servicing, but it is worth noting that the barrel will be extremely thin on one side so that the smallest damage may cause a leak. Assuming that the barrel is sound, new corks can be fitted as described for Onotos.

Most repairers report problems with getting Magnas to fill reliably; there are a number of good reasons for this. Magna barrels do not all have the same internal diameter. They were made in at least four sizes whilst retaining the same external dimensions, so it is vital to measure the diameter in order to select the correct size seal. The margin for error is not great, and it will be found that plunger seals designed for the smaller pen will not work for long, if at all, in the larger pen. Conversely, the larger seal, if fitted to the smaller pen, will not allow ink to flow past it in the release groove. The roundness, thickness and flexibility of the seal are also important.

Onotos were originally fitted with a cup-shaped plunger washer but it is possible to use flat washers as seen in the Sheaffer Vac-fill pens. Sheaffer and Eversharp used a dished backing washer to encourage the flat plunger washer to adopt the correct profile. We have found this to be effective on Onotos. A dished washer is easy to make on the lathe, but it can be carved from a thick plastic washer using a countersink or burr in a drill chuck. A flat backing washer works quite well on the standard Onoto, but not so well on the Magna.

The backing washer should not be much smaller than the barrel internal diameter, bearing in mind that the ink must be able to pass it when the pen is being flushed from full. If the backing washer is

Barrel	Backing Washer	Plunger Washer
ID mm	OD mm	OD mm
9.1	8.5	9.45
9.75	9.1	10.15

Dimensions of flat rubber seals for two extreme sizes of Magna. Seals are 0.8mm thick and 2.7mm ID

too small, the plunger washer may try to fold back the wrong way and not seal properly.

A potential complication in fitting flat plunger washers to Onotos is that the seal drops into the release groove slightly later on the stroke than a moulded washer would, and occasionally, does not release at all. This problem can be cured if a thicker backing washer is used so that the effective length of the rod is increased. Alternatively, the release groove can be lengthened in the lathe.

Magnas often present themselves with a separated or missing knob. This happens more often in Magnas than other Onotos because the knob is larger and offers more leverage on the weakest part of the rod. Unfortunately, the wire reinforcement does not reach the end of the rod because that would prevent the locking pin from being inserted. There is, therefore, only a thin wall of hard rubber to break, and it is made even more vulnerable by the thread cut for attachment of the button. Once broken, the rod cannot be glued successfully, so a new rod must be fitted. The stub of the old rod may have to be removed, usually along with adhesive left behind by previous abortive attempts at repair. It is best to drop the knob is boiling water for a few seconds and then use a sharp jeweller's screwdriver to remove the stub from the inside using a clockwise motion. A replacement rod may be obtained from a scrap long Onoto, but it will

CAUTION *If the head of the piston unit is modified in any way it must end up the same length over all or the ink cut-off facility will not work, or the knob will not screw on fully. Adjustments may be made to the back of the plunger cone if necessary.*

have to be cut down to fit. The piston end can be cut down and threaded (5BA l/h). Alternatively, the knob end can be cut, but you will not be able to screw and pin the knob as before, so the knob threads will have to be drilled out to enable the rod shaft to be glued in.

Happily, the pens with the brass locknut attachment are more robust, but the knobs on these can also be sheared off by the application of too much force.

Cap, clip and trim

Magna clips can be sourced from smaller Onotos by softening the back of the clip washer to enable the washer to be expanded by careful hammering against a steel mandrel. A little filing and smoothing may be necessary followed by replating. Black Magna caps have a habit of shrinking so that the bands become loose, but the caps can be expanded again (see Cap Bands).

Nib & Feed

These pens were fitted with either No6 or No7 nibs and some of them are two colour. The nibs have a tendency to crack. Curiously the feeds are too small for the nibs and some nibs have a necked root (see main picture). Be sure to use a

coned drift rod to knock out the feed or it will be damaged.

Variety of Magna nibs

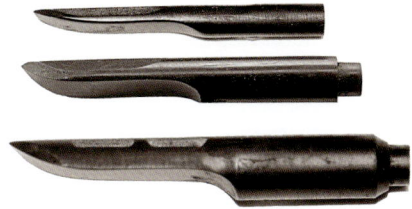

Standard, Magna and Mammoth feeds with delicate shut off recess.

CUP WASHERS

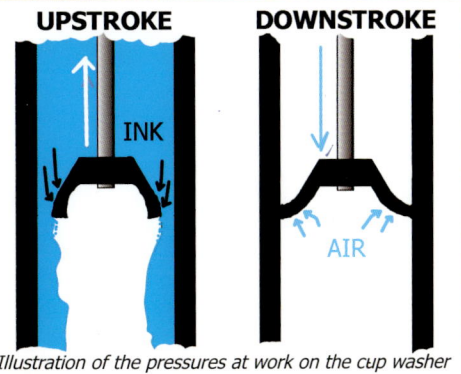

Illustration of the pressures at work on the cup washer

Onoto piston pens were all fitted with cup washers but until recently these were unobtainable. Pens continue to be repaired efficiently with flat washers, deformed to adopt a curved shape but we were interested to consider how the cup washers might perform in comparison. Our conclusion, illustrated in the diagram, is that cup washers are less likely to create top end leaks; they give a very efficient filling action and are unlikely to be inverted or torn off the plunger.

Upstroke. *If the pen is empty a tapered cup washer slides up the barrel easily. With liquid and air above the washer, it creates a pressure which forces the skirt away from the barrel wall and makes it easier for the liquid to escape without over-pressuring the top seal.*
Downstroke. *Air or liquid located below the washer is swept out of the pen so air pressure pushes the cup skirt towards the wall. This possibly gives a more reliable seal than that achieved by a flat washer.*

ONOTO LEVER FILLERS

Most barrels were engraved 'The De La Rue Pen' but occasionally 'Onoto the pen' ; nibs were stamped De La Rue not Onoto

The piston fillers were successful, but De La Rue did not want to miss out on the popularity of the more recently invented side lever sac pens, so in 1924 they introduced a lever pen. The basic range was equipped with a simple straight lever held by a C-ring located in a barrel groove. This implementation was similar to that used by Conway Stewart except that a J-bar was used to return the lever and compress the sac. The better quality pens, including the Magna lever filler, used a lever box in the same style as used by Waterman. The pressure bar was attached to the lever and did not have to be sprung because it latched in the closed position against the sides of the lever box. Maintenance and lever replacement is the same as for Waterman pens

TdLR logo on lever thumb tab

ELFIN PENS

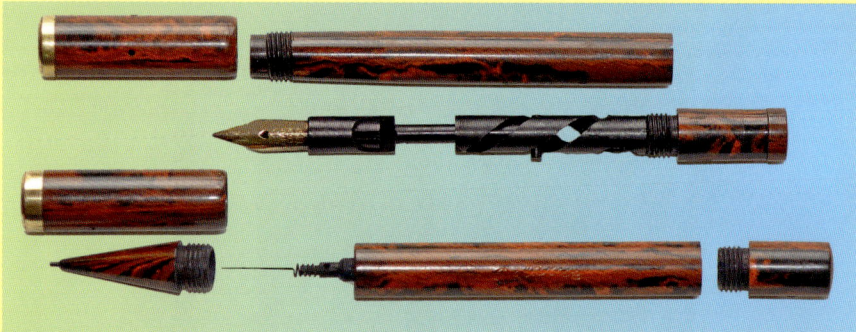

Rare De La Rue Elfin safety and stylo set

Most companies dabbled with 'mini' pens in the 1920s and 30s. Eversharp had small metal lever 00 pens and plastic bulb fillers; Parker had their 'Pastel' range; Conway Stewart had Dinkies; Watermans had V 1/2 models: Unique had slim lever and stubby eyedroppers and De La Rue had their Elfin range.

The Stylo is a sprung point eyedropper and repair is essentially replacing damaged points and cleaning. The retractable nib Elfin is a 'Whytwarth' style design with the turning knob and shaft attached to a separate spiral by a pin. This pin must be removed to replace the top end cork seal. If the pin is steel it is likely to have corroded and it will then be impossible to knock out without the shaft or the spiral breaking. It must be carefully drilled out. The spiral is fragile and if broken has to be repaired or preferably replaced. Glue is rarely an effective or long lasting solution. Good spiral repair involves complicated pinning and reinforcing plates. It is not impossible to cut new spirals but this is rarely a cost effective repair.

ONOTO MINOR

The dismantled pen

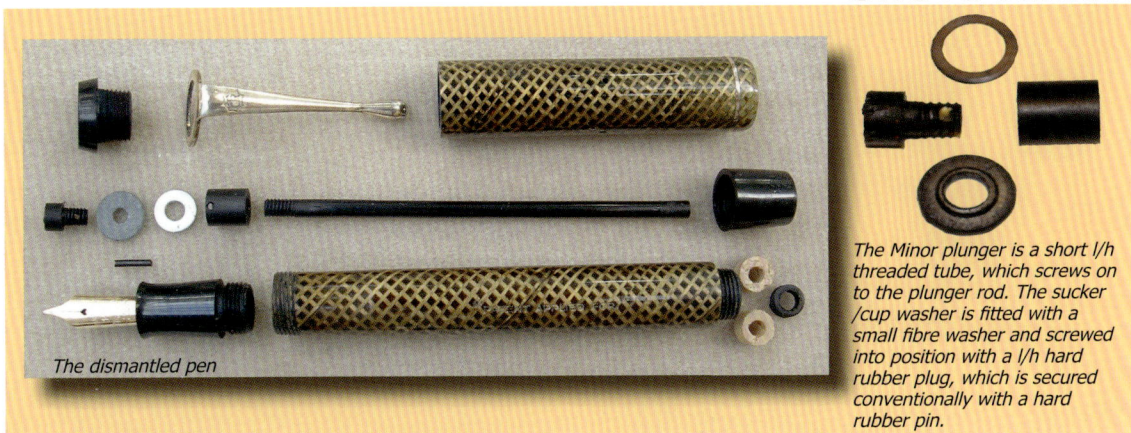

The Minor plunger is a short l/h threaded tube, which screws on to the plunger rod. The sucker /cup washer is fitted with a small fibre washer and screwed into position with a l/h hard rubber plug, which is secured conventionally with a hard rubber pin.

These beautiful transparent lattice pens belong to the pre-war era of 1938 when the gold and silver Magnas were produced. Like some of the Magnas, the Minors were fitted with black plastic knobs rather than hard rubber ones. Unfortunately, they are glued to the rod. The Minor has a simple but different short seal holder and no ink shut-off valve like other Onotos.

Servicing

While the Minor appears similar to other plunger filler Onotos, it can be more difficult to repair because the knob is not easily removable; it is glued to the rod rather than being threaded and pinned, so a different servicing strategy is recommended. The rod is also different from other Onotos in that there is no shoulder for the piston seal assembly to thread up to. However, this difference allows us to service the pen without removing the knob because the rod can be removed from the end of the pen when the piston seal assembly is unscrewed. This is where difficulties can arise because there is no obvious way to grip the piston head. Onoto service engineers used a special clamp with jaws thin enough to enter the barrel mouth. However, it is not difficult to make a similar tool from cheap (unhardened jaws) pliers (see pic.). An alternative technique is to cut a slot in the plunger end with an engraving tool which makes it possible to use a screwdriver. Soak the seal holder/rod joint by supporting the barrel in a stand and fill it with water/detergent mix or a mild alkaline solution. Leave it for at least an hour.

It is only if all this fails, remembering of course

that the thread is left handed, that it is necessary to consider removing the knob. Knob removal requires a punch ground to just less than the rod diameter and a firm support, which is ideally provided by a robust wire gauge on a tall metal tube. The adhesive may be weakened by heating, but the rod and knob will be softened, and may be distorted or even cracked by the punch. Bearing in mind that the hardened wire core of the rod will prevent drilling out, you are strongly advised to leave the knob alone!

The washer can then be replaced with an 8 mm flexible flat washer plus a hard washer (same as standard Onoto) or a cup washer. Note the different design of plunger illustrated above.

The barrel seal replacement is similar to other Onotos and the same diameter cork seals are used. Use a small amount of silicone grease with the corks. Press them into the recess using an old rod as a guide or with the actual rod in position, and then screw down the cork seal screw plug.

Two methods of getting access to the seal holder; A - with a pin punch to remove the rod or B- with special pliers to unscrew the plunger unit without removing the rod.

ONOTO K SERIES PISTON FILLERS

Onoto K1

Onoto K4 demonstrator,illustrating metal turning screw and plastic plunger

The Onoto K series pen was introduced by De La Rue in 1955. (They were all piston upfillers), The filler knob unscrews two and a half turns to advance the plastic piston and the pen fills by returning the knob to the closed position. The K series were good quality pens but the filling system was not designed to be serviced, presumably because it was believed that the plastic piston washer would last at least as long as the rest of the pen. Perhaps this was justified because the 54 year old pen illustrated here fills as if it were new!

Hooded model K1,K2,K4
Dismantling

The shell can be unscrewed to reveal the section and tubular nib. Two rubber seals prevent leakage around the inside of the shell (later models had only one top sealing washer.) The nib fits onto a feed which is a push fit into the carrier/collector, which in turn is a push fit into the barrel. All can be taken apart easily and the nib can be knocked out and or changed as appropriate.

Unfortunately the mechanism cannot be removed because the sleeve that holds the section is glued into the barrel and does not permit withdrawal of the piston head.

Open nib model K3

This has a conventional section and does allow withdrawal of the mechanism. The knob advances the piston to the mouth of the barrel so that it comes off the spiral and can be pulled out. The plastic seal is a click fit over the piston head. Reassembly of the pen is not difficult provided the knob is in the correct position as the piston is pushed down onto the start of the spiral. The knob must be withdrawn two and a half turns (1.8mm) at this point; this will ensure that when the knob is screwed up, the piston will be able to retreat to a position just short of its end stop.

Cap and clip

The gold-filled cap and clip are constructed in the same way as the later Parker 61 caps. It has an internal clutch and is dismantled by removing the clip screw.

Solid colours and plastic caps; the K4 hooded pen has a screw cap; all other K series have push on caps.

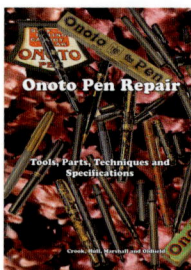

For more details of Onoto step by step repair guidance, history and specification please refer to our publication Onoto Pen Repair.

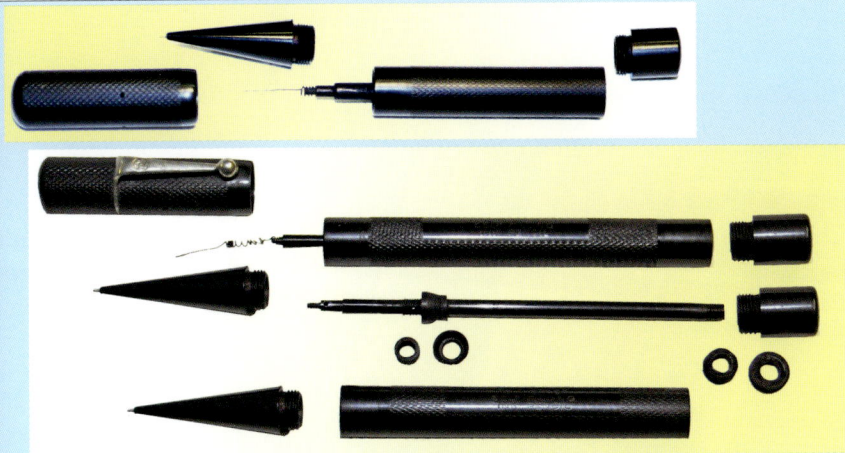

The early stylos were designed with a sprung point and this was also used with the Elfin. The self filling stylo based on a plunger mechanism was a very complex design with a hollow rod and complex filling procedure, which involved sealing the top airhole.

These models were replaced after the war with a redesigned nozzle system.

There are various designs of Onoto Ink pencil and at least three filling systems. The 'stylo' designs were either :

- a **'spring point'** which retained its 'at rest' position by having part of the wire 'point' coiled into a spring
- a **'gravity point'** which kept its position by being attached to a heavy lead slug.

Ink is transferred to the paper, when the inner 'needle' is pressed up and this allows ink to feed down the annulus between the needle point and nozzle. To achieve continual flow of ink air must somehow feed back into the ink reservoir. Problems of flow are usually related to dirt, blockages and bent 'needle points. (For details on how a stylo works see www.penpencilgallery.com).

Filling systems

Eyedropper- illustrated at the top of the page and developed from the de La Rue Nota Bene ink pencil.

Plunger filling. The early 1920s design was very complicated with a 3.7mm hollow tube rod and a solid end onto which the sprung point is attached. The hard rubber shank, with a breather hole, screws onto the rod at the other end (and there is no securing pin). The plunger cup washer, mounted almost midway up the rod, is fixed in position with a threaded tube. Filling requires the hole at the top of the shank to be covered. The 'modern' post-war plunger stylo (see below) used a simple Onoto Minor plunger with a separate cone and gravity point.

Lever Filling. This model also has a separate cone and point system which can be easily screwed out. The section is a push fit and can be removed for resaccing.

The self-filling stylos were introduced after the war with a new nozzle design. The sprung point was replaced with a cone which had grooves and air holes just below the threads. The design was the same for both the plunger and the lever fill. The plunger model illustrated has an Onoto Minor style of plunger and a solid metal slug with a short piece of wire, which facilitated flow.

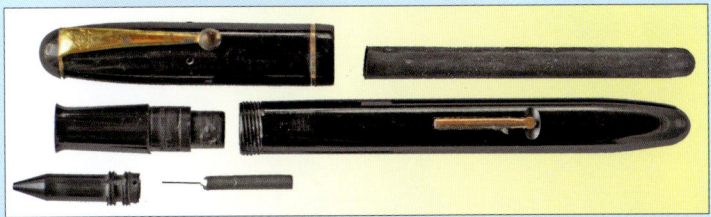

ONOTO PENCILS

Lead size -1.2 mm diameter;
25 mm long.

The dismantled Onoto pencil.

The dismantled Magna pencil.

The Onoto pencils were made to match the range of Onoto pens and that included a range of Magna pencils. They are well made and easy to dismantle for parts replacement, adjustment or lubrication.

The exploded images illustrate that all the parts are threaded and screw off. Sometimes the threaded tubes have rusted or the plastic has shrunk so it is important to use heat. It is worth making a pair of 'cone' pliers if you are intending to work a lot with pencils.

The mechanisms are complicated to dismantle and repair, so if parts are broken it is usually best to look for a replacement mechanism. The mechanisms were made by Johnson Mathey and similar mechanisms were used in many post war pencils. Fortunately, most problems arise from jammed leads (easily sorted with a fine drill) or lack of lubrication.

Two designs of mechanism are common, one of which requires the adjustment of a small nut to put the mechanism into correct alignment with the barrel.

A steel tube with the end cut to form two lugs is the only tool required for this adjustment.

The clip is held by a brass or plastic bush.

Eraser renewal will require a new one to be cut from a block using a sharpened tube.

Two JM pencil mechanisms

Spanning tube for releasing locking nut

Magna silver/transparent pencil.

KNIGHT RIDER

The idea for this pen was patented in 1937 by Knight in collaboration with De La Rue, and pens were subsequently marketed following the style of the Onoto 5601 plunger filler. There is no evidence of DLR involvement from imprints on the barrels or nibs, but the clip shows the familiar crysanthemum logo. The Knight Rider is a bulb/diaphragm pen similar to the Vacumatic and Ink Vue. In this case the bulb is compressed with an ingenious button operated tongs.

Servicing

Dismantling starts with unscrewing the section and breather tube, followed by unscrewing the two parts of the barrel to reveal the attachment of the bulb by means of a brass ring. The clear part of the barrel is cleaned and the new bulb attached with shellac. The brass ring is probably not essential, but it gives an added sense of security when the bulb is squeezed. If the tongs operate properly when the button is pressed, there is no need to dismantle the button assembly. If it is necessary to dismantle then a means to grip the threaded bush is required. A rubber tube gripped with section pliers may work, but the best method is to use a correctly threaded C-ring if you have a lathe to make one.

ONOTO TIT BITS

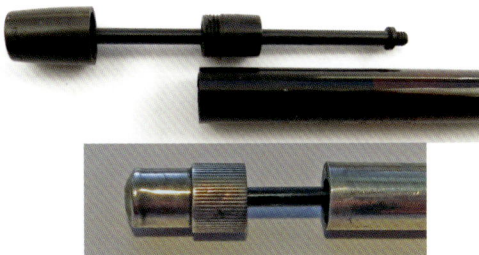

An Onoto cartridge seal

With later Onotos such as the one illustrated, the construction incorporated a separate seal cartridge at the top end of the pen. You can make such a unit by turning and parting the top of an old barrel. If your Onoto top has broken off at the threads the barrel top/seal unit can be drilled out and replaced with your fabricated seal cartridge. This is particularly practical if you have a barrel overlay. (You will still have to take the overlay off the turning knob).

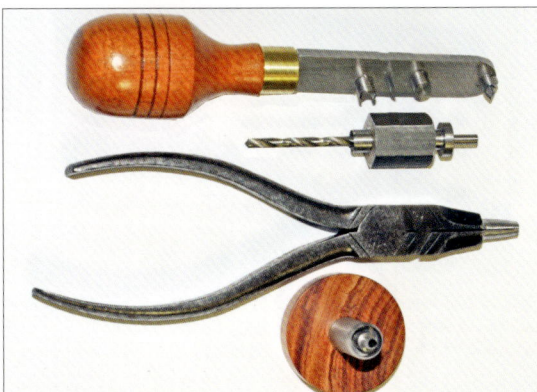

Tool kit The increasing popularity of new Onoto pens has increased the interest in using quality older Onotos and de La Rue lever fillers. The consequence is that more and more collectors are asking for the suitable tools to repair the plunger fillers and searching for spare parts. These are the key tools you can purchase for repairing Onotos.

BRITISH PENS

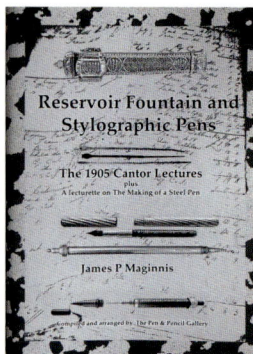

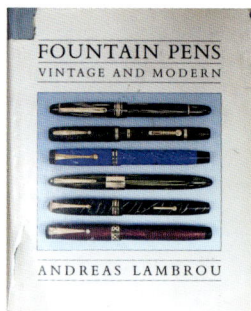

Our focus is repairing pens but as enthusiasts we cannot avoid being influenced by attractive colours and unusual designs. Considering our location during the last 25 years we have probably spent more time repairing British pens than any others and yet many of these are relatively unknown internationally. Conway Stewart, Onoto and Mabie Todd are of course international but the other lesser known makes are often relegated to the second division and this is unfair both from a quality and design standpoint. This is sad because the variety of these British pens provides a great opportunity for collectors.

From a repair standpoint there are few complications with the run of the mill lever and button fillers but complexity always seems to be introduced when companies become more successful and start to patent their innovations.

There is no better introduction to the design and development of early pens than the patents referred to in the Maginnis Cantor lectures. These are worth mentioning in a repair book as a source of information on the intricacies of feeds and ink flow. Our brief summaries of any British pen development in the next few pages is completely influenced by Steve Hull, whose working notes on English pen manufacturers are essential browsing and reference for anyone interested in English pens. The first collector information on English pens compiled by Andy Lambrou was published by Sothebys and then expanded in his large book. You will need few other references than these to start collecting.
Repairing is another matter!
Fountain pen manufacture in the UK developed very quickly in the late C19th century. The first pen made was possibly the 'Anti stylograph' licensed to Thomas

De La Rue in 1881. Steel nib makers entered the market to protect their own interests and companies such as Perry, MacNiven & Cameron, Mabie Todd and Bard and John Holland were all very active in the UK (John Holland was represented by Jewel in 1884 and by 1895 Jewel were making their own pens).
There is often doubt with small brands as to who made what! Some small firms had their own manufacturing facilities but many used third parties at least at some stage of their growth. This is illustrated in some way by comparing the similarity of lever bars of 10 British pens below.
Major stores had their own brands such as Harrods, WHSmith, John Lewis and Boots; promotional pens were produced such as OXO by Conway Stewart and Typhoo tea by Wyvern; pens such as Battleaxe were produced for catalogue houses.
Many makers showed little original thinking in the first quarter of the C20th. National Security's early models, for example, were direct copies of Parker Duofold button fillers and Valentine pens (parts can even be exchanged). However that did not apply to all and companies such as Onoto, Mentmore and Wyvern were very innovative.

Similarity of lever boxes of some British pens 1.John Bull, 2.National security, 3.Stephens, 4.Mc Niven & Cameron, 5.Summit, 6.Wyvern, 7.Croxley, 8. Chatsworth, 9. The Treasyury pen, 10. Typhoo Tea

Francis Mordan's eyedropper from about 1910

Unused Spa pen with barrelstamp and interestingly a Brandauer pen nib

Camel silver overlaid eyedropper with manifold nib.

From the top WHS self filler with synthetic seal; Unmarked small under/over feed pen; The Improved Post Pen (1901 Patent)

Largest eyedropper pen The Teddy pen and the very small stylo The Tom Tit.

Unused Croxley pen from 1949.

BRITISH PENS

EYEDROPPERS

Eyedroppers -some of the earliest British practical pens were stylographs and after these eyedroppers dominated until the early 20th century. These were produced in vast numbers with names such as Fleet, Newman, Spa and even now mint examples turn up.

Repair - usually a good clean and they will function. Sometimes nibs have been changed so always examine the pens - you may find a rare Parker in a decrepit Chad Valley pen. Take care with fitting under/over feeds and to secure the nibs fit with warmth.

EARLY SYRINGE PENS

There are a surprising number of these pens in the UK; they were sold by WHSmith and by Pitman for shorthand.

Repair - often regarded with curiosity they can easily be made to fill by replacing the corks or in some cases a synthetic rubber seal. Usually access to the piston involved screwing off the nib section and refitting a new cork with a small amount of silicone grease (See Corks and Piston pens). In the lower example the piston is withdrawn by unscrewing the plunger end and replacing the cork seal, which is secured by a threaded plug .

ORMISTON & GLASS

Better known for their hard rubber dip pens they produced some unusual fountain pens and stylos such as the minute Tom Tit and the extra large Teddy. Both these eyedroppers were available as stylos and pens.

Repair as for stylos and eyedroppers

CROXLEY

Croxley was a brand made by the paper retailers Dickinson in Liverpool. In 1947 they bought Lang's old equipment, producing a lever filler with a feathered arrow clip and lever. Production lasted for only two years (1947-49) but they can still be found in mint condition.

BURNHAM

Burnham pens first appeared in 1927; they bear a strong resemblance to Conway Stewart pens, and like Conway, they used many very decorative plastics including some casein materials. Pre-war pens were made as button and lever fillers but these are rare and post war pens were all lever fillers, with an emphasis on simplicity and value for money. They were perhaps a little down market on Conway, having very poor gold plating and some non-gold nibs.

Servicing

In contrast to Conways, Burnhams have screw fit sections; most come apart very easily. A conventional lever operated pressure bar is used, and sac changing is straightforward.

Burnham pens have a lever held by a wire ring located in a groove in the barrel. However, except for the earliest pens, the lever is straight so it is possible to insert it into the slot from inside the barrel.

Cap, clip and trim

At least three different methods of clip attachment were used. Pre 1948 pens used a flat washer-type clip held by a large button. The early 1950's models were similar to Conways with a conical button recessed in the clip top (main picture). Later 1950s models used a stud attachment. The stud can be removed from inside the cap after any dried ink and dirt has been cleaned out to expose

the screwdriver slot. It is necessary to use a narrow screwdriver as the head is recessed and to turn it clockwise to expel the stud.

Stud-type clip attachment

Four examples of Burnham washer clips, including an austerity post war clip- number 1 lhs.

CAESIN DETERIORATION WITH TIME

Some Burnhams are made of casein, so beware of leaving them in water for more than a few minutes.

CAUTION

Use sacs one size smaller than you would use for Conways to avoid the possibility of the sac twisting as the section is scewed in.

INFO

PERRY & CO

Perry were a major stationers supplier and steel nib maker but theirr fountain pen digressions were few. This large Perry nib required a tab to secure it to the feed.

JOHN BULL UNIQUE

Unique pens are judged by war babies as school pens made from cheap plastic; however in 1924 they had 60 different models on show at the 1924 British empire Exhibition. The small hard rubber eyedropper contrasts with the attractive lapis button filler.

Repairs are mainly sacs for post war marbled lever fillers and nibs.

CURZON - SUMMIT

Lang, the manufacturer, was established in 1895, near Liverpool and linked with Curzon in the early 1920s to become a major pen player. One of their 1927 quality products was the Debrett/Curzon, which had a unique top level filling system as well as a rather 'posh' brand name. Some of the Curzon 1930s pens were in spectacular plastics such as their Sunray Coral and the Moire patterns.

Summit was a brand name in the 1920s and Curzon and Summit pens were produced until the 1940s. In 1945 Curzons Ltd changed their name to Summit Pens Ltd and few Curzon pens were made after that. Quality pens were produced until 1954 with some wonderful intense solid colours such as their rich forest green and advanced innovations like their spring clip.

The illustration show an excellent prewar Summit lever fill lizard disassembled; a green moire ring top Curzon; a Coral Summit and an S106 with the special spring clip

MACNIVEN & CAMERON

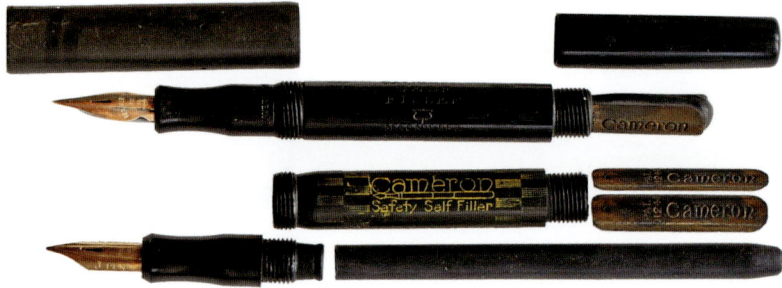

Not a bulb filler but a long sac with bars to squeeze the sac

This Edinburgh based company, founded in 1770, were well established steel nib makers. The distinctive shape of their Waverley steel nib was used as the template for gold nibs when they started to make fountain pens in Birmingham in 1906. The first products were a variety of eyedroppers in black hard rubber after which they adopted various filling systems, mainly using rubber reservoirs.

Repair

The variety is surprising and includes a squeeze plate design, a push/pull system and conventional lever fillers. Both screw and push sections were used so always try to screw the section out. Most pens are black hard rubber with little decoration and require little attention other than resaccing.

Cap clips are frequently riveted thistle design or ring clips with embossed Robert Burns images. Coloured examples are rare and overlaid examples even rarer. A modern eyedropper, the Waverley, was produced in the 1940s and 50s for Civil Service use in hot countries where rubber sacs deteriorate dramatically.

Waverley nib with over support

Rare silver overlay eyedropper

Red mottled vulcanite lever filler

Thistle clip on red lever pen

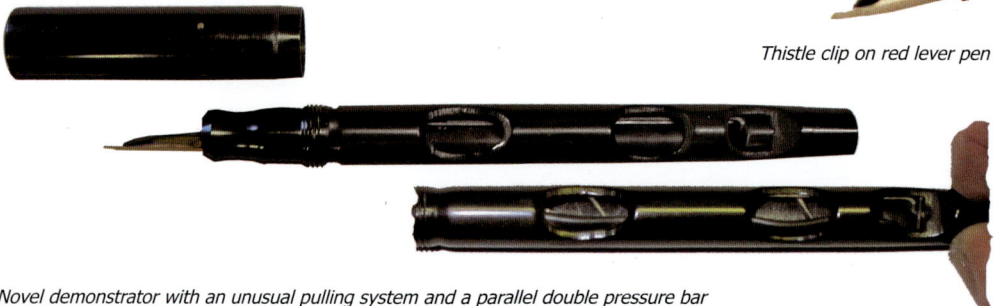

Novel demonstrator with an unusual pulling system and a parallel double pressure bar

Spot pens were very well made and the red and black mottled vulcanite and small metal pens are as good as any of the major manufacturers quality pens

The Mentmore Manufacturing Company was founded in 1919 and started manufacture in 1923. One of their main corporate aims was to produce sufficient quantities of pens for school children and families, who could not afford quality pens. The early MMC Ltd brand 'Spot' had a range of quality products with a prominent white dot on the cap, which possibly predated Sheaffer's use of the dot. In general one can split their activities into the Mentmore mid-market range of products such as Diploma, Moderne, Celeste, Auto-Flow and Ink-Lock, and the Platignum products with iridium tipped steel nibs for the mass market. Platignum also offered gold nibs as an option on earlier pens, but from 1931 MMC had a policy of gold for Mentmore and steel for Platignum.

The fascination with this company reflects the range of filling systems used, experimented with and patented. A great success story from a garden shed in Hackney!

Platignum Visi-Ink and Mentmore Ink-lock

In the late 1920s the Platignum range was launched, and with it, the claim that metals other than gold could make very good nibs.

These pens have a breather tube (air tube in the patent descriptions) that is not connected to the feed. The air tube is connected instead to a means for varying pressure within the barrel – typically a rubber bulb. By squeezing the bulb, air is forced down the tube and through a hole in the end of the feed, the feed being in close proximity to the chamfered end of the air tube. The hole in the feed is connected to the ink channel, so air exits via this route. On release of the bulb, pressure in the barrel is reduced and ink enters. Air remaining in the barrel enters the bulb through a small hole or groove in the upper part of the air tube. This aperture is of much smaller size than the bore of the air tube so that it offers more resistance to airflow than the air tube when the bulb is squeezed.

An early hard rubber Visi Ink Platignum. these early Platignums were high quality.

The process is repeated about six times to remove all the air and fill the pen. The Platignum Visi-ink holds 2.28ml.

The Mentmore pen was patented two years later, but it is essentially the same mechanism. The bulb, rather than being compressed by a button,

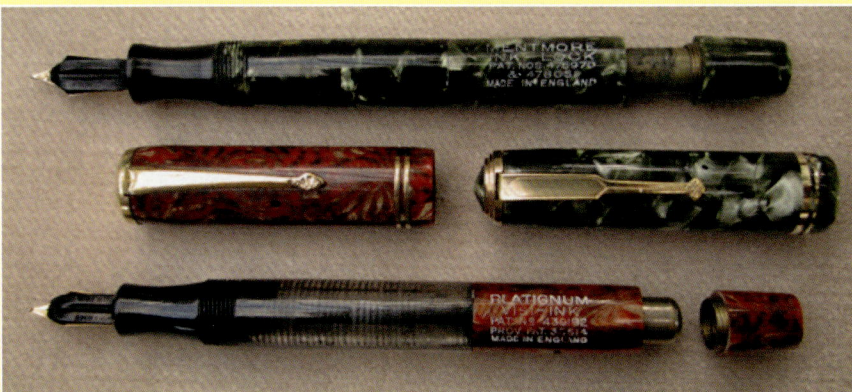

The Mentmore Ink Lock and the Platignum Visi-ink share the same filling principle.

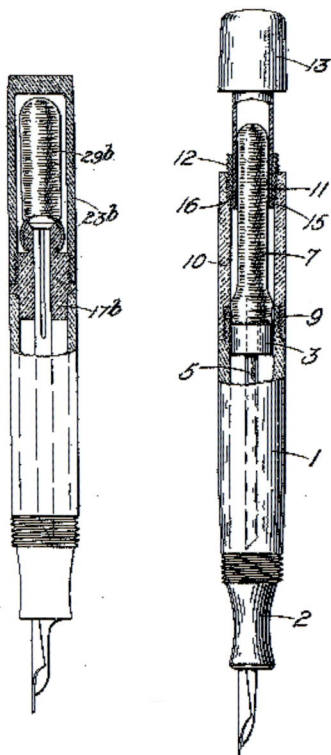

Platignum patent GB 439182 May1934
Mentmore patent GB 475970 June 1936

is compressed by air in a piston, just like the
Chilton. This pen has a pin within the cap that
engages with a hole in the front of the feed to cut
off ink flow when the cap is in place.

Servicing

Both pens unscrew in the centre of the barrel.
This enables sac replacement and removal of
the air tube. Air tubes have been found to be a
tight fit so they must be driven out with a drift
rod following heating of the central bush. Careful
ultrasonic cleaning will ensure that the airways

are clear.

Mentmore lever and button fillers

The pre-war models were upgraded and
the 45, 46, 69 and the semi hooded
Diploma launched.

Quality pens were offered with sterling
caps. The Autoflow was made with lever
and button fill, with a clip having an M
logo in a diamond and M stamped on
the lever tab.

So many of the British pens from the
1930s have a similar appearance and
were made with similar plastic. It is
likely that Mentmore made a number of
these pens as they were skilled in the
mass production of lever, button and
also simple bulb fillers; there are many
unstamped pens from this period, which
are undoubtedly of Mentmore origin.

Repair

These pens present few problems and
typical procedures can be referred to
in Lever and Button Fillers (Section
1). Levers were secured with C-clips
and the pressure bar is a simple J-bar
wedged in the barrel end.

Early buttons were made of hard rubber
with a short length of thread which
screws into the barrel and acts as a
retainer. (DO NOT TRY and pull this
button out like Parker or Summit pens).

Elegant Mentmore Paramount w transparent

The Mentmore Ink Lock dismantled illustrating the parts referred to in the patent and the text.

Dismantled Mentmore Diploma early button filler in very good condition

Brass buttons were used in pens made from the late 1930s.

The Diploma was a button filler with a small diameter feed and small nib. Knocking the feed out requires a shaped block. Button fillers were not made by Mentmore after 1950.

The 1965 cartridge model

Many will remember The Golden Platignum from school; robust and modern looking with a small nib but also produced with an open nib. The Platignum products made from 1929 were initially good quality when made with hard rubber but the early plastics of the 1930s have rarely stood the test of time. Shrinkage and corrosion of nibs are the main problems.

Repair

The pens screw apart (shrinkage permitting) and the early models had a simple J bar which is easily replaced In the 1950s they adopted an aerometric filling system and the sac protector is frequently corroded. Parts for such pens are now hard to find. From the 1960s the adopted screw in nibs. They continued to make pens with steel nibs until 1975.

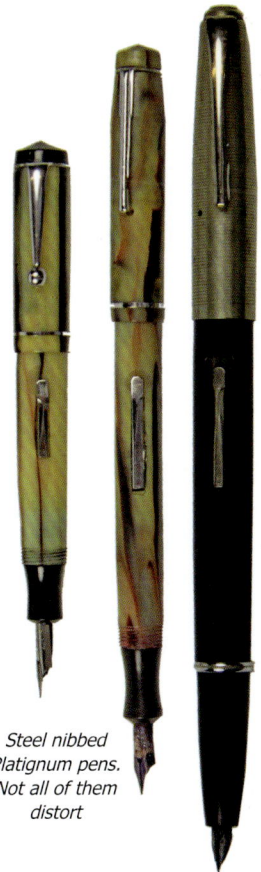

Steel nibbed Platignum pens. Not all of them distort

The classic school Platignum

VALENTINE

Two very collectable lizard and 'red' Valentines .

Two Whytwarth silver overlaid safety pens

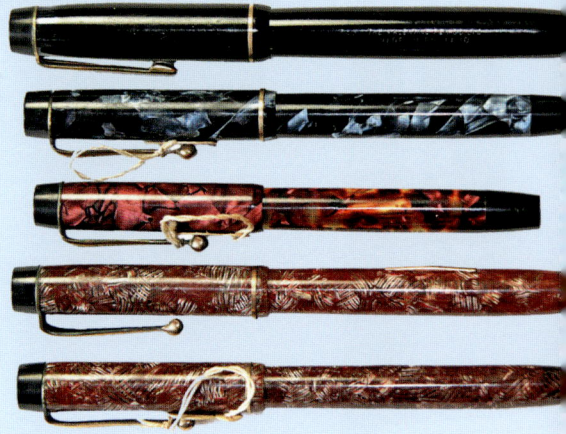

Five mint Valentine 'factory' reference pens.

Valentine existed as a Dundee greeting card company (established in 1825) but diverted into pens, after acquiring Gold Nibs Ltd and Whytwarth in 1929. The 1930 range of Valentine pens included attractive lever fillers with a choice of pocket clips and the Whytwarth range of safety pens. In the 1930s, the Valentine Pen Co was making pens for a number of companies including National Security and Parker. Valentine branded pens were made until about 1950, and this was after Parker took over the company in 1945. The most common Valentines are almost identical to Parker Victory pens.

An unusual pen, the Securite, is large for a ring top; 140mm long capped and uses a very similar plastic to the Onyx Patrician. It has a twist filling system like the Swan Leverless, but it is better engineered and the patent (Nov 1930) predates the Mabie Todd patent. It also has a unique spring-loaded ink cut-off system, operated by a pin within the cap.

Whytwarth's focus was on safety pens; most

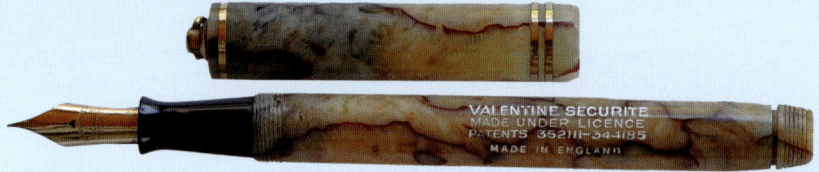

Unusual onyx Valentine Securite

models were slim black hard rubber, but the larger models with silver overlays and some very rare enamelled or red and black hard rubber examples are the most desirable (for repair see Safety pens).

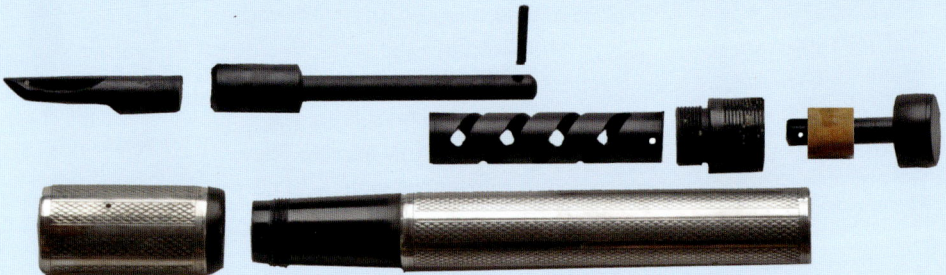

Dismantled large Whytwarth, ready for reassembly

WYVERN

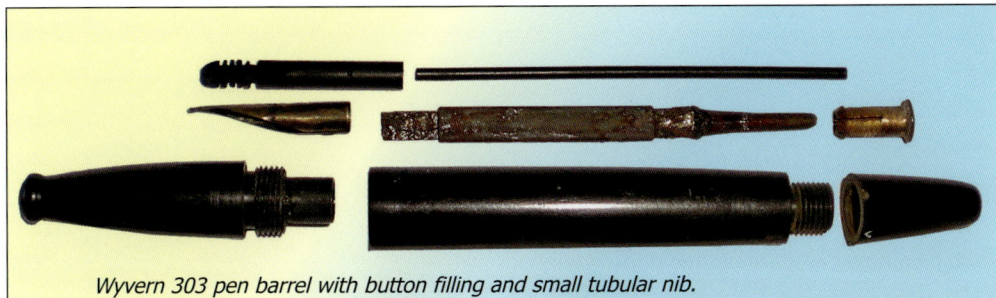

Wyvern 303 pen barrel with button filling and small tubular nib.

The Wyvern pen company was established in Leicester by the Finberg brothers in 1929. They produced a variety of pens, ranging in quality from cheap school pens to the exotic leather covered pens used by George VI. The most popular pens were similar to the Mentmore, Croxley, early Burnham and Summit range of button and lever filling pens.

Wyvern were a progressive company and adopted hooded shells even before the advent of Parker 51s. These were in some ways similar to the Eversharp 5th Avenue but with good ink capacity (note the very long breather tube!).

The 303, 404, 505 and 707 ranges of small nibbed pens, with griffon clips, were memorable to repairers because most had left hand thread sections (even more memorable were the few right hand threaded 404s!

Problems
- plastic quality of post war pens was poor
- pressure bars rusted badly
- some caps were a poor fit

Servicing
The repair of most of the open nibbed pens is straight forward. The sections vary from push fit to both standard and reverse thread fits; the nibs knock out through the section and tapering sections must be held firmly in a conical shaped knocking block (see Taperite), to avoid damaging the shell.

The cap/clip
All early pens had clips secured by a hard rubber clip screw, but with the introduction of streamlined shaped pens, the clip screw was reduced in size and metal inner collars were also used.

Wyvern developed a unique inner cap system to secure the pen and cap. The rim on the section clicked into a groove in the inner cap, which was spring loaded.

Inner cap with spring, which fits into the moulded cap.

Wyvern 808
One of the exotic pens made by The Wyvern Pen Company was the 808 which is illustrated below.

Introduced in 1950 it followed a trend in the UK for bulb fillers, but it is fascinating because it is sculpted into a stylised transparent acrylic frame.

The breather tube can be seen extending through the ink chamber into the bulb. The bulb section screws onto the ink chamber.

Range of Wyvern pens from 1930s to the last 808 model

It has always been claimed by Mrs Hannah Finberg that Fords were made by Wyvern; this is one of these typical UK manufacturing mysteries. There is no doubt that Wyvern could have made the Fords because they produced some meticulous quality pens.

STEPHENS BUTTON FILLER

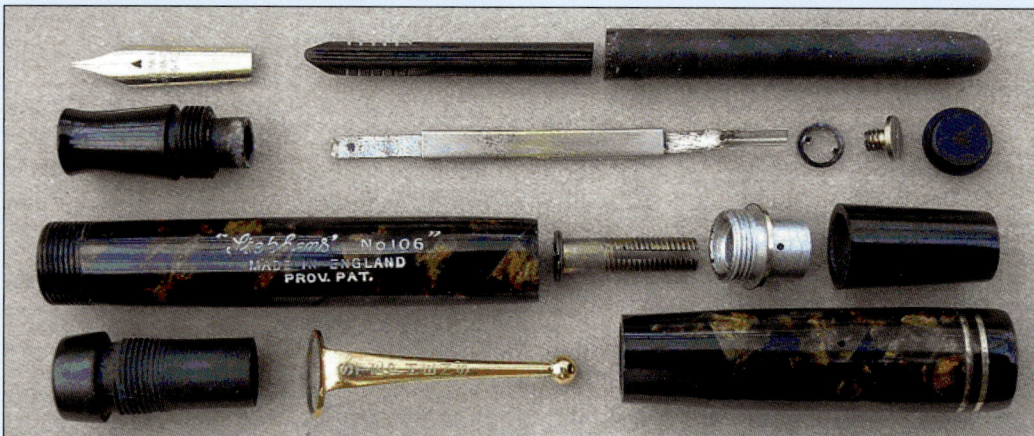

Stephens were well known for their ink and their steel pens, but not for fountain pens until the button (or stud) filler appeared in 1935. This filling system had been patented by Lang (Lang was the probable maker of Stephens' pens and most were economic lever fill products targeted for school use).

This pen was novel in that it was probably the first to have a blind cap permanently fixed to the pen. Four models were produced, the 56, the 76, the 106, and the deluxe model 21. The model numbers reflected the prices in shillings and pence.

Problems
- button does not unscrew
- button unscrews but does not depress

Dismantling
First unscrew the section after the usual cold water soak and hot air. When the old sac has been removed, pull out the pressure bar and inspect it for corrosion.

If the filler button unscrews and is free to move, only the refitting of the pressure bar and a new sac is required. If the filler button is not free to move try warming it and rocking it and if it still does not move, the button assembly must be dismantled. Do not force it or the hard rubber threads inside the button will be damaged.

The filler button is held in place by a screw located beneath a small hard rubber end cap. The aluminium bush provides the mount to the barrel and prevents rotation of the brass push rod. The internal end of the rod has a recess that provides the location for the end of the pressure bar. The other end is threaded and slotted. The slot aligns with a pin in the aluminium bush and the thread holds the hard rubber button.

A small screw and keyed washer prevent the mechanism from coming apart in use. The nice finishing touch is the hard rubber cap that screws into the button so snugly that it is often impossible to see the joint.

Button unscrewed and ready to be used

The filler button and mechanism

Hot air will be useful to help the process of unscrewing the button cap, but it will be necessary to use a thin rubber sheet to achieve adequate grip. If it still cannot be removed, use superglue to attach a short length of tubing to it (preferably wood so that you can remove it easily later). Beneath the button cap, the slotted top of the brass screw that attaches the button to the brass plunger will be seen. When this is unscrewed, be careful not to lose the small two-pronged lock washer. The button can now be unscrewed from the aluminium bush, and it will probably be apparent that the brass plunger is fused in position by corrosion. Now use section pliers or a C spanner to remove the mechanism from the pen barrel and soak it for a while before putting it in the nib knocking-block for a little gentle persuasion.

Reassembly

Clean and lubricate all the parts and assemble the pen without the sac to make sure that the mechanism is working properly. The end of the pressure bar must be located correctly into the end of the brass push rod and the pressure bar must be the correct length.

When fitting the sac, allow plenty of clearance on length and diameter or it will become strangled when the section is screwed in. A liberal coating of talcum powder on the sac will help. If the pen holds a reasonable quantity of ink (at least 16 drops) it can be assumed that the sac is correctly located.

A popular Stephens lever fill school pen with a high price of 15/6 (78p).

NATIONAL SECURITY

'Look alike' Parker Duofold probably made by Valentine.
Quality chased hard rubber and rarer lizard and marble examples are very attractive. Often they were advertised together with another BCP Co brand Rosemary 'Lest we forget' pens.

National Security was a brand name of British Carbon Papers Co. Early models were imitations of current popular pens of Watermans, Mentmore, Parker and Valentine and made under contract in Newhaven by Valentine. In the 1940s they continued to imitate Parker, and copied a 1930's Vacumatic shaped pen as a lever filler.

Repair

The repair of such pens is the same as the original for the 'lookalike'. Parts for button and lever pens are often interchangeable with Parker and Valentine pens except that they usually have a smaller feed. Warranted nibs were used and a range of generic ring clips.

A turquoise bulb filler typical 'look alike' to the Mentmore bulb fillers.

FORD

Features

The Ford Patent Pen, developed in the early 1930s, was probably the most advanced of its generation of high-tech pens.

Several sizes of pen were produced, the Magnum, the Standard, the Short Standard and the Lady fabricated from black and red/black vulcanite; some had silver, gold or enammelled overlays. Fords had a number of interesting features:

- they fill on the syringe principle (fills on the pull

stroke) and it has many advantages over modern syringe fillers.

- they may have been the first to incorporate a full-length breather tube to enable the escape of air so that the whole reservoir can be filled.
- they have excellent thermal insulation
- they have a cut-off valve to prevent leakage when the pen is not being used.

The Lady pens have internal components made of nickel silver, making them more robust than the other models where hard rubber was used. The earlier Fords have a brown tinted celluloid ink chamber threaded at both ends whereas later pens had acrylic chambers with integral barrel seal. In general the celluloid chambers have survived better than the acrylic ones, some of which have developed networks of fine cracks that have made them very fragile.

The main picture shows a Ford Standard with an acylic chamber in exceptionally good condition and with gold plated support rings on both ends.

Fords Magnum, Standard, Short Standard and Lady – the Magnum is 159 mm long and has a hidden clip washer

The two styles of ink chamber in less than perfect condition

Problems
- crazed or broken ink chamber
- chipped and cracked cap lips
- split outer casing
- broken internals

Fords have a reputation for being difficult to repair, but with the knowledge of how they are assembled, there should be no major problem. It is important to remember that the filler components are quite delicate.

How they work

The heart of this pen is the piston seal that is allowed to move on the piston rod such that the configuration of the pen changes between the pull stroke and the push stroke. This change allows ink drawn in on the first cycle to bypass the seal so that it is not ejected again on the second cycle, as would be the case with a simple syringe.

On the pull stroke ink is sucked in through the feed channel while air is expelled from the end of the pen via a hole in the plunger rod, the breather tube and a vent in the under side of the feed.

On the push stroke the piston rod slides through the seal to expose a slot through which ink passes rather than being expelled back through the feed. The ink

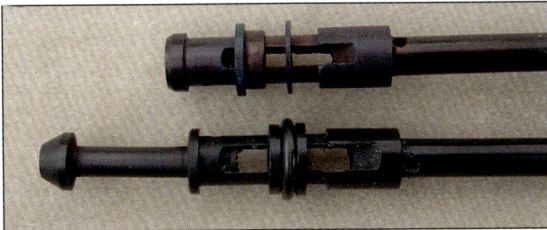

Piston seal carrier in a Short Standard and the modified seal in a Standard Ford - both are short carriers.

transferred to the end of the pen is prevented from escaping by a cork barrel seal surrounding the piston rod. This seal (unlike the similar one in the Onoto pen) is not critical for filling, but if it is not good the pen will flood and leak during use.

The repair process involves replacement of both seals. The original seals were made of cork or leather. Similar replacements can be fabricated, but better performance is achieved by using modern O-ring seals.

Servicing

The section is easily unscrewed from the reservoir, with a little warmth; be careful withdrawing the unit because of the long breather tube.

Removal of the mechanism

For pens with reservoirs threaded at both ends you can extract the mechanism either by removing the knob, or the reservoir end-plug. For later pens, unless the rod can be unscrewed from the seal carrier, (not usually possible without risk of damage) there is no option but to remove the knob. This is not threaded on like the Onoto knob but a push-in fit, held by a hard rubber crosspin that it is sometimes quite difficult to locate.

First mark the alignment of rod and knob at the end and then punch out the pin only so far as is necessary to remove the knob. After removal of the spring (usually crimped to the rod and also corroded), withdraw the mechanism carefully through the front of the reservoir. The plunger rod is three pieces screwed together. It must be gently unscrewed after soaking/heating to allow replacement of the filler washer.

Whilst most Fords have left hand threaded piston components this must not be assumed. It seems likely that Fords changed at an early stage from right hand to left hand threads because of problems with early mechanisms becoming unscrewed. This change coincided with the introduction of the shorter carrier, which has the benefit of lengthened filling stroke (see Webnotes).

Replacing the barrel seal.

The cork seal at the top of the reservoir is held in a similar way to the Onoto pens and is removed using similar tools. Heat the hard rubber retaining ring and press the teeth of the extraction tool into it. Unscrew on a right handed thread. When the ring has been removed, the old cork seal can be picked out and the reservoir thoroughly cleaned.

Unscrewing the threaded ring that holds the cork barrel seal in place

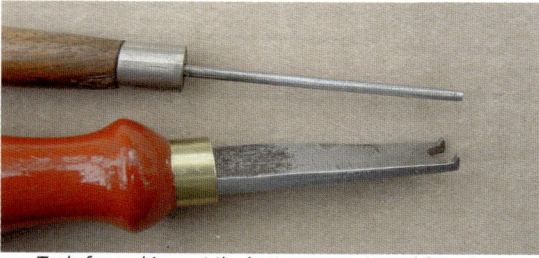

Tools for pushing out the button cross pin and for gripping the barrel seal retaining ring

A new seal can be made using a piece of good quality cork. First bore a hole slightly smaller than the piston rod diameter and then trim it with a sharp knife to the approximate finished external dimension. Mount it in a drill and hold it against sandpaper to achieve a good tight fit in the seal socket. Alternatively use a lathe to make a cork seal cutter. The seal can be replaced with an O-ring (3.7mm ID by 1.5mm), but you will have to make up a precision spacer to fill the rest of the seal socket. The O-ring must seal as well to the socket as it does to the rod so make sure that the socket is clean and smooth on the inside. The new seal should be fitted with silicone grease all around it. It is best to tighten up the retaining ring after refitting the piston rod.

The piston seal (and its replacement)

This can be cut from a 3mm thick sheet of cork to match the original, but this is a tricky operation, and would require a flawless piece of material. Clearly, Ford considered this seal to be a weak part of the design, because in order to extend the life of the seal, they recommended that the pen should be kept filled with water if it was not to be used for a while. We recommend that the piston seal be replaced with an O-ring because this will be longer asting and it will also give better performance. The old mount and washer can be discarded and a new mount made to the dimensions illustrated in the drawing and table.

A new unit is illustrated in the main picture. The new seal mount must be carefully finished on the front face because it must be able to make a good seal with the back face of the piston nose. If these two components do not mate properly the pen will not fill.

If the seal does not move reasonably easily within the chamber, fit the mount on a tapered mandrel in the lathe and use a round swiss file to deepen the

groove. The mount must also be able to slide easily on the rod during the pull stroke, and be free to slide back again to transfer ink above the seal during the push stroke.

Fit it with a trace of silicone grease. Remember to refit the spring and to crimp it onto the rod before replacing the knob. When the cap is screwed on, the barrel sleeve is drawn up further over the reservoir against the spring so that the piston nose seals the mouth of the feed to prevent the pen from leaking. This spring is often found corroded; replacement springs may be sourced from the mechanism of liquid soap dispensers. The length and strength of the spring is important.

If it is possible to push the section in a few mm against the spring, and it returns to its original position when released, then the spring is OK. If not, a stronger one should be fitted.

The nib/feed can now be adjusted for good ink flow.

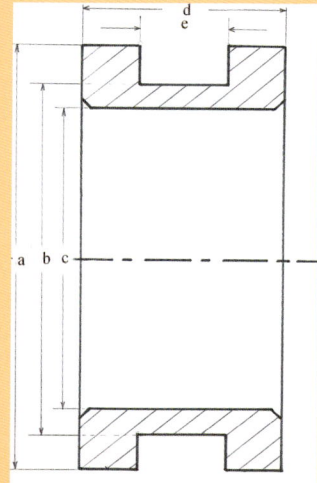

**New piston seal mount for the O-ring
-to be made from a durable plastic**

Dimensions (mm) of the O-ring seal mount

	Magnum	Standard	Lady
Chamber ID	10.7	9.5	7.7
a	10.2	8.5	6.5
b	8.1	6.9	5.2
c	5.8	5.8	4.5
d	4.0	4.0	3.5
e	1.8	1.8	1.7
sealID	8.0	6.5	5.0
Thickness	1.5	1.5	1.4

Replacing the ink chamber

The later style chambers are frequently found in unservicable condition due to cracks and broken ends. New chambers can be made faily easily on a screw cutting lathe. Clear acrylic (perspex/lucite) gives pleasing results but it is essential to use cast rather than extruded material in order to avoid later development of fine cracks. The internal boring must be carried out at slow speed with water. The ends are threaded 36 tpi.

The early chambers are simpler to make and should replace later ones if the end fittings are available.

Cap lip replacement

Ford caps have very thin lips so cracks and chips are common. Assuming there is a source of hard rubber stock the defect lip can be sawn off and replaced (see Section 3).

Filling the pen

Filling should not take more than three operations of the plunger, but if the pens are dry inside they may need persuasion to start. After servicing or long periods of non use the O-ring settles and may be reluctant to move. To get it moving push the plunger hard against the spring first rather than trying to pull it.

LADY FORD

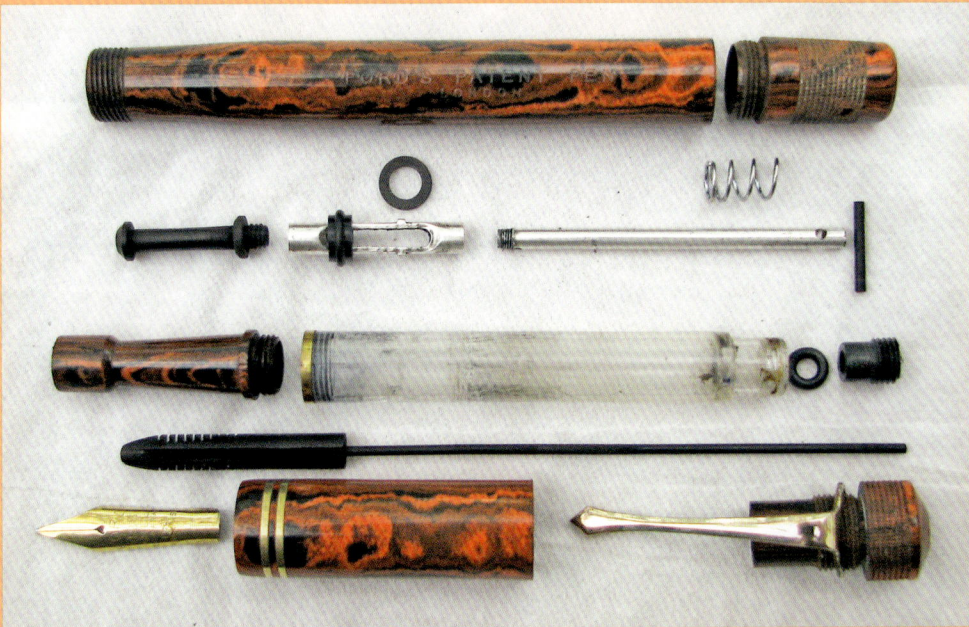

This small Ford was promoted for use by ladies and was particulary attractive with the outer case made from 'Cumberland' vulcanite - a popular name in the USA for red and black mottled hard rubber.
The construction of the internal components however were made from nickel rather than hard rubber. It is a more durable pen and easier to service. It is possible to use Onoto corks to service the end seal but otherwise servicing is as described previously.

Lady Ford pens had status. This one was formally presented to Ruby Murray the 1950s Irish singer as an award.

PULLMAN AND BRENNA

The Pullman was a novel button filler 'safety' pen made in metal with a thin plastic overlay in stunning colours. It was also made from black and mottled hard rubber. The 'pen' is hidden in the barrel and when the carrier tube is pushed the nib pops out through a hinged lid. When the carrier tube is pulled the nib disappears back into the barrel and the lid snaps shut. Although it was promoted in the UK it was most likely made in France by Meteore as was the Brenna pen. There were a few different designs and similar pens were made in Italy.

Problems

The instruction sheet states *'The Fountain pen must only be taken apart by a fountain pen expert'*

Mottle hard rubber with replaced brass screw and black Brenna

so perhaps problems were expected.

- the thin plastic coloured outer casing, on the metal barrelled pens, cracks. Black pens do not suffer this dramatic defect.
- the lid hinges break
- the lid casing pulls away from the top of the barrel
- pressure bars deform badly, often because they are refitted incorrectly
- lid actuating bars are easily dislodged
- the internal metal carrier tube deforms often by jammed or out of position actuating bars and pressure bars

Dismantling

There were two main models and in both cases the dismantling depends upon the state of the pen. e.g. a broken hinge or missing lid can make life easier!

The hard rubber barrel pen

If total dismantling is necessary the first step is to remove the linkage between the lid and the carrier bar. To do this it is easiest to remove the section to make access easier. The pen is extended and the section is either screwed or gently rocked to ease it out. If it is a simple job of sac replacement, and everything else works, the section can be resacced and screwed or pushed back into position making sure to line up the nib correctly. The button pressure bar need not be withdrawn in most cases.

With a hard rubber pen the lid is complicated because it has a hinged metal small cap which is screwed to a larger hard rubber disc. The actuating lever is fixed to this hard rubber disc. Removing the pin can be tricky but it has to be done unless it is easier to unroll the actuator bar lug. The bottom barrel bush in hard rubber (or brass) screws off in some cases but in others pulls out like the metal barrelled pens.

The metal barrelled pen

The same steps are taken but in this case the lid is larger and only metal. It is much easier to remove the tapered pin and then the pen holder can be pulled out through the bottom of the barrel. It requires a firm pull to extract the pen. In fact the carrier units can sometimes be pulled out without removing the lid actuating bar but this is not recommended as it at least deforms the inner carrier tube and can jam the mechanism entirely. With the carrier and barrel separate one can now repair the parts.

Hinge and lid problems

The majority of problems are with the lid and hinge and the two most severe are a broken hinge or when the hinge and lid casing has broken away from the barrel top.

Replacing a hinge

Remove the hinge frame after pushing or drilling out the two retaining pins.

The task is now to restore or make a hinge. The most frequent problem is that the hinge has torn off the frame but the lid hinge lugs are still in place. A neat job can be done with small diameter brass tube. It is easier to silver solder a slightly longer length than is required and then file to fit. Do not even think about soft solder because not only will the joint not be strong enough but it would not take the plating, which will be required.

If you are nervous about tackling a hinge, it is a simple job for a good silversmith.

The repaired lid unit can be refitted to the barrel top with new pins. Riveting is impractical; glue can be used but a better solution are 'jeweller' micro threaded pins which are then trimmed and polished. (Often lids are missing but it is not too onerous to make a lid from sheet brass, small diameter tube, using a doming punch and silver solder).

If the barrel top is broken away, which only happens with the hard rubber models, it will have to rebuilt and this is best done with a metal insert which

The top of the Brenna with replaced lid hinge and rubber sealing washer inside the lid. note the nib is ready to emerge

can be pinned in place. This then gives a stronger foundation for the hinge/lid frame.

Pressure bar/actuator bar

The pressure bar is a sophisticated triple bar which has an attached button and a bottom lug, thatfits into a slot in the carrier tube. If it is fitted badly it will become sprung and it is difficult to reset it without removing the rivets and refitting. Take care to line it up with the slot when refitting.

The lid actuator bar is frequently missing or twisted. Fortunately it is a simple shape and can easily be made from thin brass flat but make sure the length is correct.

Nibs and sections

There are both push and screw sections, but the dimensions are critical and they must align correctly into the carrier tube to retract 'just right' and extend with sufficient nib to write with. Never try and adjust the fitting by shortening the section otherwise the pen will not extend correctly.

Assembly

The carrier tube with the actuator bar in position is lined up with the groove in the hard rubber barrel or the stamped groove in the metal barrel and pushed into position. To ensure the actuator bar stays in position, fine brass wire is attached to the actuator lug so that it can be pulled as the barrel is pushed. The actuator bar is then fitted to the lid with a new tapered metal pin, which is then trimmed. Check the lid action and the position of the carrier tube when it is pulled out.

The brass/hard rubber barrel ring is screwed back on and the pressure bar and blind cap are fitted and the sacced section is pushed into place.

Testing

Make sure the mechanism works and that the nib clears the lid! It is easy to clip the iridium off a very expensive nib .

Please refer to the webnotes for recent activity restoring Brenna and Pullman pens

WEB
NOTES
www.........

PELIKAN

Early model 100

In 1929 Pelikan became the first to introduce a compact piston upfiller (syringe) method for filling a pen and that catalysed a worldwide activity in using this principle for filling. Conway Stewart, Conklin and almost reluctantly Montblanc became 'piston' pen makers, together with most German manufacturers. Pelikan used a screw thread to drive a piston up the barrel so that syringe action could take place without the inconvenience of a rod protruding from the barrel end.

Pelikan have a reputation for quality and responsive nibs (Arthur's favourite pen!). They have changed little over the last 80 years, although a collector might dispute this. From a repair standpoint, apart from changes in materials and a few design quirks, the mechanism is the same today as it was in 1929.

Servicing

There are three areas

- filling defects
- nib replacement
- body/cap/clip repair

Filling is undoubtedly the most significant challenge, so that will be the main focus.

Pelikan used cork seals until 1940 when they were replaced by rubber ones. These were used until the early 50's when plastic piston heads were fitted to the Pelikan 400s and 140s.

The early 100s and 100Ns.
Replacing the cork seals

We have emphasised elsewhere that rejuvenation is always a possibility with seals. This is less likely with dried out cork, but if the nib is easily screwed out, try soaking with warm water (about 40⁰C) and detergent.

If it is not effective then the mechanism must be removed from the barrel.

Removing the section is very difficult and unnecessary. The only action is to remove the nib to allow access of water to the inner workings during soaking.

Soak for a long period and then remove the barrel sleeves by holding them firmly with a rubber pad and pulling.

The most important feature is that the mechanism is screwed into the barrel on these pens and it has a left hand thread.

Heat should now be applied to the end of the barrel while slowly rotating and making sure that the heat is not too much. Never try to open an old Pelikan 100 without soaking and heating because the barrel threads are delicate and will break. (The later and bigger models (100Ns) are easier to handle, but they also need heat)

Take your time and be patient.

The mechanism should screw out by hand but section pliers may be required. Grip carefully and gently ease the threads. If necessary reheat and move a little at a time!.

With the mechanism out the next step is to change the cork seal.

The piston of the Pelikan 100 has a seal securing plug that is pushed tightly into the piston head. After removing the old cork ease the plug out.

Fit the cork (see Cutting cork seals) and secure it with the plug. Occasionally there are variations in the internal diameter of the barrel, but it is most important that the seal is tight in its final resting place (after filling)

The early Pelikan 100N piston is a special one because the cork is secured with a 'top hat' which unscrews with a left hand thread. Remove this and leave the supporting washer in place; measure the distance to the threaded area and cut the cork to fit (the piston seal shaft is slightly bigger than the one on the Pelikan 100 so the centre of the cork must be enlarged or it will split!)
Screw on the retaining 'top hat' and start the fitting procedure with razor blade and sandpaper. This fitting stage can be tedious but necessary. Repeat and repeat and repeat this process until a snug and smooth motion in the barrel is achieved.

Lubricating and treating the cork

Two early hard rubber piston holders; top-for the 100 and the lower 'top hat' screw unit for the 100N

Once the cork is a perfect fit, it must be impregnated with wax or soaked in liquid paraffin (the cork should not be removed from the piston for this treatment).
After drying off the excess, cover it in silicone grease and re-install it into the mechanism. Don't forget the left hand thread. If you had removed the sleeve before this work, push it on the barrel gently and tightly until it touches the mechanism, covering the metal ring of the barrel.

Later plunger systems using celluloid

Later 100s and 100Ns.

Pelikan modified the barrels of the 100s and the 100Ns in the early 40's and used celluloid for mechanisms rather than hard rubber. The elements of the piston rod and the screws driving the piston up and down had different inclinations. Dismantling the later 100s and 100Ns is similar to the early ones. It is easier with these models, because they are more robust.

The main problem is finding the spare gaskets. One approach is to adapt the shrunken gaskets of the bigger 100Ns to the smaller 100s by adjusting the diameter on a lathe or by using sandpaper. The piston rods are similar, so you don't throw away any parts! What is not useful today may be very useful tomorrow.

400s and 140s

The dismantling of 400s and 140s is different. Their mechanism is fitted into the barrel only by friction, so it must be pulled or knocked out.

Later model piston holders with rubber and plastic gaskets

Knocking out the mechanism with a wooden punch

Knocking it out

The nib has been removed, so after soaking and warming the barrel top, ensure that the piston is fully retracted. Insert a wooden punch, which is as big a diameter as possible (old knitting needles are ideal) and holding the pen in your hand, give the punch a sharp hit with a hammer.

If the barrel was well prepared, one or two strong hits will move the whole unit. The piston is easily replaced with a new or better one; or the piston gasket can be exchanged. It is not vital, but gluing on the replaced gasket will reduce the possibility of it being pulled off in use.

Before fitting the whole unit with the new piston, the gasket should be treated with some silicon grease to allow a smooth movement in the barrel.

Pulling the unit out

Before your muscular exercise prepare the barrel by soaking and warming.

Hold the turning button with a spongy rubber pad and grip the barrel with a rubber sheet. It is sometimes possible to pull the unit out of the barrel. If that doesn't work it is better to pull it out with section pliers while gripping the middle of the button to avoid breakage.

Nib Matters

The removal of nibs is usually straight forward as most screw out of the section; the nib and feed are held in a gripping collar, which can be removed. There are Pelikan pliers with fancy grooves and pronged 'gizmos' but we have never found these necessary. However, they no doubt have their supporters, but treatment with water warmth and patience repairs most pens!

Clips and caps

Another repair plus for Pelikan. Washer clips are so easy to exchange, replate or repair.

A restored early Pelikan 100 circa 1929

MONTBLANC PISTON FILLERS

The main components of a typical Montblanc 149

Montblanc has produced a huge range of filling systems, and within each category even more diversification. Specialist collectors will agonise over minute detail but the repairer is primarily concerned with getting things working. The bulk of Montblanc repairs that we receive in the UK are piston fillers, although there are vintage safety, lever and vacuum fillers around, we rarely see them. Consequently we are restricting our consideration of Montblanc to piston fillers.

Early piston fillers (pre 1936)
Prior to 1936 models such as 17½, 234 and 334 had similar pistons to the early Pelikan 100s. They are not fully attached to the rest of the mechanism and can be separated from it. The only difference is the threading on top of the piston head and the small female screw that holds the cork in place. Montblanc parts have right hand threading.

After removing the mechanism from the barrel, it is easy to remove the piston rod and replace the cork in the same way as for Pelikan pens. It is useful to clean the parts and apply some machine oil to the motion before putting it together after attaching the new cork seal to the piston head.

Telescopic mechanism and prewar piston fillers
In 1936 Montblanc patented a new piston system called " the telescopic mechanism" which consisted of two tubes, which allow the mechanism to be smaller, thereby creating more ink capacity.

The piston unit was a part of the mechanism and could not be removed from it. Many models used this system until the end of the 1950s These models are the whole Meisterstüchs 13x series with their variations.

Accessing through the open barrel end to replace the cork

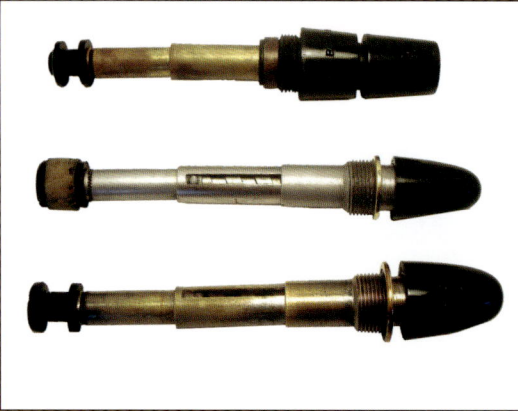

Three different telescopic mechanisms

The largest Montblanc for servicing

The section screws off

The securing flange screws off the piston head and the old cork seal can be removed and the piston head cleaned

The barrels of the 1930s' Montblanc piston fillers are very brittle and need special care while removing the mechanism. They must be soaked and agitated in the ultrasonic bath for a long time. Water has to penetrate all the parts.

Again heat is essential before attempting to screw out the unit. Gently try, and if no response, reheat and try again. As soon as you notice a movement, stop and heat it a short while again. This is really the only way to save a rare barrel.

If you are repairing a lot of Montblancs it is an advantage to have a spare piston of a later model at hand. This can be used for cutting the cork for the telescopic mechanism. The piston heads of Montblanc pens have the same dimensions, so it will not be necessary to modify the cork before changing pistons. (The manufacture of cork seals is discussed in Pelikan, Nozac and Seal Cutting).

Caution is necessary while putting the mechanism back into the barrel with the new cork. Since these barrels are fragile, do not put too much pressure on the mechanism while closing the threads. Reassembly with heat is strongly recommended together with silicone grease.

Telescopic mechanism and postwar Meisterstüch

The telescopic mechanism was used also in the post war Meisterstüchs like 142, 144, 146, 149 and their variations. In these pens replacing the cork seal or replacing the plastic gasket with a cork seal, one works through the 'business' end by first removing the section.

It is not always necessary to take out the mechanism. After removing the section the piston can be extended sufficiently out of the barrel to remove the old cork or the old plastic gasket.

The new cork cut on a spare piston can then be fitted and tested.

Many of the post war Montblanc joints were sealed with a pine resin (mastica resin) that petrified after so many years making it a challenge to open them. It is absolutely crucial to soak pens thoroughly and use heat.

It is desirable to remove the residual resin from the barrel with a thread chaser.

It is occasionally necessary to dismantle the mechanism as well. This can only be removed after the piston head has been withdrawn through the open barrel end.

Replacing plastic piston seals with cork

It is an opinion, but since cork is a much smoother material, it is actually better than plastic and we recommend to replace a plastic seal with a newly prepared cork seal. If this is to be done then a minor modification is required to the screw in order to accommodate the new cork. The new seal securing screw (female screw) should have a larger diameter than the regular ones in order to hold the cork in place. The whole mechanism should be cleaned and oiled before returning it back into the barrel, re-assembling and testing.

Pens with spiral driven pistons

These pens are 244s, 246s, 332s, 342s, 344s, 442s, 444s, the later version 232s, 234 1/2s, 334 1/2s and their variations.

These piston mechanisms can be removed from the barrel and fitted with a new cork seal outside of the barrel. The only way to get into the guts of the pen is by removing the section after the usual soaking and heating treatment. It is important to remove the residual pine resin from the section threads and from the threads inside the barrel. The cork is cut and shaped on the piston, and after checking the suction from the top, it will be put back into the barrel. This is a tricky process and needs some patience. First push the piston inside the barrel and find its alignment with the button thread, then pull it down by turning the button. After finding free motion in the barrel, push it up and stop almost 10mm before the top of the barrel threads. Push

the cork into the barrel and set it in its place on top of the piston head. Using tweezers, set the small female screw in place and tighten it. Check the suction with your finger and also the motion of the piston in the barrel before fitting the section into the barrel.

The later version 244s, 246s (like the tiger's eye and the grey laminated models) and the special model of the 234 1/2s with the Meisterstück clip have a slightly different piston which is made out of metal. Piston replacement is easier with these models.

Montblanc models from the 50s with plastic gaskets

Plastic gaskets were used in the early models of 14x series. If they work well leave them alone and do not bother changing them. But if they do not perform well and have to be repaired, it is advisable to replace them with cork.

The other models that are equipped with plastic gaskets are 252, 254, 256, 262, later version 342, 344 and the 042 Monterosa.

After the introduction of the series 12, 14, 22, 24, 32, 34 and their variations in the 60s, only plastic gaskets were used. All the pens produced after 1960 can also be repaired in the same way. The difficulty will be to find the spare parts needed.

Dismantling

This is quite easy. After the usual soaking, push the piston up sufficiently so that a pair of tweezers can grip onto the threads. Turn it anticlockwise. After a little resistance it will move. Just screw it out and remove the piston from the mechanism. You can now either change the whole piston or just remove the screw on top of the piston and replace the plastic gasket with one that is either unused or at least in working shape.

SOENNECKEN PISTON FILLERS

Attractive click lizard Sonnecken 111

There are three different Soennecken piston filler mechanisms.   While similar, each has a slightly different means of disassembly for repair.

Early mechanisms -Model 507 from the 1940s   These can be identified by having a separate turning knob and a middle section to which the piston assembly is attached. They do not have a clicking mechanism. The assembly is similar to those of the Montblancs with the early telescopic mechanism that has two separate pieces, like the MB 134.

Early piston mechanism

Disassembly
Soak the barrel in water to loosen the nib and section assembly and then unscrew it. Soak the barrel again in water to soften or dissolve the dried debris and then gently warm the turning knob end of the barrel with a heat-gun.
While holding the barrel with a rubber sleeve turn the mechanism unit clockwise (or hold barrel tightly and turn middle section anti-clockwise).

The mechanism will unscrew and the piston can be withdrawn.   Note that the piston has a brass bottom ring with a protruding thick pin which fits into a linear groove in the barrel.
Usually the piston assembly cork has to be replaced, so unscrew the retaining ring and remove the old cork. As with all piston pens cut and fit a cork that has been soaked in paraffin oil. Coat the cork with a small amount of silicon grease.

Reassembly
The piston is inserted into the barrel with the brass guide peg aligning with the groove in the barrel. Push the piston assembly as far as possible into the barrel and screw the threaded portion of the middle section into the barrel and tighten. Refit the nib and section unit after examining and cleaning

Second series mechanisms use a single turning knob assembly, to which the piston mechanism is attached. Again there is no clicking mechanism.

Note the lug

Disassembly
Soak the barrel in water to loosen the nib and the section assembly and carefully unscrew these from the barrel. Let water get into the barrel to make it easier to dismantle without strain. Ultrasonic, heat and patience! Again heat the end of barrel and internal threads near the turning knob and turn it anticlockwise to push the piston up towards the section. There will be a gap between the knob and the end of the barrel showing a cylindrical tube that is attached to the barrel with threads. Hold this piece with thin pliers

and turn it gently anticlockwise. Unscrew the mechanism and pull the piston out of the barrel. Unscrew the retaining ring and remove the cork and replace. Refitting the piston into the barrel is a process of turning and then moving back and turning the collar again like most safety and piston pens. Refit the nib and section.

Piston systems for later models

Click filler mechanisms 111 Extra, 22 Extra, Superior and Lady.

Loosen the nib and section assembly and then soak the barrel again in water to permit water to lubricate the inside of the barrel. With a heat-gun warm the barrel and internal threads near the turning knob.

Pull the spring loaded knob assembly in a direction away from nib. Often there is a strong spring pressure, which must be overcome. (Unlike the 1 series, there are two protruding keys that engage into two slots on the end ring of the piston mechanism). This causes the clicking sound when they engage. To disengage, pull the turning knob against spring force and turn counter clockwise. Then while continuing to pull on the knob, grip the area between the turning knob and the end of the barrel with narrow serrated medical pliers. Holding tightly, turn the barrel clockwise (or hold barrel tightly and turn the middle section anti-clockwise). The mechanism can be unscrewed from the barrel and the piston withdrawn. The piston has a brass bottom ring with a protruding thick pin which fits into a linear groove in the barrel.

Cork replacement is as per normal and the piston is inserted, aligned and the threaded portion of the turning knob can be tighten by hand. Finally pulling laterally on the turning knob, use the slim pliers to tighten the piston and turning knob assembly.

Refit the nib and section assembly.

Pull back top button to grip turning knob

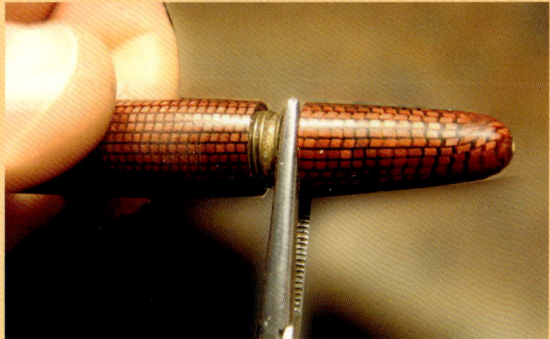

Twist anticlockwise (right hand thread)

Refit the piston unit

DUNN

A typical Dunn - characterised by the black barrel and red filler button

The 1920 Charles Dunn patent (US 1,359,880) was a key milestone in fountain pen design, being technically superior to anything offered by the major pen manufacturers at that time. The Dunn is a single seal pen looking like a syringe filler, but it actually belongs to the same class of pen as the Vacumatic, and is the first we are aware of to demonstrate the principle of a breather tube linked to the ink channel. In this class of pen, filling relies on cyclical variation of the air volume in the barrel; the Dunn achieves this by moving a hollow piston rod. When the piston is raised, the reduction in air pressure causes ink to enter through the ink channel. Although some of the ink is returned the same way on the down stroke, a greater volume of air is expelled down the breather tube because air flows more easily through the channels than ink does. It takes about 6 cycles to fill the barrel.

Problems

- The barrel seal is worn
- The piston rod is damaged
- The knob is broken so that the end of the piston rod is not properly sealed
- The knob will not thread into the barrel
- The breather tube is blocked/broken

Special tool for turning the guide ring and barrel seal retaining ring

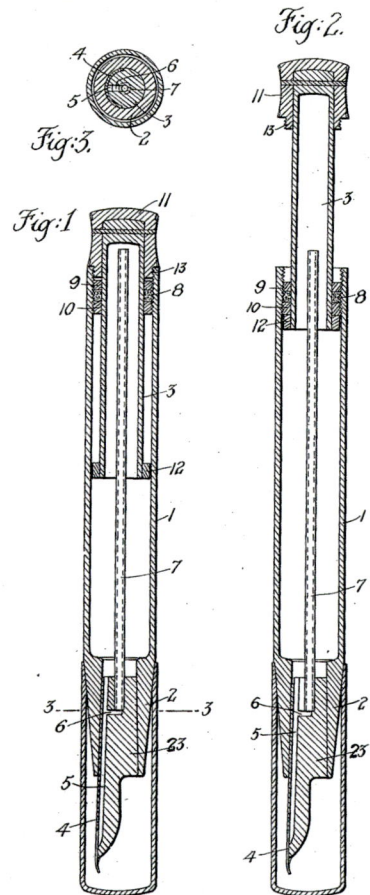

The 1920s patent- Note the breather tube linked to the ink channel and the hollow pistons by which the air volume is cyclically varied in filling.

Servicing

First the section must be removed (36tpi r/h thread). Unless the pen is damaged, servicing is limited to replacement of the cork barrel seal. As with the Onoto, there are two ways of doing this – with and without the piston in place. If the pen barrel is in a fragile state and/or the piston cannot be removed, the split seal technique is the only option (see Onoto).

The piston can be removed from either end of the barrel. The piston head is a guide ring and end stop (not a seal), and it is screwed r/h to the piston rod. It normally has four flats filed on it, and these may be engaged using two fine bladed tools pushed down the barrel to prevent the ring from rotating as the piston is unscrewed.

Alternatively, a special tool can be made consisting of a thin walled cylinder with a toothed edge. It is well worthwhile making this tool because it is also useful in removal of the barrel seal retaining ring. If the guide ring will not unscrew, the knob will have to come off. Knobs were made in a number of materials, including casein, red hard rubber, celluloid and bakelite. Some are now very fragile and they are difficult to replace because they screw into the end of the barrel to prevent movement of the piston during normal use of the pen. Most are held on with a stainless steel pin 0.85mm in diameter. Following removal of the pin (using a pin punch), the knob may be unscrewed (usually 48tpi l/h thread, but some earlier pens have r/h thread) following gentle heating – not too much heat because the piston is thin-walled hard rubber and is easily distorted.

The piston should have a small plug of wax in the end to prevent leakage from the knob joint and pinholes. With the piston out, access can be gained to the cork seals beneath a threaded ring (36tpi r/h thread). The ring can be removed with the tool illustrated, or with the end of a triangular file. New cork seals will have to be made (see seals). Before these are fitted, make sure that the recess is clean and lined with a film of silicone grease. It is easier to fit the piston from the rear, provided the tool is available to fit the guide ring within the barrel. Fitting from the front will require a rod to guide and push the piston through the seal.

The Dreadnaught cap is in two parts. The pen is filled with the bottom part in place so the section does not get inked and the nib is protected from damage

Proper fitting of the knob is important because any leaks will prevent filling and cause flooding during writing. Sealant must be used on the screw thread and the pinholes. The wax plug in the end of the piston should, ideally, be replaced to create the first line of defence. Check for leaks by immersing the knob end and blowing through the barrel.

Some later pens have two holes behind the guide ring (not specified on the patent). These are to reduce the syringe effect on the down stroke so that less ink is returned to the bottle. Pens with these holes therefore fill in fewer cycles. The ink capacity of the Dreadnaught is 2.65ml.

The standard model and the 'Dreadnaught'

CHILTON

Dismantled small Chilton with waxed wound cotton thread seal exposed and friction brass connector

The Chilton Pen Co spun out of Seth Crocker's Boston company. The blow filler was the foundation for the mechanical pneumatic system adopted for the Chilton pens. Some of the 1930s Wingflow pens were stunning.

Principle

The sac is compressed by pressure from a plunger pump system. The outer barrel in early models is pulled back and then pressed firmly down with the end hole sealed with a finger. Removing the finger releases the barrel pressure and the sac pulls in ink. In later models an internal tube attached to an end button is withdrawn and pressed down with the same effect. The sealing system, except for early hard rubber pens, used waxed thread wound around the brass internal tube.

Problems

- does not fill
- barrel cracks
- pen pulls apart

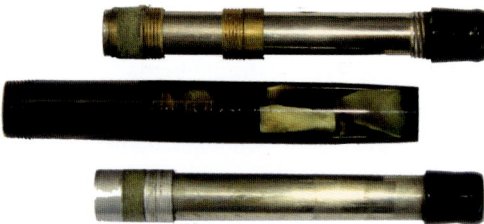

Later model illustrating different materials for friction connectors

Dismantling

The section is a screw fit and easily removed. Residual sac debris must be removed and the tube vent must be clear.

Early models (*hard rubber*) - the extended barrel is a close fit and needs only grease to make a seal. It should not need futher work but if it does it can be separated by heating the barrel by rotating it over a heat gun and with patience the parts will separate.

Later models (*plastic*) - the same procedure will separate the tube with top button from the barrel. In both cases it is practical to have the heat gun clamped in order to use both hands for rotating and pulling.

The connector design varied; some used one two or three brass rings and aluminium was also used.

Later model ready for seal rewinding

Examination and repair

Look carefully for cracks, which will either require sealing (difficult!) or replacement (preferred). The waxed thread is usually in good condition but if badly frayed or missing can easily be replaced. Polyester/cotton mix has been suggested by Victor Chen and it is important to ensure that the thread is well impregnated with wax/grease. Soak the coarse dernier thread in liquid paraffin and then dip in melted wax; work it well into the fibre. Wind round the base of the tube, to give a seal of about 6mm passing the thread under the last loop to pull tight.

Reassembly

This should be done with heat and the parts are pushed together; in later models ensure the button is flush when secured.

CAUTION *If the end button is damaged then it will have to be removed and this is not an easy task as the plastic has usually shrunk. Also the tube is knurled to ensure good attachment. You may have to remake a top button.*

CONKLIN NOZAC

The Nozac syringe mechanism appeared in 1931. It operates with a metal spiral and a carrier tube. Conklin adopted the Pelikan design with a filler that could collapse on itself, thereby halving the length of a simple syringe. There were a number of variants but all essentially had the same innards.

Servicing

The Nozac is an easy pen to service because the single seal can be accessed from the section end. First remove the section, remembering that it is threaded into the barrel and that a sealant was used to prevent leaking. By turning the knob in an anticlockwise direction, the piston section will come to the mouth of the barrel and can be removed with an anticlockwise twist.

Making a cork seal

The cork seal will probably have gone hard, so it must be cleaned away together with any residual adhesive. A new cork seal is not difficult to make; there is information in 'Cutting Seals' and in chapters on piston pens. All that is needed is a good quality piece of cork, a sharp craft knife, a small rat-tail file and an electric drill.

First cut a slice about 10mm square to the correct thickness and make a small hole in the centre. Enlarge the hole with the file to the right diameter. There seems to be no way to remove the piston end so make a radial cut so that the cork can be clamped and glued in position. Finishing it to the right outer diameter can be accomplished by trimming with the knife and then by mounting it in the drill and holding a piece of glass paper against it. Then treat the cork with wax, liquid paraffin and silicone grease. The seal should not be too tight in the barrel – just tight enough to be effective.

Before final fitting and reassembly remember to clean out the inside of the barrel to restore transparency, and smear a little silicone grease inside. Fit the section with a little shellac.

Modification

Some restorers fit rubber seals that must be stretched over the piston end. They work well for a limited period but rubber seals can harden or

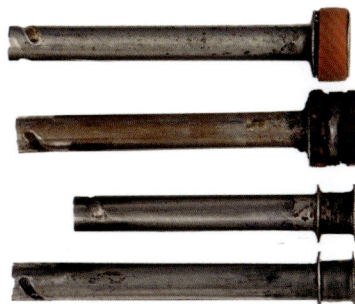

Variety of of pistons dismantled for spares; note the different lengths; the rubber and double cork seals ; two pistons without seals

stick to the plastic wall.

Twist mechanism

Accessing the pen via the section end assumes that the filler button will turn. Often it will not, even after soaking and heating, so the button must be removed. The knob is fixed to the shaft with a metal pin that is easily pushed out with the shank end of a small drill bit. With the knob off, the end of the piston rod can be tapped lightly to get the seal moving. It is then straightforward to dismantle, clean, replace parts and grease the components.

A A WATERMAN

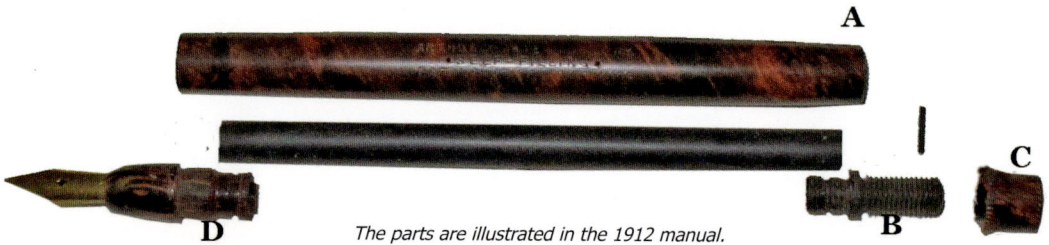

The parts are illustrated in the 1912 manual.

Arthur Waterman's twist filler was an adaption of Moseley's 1859 patent and was very popular in the first decade of the C20th. The sac is twisted by rotating the knob at the end of the barrel; with the pen immersed and the knob released ink flows into the sac/tube. Twist filler repair is interesting and not difficult.

Problems

Frequent twisting ages the sac quickly

Dismantling

The nib/section and the screw plug must be removed. Contrary to Frank Dubiel's manual, we have never found this an easy task. Older pens have section wear due to repeated sac replacement and there is a tendency for the section to rotate. To eliminate this a section may have been seriously glued, and if this is the case, it can be a problem.However if you are lucky and section removal is not a problem it can then be cleaned ready for resaccing.

The screw plug has to be removed and the first step is to remove the metal pin from the button. Mild steel pins rust and cause the pin to swell, so soak and warm before attempting to knock out the pin. The end unit can then be screwed out of the barrel with a long thin screwdriver (l/h thread). This plug should be cleaned.

Repair

Use a 14/15 sac (at least 70mm) long and cut to the required length. This is determined by placing the parts beside the barrel and measuring the distance between the end flanges. The sealed end of the sac is cut very near the end so it acts as a necked sac when it is fixed to the plug. Glue the sac with super glue or shellac (the grooved plug facilitates good adhesion). The sac selected should be reasonably thin and elastic. The end is then screwed (l/h) using a screwdriver inserted into the recess of the plug. Fix the turning knob on with a pin and screw down until flush with the barrel top.

The sac is pulled out of the open end and secured with gripping tweezers. The section unit is then attached to the exposed tube and left to set before the tweezers are removed. A dab of shellac should secure the section from turning. The pen is then ready for filling.

Modern Repair Department PRICE LIST(1912)

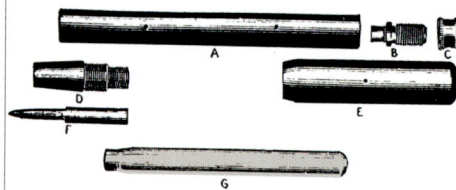

Parts of Modern Self-Filling Fountain Per

		Nos. 20 to 40.	Nos. 50 to 80.
A	Barrel	$ .60	$1.00
B	Screw plug		
C	Button	.25	.25
D	Section	.50	.85
E	Cap	.25	.35
F	Feed	.30	.50
G	Sac	.25	.25

FITTING AA WATERMAN SAC

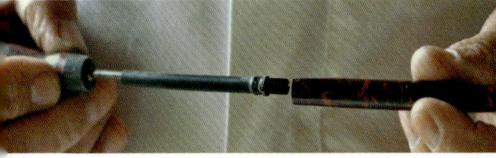

Unscrew end plug with a thin driver

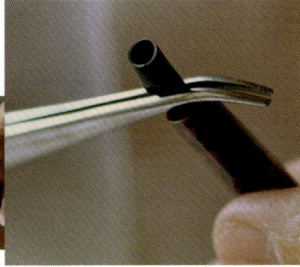

Use of sprung tweezers to aid fitting section/sac

EAGLE

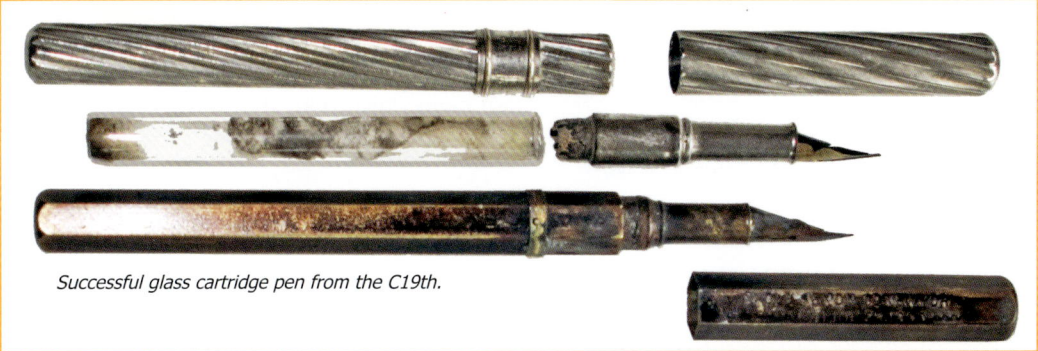

Successful glass cartridge pen from the C19th.

Pen manufacture was started in 1887 as a diversification from pencils. Henry Berolzheimer who, with two others, founded the Eagle pencil company, shortened his name to Berol and that is still with us today! Many of the products were quite innovative. The early glass cartridge pens were well received and sold in Woolworths and their range included stylos, lever fillers and unusual fillers such as the Eagle Flash. This pen has a lever system, which presses a bar into the sac when the top button is pushed in. When coloured pens became fashionable they produced 'look-alikes' at a fraction of Parker and Sheaffer prices. In the 1930s the Epenco brand was established; these are rarely found outside the USA and are a mixed bag of great coloured pens, which are often deformed.

Eagle Flash pen

Eagle utility pen with J-bar, simple lever with C-clip and with a 14kt nib

EAGLE 'FLASH' Self filling Pen

YOUR finger never touches ink or any ink-filling contrivance. You press the button at top of pen and by this simple operation the "Flash" fills in a flash. Impossible to spill the ink or stain the fingers. The Flash can be refilled wherever you are and from any ink-well in reach—no filler to carry. No spilling—leaking or blotting. Guaranteed to write the instant it touches the paper. All Eagle "Flash" Fountain Pens are supplied with the celebrated Eagle 14 Karat

ESTERBROOK

Red/black mottle vulcanite English made eyedropeper (1930s) and 'ReNew-point' calligraphy model

In 1859 Richard Esterbrook successfully persuaded five craftsmen from the firm of John Mitchell to accompany him to the USA, where he established a small nib-making workshop in Camden, New Jersey. The development of the Esterbrook Steel Pen Manufacturing Co was rapid, and by the 1950s, Esterbrook could claim to be one of the world's major pen makers.

The main activity was US based but the famous Esterbrook Relief nibs were introduced into England in 1886. The company's move into fountain pens was probably in the early 1900s, and by 1922, manufacturing had begun in the UK. 12 fountain pen models were available in three styles: a slip-cap eyedropper, a safety-screw cap eyedropper and a lever-filler, all imprinted 'R Esterbrook & Co, Relief. In 1933 the first three English-made Relief lever-filling models were available, all with a red band above the clip washer. Two more models were also made, with a patented stud-filling mechanism.

Repair of these is straight forward, as they were made by Conway Stewart and so follow all the guidelines given for lever, button and pump. Relief pens had the advantage of a simple ring clip and for some reason the thumb tabs on the levers seem more robust.

In 1938, new Relief models were introduced but more significantly the 'ReNew-Point' models with unscrewable 'Duracrome' nibs (which were imported from the US).

This was a major step forward in replacement repair. After the war the Esterbrook 'ReNew Point' range was promoted in the US and became a popular school and office pen.

By the early 1950s Conway Stewart were manufacturing Relief lever pens-identical in style and colours to the Conway Stewart 58, 24, 27 and 28 except with Relief nibs and 'R' logos on the diamond-ended clips. These Conway Reliefs were probably only available for four or five years. The last Conway Relief to be marketed (c1955) was probably the No 12, with 2 cap bands.

Problems
- Broken clips and levers
- Cracked inner cap
- nib damage

Repair and servicing
The repair of the Relief range is identical to Conway Stewarts.

1930s slim Relief with red trim band and R on lever and Relief stamped on clip; cracked ice Relief piston based on the Conway stewart 80

The 'ReNew-point' lever fill models have the basic repair issues of pressure bar/lever, sac, clip and nib unit.

Filling system. The section is a push fit and rarely gives problems in dismantling. Removing the pressure bar from models before 1945 requires a screwdriver and a pair of long nosed pliers. The standard bar is a double J-bar and can be released by twisting a screwdriver on the bar. Do not do this if the barrel has an acrylic sac support liner. In this case it is usually possible to withdraw the acrylic liner and pressure bar with an appropriate hooked dental pick or long nosed pliers.
When refitting a pressure bar to the later models with acrylic sac support make sure the pressure bar lines up correctly.
The lever is easily removed by pressing down on the C-clip and, after turning 90^0, it exits through the barrel slot. Replacement involves the same actions but in reverse.

Clip

This is fixed on by a crimped brass tube over the clip flange. For clip replacement the broken clip remnants must be removed. First remove the inner cap and then ease off the black plastic plug. (Sometimes the inner cap is polythene, sometimes acrylic, which usually cracks as it is removed. Replace it with hard rubber or nylon).
 The crimped tube can be prised up with a flat dental pick. Pulling gently and more prising will release the clip remnants. To refit a donor clip, first refurbish the brass tube by rolling it straight again on a suitable bar. Assemble the items and recrimp the brass to the clip. One way to crimp the clip in position is to use an appropriate sized/shaped nut with a taper and, with a screw headed bolt inside the cap and through the brass tube and clip, tighten the nut.

Nib

The nib unit screws out and the nib can be knocked out of the bushing to replace the feed if required.

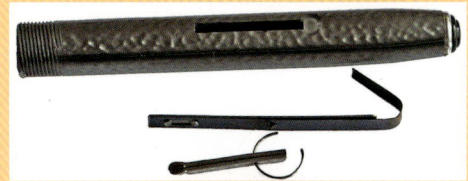
Lever, C-clip and barrel

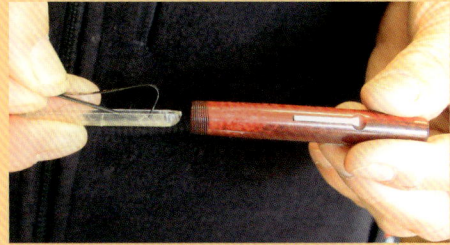
Fitting the pressure bar with acrylic sac support

Components of clip/securing system

Nib and feed in threaded bush

Demonstrator showing inner cap and sac support

JAPANESE PISTON

This type of pen, apparently rather similar to the Onoto, is usually thought to be an eyedropper with a piston rod merely to provide an ink cut-off facility. However they can be self fillers when the right filling technique is adopted.

Filling occurs on the up stroke by the displacement principle. As the rod is withdrawn through the barrel seal, the air space is increased, so the pressure is reduced. The volume of ink entering to equalise the pressure is equal to the volume of the rod withdrawn. If the knob is pushed down again, the ink is returned to the bottle, but if the pen is removed and held nib upwards, ink runs away from the ink channel and only air is expelled as the piston is pushed back in. The pen is returned to the bottle and the cycle repeated about six times to fill the barrel completely.

Although a little inconvenient as a filling technique, the method can be used with other pens, particularly when a piston seal has failed. As an example, the piston seal from an Onoto 6233 was removed and the above method was used to fill it. The ink capacity using the displacement filler technique was 1.8ml, whereas with a good piston seal using the proper one stroke down-filling technique, the pen held 1.45ml. The advantage with the displacement method is that the whole barrel can be filled.

Servicing

These are simple pens, but it is not usually possible to remove the filler knob in order to change the cork barrel seal. The split seal technique as described for the Onoto has to be used.

UTILITY PENS

A professional repairer must be ready to deal with any pen, even if the quality of the item may frequently make the repair cost greater than the market value of the pen. Many pens are deeply personal items and the sentimental attachment to a father, mother or spouse's pen can outweigh any pecuniary value. Such items are usually more tax-ing than a standard collector's pen.

Problems

- shrinkage of plastic
- broken clips, levers and feeds
- rusted corroded nibs

Examination

The repair approach with such pens is to try and preserve as much of the original pen as possible. Don't waste too much time. Adopt a replacement strategy that will preserve the outer but make a working pen. Usually a better quality feed and nib will make a big difference so upgrade to a second hand gold nib; use push in J-bars with levers and Parker aero sac covers if they fit. These pens are a creative challenge but the customer is usually ecstatic with the result.

A typical cheap pen in plastic that deforms, a lever that fits badly and a steel nib - but to someone it meant something to someone with the cap top image of a young Princess Elizabeth

OMAS AM87

This elegant modern pen with a burr wood overlay is a piston filler. The piston, attached to a coarse threaded spiral, is moved by rotating a fine threaded turning knob. One rotation of the knob will drive the piston down the length of the barrel. The piston will only drive up and down if it is does not rotate and this is prevented by a peg within the barrel. This is similar to the Mabie Todd button bar, except that a piston is driven rather than a pressure bar. This example suffered from a broken peg so the piston would not move. The peg before it was broken off was an integral part of the barrel liner, which unfortunately could not be withdrawn. Consequently the effective solution was to drill a hole from the outside and glue in a brown plastic replacement peg.

GLASS NIBBED PENS

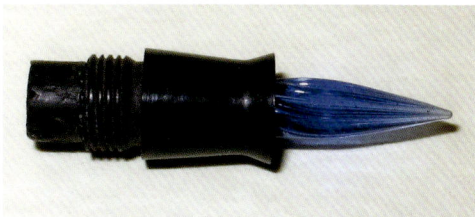

Glass nibbed dip pens were very popular in the C19th and nibs as illustrated have been used in self filling pens for over 100 years. The advantage of cost is offset by their fragility but they were used extensively during the wars. The rigidity of the nib was a great advantage when carbon copies were required, and they were sometimes referred to as glass manifold nibs.

The diameter of a glass nib is typically similar to a 4.5mm feed.

Repair

Small chipped edges can be smoothed with a green grit-grinding wheel but replacement is usually necessary. Warm the section and knock the old nib out. The section should be heated and the new nib immediately pushed into the section to get a good seat. If ink flow is too great then the section might require heating again and the nib pushed in further.

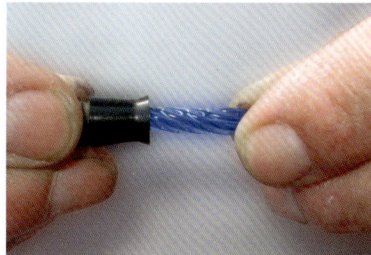

SAFETY PENS

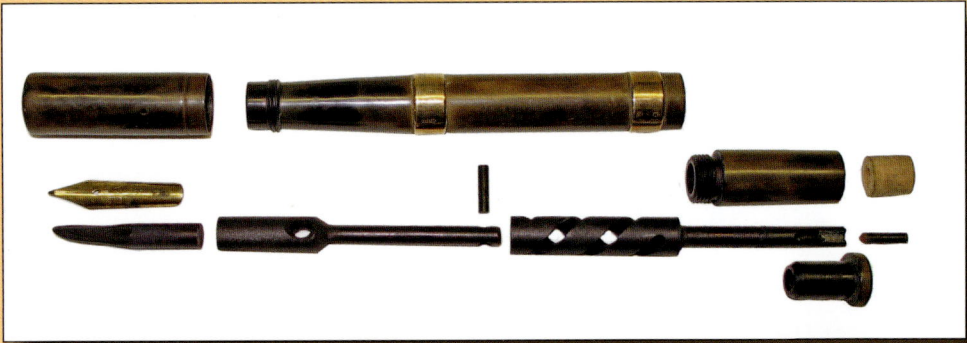

Waterman Safety 42 SF; quite a robust pen and strong spiral

Safety pens use the barrel as the ink reservoir and have a retractable nib. The pen is filled with an eye-dropper and the cap acts as the ink seal when not in use. When the pen is to be used the cap is removed with the barrel in a vertical position, open end at the top. After the pen is full of ink the nib is propelled into position by turning the end of the barrel. The section of the pen seals on the inside of the barrel end to prevent ink leakage.

There are a number of internal variations of the sealing system and nib/feed holder with different safety pens, but the differences are minor.
The majority of safety pens extend by turning, but the Moore safety pen uses a slide system.

The Propelling Mechanism

The mechanism for propelling the section/nib unit consists of a turning knob and a hard rubber spiral linked to a nib/feed holder via a propelling rod with a spiral follower. The 'spiral' peg also locates in a groove in the barrel to ensure the pen propels straight and does not spiral out. The turning knob passes through a sealing unit, which screws into the main barrel.

The propelling train (turning knob to nib) is a fragile unit that often requires repair. It can be withdrawn as a whole unit and serviced.

Main problems

- cork seals deteriorate and the pen leaks at the 'turning knob'
- the pen nib does not propel out because the internal mechanism has ceased to work (most likely because the spiral has broken or the pin has deteriorated.)

- the nib is damaged usually by attempting to propel the nib with the cap on
- the pen leaks in use

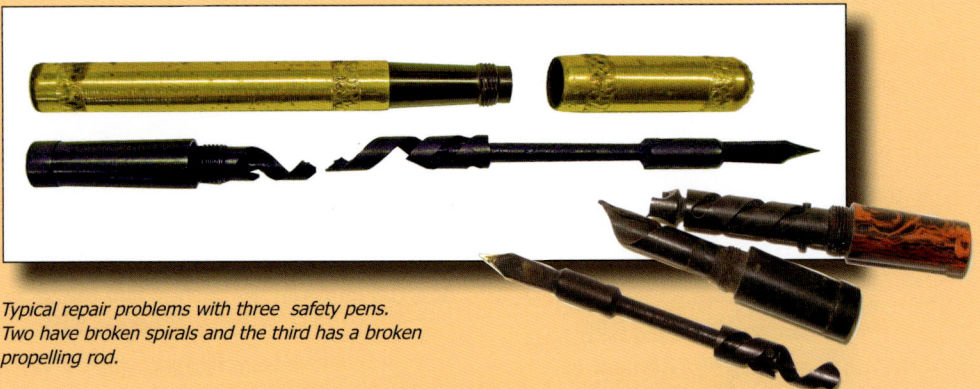

*Typical repair problems with three safety pens.
Two have broken spirals and the third has a broken propelling rod.*

Dismantling

Removing the propelling train

The aim is to remove the working unit and the first step is to soak the pen internally. This is best done by removing the cap and in a vertical position fill it using an eye dropper and a mild alkaline detergent mix. Leave the pen for at least five or six hours, preferably overnight. Do not try and turn a safety pen which has dried out as you will definitely strain it and possibly even break the delicate spiral.

After soaking attempt to remove the seal unit. Gentle warming will soften shellac if it has been applied to the threads. First check to see if the turning knob moves; if it does then you can begin to unscrew the seal unit. If it does not then it might be seized because of deteriorated cork or dirt or, more sinister, it might be jammed because of a broken spiral or solidified debris. This might impair the removal of the spiral system so try again with ultrasonics; even penetrating oil can sometimes work. It is not the end of the world if the knob will not turn, particularly if the seal unit unscrews easily, and most of them do. Take care towards the end of the threads as the pins sometimes are dislodged and can jam.

If the safety pen has an overlay, like many attractive Italian and French pens, then soft jawed rubber section pliers are essential to avoid damaging the tapered end. With sufficient warming and soaking most units unscrew without section pliers.

Dismantling the parts

Once the working unit is out of the barrel it can be dismantled into the component parts to check and service them.

Three different barrel ends and tracking grooves

Removing the nib/feed carrier

The examples illustrated have a tubular holder with an ink access hole. The holder acts as a section and accepts a nib and a short feed in the normal way. This nib/feed carrier is either machined from a hard rubber rod (which is integral with the propelling shaft) or is a separate shaft pinned to the holder. The end of the holder

The nib holders vary

is profiled to seal at the barrel opening, when the nib is exposed. The nib and feed can usually be extracted by pressing a conical wedge into the ink access hole.

The Whytwarth has a sliding collar for the nib and a collar to effect a seal on the barrel. In this case the feed is the propelling shaft.

A black hard rubber Whytwarth

Three Waterman style turning knobs, pinned eccentrically with a hard rubber rod

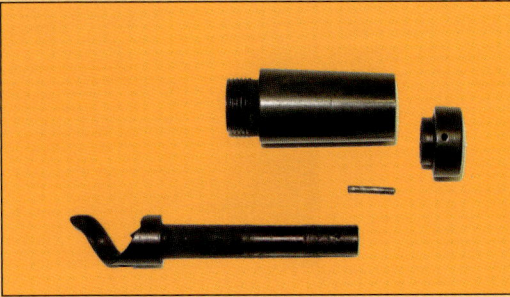

Turning knob with a push on fixture to the spiral shaft; fixed with a metal pin

Grooved punch for knocking out the spiral shaft

The spiral/propelling shaft

In all cases the propelling shaft engages the spiral with a hard rubber pin. This can be a long pin which extends through the shaft and has a double bearing surface on the spiral, or it can be a short pin with a single contact. This pin extends about 1mm in order to fit into the guide slot in the barrel. If the pin is broken it is possible to use a metal pin but plastic knitting needles are a good source of material to avoid corrosion.

Removing the turning knob/spiral

The spiral is attached to the turning knob so it must be disconnected in order to access the cork seals. As with the nib holder, some spirals are attached to the turning knob by a steel pin through the spiral (Whytwarth). In other cases the spiral is integral with the turning shaft (Watermans and most French and Italian safety pens) and is pinned or wedged to the turning knob. The Swan and Blackbird safeties have a turning knob, which accepts a D shaped profile turning shaft.

Removing metal pins requires care and precision. The staking tool is ideal but if a punch and hammer is used make absolutely certain that the spiral is firmly supported otherwise it will crack.

Corrosion of metal pins is a serious problem because it can cause breakage of the shafts if the pins are punch driven without warming or preliminary probing to loosen the pin. It may be necessary to drill other pin holes.

Small French safety from the 1930s

With the Waterman unit (and most French pens) the shaft is fixed by a hard rubber rod, which fits into a keyway in the spiral shaft. The shaft must be knocked out and it is easy to make a suitable punch from a nail as illustrated. When the shaft is knocked through, the turning knob pulls out to reveal the cork seals.

It may be necessary to replace a broken spiral; if the correct spare is not available it will be necessary to adapt other spirals to fit with the use of pins and joints.

Knocking out spiral

Special lathe tooling is required to produce a new spiral but given the correct diameter stock tube one can be made by hand. Begin by measuring the perpendicular distance between the grooves, then cut a strip of masking tape to this width. Wrap the tape spirally so that the edges come together. Drill through the wall to the start and finish of the spiral and saw on the tape joint between the two holes. For a double spiral (pens with twin tracking grooves)use double width tape and saw also along the mid line of the tape. Widen the slot with a Swiss file to suit the drive pins - not easy but could save your pen.

Replacing the cork seals

Pen diameters vary but the spiral shafts are reasonably uniform. Corks can be turned on the lathe or with a drill against a surface grinder and then fitted into the seal compartment with a little silicone grease (see Making Seals). The spiral shaft is refitted and the top repinned or the key pushed back in place.

Reassembling the pen

The nib is fitted and the propelling shaft engaged with the spiral. The 'train' is now fed into the barrel ensuring that the drive pin lines up with the barrel slot. The unit should slide in easily. If not then you may have cut the replacement pin too long and it will require shortening. Do not force anything at this stage otherwise you will stress the spiral.

The seal unit should screw in easily. It is necessary to retract the nib, then screw the seal unit, then retract, then screw the seal unit and so on until the end unit is tight.

The pen should now be tested for leaking at the seal end and in the writing mode.

Safety pens do work; at times it seems as if they are bound to leak in use but it is always a surprise that they do not. The biggest problem is forgetting that they are safety pens and unscrewing the cap with the pen not in an upright position.

There are a lot of attractive overlays on safety pens, mainly from Italy and France. The Whytwarth range of silver and enamelled overlays are much sought after.

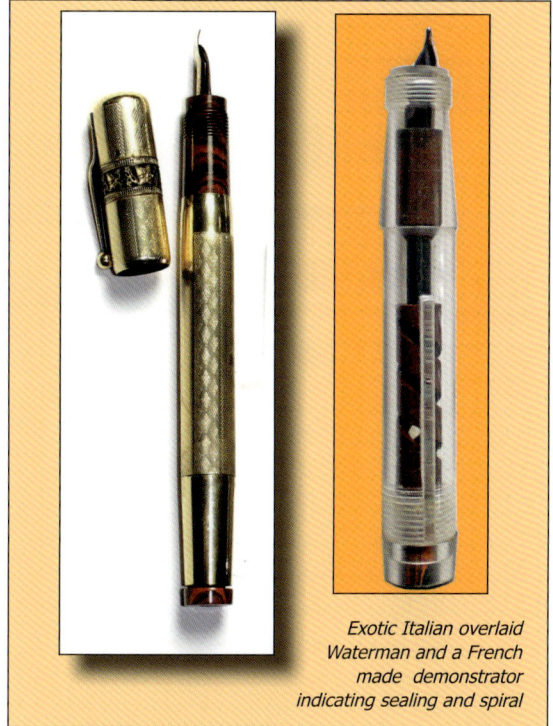

Exotic Italian overlaid Waterman and a French made demonstrator indicating sealing and spiral

a collection of safety parts

Rare Mabie Todd Safety pen

STYLOGRAPHIC PENS

Mabie Todd ; typical design of economic priced stylo. Cylinder body has an inner tube to which a rod and sprung needle is attached. The tube and rod are push fits, secured by shellac

Stylograph Co of Rhode Island with intricate turned 3 piece end unit with needle point and separate spring push fitted into tubular holder. The end vent unit screws off.

These pens are very significant in the history of fountain pens as they were the first pens to be produced in large quantities in hard rubber. Most collectors are aware of the early Cross and McKinnon pens but perhaps do not appreciate that Companies such as Conway Stewart, Onoto, Mabie Todd and French and German companies made 'stylo' pens well into the 1950s. Rotring, Tintenkuli and Staedtler are still popular as drawing pens.

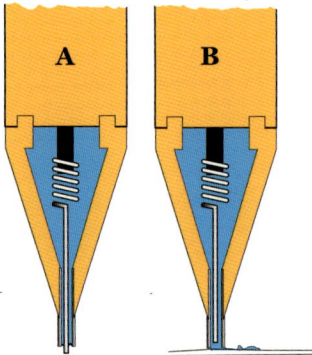

Ink starts to flow as the needle is displaced by the paper.

Principle

A 'stylo' feeds ink to the paper through a thin nozzle feed tube. Flow is controlled by a thin rod or wire moving up and down within this tube.

In a static state (A), ink is retained within the tube by surface tension but when the inner wire is moved it disturbs the equilibrium and ink is pulled out on to the paper (B). The line on the paper is a parallel line, the same thickness as the feed tube diameter. When the pen is lifted from the paper the ink flow stops, as the wire moves back to its original position.

Two common designs are used:
- a 'spring point' which retained its 'at rest' position by having part of the point coiled into a spring

- a 'gravity point' which kept its position by being attached to a heavy lead slug.

Problems

- inner wire jammed/broken or missing
- outer tube squashed
- self filling system does not work

Dismantling and repair

This depends upon the model but many stylographic pens are eyedroppers, they simply unscrew at the cone end.

The majority of stylos do not work because the wire is deformed or does not move properly in the nozzle feed tube. A new wire sprung unit can be made and fitted. It is easy to make a spring on a lathe by slowly rotating a steel rod and wrapping the wire under tension around the rod. In some stylos the wire is pushed on to a peg but in other examples it is pinned or pushed into a tube. Gravity stylos have a lead or heavy plug with a fine wire moulded into it. These can also be made by casting a wire into solder.

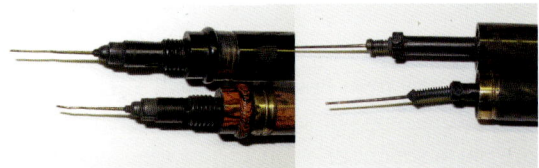

Needle points of early Stylograph company and A T Cross

Filling systems.

These can be quite complex as in the later Onoto self filling ink pencil or very straightforward as with piston and lever fill pens. Air has to replace the ink in the reservoir otherwise the pen will stop flowing. In later models this is done by having vent holes in the stylo 'nib' unit. Quality drawing pens from Germany used a piston system.

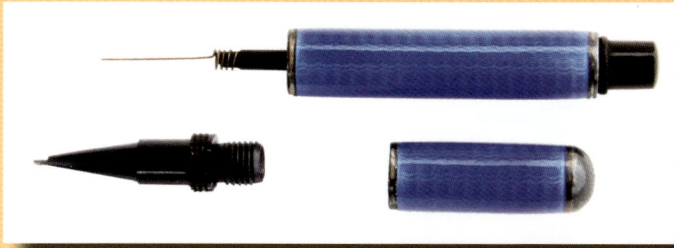

Small enamelled stylo of conventional design with spring needle and rod

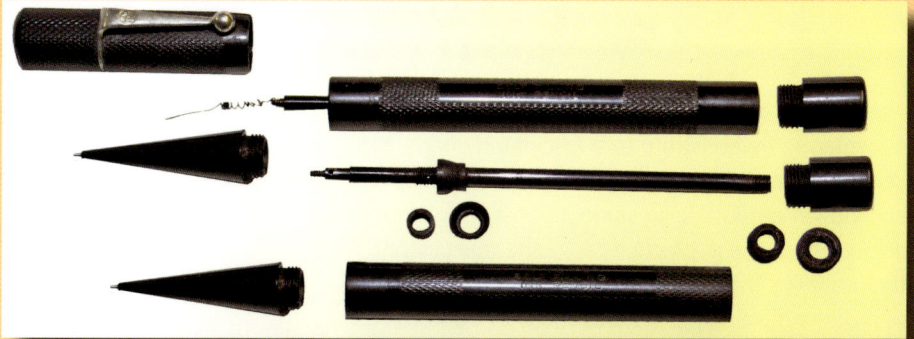

Complex self filling Onoto with a tubular shaft attached to a plunger rod with a washer system on the shaft

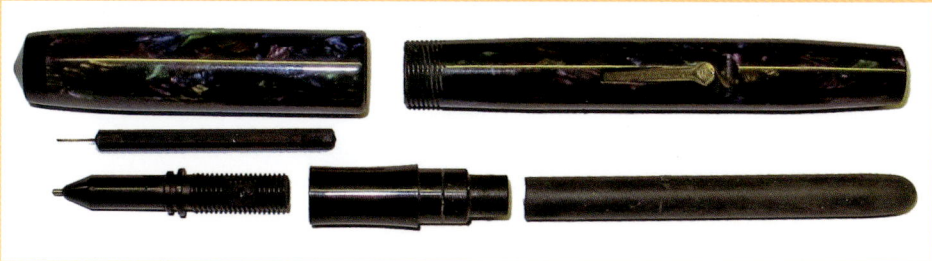

Lever fill Conway Stewart; section is push fit; the stylo unit with a removable gravity hard rubber grooved point unit can be screwed out.

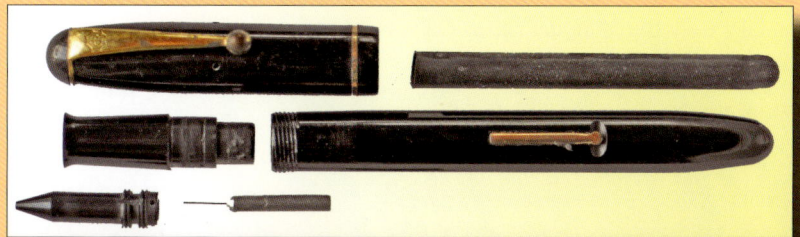

1950s gravity feed Onoto ink pencil with gravity needle control and lever fill

Three UK stylos almost identical in design; Mabie Todd stylo; Conway Stewart Dandy ink pencil; Onoto 'Nota Bene' stylo

DEMONSTRATORS

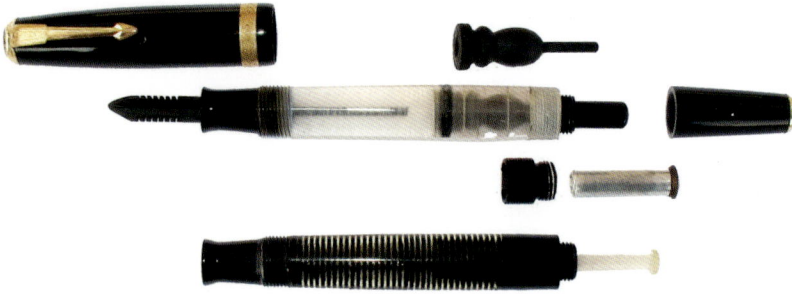

Such demonstrators as this rare Parker with a Sager unit installed help clarify product issues and allow comparison with existing products.

Acrylic transparent pens were not only for the salesman to demonstrate to a fascinated shop keeper, but also very useful for instruction in repair and vital in product development. Observing what actually happens in practice can sometimes clarify the problems that might occur. A typical example of product development is illustrated by Parker's work with the Sager pump units to replace the complicated vacumatic pump.

Demonstrators are also very collectable and often expensive, but it is possible to get hold of cracked and damaged examples for very reasonable prices. During the 1990s a lot of transparent Parker 51 shells and barrels were made in Brazil and Argentina. These are excellent for allowing the mechanism to be viewed, but take care if they are being offered as collector items; examine the barrel for Parker imprints and date marks. It is usually easy to distinguish such copies as the quality is not as good as the originals.

CAUTION Take care with section pliers when dismantling demonstrators as they are often rather brittle and craze easily.

Some piston and lever Sheaffer demonstrators were made in the 1930s but these were usually made by cutting sections out of solid pens.

With the introduction of the Snorkel range and ball pens, Sheaffer produced quite a wide range of demonstrators. The mechanisms of both snorkel and ballpoint were becoming increasingly complex, and such demonstrators make it much easier to comprehend the internal parts and their function in the process.

It is important to remember that even professional repairers need to remind themselves of mechanism detail; drawings are useful but a demonstrator is even better.

Onoto and Mabie Todd were two other companies who produced demonstrators for their sales force. Again the filling systems were different so such pens helped to educate the sales force and the retailer.

You can make your own demonstrators by cutting up old pens. This was practised by manufacturers even until the late 1950s and the previously illustrated Watermans, McNiven & Cameron and Esterbrook examples were made by the factories and sent out with the salesman, who used these in their sales promotion.

We do recommend that you try making a demonstrator yourself. Purchase a piercing saw and file and operate on a pen or pencil. It is excellent practise in understanding the materials, the position of the pins, clips, innercaps and levers; in fact a perfect anatomy practical. You can then use such examples with students or customers or to remind yourself later on.

The Matador safety pen is an excellent example of a cut away pen and the somewhat crude but effective example of a French Visofil Gold Starry has been a great asset is selling such pens.

Onoto traditional filler, which clearly illustrates the plunger system with cup washer and shut off valve.

Onoto K series twist with plastic sealing washer and screw/twist mechanism.

Argentinian made Parker 51 acrylic shell and barrel.

Genuine Parker 51 Vacumatic demonstrator. These frequently show crazing/small cracks.

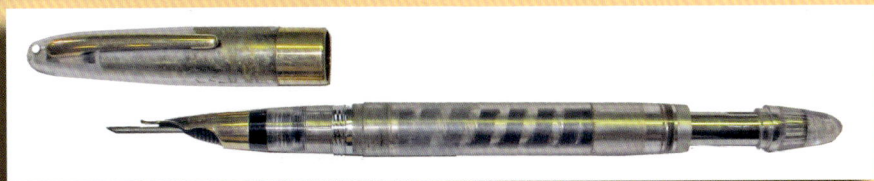

Sheaffer Snorkel triumph nib model. These are wonderful for illustrating the extension mechanism and filling system.

A PFM demonstrators in mint condition can cost a lot of money but they were difficult to make.

Sheaffer Ballpen illustrating spring and plastic actuator system.

Matador safety pen made in France with detailed cut outs.

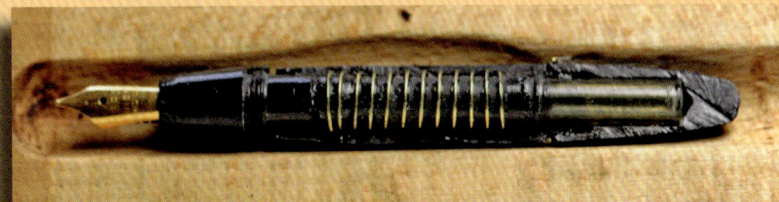

Gold Starry cut away to illustrate the replacement of a concertina sac with a straight sac and spring.

YARD O LED PENCILS

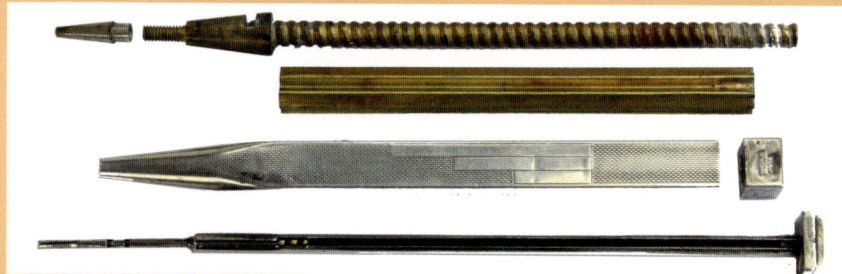

Square cross section early pencil illustrating components

Recorder model, with more complex ring clip and cone nozzle

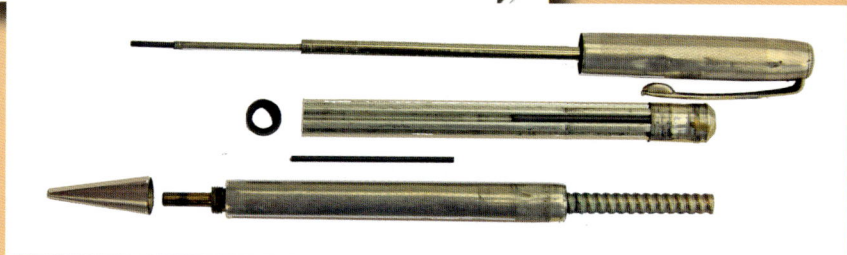

Yard-o-Led was founded in 1934 by L F Brenner, who patented a new propelling pencil system. They are still producing pencils not very different from those of the 1930s, including some classic old Baker models.

After being bombed out of business in 1941 they started again in 1946 with an excellent new product range. The post war models were robust reliable and elegant.

Perhaps a good reason for their popularity is that they are easy to repair and there are many interchangeable parts between the models.

Repair problems

- Broken clips
- Mechanism jammed
- Ejector and carrying tube twisted
- Lost nozzle

Preliminary actions

If a pencil is not propelling there is a high probability that there is a lead blockage in the nozzle. Cleaning this blockage will, in at least 50% of cases, make the pencil work. A small 1mm drill and pin vice is required. Retract the mechanism anticlockwise and then insert the drill into the nozzle and slowly rotate the pin vice to remove the compacted lead. As soon as you meet resistance STOP! Try the propelling action and if this does not work drill out more compacted lead. It is a slow process but it will amaze you how such a simple action gets a pencil working again.

If this does not work then you will have to take the pencil apart.

The components/how the Yard -o-Led works

The basic components are an outer case, a lead reservoir and a terminal which propels and repels the lead and the mechanism.

Mechanism. The 1.18mm lead is held in position in a short tube, which is attached to a drive pin, which also acts as the lead ejector. This carrier unit moves up and down a slotted support guide tube, which is attached to the end terminal of the pencil. The lead unit is propelled by the rotation of this guide tube. The drive cogs on the drive pin mesh with a drive spiral, which is rigidly secured in the pencil case and this causes the carrier unit to move up and down. The drive spiral is frequently fitted to a tapered end unit, which may be secured in position in the outer case by solder or often is

Mechanism components- lead carrier, spring and lead ejector with notched drive propelling pin.

Slotted guide tube and propelling pin

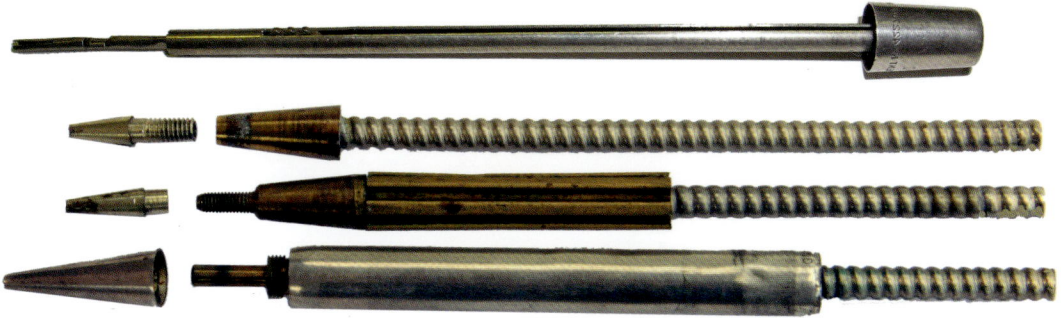

Three designs of nozzles and attachments to drive tube

pulled into position by a threaded nozzle.

Lead storage is created by a fluted insert, which fits around the spiral tube and has the capacity of 36 inches of lead or one yard of lead. The lead can be retained in the reservoir unit by a small knurled nut or a cast block.

Outer case The majority of cases are hexagonal or round made from silver, gold, plated metal and gold filled metal. There are desirable square and triangular examples.

Clips are either riveted on to the outer case or fitted as ring clips, secured by the knurled top screw. The smaller Yard-o-lette models usually have no clips and a suspension loop.

Disassembly

If the pencil is not jammed screw the top anticlockwise and remove the guide tube completely. If there are case problems then this can be dismantled by first unscrewing the nozzle and then withdrawing the spiral/cone/lead

Twisted guide tube as a result of overturning

reservoir. This may require heating at the lower end and suitable grips for withdrawing the tube.

Repair

Mechanism Twisted guide tubes and carrier tubes are immediately obvious, and the mechanism will

have to be taken apart. The lead carrier and drive pin must be removed and this sometimes can be effected by unsoldering the terminal tube joint and sliding out the carrier/drive unit. However it is easier to prise open the guide tube lower seam and withdraw the unit. This tube can be reformed to shape by refolding and rolling on a suitable rod or drill shank. The drive pin may be worn, and as it is flat, it can be cut and filed from brass sheet (however this is rarely necessary). The spring rarely gives problems.

Using direct flame to remove silver overlay on terminal

Body Problems are mainly dents, which can be worked on with suitable shaped round and square arbors. Broken clips are best cut off and replacements re-riveted not soldered. The terminals can be replaced and also the early model flat terminals can be refabricated.

Reassembly

Relocate the repaired drive unit into the guide tube and either resolder the guide tube into the terminal or reform the lower seam. Check the spring action of the lead ejector and make sure that leads are held securely in the carrier tube. The pencil can then be put together and tested.

FILLING INSTRUCTIONS

Onoto the Pen

MADE IN GREAT BRITAIN.

PLUNGER FILLING—SAFETY.

To Fill.—Unscrew the shank and withdraw the rod to its fullest extent—insert nib and the end of nib carrier into the ink—press the rod home and screw up the shank keeping the carrier in the ink until filling operation is completed. The pen fills at the completion of the downward stroke, the opposite action to a syringe.

To Use.—Unscrew the shank about half a turn, take cap off and place it on the other end, and the pen is ready to write. When you have finished writing replace the cap, screw the shank right home and the pen is then perfectly sealed and cannot leak.

To Clean.—Immerse nib in ink and go through the process of filling two or three times.

THE COMPLETION OF THE DOWNWARD STROKE FILLS THE PEN.

TURN ON INK TO WRITE.

GUARANTEE.

We unreservedly guarantee that the ONOTO PEN is perfect in every detail. Should the Pen not function to your satisfaction, please return same to your stationer, or the makers, within ten days, enclosing stamps for return postage.

Why the Chilton Pen Principle Provides Greater Ink Capacity

Read Carefully —how to fill and care for your

CHILTON DOUBLE WRITING MILEAGE PEN

1935 CHILTON FILLING INSTRUCTIONS

HOW TO FILL AND USE THE FORD PEN

ALL BRITISH — MADE IN ENGLAND

1 Unscrew the Cap "A" and lay it aside.

2 Remove the Sleeve "B" by unscrewing and detaching. The pen is now ready for filling.

3 Dip the nib in the ink so that the ink entirely covers it. Hold the pen with the left hand and with the right hand holding the head of the pumping rod pump up and down (3 or 4 strokes) until you see the pen is full. Do not remove the pen from the ink with the pumping rod extended, but complete the pumping action. Continued pumping merely flushes the pen. It cannot harm it.

4 After wiping any surplus ink from the barrel, replace the Sleeve and the pen is ready for writing.

HINTS ON USING THE

'SPEEDY PHIL' PENS

Hold section in left hand and with right hand rotating in an anti-clockwise direction (fig. 1). Immerse nib in ink (fig. 2) rotating knurled end 'A' slowly in clockwise direction for one click. Hold pen in this position for ten seconds to ensure maximum filling. Remove pen from ink and wipe nib and section free of all surplus ink. Replace barrel.

NOTE.—The tube filling unit must not be removed from section.

CONWAY STEWART & CO. LTD. 36/44 Copperfield Rd. London E.3.

INSTRUCTIONS FOR USING THE JOHN WHYTWARTH SCIENTIFIC SAFETY PEN

Platignum Visi-ink Vacuum Filling FOUNTAIN PEN.

Fill with water two or three times before filling with ink

1. Unscrew back end of barrel as illustration revealing small rubber "air ejector."
2. Dip pen in ink so that nib is completely immersed. Compress "air ejector" between the forefinger and thumb four or five times, releasing sharply, allowing "air ejector" to expand to its fullest extent each time. The ink will be seen to rise in the transparent barrel. Replace end of barrel and pen is ready for use.

FOR PERFECT SERVICE FOLLOW INSTRUCTIONS

Waterman's THE SAFETY TYPE.

When the Safety Type Waterman's Ideal is closed, it is, in effect, a bottle, with the cap as cork. Consequently, when the cap is removed the pen must be held upright or the contents will spill, but when closed it can be carried in any position and will not leak.

TO OPEN: Hold the pen upright in one hand and unscrew the cap with the other (see Fig. 1). Next, fit cap on the other end of the barrel (still holding pen upright) and screw until the nib is in the correct writing position (see Fig. 2). Do not overscrew—force is not necessary—you will know when it is tight enough just as you know when you have wound your watch sufficiently.

TO CLOSE: Hold the pen upright, reverse the process, unscrewing until the nib is entirely below the top of the barrel. This is important, for if the nib is left above the level of the barrel, the point will be bent or broken. Then screw cap on firmly and you may carry the pen in any position.

TO FILL: Hold the pen upright, unscrew the cap and while the nib is lowered in the barrel, drop the ink into the open end drop by drop (see Fig. 3) to within a quarter of an inch from the top.

TO CLEAN: Remove the cap and hold the barrel underneath tap and let the cold water flow into the holder for a minute or so. Do not take the pen to pieces in any circumstances.

Waterman's Writing Sets—over 40 different styles.

Waterman's THE SELF-FILLING TYPE.

(Pat. No. 5790/15) With boxed-in lever.

The Self-Filling device incorporated in this type of Waterman's Ideal is not only the simplest, it is easily the most efficient. It operates quickly and reliably, does not get out of order and is never in the way.

This Pen being fitted with the "Spoon Feed" will continue writing without flooding until the last drop of ink has been used.

TO FILL: Raise the lever, immerse the nib in the ink until entirely covered, let the lever go back, pause for a second, press it home—and the pen is filled.

TO CLEAN: Proceed as in filling, using cold water instead of ink. Raise the lever several times and the pen is cleaned.

IMPORTANT.

To remove the screw-lock security cap, give short turn from left to right. To replace, turn reverse way—right to left—until it is firmly screwed.

If there is any ink in the barrel always hold the pen over an ink bottle when raising the lever.

After filling, at once wipe off any ink there may be on the point section.

Always hold the pen upright when putting on or taking off the cap; it is better, also, to carry the pen in an upright position.

There is a Waterman's Pencil to match every Pen.

The first collector pen books and magazines of the 1980s were essentially a collection of copies of advertisements. This should not be derided because they can provide a wealth of information for the repairer. More details are available from instruction leaflets; in Section 1 we suggested assembling a collection of these to be able to send filling instructions to customers. Frequently such documents include details on pen parts or filling systems; where else would one discover how to fill a Ford, Chilton, Whytwarth, 'Speedy Phil' Conway Stewart or a Platignum Visi Ink properly!

PART THREE

Special procedures and information

Cutting seals	230
Adhesives	232
Tools & tips	233
Nibs general	235
Nib grinding & smoothing	236
Nib repair	238
Cap bands	240
Cap lip replacement	242
Barrel thread cracks	243
Cap to barrel threading	244
Materials	245
Cosmetic treatment	246
Hard Rubber restoration	248
Plating	249
Machines & equipment	250
Machining practice	252
Dismantling metal caps	254
Extracting inner caps	255
Dents and refinishing metal caps	256
Finishing a stainless steel cap	257
Threads	258
Thread Reference data	260
Reference Information	261
Bibliography & internet	263
Supplier advertisements	266
Index	279

CUTTING SEALS

Typical cutter sets for cork and rubber seals. The rubber seal cutter shows two different outer diameter cutters and an inner cutter.

Cork and Rubber

The first option is to look for ready made seals from a commercial supplier. It is possible to buy seals for many popular makes of pens, and if they are not exactly the correct specification, they can often be modified to suit. (see for example Nozac)

Replacement of the original cork or felt barrel seals with elastomeric O-rings is possible (and desirable in pens such as Ford, Onoto and Sheaffer Vac-Fil) and there is a wide range of sizes available to facilitate this modification.

Typically, upfiller pens have cork piston seals and downfillers have rubber washer seals.

In previous sections we have outlined how to cut and fit corks by hand processes, but this is never a quick or reproducible method. If one is doing a lot of repairs of a particular model it is possible to make simple tools to cut cork and rubber seals, providing you have a lathe.

Making a cutter

Most seals require a central hole, so the tools must be in two parts and machined to close tolerances so that concentricity is maintained. The tools should be treated as cutters, not punches, so the steel does not need to be hardened if a soft backing plate is used. Mild steel can be used, but silver steel is better. The cutting edge needs to be very sharp, and also to be thin for the cork cutter.

Using the cutter

The outer cutter is best operated by hand with a firm rotational movement, making sure that the rubber or cork is cut all the way through before the tool is removed. If the cut is made too quickly the rubber can deform so a slow rotating action is preferred.

It is best to cut the central hole first (this one can be tapped with a light hammer), leaving the inner cutter in place to align the outer cutter. We are all familiar with rubber washers 'off centre' and by using the concentric cutters, this is avoided.

Rubber

The sheet for making the seals should be between 0.8mm and 1mm thick and durable against ink. Neoprene seems to work well.

A cutter set where both inner and outer cutters have been fitted with knobs.

Cork

Cork, being the bark of a tree, is a material where numerous flaws may be encountered, so the material needs to be carefully selected and we suggest avoiding reconstituted cork. Corks from fortified wine bottles are often most suitable, but the best quality material can be obtained from musical instrument makers. Cork seals are usually thicker than rubber so one requires a firm surface and again a slow and deliberate cutting without deforming the cork with too much pressure.

Cork seals for pistons should be finished by hand with fine sandpaper in order to ensure a good fit to the pen barrel and to obtain a smooth surface. When the seal is completed it needs to be coated in order to repel ink and ease its motion within the barrel. It may be boiled in wax or soaked in liquid paraffin for a while. Any excess should be dried off and then the seal can be lubricated with silicone grease. Cork seals made in this way are superior to the modern plastic seals and many pens are improved by the modification.

Hand cutting

Most repairers will not have machining facilities so hand cutting cork seals is a reality! First cut a round slice slightly thicker than required then drill a hole in the middle of the slice and slowly enlarge it with a needle file until the piston head can be firmly pushed into it.

With the seal in place on the piston head, it can be sandpapered either by hand or in a drill or lathe using 150 grade to start and 350 to finish. During the process it is advisable to test it many times before taking too much material from the cork. Check the fitting all along the barrel and especially in the area where it is going to rest after filling the pen with ink. This is because some pen barrels are not uniformly cylindrical. If the piston sits tight at the end of the filling it will not leak.

SUMMARY OF STEPS FOR HAND CUTTING CORK SEALS

Use good quality cork not composite

**Rough cut a large slice, put a small hole in it and enlarge
with a round needle file until it fits the peg**

Trim to slightly oversize -with razor blade or drill/lathe & sandpaper

Fit and sand   Fit and sand   Fit and sand   to perfect fit

Ensure good seal at final position   AFTER FILLING

Treat with liquid paraffin or molten wax

Final filling and testing

ADHESIVES

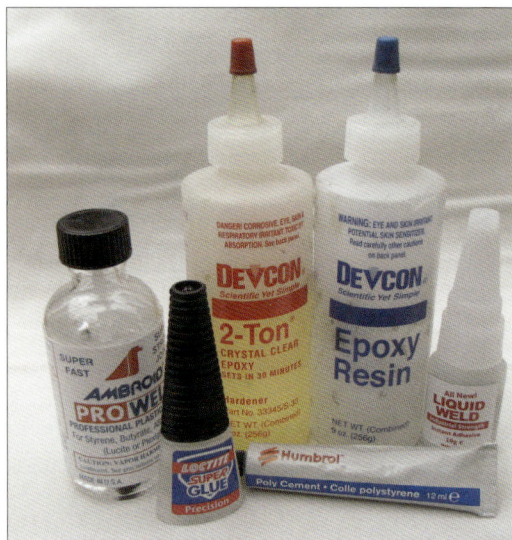

A range of useful adhesives

For the first two editions of this book we did not cover adhesives. This was because the content of proprietary adhesives is known only in general terms, and it is not possible to recommend any specific adhesive unless the properties of the materials are known. In addition, there are significant health and safety issues with some adhesives.

There have been no changes in these issues since the last edition of the book, but due to the wide interest in this topic, and as it is scarcely possible to do pen repairs without adhesives, we decided to include some recommendations of a general nature.

Firstly, we need to consider some of the properties that we might expect from our adhesive:- welding ability, range of material applications, set time, crack penetration, gap filling, tackiness (do we need clamps?), temperature sensitivity, water/ink tolerance, lifetime, toxicity.

We next need to consider the range of adhesive jobs we need to undertake. These may include:- repairs to broken plastic parts, sealing parts that we may need to open again, repairing hairline cracks, metal to plastic joints and filling or replacing lost material.

Hairline cracks

If possible a solvent weld should be used. However, an experiment is required to determine whether the chemical at hand is suitable for the material. For many vintage plastics (especially celluloid) MEK (methylethylketone) or THF (tetrahydrofuran) are often used. However, these chemicals are hazardous and should be used with protective gloves in a well ventilated area. Other solvent weld options are available for acrylics (see http://www.shop4glue.com). Plumbing weld materials such as 'Weld-on-3-Acrylic' and certain model kit glues are also useful, and some of these have a wider range of applicability including Sheaffer and Montblanc materials. However, without sure knowledge of the properties of the pen material, it is essential to do an experiment on a scrap pen or on a part of the pen where residues can be polished off afterwards. With solvent welding it is essential to remove any excess immediately.

If none of the available solvents produces the required reactivity, cyanoacrylate (superglue) may be the best option. The low viscosity 'liquid' type has very good penetration in hairline cracks, but be sure to use a waterproof version if the surfaces are to be exposed to ink.

Separable parts

If the parts are separable, other options are available, especially epoxy resins. Always use the long set time version and warm the components and the resin first so that the closest possible contact is made between components. Devcon '2-ton' epoxy is able to bond most materials, is unaffected by moisture and heat, is clear and it sets hard. It can also be coloured as required, but for scratch and dent filling, it is better to use it clear. Cyanoacrylate glues seem to have had a bad press in pen repair, but when used properly, they can be most useful. Clear, hard setting and moisture resistant versions are available and they have an advantage over epoxy for some applications in that they are very fast setting so that clamps are not necessary. We have had very good results from 'Liquid Weld' (www.liquidweldglue.co.uk) a UK product similar in some

A Liquid Weld joint between hard rubber components tested to destruction

rubber block shattered under extreme testing leaving the joint intact.

We emphasise again, that with the vast range of adhesives available, it is always desirable to do some experiments before using any adhesive on a valuable pen. Having discussed these modern adhesives, we emphasise that a permanent glue should never be used where traditional shellac or other reversible material would have been used. Shellac can be difficult to release sometimes, so for tasks like thread sealing, rosin based materials or even silicone grease, are much kinder for the pens and the next repairer.

respects to cyanoacrylates, but the distributors seem unable to provide details of the formulation. Tests have shown it to be particularly effective with hard rubber, where a 2mm wall thickness 10mm diameter hard rubber tube butt jointed to a hard

For fine work use an applicator such as a fine dental pick or a toothpick - always wipe off excess adhesive as soon as possible. **TIP**

TOOLS & TIPS
Most of us have personal ways of doing things and sometimes a simple idea can make things so much easier.

Tea bag holder
Great for washing that small part in an ultra-sonic bath or or warming a section and feed in very hot water.

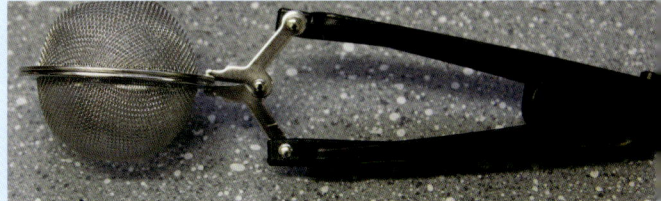

Making a threaded holder from a metal connector
It can be quite awkward to secure a small item for turning in a lathe. It is possible to make a threaded holder from a Bexley metal connector fitted on to a steel rod. This was used to turn down a plastic threaded insert for a metal 51 flighter from a normal barrel. The threaded connection gives solid support for the barrel to be turned to the necessary thin wall thickness.
The same procedure can be used for Parker 61 inserts.

Parker 61
Parker 51

Feeler gauges
These are ideal for cleaning feeds and channels.

Measuring
Vac sacs must be cut to size; because we were repairing a lot of Vacs we cut two notches in the bench to make it easy to trim the sacs to length. Later we became sophisticated and nailed a plastic ruler to the bench!

TOOLS & TIPS

Keeping your adhesives in order

It is so easy to knock over a relatively unstable bottle of shellac or any adhesive. This is where an ink bottle can be very useful. Make up the shellac and drill a hole in the lid of an ink bottle. If you wish to use PVA or solvent adhesive use smaller pots and keep them in a polystyrene box. Small brushes, steel rods, cocktail sticks or toothpicks are ideal applicators.

Wire and cork

Guitar string threaded through a cork, so one does not lose it, will clean most breather tubes.

Making a small grinding wheel for a Dremel

Sometimes you require a small slim grinding wheel e.g. to modify a lever box or an internal C groove in a barrel. Run the Dremel with a large disc against your UNSWITCHED ON BENCH GRINDER and you can very quickly reduce the diameter to what you require.

Masking tape, plastic ties and Blue Tak

These are invaluable for holding, marking and clamping. To ensure you do not drill in to far use masking tape on a drill or for fitting a cap to the right position. A plastic tie is great for holding a Waterman clip in position for rivetting etc...

Boxes and Boxes

After plier fetishes most repairers have box fetishes- but small boxes within large boxes are essential if you are doing a lot of repairs. Purchase lidded boxes so you can close them and store them,

Using your Dremel accessories manually

The range of Dremel and model making kits is amazing and these are often of advantage to use by hand. Use a pin vice.

A simple Vac Tool

The Parker 51 blind cap makes an ideal Vac pump tool. When a single slit is cut, it can be used with section pliers, as shown, to remove Vac pumps. If a stronger tool is desired, the top dome can be cut off and the blind cap glued into a metal tube; two or three slits cut in the metal tube and blind cap. This can be used for all standard size Vac pumps.

80 Needlepoint
An extremely fine point for precise figure work. Not intended for general writing.

X Extra Fine
For fine line writing with a light touch.

F Fine
Excellent for general writing and note taking. Moderate pressure produces a fine line.

M Medium
For average writing pressure, average line width. General all-round use.

B Broad
A heavier, rounded point for wide lines.

85 Extra Broad
A large rounded point excellent for heavy lines and bold signatures.

86 Extra Extra Broad
Developed for people who like to write boldly and rapidly and want a special flourish to their signatures.

Oblique nibs

Italic nibs

Right

Left

93 Reverse (M) Oblique nib
Generally used by left-handed writers

88 Oblique nib(M
Generally used by right-handed writers.

94 Straight Italic(M)
Generally used by right-handed italic writers. Can be used by left-handed italic writers.

15° Oblique Italic
Generally used by right-handed italic writers. Can be used by some left-handed italic writers

30° R Oblique Italic

30° L Oblique Italic

LEFT HAND OBLIQUE

LEFT FOOT

There can be confusion defining 'oblique' nibs In the US the convention is to describe a 30° R oblique as a LEFT HAND OBLIQUE.

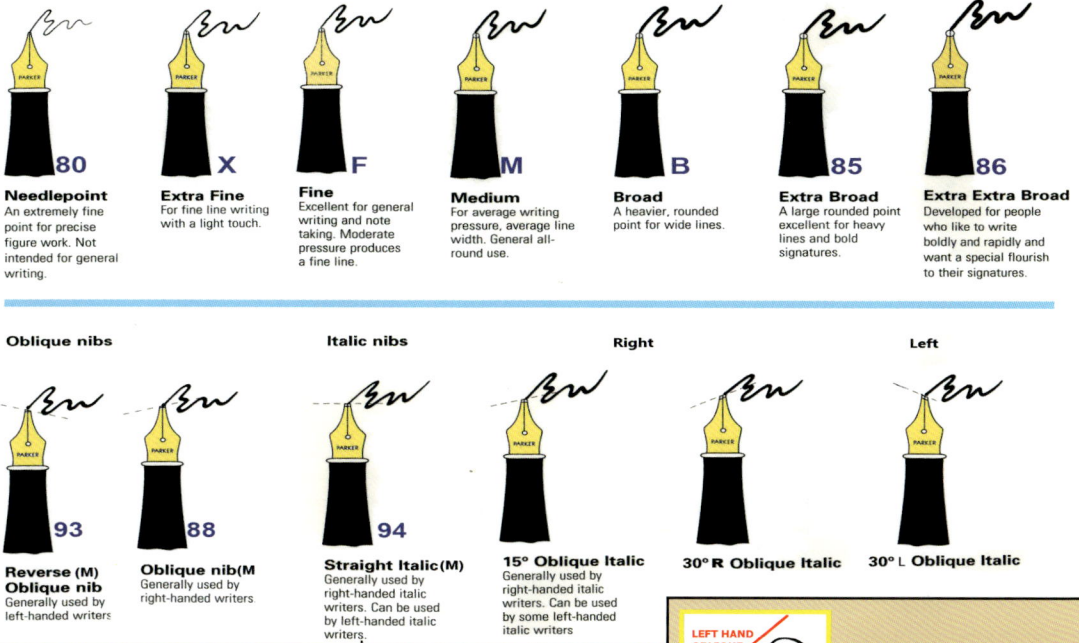

A high percentage of repairs relate to nibs. They are either damaged, scratchy or simply wrong. Without a nib working well, the remainder of the pen is superfluous. In most cases the nibs have to be removed in order to be corrected in some way.

Repairing nibs is a skill that can be acquired with practice but it requires a lot of old nibs, direction and some

What can be done to a nib

It can be reprofiled

It can be smoothed

It can be repaired for cracks and dents

It can be retipped

Finally it can be changed!

a smooth aligned nib and hope that it suits. The interpretation of italic, stub, oblique is subjective, so if you have a request for an accountants left hand oblique italic, then refer them to a friend!

John Mottishaw's comment 'One persons dream nib can be anothers nightmare' is based on personal experience!

patience. Furthermore it is vital to understand that the way a nib is used is very personal. It is very difficult to adapt a nib without the user being there to test it; all that can be done is to produce

We draw your attention to the Winter issue 2005 of Pennant which was dedicated to nibs. It is full of useful tips and information and significantly it also has a US tribute to Arthur.

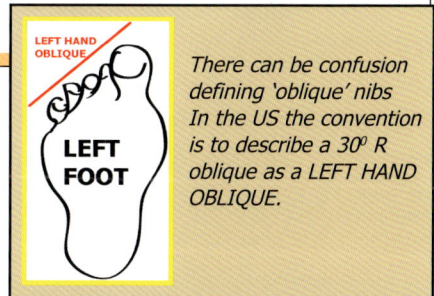

The sizes of nibs and other marks on the nib

Early fountain pen nibs were made by the gold dip pen makers; their convention of low numbers for small nibs and large numbers for larger nibs was adopted for fountain pens. There is no agreed standard but most working nibs range from 2 to 4 for smaller slim pens and 5 to 7 for larger ink capacity pens.

Most quality nibs are stamped with the maker's name and some have logos or ornate scrolling, which may be enhanced with two tone. The vent hole shape can define the age and a letter may indicate the factory. e.g. N = Newhaven. Specific words such as Eternal or Manifold or Maniflex indicate stiff nibs with more gold in the shoulder of the nib. Such robust nibs were originally designed for marking through carbon paper.

NIB GRINDING & SMOOTHING

Re grinding may be required when a pen has been dramatically adjusted after trauma or when a person requests a totally different point profile.

It is an important repair activity, not only because pen manufacturers produce so few variants, but also it is often necessary to re-grind older nibs in order to change the worn tip profiles.

However all manner of things can go wrong with old nibs, or even new, so you must practise. Practise on scrap steel and then gold nibs to get the feel. Start simply e.g. by changing a medium to fine before going on to the more difficult oblique stub. Arabic and accountant profiles.

There are 3 important points;-

You must know where you are starting from and where you are going to in terms of nib profile. Study the tip profiles of a range of nibs before you start. You must continually, and we mean continually, look at the effects of any action. There must be sufficient tip material to accomodate the modification.

The manual method for smoothing

Arkansas natural stone (obtained from woodcarver's suppliers) is ideal for final smoothing. A rolling/

rocking motion generated by first finger and thumb will reduce the point to a rounded profile.

For stub and oblique nibs, the best plan is to write on the stone as you would with these types of nib. A final polish is imparted by smearing jeweller's rouge on a piece of paper and writing over it.

The use of sponge backed emery is an option to the stone and can be just as effective.

The mechanical method for profile changes

This can be achieved on a small scale by using an electric drill or a Dremel set at a low speed and fitted with appropriate grinding wheels.

One can do all that one does on large professional diamond wheels with small hobby cutting discs. Diamond, rubber abrasive and hard felt discs are all available from Hobby shops.

Always have the wheel working away from you and make sure that your 'Dremel' or small drill is secure. Most small kits have accessory stands like the ones illustrated below and that makes holding the nib much easier. If you have a small lathe the various discs can be mounted in the chuck.

Gentle grinding or smoothing using foam backed abrasive pads and Arkansas stone for profile change

Eyeglass

Two Dremel models with stands

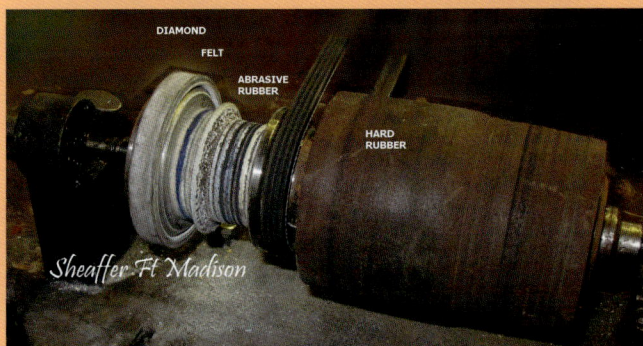

Range of foam backed abrasives of different grades, arkansas stone and two rubber wheels

DIAMOND

FELT

ABRASIVE RUBBER

HARD RUBBER

Sheaffer Ft Madison

Older belt driven grinding rig with diamond wheel, then felt, then abrasive rubber and finally large hard rubber cylinder; from the Ft Madison factory.

A semi professional set up

If one is frequently re-grinding nibs, then an investment in a professional set-up is well justified. The order of wheels illustrated opposite is based on typical set ups in the Sheaffer factories in the UK and USA. Diamond, rubber abrasive and hard felt wheels are firmly mounted on a shaft with appropriate spacers. The shaft is then aligned and attached to the motor drive and carefully balanced. In some cases two support roller bearings are used. Occasionally factory grinding equipment will have glass, leather-covered, rubber/abrasive and hard rubber grinding wheels but most work can be done with the three wheels illustrated above.

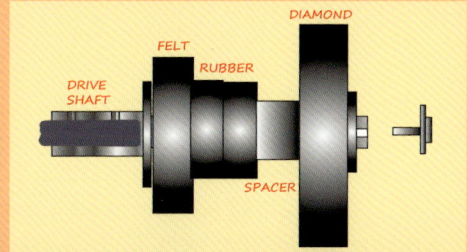

Illustration of a typical grinding set up

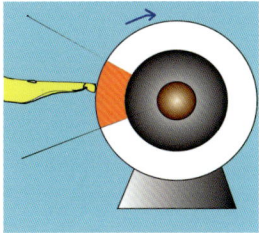

The wheels must move away from the operator and the nibs are usually presented to a small segment of the wheel.

Note in the adjacent photographs the positions that Letta Grosskemper, with her 60 years experience, adopts at the wheel.

We can write down good practice but smoothing nibs requires a lot of practice:

- the angles of presentation of a nib to grinding wheels is important. A steady progression across the wheel is imperative with moves at an angle up or down across the wheel for obliques.
- the sides of the wheels are extremely useful to produce a 'flat face' for italic nibs
- make a firm 'one pass' across the diamond wheel
- use the rubber wheel sparingly after your main profiling
- rotate the nib only on the felt wheel
- attach a plastic plate to the bench as a softer support for tine alignment and adjustment
- fix in your mind the profile you are intending to achieve or use nibs as your templates to work to. Keep examples of each cut so you can refer to it to remind you where you are going!
- one should spend more time 'looking at' than grinding

Letta demonstrating some of the points in the text.

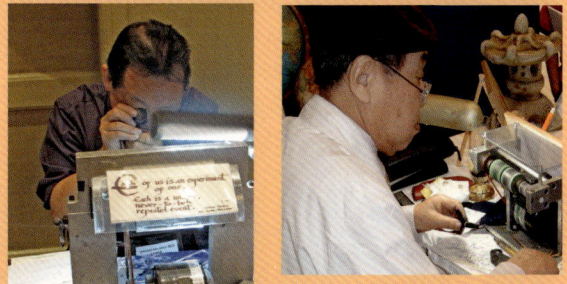

Two nib cutters at US pen show.

NIB REPAIR

Cracks can be soldered and tines can be straightened, but tips cannot be replaced without resort to very expensive equipment. It is important therefore to take care of tips and not to exert stress on the gold/iridium weld. Note that there is no actual iridium in the tip, which is usually an alloy of ruthenium, osmium and other rarer metals. However 'iridium' is the common word used to describe the tip material.

Nib straightening

Straightening can be undertaken with a very simple tool set. A pair of smooth jawed long nosed pliers, a fine file, abrasive sticks, a fine abrasive stone, jeweller's rouge and a measure of patience are the essentials. An expensive nib block is not essential but it is necessary to have a smooth hard surface like an engineers surface plate or a smooth rod.
Work on the tines alternately, gradually bringing them back to the correct angle and alignment. Arthur used to say 'Work from the vent hole', first one tine then work on the other.

If a nib has been inexpertly straightened previously, it may have obvious kinks. In such cases it may be necessary to re-bend the tines and bend them straight again at the right location. If the tines need to be bent laterally to enable the tips to just touch each other, be careful not to exert stress right at the tip.

When all is in good alignment, it is time to remove the vestiges of bend creases. This can be done with a very fine file while using the finger for support. Take off just enough gold to restore the smooth continuous curve of the nib profile. Finish with increasingly finer grades of abrasive stick and finally with metal polish. The nib is then fitted to the feed and section and tested for writing performance (see 'Testing a fountain pen').
Do not expect the point to be as smooth as new at this stage, it will need grinding and polishing to regain its former performance. (see Nib Grinding)

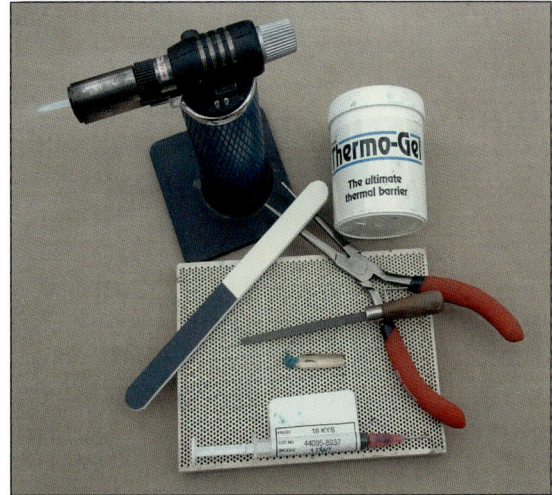

Items for repairing cracks

Nib cracks

These are repairable and it is quite possible to achieve a repair that is so good that you would not know from the front of the nib that the repair had been done. 18ct gold solder paste is much easier to use than any other gold solder and it is readily available from jeweller's suppliers. You will need thermal gel to protect the temper of the nib tips, a ceramic plate to support the nib and a small micro blow torch.

The repair is done from the back of the nib, but first make sure that the edges to be soldered are in close contact because the solder does not fill gaps. It might be necessary to bend the nib a little if the crack is across the tines and to hold the edges together with spring loaded pliers if the crack is longitudinal and widening towards the tail.

Clean and degrease the nib, and then support it so the crack is horizontal and at the low point

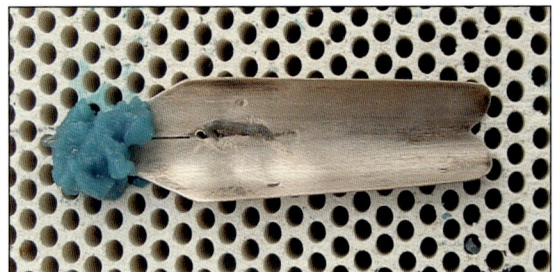

This nib has a crack extending from the vent hole. Note the thermal gel and the gold solder paste

of the support. Heat the whole nib gently and then apply the solder paste along the length of the crack. Do not use too much solder. Set a fine flame and direct the tip of the blue part on to the centre of the crack (do the job in several stages if the crack is long). The paste will tend to gather into a ball and then begin to flow as it reaches red heat. Remove the heat as soon as the solder flows or you may burn a hole in the nib. Keep the flame perpendicular to the surface avoiding the edges of the nib or they will curl up and disappear. Cool the nib rapidly in cold water.

This operation requires having a clear space and the correct tools at hand including tweezers or grips to handle the hot nib. Have some cold water in a small dish and a small fire extinguisher in case

you drop the torch as your Big Red nib vaporises! Seriously, if you are going to use any direct flame, you should have a small extinguisher and know where it is!

Now inspect the front of the nib. If the crack has been successfully soldered, the solder will be visible as a thin line where the crack was. This can be smoothed with the aid of a fine file, abrasive sticks and metal polish, usually without damage to the imprint. The rest of the nib may be blackened and will also require some attention from the abrasive sticks. Any excess solder on the inside surface of the nib should not be removed completely, so the feed may have to be adjusted to ensure that it fits snugly to the inside of the nib.

Useful tools for nib adjustment

Pliers-
Smooth jawed pliers are essential but they ideally should be profiled to make a parallel grip. Parallel pliers are ideal if you can find them so small. Curved jaws are sometimes invaluable. We have made nib pliers with a notch cut into them as shown. This allows one to work around the tip when straightening a nib

Burnishing
The use of agate burnishers is well known when dealing with gold. Make a hardwood block with channels routed out to different depths. This is useful for activities other than nibs but with the nib face down and an agate burnisher it is possible to remove many dents without any other activity required

Ball bearings
With the nib on an engineers surface plate use a ball bearing of the right diameter as a dent remover. Roll it along backwards and forwards along the nib exerting pressure on the ball with a wooden stick domed out for the ball.

Hammers and anvils
Perhaps extreme, but small plastic headed hammers are useful for taking dents out. A solid rounded surface plate or anvil is essential. A tapered polished rod or a triblet in a vice will act as a nib support.

Small jawed pliers are most useful for nib work and curved jaw options can help restore profiles

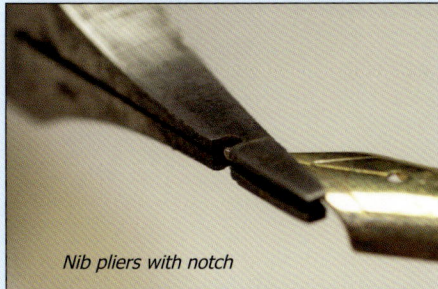
Nib pliers with notch

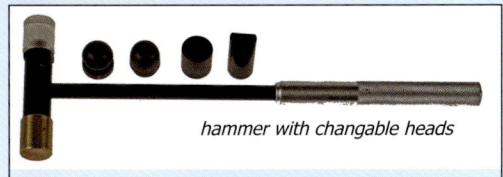
hammer with changable heads

Nib repair kit with two taper anvils which can be held in a vice for straightening nibs and two burnishers.

CAP BANDS

Typical band problems - missing and brassed

We have mentioned that cap bands were introduced to prevent the splitting of cap lips in the days before threaded plastic caps were introduced. The decorative value of cap bands prevented them from being phased out when their mechanical benefit was no longer required. Most good quality vintage pens were provided with bands despite the problems of fitting them. There is much discussion about the original fitting method for cap bands, but it seems likely that a band would have been fitted by starting with it being oversize and then by rotating it under pressure so that it was compressed into the groove. The machinery to do this is no longer easily available, so alternative methods should be considered for restoring caps that have missing, damaged or ill-fitting bands. Loggerhead pliers with or without a protective metal shim can

sometimes be effective. (There is less marking with a shim)

Band Replacement

The easiest way to replace a band is to find one that will just fit over the cap and to fix it in place over the groove with a gap filling glue. This can be reasonably effective if done with a slow setting glue (like epoxy), so that the excess can be cleaned away with methylated spirit before final curing. However, the band will be left proud and the removal of any remaining glue residues will probably take the gold plating off, so it is not recommended.

Two other options can do a better job, but they require a certain degree of skill and courage.

If the material is black hard rubber or any other material without a large scale pattern, and identical material is available, the bands can be replaced very convincingly by using the cap lip replacement strategy (see Cap lips). This approach is similar to that adopted by modern marbled Parker Duofolds where the cap lip and the cap tube are separate parts.

The alternative method requires hot air to make the cap lip sufficiently pliable that the band can be forced over it into the groove. This requires good control of the heat source, and a metal mandrel previously turned to the inside cap diameter. The mandrel can be heated and pushed into the cap to restore it to its original circular profile. This is a somewhat risky strategy as some materials will have a tendency to shrink after the heat treatment and it may be difficult to expand them again. However it works well with hard rubber because this material when heated returns to it's natural shape.

Problems are compounded where there is more than one cap band because it may not be possible to pass one cap band over another or to stop them falling into the wrong groove. In such cases use a larger band or try one of two other possibilities, both of which will change the original appearance of the pen.

The first option is to polish the grooves off so that the cap becomes bandless. This is fine for certain pens, but it reduces the cap lip thickness and renders the lip more susceptible to further damage. The second option is to fit a band sufficiently wide to bridge the space between the edge of the cap and the furthest band. If the lathe is used to clear the material between the grooves right out to the cap lip this can be very effective. It is also a useful technique where cap splits or chips cannot be repaired.

Loose bands

These are an easier problem to solve because it is usually a cap shrinkage fault rather than a band fault. Assuming that there has been no previous attempt to glue them, and that there is no glue residue to remove, the best way to fix this problem is to expand the cap again. This may be achieved by heating the cap so that it can be moulded back to its original shape as discussed above. The easy alternative is to glue the bands, and this may be the best approach if they are only marginally loose. If they are very loose, this method will leave them uncomfortably proud of the surface, so it is better to refrain from clamping them in order to spread the protrusion evenly around the cap.

Sourcing cap bands

Ornate cap bands such as Partrician or lattice Swan have to be sourced from similar old pens, and even plain bands have a variation of diameter and width that makes it difficult to match cap bands if one is missing from a set of 3.

The first approach is to look through your stock of old caps. Bands can be recovered by burning old caps so never discard a no-name cap that has lost it's pen.

The second approach is from stock that can be purchased. There are quantities of pen cap bands on some web sites; also bands are available from Eastern pen kits suppliers but these are usually rigid and too thick for old pens.

The third approach is to make the bands by turning them from brass rod. First bore out to a diameter just less than the cap then turn the outside with a very sharp tool to a wall thickness of 0.15mm (6 thou). Part off with again a very sharp tool backed with a stick to catch the ring.

Bands do vary in thickness, band width and diameter; for example most pen cap bands fall in between 12.9mm and 15.5mm (e.g Big Red 15.3mm, Vac Major 13.9mm, Onoto Magna 15.4mm); band widths vary from 0.5mm to 4mm; the average thickness of a band is about 0.15mm. Bearing in mind that older pens were hand made there was always some variation and it was necessary to adjust the cap bands a little. This

Old stock cap bands ex Stylochap

is essential for repairers today considering the limitations of replacements.

It is easy to enlarge the diameters simply by stretching the band over a tapered mandrel such as a sharpening steel from an old carving set or a small triblet from a jewellery tool supplier.

The task is made easier if the ring is softened by heating it to cherry red but most will stretch without resorting to this. Just push the band down with the edge of a piece of hardwood until it reaches the required diameter.

Bands can be stretched with a professional jewellers ring stretcher but a very simple tool can be made from two pieces of brass or even hard wood. A split external tapered tube is made by boring a 16mm

Modest but very functional ring stretcher

brass rod with a 10.5mm drill to a depth of about 6cm. An external taper can be turned from 16mm to 11mm over a distance of 6cm and then the tube can be slit across. The opposing bar has as a slight taper from 10.2mm to 11mm over about 6cm. This crude tool shown has stretched cap bands for the last 4 years so no other sizes have been made.

Most of the bands stretched were 13mm and they can extend to 16mm usually without breaking.

Band width can be reduced on a lathe with the band firmly held on a tapered wooden rod.

One way of controlling the stretching of a band accurately is to place one opposing taper of the ring stretcher in the tailstock of a small lathe and the other in the headstock and adjust with the tailstock screw.

CAP LIP REPLACEMENT

Cap lips before and after

This is a skilled job that should not be attempted unless you have experience with a precision lathe. It is not a task to be undertaken unless you have no other option because it is necessarily intrusive on the original external structure.

However, if the lip is badly cracked or chipped like the examples shown, cap lip replacement is the only viable option provided suitable material is available for the replacement. If done well, the repair will be virtually invisible and much better in terms of mechanical stability than the alternative of using various glues and fillers.

Caps in need of attention are often black hard rubber ones; fortunately these are the easiest to do and the material is not difficult to obtain. The most difficult caps are those with marbled or patterned decoration because the repair will almost certainly be noticeable unless the band is wide enough to hide the discontinuity in the pattern.

The first step is to use a razor saw to remove the damaged lip just below the band. The best mechanical joint is the longest that can be achieved at right angles to the direction of stress, so a tapered joint is recommended rather than a stepped one. Ideally, the joint should extend between the band groove and a point just clear of the threads. Angles in the range 5^0 to 8^0 have been found to work well, but some caps with the threads near the mouth may require a steeper angle.

The cap should ideally be held in a collet chuck, but a well-centred 3-jaw chuck is fine if the cap is protected with a layer of masking tape.

The remains of the cap lip, up to the edge of the band, are removed with a sharp tool; the band can then be slipped off if it needs changing or replating. A fine boring tool set to advance at the taper angle is used to cut material out until a feather edge is reached at the band, whilst making sure that the cut does not reach the internal threads.

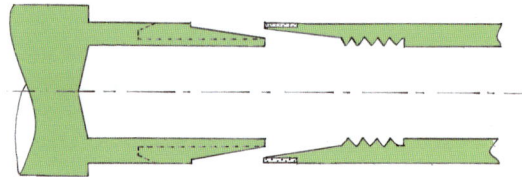

A piece of new material is then set in the lathe and bored out to a diameter slightly less than the inner bore of the cap. It is finished to the correct outside diameter and polished. It is then turned to the chosen taper angle and the cut terminated in a step equal to the band thickness. The pieces are then glued together with super glue or epoxy, and any excess removed from the outside immediately. The cap is then remounted in the lathe and the excess material cut off the lip. It is then carefully bored out to the same diameter as the rest of the cap, taking care not to touch the threads. The lip is sawn and turned to the correct length and edge profiled with a hand scraper to match the original. The job is completed using a range of fine abrasives and plastic polish.

BARREL THREAD CRACKS

A barrel crack through the threads is a serious problem for a fountain pen. Untreated, the crack will get worse and eventually the section will not stay in place. As far as we know, there is no glue that will withhold the fitting stress of a correctly dimensioned section.

The alternatives are to glue everything together (awful consequences for any future servicing), or to line the barrel throat with a thin metal sleeve, as found in many Eversharp pens. It is not necessary to line the whole barrel, only the 10mm or so under the threads.

The barrel is then mounted in the lathe and the inner surface cut out on a taper (5^0 is about right). The metal insert does not have to be very thick to give adequate strength, so there is no need to cut very far into the barrel material and possibly endanger the base of the barrel threads.

A piece of brass (or clear acrylic if the barrel is translucent) is then bored out to just less than the diameter of the section shaft, and tapered on the outside to fit the barrel mouth. This is fixed with superglue or epoxy and finished off in the lathe with very fine cuts so that the section fits tightly

Small band clamp to hold cracked barrel while glue cures.

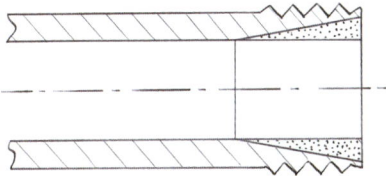

Conical liner glued in the barrel mouth

The first step is to glue the crack with epoxy or superglue. The important thing is to close the crack completely (use some heat) and to use some form of clamp while the glue cures. Clamping can be a problem, because the barrel must stay circular. One solution is to use an ordinary clamp with a piece of greased dowel in the barrel throat. A band clamp (main picture), as used by dentists, provides a more elegant solution.

again. In some pens with very thin barrels, it may not be possible to make the opening as wide as it was before, so the section may have to be trimmed down a little. Some of the glue may have spilled into the outside threads, so the final task is to clear this out with a fine knife-edge file or razor saw. This repair will make the pen stronger than it ever was.

If the barrel had a thread-fit section it is easiest to do the repair as described and convert the section to push fit, but a threaded sleeve in metal or tough plastic may be possible if the barrel material is thick enough.

For advice on cracks in any other part of the barrel, please refer to cosmetic treatment.

CAP TO BARREL THREADING

Many otherwise excellent pens are spoilt because the cap does not attach firmly to the barrel. Ideally a cap should screw up tightly after one rotation when it will be held by three rows of threads if it is the usual three-start thread. If the cap does not grip, or tightens on less than half a turn, several options exist to correct it, and these must be chosen based on the reason for the problem, the severity of the problem, the tools and skills available and the effect on the pen produced by the corrective action.

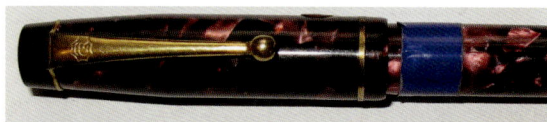

Measuring the problem

Remove the section and screw on the cap to the point where it is gripped by at least one turn. Place a piece of adhesive tape on the barrel tight up to the cap lip. Remove the cap, replace the section and then measure the distance between the edge of the tape and the cap lip when the cap is replaced. In most cases this distance will be around 2mm.

Reasons for the problem

- Barrel threads are worn
- The cap threads are worn in a similar way
- A section has been fitted that is too long
- The inner cap is not pushed fully in or is too long

The options

- Shorten the inner cap
- Cut away the worn barrel threads
- Shorten the section from the front or the rear
- Expand the barrel mouth using heat treatment and a tapered mandrel
- Shrink the cap by heat treatment and rotation between the fingers
- Create new threads in the cap by moulding with epoxy
- Machine away the old threads, glue in a liner or collar and cut new threads

The implications

Shortening the inner cap may leave insufficient room for the nib: if this is indicated by the depth gauge, the nib can be set lower or it may be possible to drill the inner cap a little deeper. Reducing the length of the barrel threads may spoil the appearance of the pen, and the filling mechanism may be affected.

Shortening the section from the front may be possible, but it could affect the fit against the blind cap. Shortening from the rear may require the sac peg to be shortened too.

Expanding the barrel end must be confined to the first few mm or the section will be loose.

How to do it

For the repairer without a lathe, the inner cap option is probably the best. It can be shortened with a hand operated end mill of the correct diameter without having to remove it from the cap. Failing that, the inner cap will have to be removed and cut down, making sure that it finishes up square. The easiest and best method is on the lathe with a boring tool.

The barrel or the section can be shortened by hand, but it is vitally important to leave the ends square or the cap will not sit straight.

Barrel end expansion and cap shrinking are not difficult if you can control the heat. Too little and you risk cracking, and too much may distort the cap so that it will not fit at all.

To create new threads with epoxy it is necessary to make sure that adhesion is only in the right place! Clean both cap and barrel threads thoroughly and then apply a thin but complete coat of Vaseline or epoxy release agent to the barrel and barrel threads. Epoxy is then applied evenly, but not excessively, to the cap threads and the cap is screwed onto the barrel without the section. Leave it for a day to cure and then unscrew it using heat, expecting it to be very tight. The threads can be loosened up using a fine grade of valve grinding compound or a thread chaser. The cutting of complete new threads is for the advanced machinist – see Threads.

This is a major topic that deserves more attention than we can give here so we have simply included some general points on the materials that pens have been made from over the years.

There are 4 main ones
- Vulcanite, Ebonite or hard rubber
- Cellulose nitrate and acetate polymers
- Casein polymers
- Acrylic polymers

The chemistry and the physical processes to make marbled and patterned materials is beyond the scope of this book, but it is necessary to know what materials you are working with. A quick test on any material is to use a red hot needle to produce an odour.

Hard rubber (HR)
Before 1920 the majority of pens were made from hard rubber. Thomas Hancock patented the process of vulcanization in England in 1844 noting the qualities of hard rubber, and it was also patented by Nelson Goodyear in 1851.

It proved to be an excellent material for pens and particularly the parts that were in contact with the ink. It is easy to recognise by it's sulphrous smell. It is stable in the dark but unstable to light and over time becomes brittle, loses sulphur and develops that greeny brown tinge with loss of surface gloss. Washing can reduce surface acidity but there is no reversal of degradation.

Cellulose nitrate (CN)
Known by various names Parkesine, Xylonite, Celluloid, Radite, Permanite. It was adopted by pen makers in the 1920s. Some of these materials can be flammable. Mixes after 1928 are quite stable.

Cellulose acetate (CA)
These polymers were similar to CN but they had a wider range of hardness. They were used in many European pens.

Casein
A natural polymer from rennet and skimmed milk, hardened by formaldehyde treatment.

Acrylic
A general name for a multitude of poly methyl

A mix of celluloid tubes and hard rubber rods.

methacrylate polymers. The properties of these materials vary but have the characteristic of a hydrophobic, glassy material, which can be plasticised.

Some practical observations relating to pens

 Hard rubber varies considerably. Take care with some of the 1940s rods, which are porous and also part filled with bitumen. They can give off a really irritating odour, when turning them. It is good practice to wear a mask.

To date no one has reproduced authentic looking red hard rubber as a material for restoration. Other colours have been made but red still seems to be beyond the rubber supplier's capabilities.

Modern black hard rubber and the green and fawn ripples make excellent pens and can be worked easily with the help of a lubricant.

Cellulose acetate and nitrate tubes are still available and can be used without problems. They may require some soaking and straightening. It is recommended that they are left soaking for about 2 hours in warm water 60°C and then allowed to dry out with a wooden or steel rod in them. They are then straight and are less brittle to turn

Cutting Acrylic on a lathe is not as easy as other materials. It is particularly important to have sharp cutting tools and work at a slow speed with a coolant (water). Post turning crazing is much worse with extruded acrylic than cast material so beware of using rods when making demonstrators.

COSMETIC TREATMENT

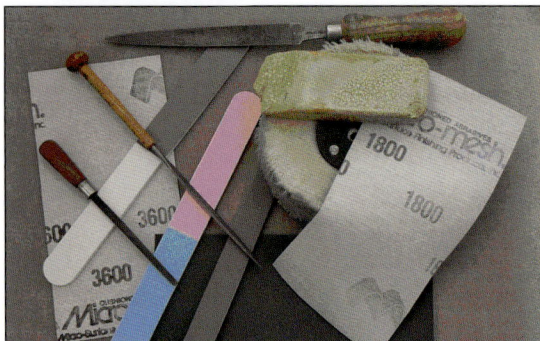
Materials used in cosmetic restoration

Many pen enthusiasts do not need their pens to work – only to look as though they have just left the factory. After perhaps 60 years or more of use, it is quite a challenge to find the elixir of youth for such pens!

Many faults may have developed over the years, such as scratches, cracks, stains, discolouration, burn marks, bite marks, plier marks, chips, engravings, damaged bands, worn plating and distortions.

Dirt, stains and minor scratching

This is about cleaning and polishing, where cleaning is defined simply as the removal of dirt, and polishing is the removal of surface material. Cleaning should be the easiest of all restoration tasks, but it is possible to get it wrong. The main rule is never to use a technique that is more invasive than necessary. If the pen is just greasy and dirty without any obvious scratches or unwelcome surface features, soap and water are probably all that is needed. A good wash would improve most pens inside and out!

Minor scratches may need to be treated with a polish, but some collectors prefer a pen to have a 'patina' that characterises its period of useful service.

Pens are sometimes polished to a glassy (ghastly?) shine that they would never have had when new. Very fine abrasives are required to achieve such a shine, and these do not touch wear scratches, so all they do is polish the gaps between the scratches and thereby create a 'tarted up' appearance. Paradoxically, an aggressive polish gives the pen a 'VGC' appearance because the wear scratches are reduced and other fine scratches are introduced to create the impression of a good life.

Very good results are achieved with cutting agents for cellulose paint on car bodies (T-cut).

Metal polishes such as Simichrome have achieved widespread popularity but these in common with cellulose polishes contain solvents which could cause damage to vintage plastics. It is wise to clean the surfaces thoroughly but safer to use water based polishes such as Micro-gloss (formulated for military use in cockpit canopies)

Many pen repairers use a number of buffing wheels each loaded with a different grade of abrasive. However if incorrectly used wheels have their hazards and it can be a quick and easy way to finish a pen - in both senses of the word. During a moment of inattention, the surface may be melted, the edge taken off a feature that should remain crisp and the pen could even be thrown across the workshop when the clip catches in the wheel!

Macro scratches and scuff marks

These may be filled as for engravings or they can be treated with files and abrasive sticks. Select the finest file that is sufficient to remove the damage, and progress through to the final polish. It is usually necessary to work on a much wider area than the local damage so as not to change the surface profile in a noticeable way. Extra caution is required when near trim or edges; a small piece of masking tape can give protection.

Plier and bite marks

The effect of these defects is reduced by applying heat, as most pen parts are thermoplastic. Plier marks on sections are a common problem (why do they do it?). Before using any abrasives, put the section in boiling water for a few seconds. If none of the original material has been scored away, hard rubber will recover its original profile. Boiling water will spoil decorative plastics, but hot air in moderation is fine, so it is worth a try for the reduction of bite damage. Finish off with abrasives as you would for scuff marks.

Engravings and burn marks

There is no perfect method for these problems because original material has been destroyed. Shallow engravings and burns can be taken out by removal of the surrounding material with files, abrasive sticks and polish, but to do this with deep engravings or other deep surface damage would change the original profile of the pen in a noticeable way.

A deep engraving filled with paint

The engraving cut back to virgin material

The engraving filled

The surface is reprofiled

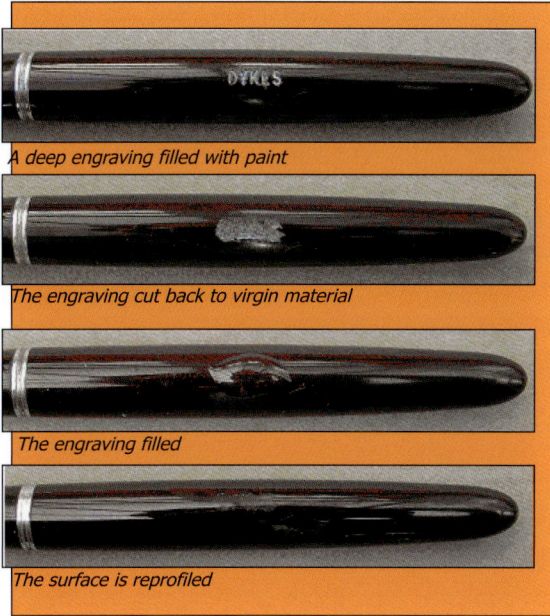

Superglue gel or clear epoxy resin is useful for filling defects in plastic. Choose a make that sets hard and will take a good polish. If the defect is shallow use layers of superglue.

First, the engraving must be cut back to virgin material with a small engraving tool, leaving no trace of dirt, paint filling or burn debris. The clear filler will appear to take on the colour of the base material and will make a good repair when hardened and abraded down to the original profile.

Engravings on gold or silver can be polished out if shallow, and can be filled with gold or silver solder if deep, but this is a risky job, especially with a fragile overlay.

Clear epoxy and a collection of colouring materials

Chips and cracks

Chips in a cap lip are best dealt with by lip replacement, but when this is not possible, the chip can be rebuilt using an epoxy resin that is known to set to a hardness comparable with the pen plastic (e.g. Devcon).

Epoxy can be tinted with dyes designed for the purpose, but other substances can be used including powdered original plastic and cosmetic make-up materials. With care, a passable imitation of marbled plastics can be created this way. Test the additives first because they may affect the curing process.

The base surface should be cleaned and roughened; some support from masking tape may be needed while the epoxy cures. When the epoxy has had several days to harden, it may be cut to shape with files and polished.

Closed ended cracks (not cap lips) are best treated with thin superglue that can penetrate hair lines. A band clamp will be useful in holding wider cracks together. Cracks in plain materials are much harder to disguise than those in patterned material. In some difficult materials (e.g. red hard rubber) the glued crack can be surface etched and filled with a matching colourant. Cap lip cracks are problematical because of the thin material and high stresses. Repairs are rarely sucessful but a plastic weld using MEK (methyl ethyl ketone) can work reasonably well. But take care, this material is hazardous.

Surface crazing

This fault is a characteristic of casein. It is probably due to exposure to heat and light over the years.

The surface will be dull and unresponsive to polish; under a glass the cause will be seen as a network of fine shallow cracks. The use of abrasives may help the situation, but it is not always possible to remove sufficient material to provide a cure. The best treatment starts with

The engraving tool used to clear out the engraving on the pen

a thorough clean followed by a coat of clear cellulose varnish or thin superglue. This will bond the surface by filling the cracks and then the pen can be lightly abraded and polished.

Discolouration/loss of colour

This is often the result of a chemical reaction with the sulphur in rubber ink sacs, but it is also caused by contact with ink and by prolonged exposure to sunlight. Unfortunately, there is not a lot that can be done, but if the material has lost most of its colour and is verging on transparency, the inside surface can be painted the relevant colour.

Distortion

If a pen appears bent, check first that the lip of the inner cap is not damaged, because this can result in the cap being pulled off axis as it is tightened. The same effect will be seen if the end of the section is damaged, or mounted off the central axis of the barrel.

A bent barrel can only be fixed by heat. The main problem is to know by how much to bend it back. By holding the end of the barrel in a lathe chuck, the extent of the distortion will be apparent as

the lathe rotates. A close fitting metal rod can be placed down the barrel and heated so that heat can be provided from both sides. The rod will give leverage, keep the barrel round and provide an indication of the straightening achieved.

Metal trim

Levers, clips and bands can be replated without removing them, but they must be cleaned thoroughly, and the old plating either removed or polished down to a feather edge.

Loose bands (see Cap Bands) are usually loose because the plastic beneath them has shrunk. The best way to fix this problem is to heat the cap and force a heated tapered rod inside the cap to expand it again.

However, the rod will have to be specially made for the particular cap. Bands can be glued, but they will stand proud somewhere, so it is often better to replace them if the cap cannot be expanded. Band fitting is problematical, but it can be done if heat is used together with a mandrel to restore the roundness of the cap lip afterwards (see ' Cap Bands').

HARD RUBBER RESTORATION

One can improve an oxidised pen but there is usually a downside to any 'colour' restoration. There are various techniques:

- using 40 wire wool gently abrade the surface, then dust off and smear on petroleum jelly, wrap in a cloth and leave in a drawer for a month or so. Remove and wipe. It usually seems much better, but that is to some extent the 'grease' which has improved the reflectance.

Just the thing for a wet afternoon! Get this one back to black!

- bleach the item with active hypochlorite diluted 60% with water, immersing the item for 3 minutes and then drying off with a cloth. (Do not rinse.) Repeat until there is improvement. This method can give short term improvement to filigree silver overlays. Seal and polish with pure linseed oil. beware thatb the use of bleach can also soften the surface and destroy.

- immerse in black dye and leave to soak for a day or so. Take out and dry.

- where there is no surface decoration, remove the oxidation on a lathe using hand held scrapers and abrasives.

Experiment yourself - Try T-cut for synthetics, try toothpaste, try anything that is a mild abrasive. Our experience is that the appearance can be improved, but rarely brought back completely and surface detail is usually sacrificed with the methods that give the best colour recovery.

PLATING

Peter Ford's set up for plating clips and small items; the plating solution is poured back into a sealed dark container after use; the powerpack is wired up for three stations so one can have gold, silver and electro cleaning .

Practical electrode made from a stainless steel spoon

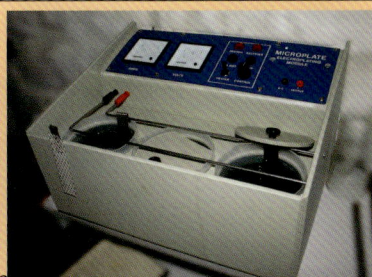

A 'Microplate' plating system, which we use, has heating elements for copper/gold and three one iltre tanks.

The replating of clips, lever boxes and trim can be an excellent way of sprucing up the appearance of a pen. Polishing brassed items can give a temporary improvement but where the plating has worn through to the copper or nickel the tarnished appearance will reappear very quickly.

Quality plating is not beyond the repairer and it does not require a massive expense in equipment or chemicals.

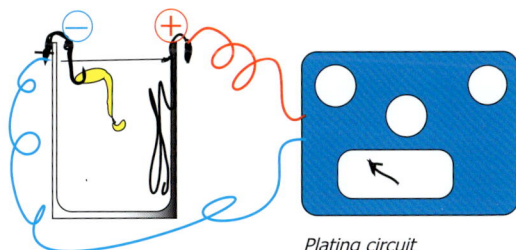

Plating circuit

Basics

The principle of plating is to pass a current through a gold, silver or copper solution using a stainless steel anode and the cathode as the item to be plated. Electroplating from solution in our experience is safer and more efficient than pen plating.

A simple set up which can be easily stored and reused uses a DC laboratory power pack, a small beaker, a stainless steel spoon, a paper clip and two crocodile leads.

A variable voltage allows current to be optimised to get the best plating conditions. For most small items such as clips and lever boxes, an efficient current for non porous plating demands around 5 to 6 volts using a 250ml beaker with the normal recommended concentrations of gilding or plating electrolyte at room temperature. Plating is completed in about 10 seconds and can be repeated if necessary.

Cleaning the item to be plated

All traces of grease must be removed and after a good scrub with detergent the item can be boiled in non foaming detergent. Rinse thoroughly and leave the items in a rinse beaker ; grease will spread from your hands and affect the efficiency of the plating so handle with clean tweezers.

With industrial plating, the first step after physically cleaning the item is to electrolytically clean the item. This can be done in a home set up by using the item as the cathode in an alkaline cleaning mix (obtained from a plating chemicals supplier). The item is then rinsed and transferred to the plating beaker and the current switched on for 10 seconds (about 5V for gold 2V for silver).

Remove the item and rinse well and then dry. You may have to experiment a little with conditions. Gold is plated at 60^0C in a commercial plater, silver is plated at room temperature. You will be amazed at the results and how easy it is.

Materials can be obtained from plating supply specialist such as Balco in the UK. Gilding, silver, copper, nickel and cleaning salts are not expensive. Enough chemical for a litre will last for years.

Rinsing is very important and the safety instructions must be obeyed.

It is imperative to understand that some of the materials are 'dangerous' and have to be handled as per the recommended instructions. Most gilding silver and copper salts contain amounts of potassium cyanide so care is essential. Rubber gloves, glasses and a lab coat are recommended and the solutions MUST be kept well out of the reach of children.

CAUTION

MACHINES & EQUIPMENT

Myford ML7

A variety of machine tools can be used for pen repair ranging in size from micro lathes to the machine illustrated above.

Small power tools and hobby kits prove useful for certain jobs. Machine equipment can appear daunting, but a lot of hand work can be carried out with lathes when making pen parts.

The benefit of having workshop machinery is that it is possible to make tools for repairing pens as well as replacement parts.

Lathes

Any small lathe can be an asset and even one with an inordinate amount of backlash can do useful jobs. When you can buy a Chinese made screw-cutting lathe for $350, it is hard not to become a model engineer. Screw cutting is essential if you wish to make sections and clip screws for caps. Collets are a great time saver for aligning and a swivel tool post is useful, particularly, when turning curved shapes.

Some options are:-

The Myford ML7 This is illustrated at the top and can do most of what is required – it has robust metal screwcutting change wheels for the various threads used in pen making and has a good indexing gauge. It can be used for heavy metal work. However it rarely comes with collets and usually has a 3 jaw chuck. Make sure it has a good one otherwise you will become very

frustrated when setting up and aligning.

Pultra This was one of the most popular lathes used during the war for instrument manufacture and still is very popular. It is larger than a watchmaker's lathe but with no screw cutting; however it comes with collets and is ideal for making push sections and small work.

Clarke/Chester These Chinese made lathes are known by many trade names and they are a great buy for pen work. They have excellent variable speed and with practice can be accurately set up for a wide range of screwcutting. They are not made for very heavy metal work but great for plastics and soft metal. There is a lot of internet information and parts available so check out www.mini-lathe.com and www.LittleMachineShop.com for background and parts and opinions. These are not precision lathes for Swiss watchmakers but do not be put off, as there are so many in service it is easy to get advice by phone or email.

The Emcomat 7

A heavier duty lathe in our case fitted with Schaublin collets. It is a great lathe for making parts and screw cutting. It also has a milling machine which can be used for heavy work. A quick change tool post makes it so easy to switch from turning to threading to parting. It is important to appreciate that it can take more time to set up a lathe than use it!

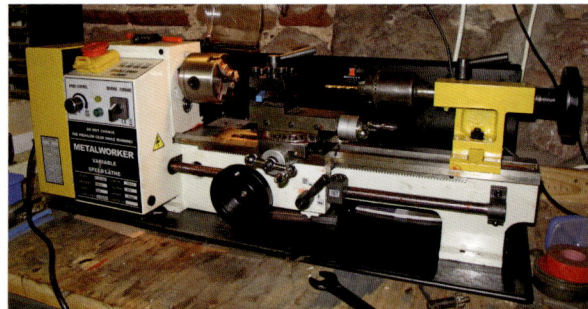

Chester Lathe

Milling machines

There may seem little point in a milling machine because most 'milling or slotting' that is required for pens can usually be done on a lathe with an end drill or slitting saw. All the spirals for the Stylochap safety pens in the 1990s were made on a small lathe using the tool post to hold the hard rubber rod. However if you want to make parts that have flats, such as Visofil pump units, accurately cut grooves or lever slots then it is an easy task with a milling machine. Stand alone milling machines such as Clarke/ Axminster take up space so the alternative is to have a combination unit such as the Emcomat above

Emcomat 7 with variable speed for milling and turning with collets and 'Elliot' toolpost (inset)

Bench grinders

Small grinders look neat but rarely have enough power for heavy work without slowing down. If you have to sharpen tools or grind frequently, then get a powerful bench unit.

Surface sander/grinder

A disc sander provides a quick way of abrading at accurate angles and making a square cut. When it is used in conjunction with a drill holding hard rubber it simplifies making conical tassies from plastic rod or clip screws from bolts.

Buffing machine

'A must for some, anathema for others' . Buffing has the wheel rotating towards you and it can be a traumatic experience if a clip or pen catches on the buff. If you are going use a buff make sure that you buy a suitable machine and learn how to use it. (Use a mask and goggles!) It is practical to use your lathe for polishing or a bench grinder fitted with a mop, however a grinder usually rotates at too high a speed (500-700rpm is best for buffing). Be sure to buy the correct type and grade of buffing compound.

'Clarke' or 'Axminster' machines can be set up for drilling and milling. Note rotating chuck. holder with indexing.

'Record' disc grinder

Set up for making a regular conical end

MACHINING PRACTICE - MAKING A NEW SECTION

We have provided suggestions on how to use tools for pen repair but we do encourage enthusiasts to broaden their activities, because it is often easier to make a pen part than one thinks. Consequently, as well as hints on general workshop, facilities, storage and tools, we have included this step-by-step instruction on how to make a pen part, in this case a gripping section.

This is a frequent requirement because sections are probably the most abused part on vintage pens. The efforts of would-be repair men armed with household pliers have ruined the sections of a great many pens and although some can be salvaged using the boiling water technique, those with deep score marks, indicating the loss of material, cannot be recovered in this way. The solution is to make a new section.

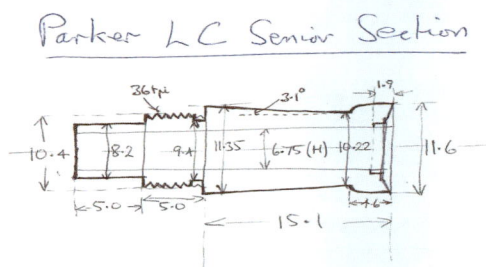

Parker LC Senior Section

Preparation before machining

You may have a broken or damaged section or it may be missing. You must have a diagram of what you are going to make and that means measuring and drafting; a simple sketch will do but it is critical to know your target sizes and lengths. Measure the thread pitch, but unless it is a Sheaffer, you can be sure that it is a 36tpi single start thread. With a pair of digital callipers you may end up with a sketch as illustrated. (Not a CAD CAM project!)

Materials and tools

Sections are best made from hard rubber. Not only is this consistent with the original but the 'thermal

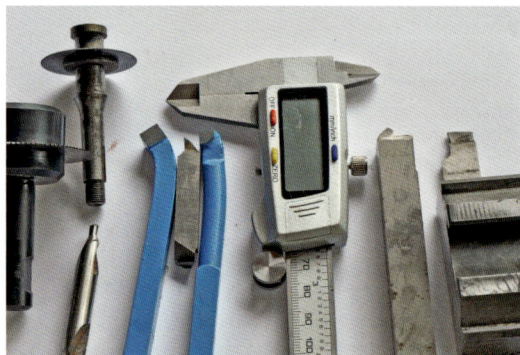

properties' make it easy to fit the nib/feed and the 'surface characteristics' facilitates ink flow (14 to 16mm diameter rod is usually used). If this material cannot be obtained, black plastic such as Acetal (engineering Nylon) is an option. An engineering lathe with thread cutting capabilities is required with appropriate lathe tools and measuring devices.

Strategy One must plan the sequential steps to convert a rod into a Patrician, Duofold or Swan section. First decide the order of cuts. If one opts for the sequence illustrated in the diagram below, the procedure ensures that the barrel fitting end of the section is first to be made. Only after that is done do we move on to the shaping and parting stages.

Sequential stages

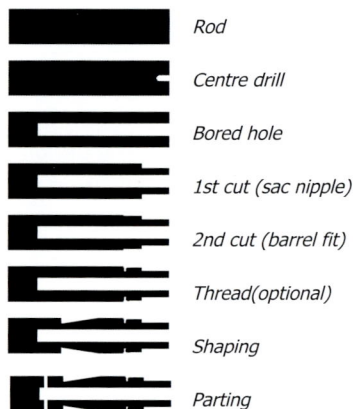

Rod

Centre drill

Bored hole

1st cut (sac nipple)

2nd cut (barrel fit)

Thread(optional)

Shaping

Parting

One can now assemble the necessary lathe and hand tools required for this specific task.

Starting-The material is mounted in the 3-jaw chuck with a little more (2mm) protruding than the final length of the section. The end is then turned square and a centre drill used to provide a starting point for the feed hole. This hole must be accurately drilled to obtain a sliding fit for the feed, so it is desirable to have available a set of number and letter drills. Use a lathe speed of about 500rpm, except for thread cutting, final finishing and parting off. During the turning keep a continual check on dimensions and lengths with digital callipers.

Centre drill and then bore/drill feed channel

on slow speed). Go slowly and catch the section on a thin dowel as it falls off. Make final adjustments to the central hole with files and reamers. The new section can be assembled with a feed, nib and sac and fitted to the barrel.

Another critical aspect of the section is its fit to the barrel, whether push fit or threaded. Push fit sections must be finished with extremely fine cuts, so it is important to stop when the fit seems a little too tight. Make sure that the length machined includes the length of the sac peg. Now turn the sac peg and include a few ridges to help with sac adhesion.

Threading-For threaded fitting to the barrel, cut a groove, using a 1mm parting tool, where the threads will terminate down to a depth equal to the core diameter. Now mount the 60^0 thread cutting tool and engage the lead screw of the lathe to advance the tool holder towards the headstock as the chuck is rotated. Use a very slow speed on the lathe or turn the chuck by hand as you take a series of small cuts down to the final thread depth.

Be sure not to disengage the lead screw between cuts and remember to withdraw the tool from the work before reversing the lathe back a little beyond the starting point for the next cut. As a confirmation check that the barrel fits without removing the rod from the lathe.

SHAPING-The external shape of the section normally includes tapers and curves. Tapers can be cut easily but they usually end in curves and this can cause problems with simple x and y fed tools. The simplest solution to this problem is to finish the curved bits with files, but this leaves a rough surface. A more satisfying approach is to use the free-hand wood turning approach with a set of curved tools. When the desired profile has been obtained, finish off with fine abrasives and polish. The final step is cutting off with a parting tool (lathe

First cut with a conventional tool angled at 10^0 to give a clean seat

Use parting tool or narrow cutter to make a recess if section is to be threaded

Threading cuts-note the tool profile at 60^0

Use a conventional tool to make the taper.

Hand cuts with a curved tool supported on a bar in tool post

Parting tool to cut section to length

Section recessed by hand with hand tool-note support bar and tape on section threads in chuck

DISMANTLING METAL CAPS

Universal puller in plastic cap mode. Fittings for Parker51, PFM and Crest shown

Dismantling is the starting process of most pen repairs and a pen is said to be 'pulled apart' even if it is unscrewed. Typically dismantling first involves pulling a section out and then pushing the feed out of the section.

Manual Pulling

The use of a pair of section pliers, or fixing an item in a clamp and pulling, are both common processes in pen repair. In most cases hand strength is adequate to separate sections and nibs, but in some cases more force is required to separate parts, and in these situations machine pullers are required. This is frequently the case with more modern pens, where push fit and strong adhesives are used.

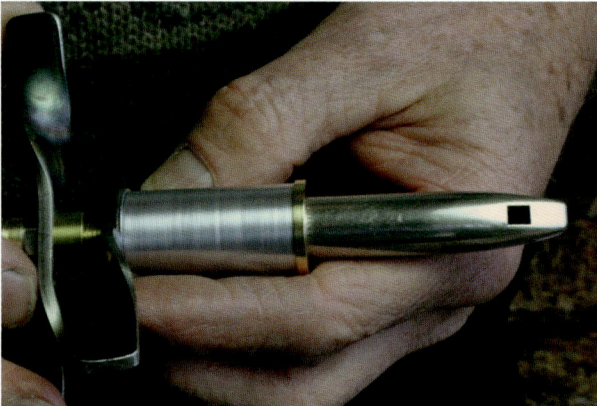

Pulling the inner cap from a PFM with a missing clip

Machine Puller

A machine puller can use a lever or a screw to apply force. With pen repair a puller is more frequently used to pull parts out of a tube rather than pull items from a shaft as is usually the case with mechanical applications.

A good puller involves three elements: -
-getting a good grip on the item to be moved;
-having something firm to pull against
-having a method of applying sufficient force.

Most pullers are used to remove parts from caps, such as inner caps, clutch springs, barrel thread and bushes.

The Universal Puller

This recent development has a range of applications. It can be applied to withdrawing any item from a cap, providing the necessary gripping partsr and shoulder plates.

To date PFM, Crest, Targa, Sheaffer Reminder, Parker VS, Jotter, 51, 61, 75 and plastic inner caps have succumbed.

It is significant to remember that Sheaffer caps are difficult because they were assembled with resin. Heat is essential.

The Lathe

If you have a lathe you already have a puller in the tail stock. It can be used to pull inner caps as well as bushes. It is always a problem gripping a cap in a lathe but it is easy to make a flanged holding tube. Fit the cap into the tube; grip it in the chuck; use the tail stock with an appropriate expanding gripper on the inner cap to pull through the holder tube base.

EXTRACTING INNER CAPS

Two models of cap extractor being used to remove an inner cap from a Waterman 7 ripple and a Conklin.
Listen for the click or squeak as the inner cap moves.

The inner cap is a short cup or tube usually made from hard rubber and its prime function is to seal the pen when not in use. This means that the ink in the nib does not dry out and the pen starts to write immediately.

The inner cap also helps to secure clips that are attached to the cap by rivets, prongs or simply long extensions. Such examples are Waterman, early Conway Stewart, Swan and Eversharp and Conklin.

When clip repair has to be carried out on such pens, the inner cap must be removed by pulling it out.

Pre-preparation

All inner caps are encrusted with dried out ink and to facilitate inner cap removal it is important to soak and soften this. The cap can be immersed in water in an ultrasonic bath. However, we prefer to invert it on a small stand (polystyrene foam) with the breather holes plugged with wax or blue tack and then fill the cap with a mild alkaline solution; leave to stand for at least 2 to 3 hours. This is extremely important as it makes pulling easier and thereby reduces the stress on the cap lip if a puller is used for inner cap removal.

Procedure

The actual pulling can be achieved in a number of ways. Threading a long shanked coarse tap into the inner cap and pulling may remove the inner cap but most situations require more refined procedures.

The inner cap must be gripped with sufficient friction so an expanding collet is usually the method designed into inner cap repair tools.

It is important to protect the cap lip as much as possible so one must take care with caps that have shrunk, making the inner cap very tight. In such cases heating the outside of the cap may be necessary. It is very easy to crush a thin pen lip. With some longer caps a 'make do' spacer might be needed like the rather large nut illustrated below.Sometimes the inner cap splits or breaks on removal but these are easy to make from hard rubber rod or tube.

Various commercial cap pullers

A large screw or tap can be used to pull out a loose inner cap but normally a slow pull with a threaded contraption is required. The Pen Sac Co. model is available from Cathedral pens and Woodbins; Pen Practice have their own Universal cap puller and Fountain Pen hospital sell an economic simple puller.

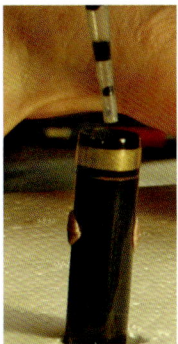

Spacer

DENTS AND REFINISHING METAL PENS

A selection of cap and barrel mandrels for different pens. Accurate shape and smooth surfaces are critical to achieve good restoration.

Dents in metal pens are a source of great irritation, even if they are quite small and not noticeable to the casual observer. The good news is that most dents can be removed with a little care, even the dreadful ones shown in the photographs!

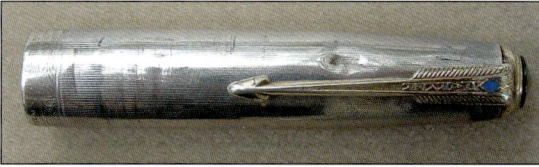

Parker 51 silver cap in a sorry state

The same cap and clip after dent removal

The main difficulty in dent removal is the extraction of the metal liner that all metal caps seem to have. Parker 51 caps have a spring steel clutch located just at the mouth of the cap: this has to be removed so that the inner cap can come out. With the cap tube empty, a mandrel can be inserted (main picture) and the dents can be rolled out with a polished steel roller. Special tools have to be used to remove Parker 51 clutches, and the liners from some other caps (e.g. Sheaffer) but these are now available.

Rolling out the dents

When the cap is dismantled, the cap tube must be thoroughly cleaned on the inside. If any stubborn deposits remain they can be removed with wet/dry paper wrapped around a pencil or a gun bore cleaning tool. This is important because the inner profile will transfer to the outside of the cap when rolling a ding.

The mandrel is a metal former that matches the inside profile of the cap; it is the surface against which the roller will press. It is not desirable that the mandrel should be a tight fit to the inside of the cap for three reasons:- space needs to be allowed for the ding, the cap needs to be able to move such that the inner surface of the cap is always in full contact with the mandrel wherever the roller is applied, and caps do vary slightly in size. For these reasons, it is often possible to use a mandrel that was made for a smaller cap with greater curvature.

The mandrel should be held tightly in a vice with the end slightly raised and the cap pushed on as far as it will go.

The steel roller is then rolled and rocked across the ding towards the cap lip using moderate pressure - only as hard as necessary to remove all traces of the ding. We have found that it is better to use the rolling technique rather than a hammering one because hammering is much more

CAUTION If there is corrosion inside which creates rough hollows, it will be very difficult to get an acceptable result.

Rolling out the ding on a Parker 51 rolled gold cap

The polished silver steel dent roller

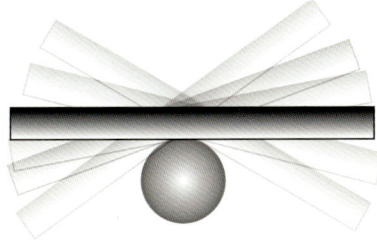

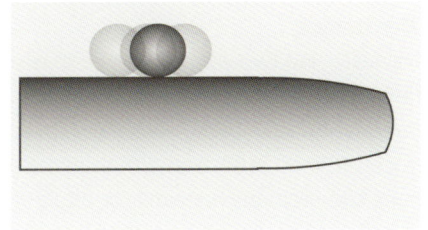

likely to cause local stretching of the material. However, for some dents, especially around the tops of caps, a leather, plastic or wooden headed hammer may be the best option. Gold filled and silver caps will not require much finishing other than metal polish.

Note that the rolling process does not affect the chasing pattern on silver and gold caps, so it follows that the technique is not effective for pin point dents.

The rocking and rolling motion with the roller

FINISHING A STAINLESS STEEL CAP

There are various methods of finishing a cap that has been restored. The aim is to get a that 'new' matt appearance without it looking scratched. Many

Before-small scuffs and scratches -shiny

After- matt even surface

abrasive procedures work such as emery paper (600 grit), 0000 steel wool or Scotchbrite best applied on a lathe with a lubricant such as cutting oil or WD40. However we have found that model makers alumina shot blasting gives that 'new' look but a good gun and compressor is required as well as dry abrasive. One must be careful and mask off the lower cap lip if a contrast and shiny band is required. The two caps illustrate the effect.

Do not use this technique without wearing a mask and goggles.

Modest 'Badger alumina shot blasting kit. Use an enclosed space and wear a mask!

THREADS

Three important pieces of kit.
Thread profile plate
TPI gauge
Most imortant 60⁰ lathe tool for cutting the thread.

The basics

For fastening two parts together in a secure and rapid manner, there are few rivals to the screw thread. Fountain pens have made much use of this since the late C19[th], and although many modern pens use click mechanisms for attachment of the cap, few of them will outlast the veritable Lucky Curve Duofold, which is as reliable now as when it was made 90 years ago.

Thread cutting is not a difficult operation with the correct tools, and much can be done without a lathe. Thread cleaning and easing is probably the main reason for interest in this topic, and these operations can be performed entirely by hand.

Thread characteristics

The important properties of a threaded rod are its diameter, its pitch, the number of separate tracks and the thread profile or shape. The triangular profile 'V' thread is the most widely used. British threads have an included angle of 55⁰ with rounded peaks, whereas American and metric threads have an included angle of 60⁰ with flattened peaks. The square thread is sometimes used where strength is a priority, but it demands a very high precision in cutting. A more practical alternative to the V

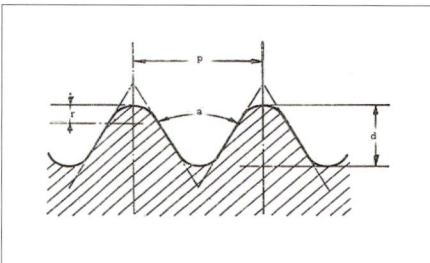

thread is the modified square thread, known as the Acme thread. This has a depth of half the pitch and has an included angle of 29⁰.

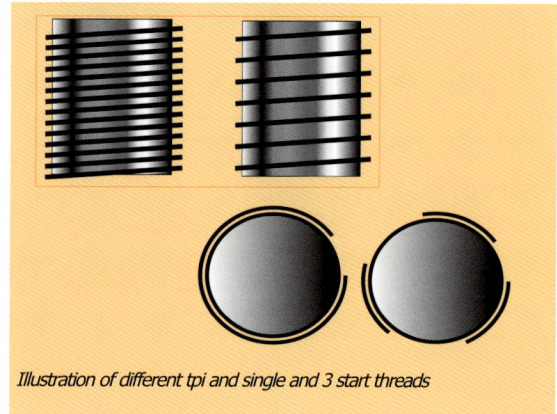

Illustration of different tpi and single and 3 start threads

The pitch of the thread defines how far the component will travel along the thread per turn, and this affects the depth of the thread.
If it is desired to advance the component more rapidly without making the thread deeper, a multi start thread is used; this is one with more than one track.

Threads on pens

Fountain pen manufacturers use multi start threads on pen caps where typically only one turn is required to secure the cap. The 3-start thread is the most popular; it gives the option of three starting points around the circumference and also enables the cap to advance further on the barrel per turn. The downside is thread strength, but that is not an important issue with pens.

Taps and dies

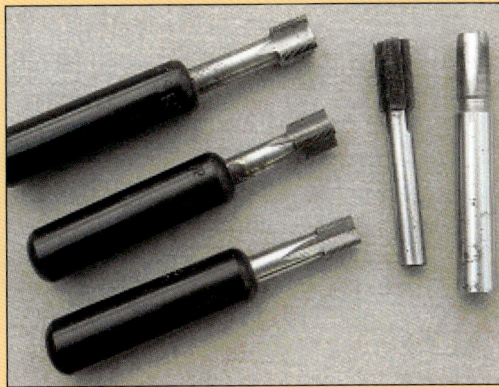

Hand chasers and taps for cleaning specific threads - in this case Parker Lucky Curve cap threads and Parker 51 barrels

30tpi external chaser and a matched pair of external and internal 36tpi chasers for use by hand or machine on single or multistart threads of all diameters

Parker codes for tools	
12876	Standard Aero barrel Tap
12878	Demi Aero Barrel tap
No37	51 barrel Filler unit threads
U	Snr Ext Filler unit cap thread
W	Jnr and Maj Ext Filler unit cap thread
N	All Lady pens cap thread
Q	Snr Lock filler and Snr Duofold cap thread
P	Jnr & Std Lock filler & Jnr Challenger
No1	51 blind cap thread tap
No 8914	Tap for clip and screw bushing

Taps and dies for internal and external thread cutting

Specialist suppliers can provide a huge variety of sizes in taps and dies. Some will even make them to your requirement and supply the correct sized drills for the taps. Even if you do not wish to cut threads from new material, it is useful to have some of these tools because you can use them to clean dirt out of old threads and to restore good fitting where material distortion or shrinkage may have occurred. However be prepared for expense if you wish to obtain 3 start taps.

Thread cutting on the lathe

The 'V' cutting tool aligned with the template (main picture) will enable the cutting of any threads that the lathe can be set up for.

Very low lathe speeds are used for thread cutting, and in many cases it is better to turn the chuck by hand to maximise control; take just a small cut at each pass.

Thread chasers

These are tools with precision cut thread profiles for internal or external threads. They can be used by hand for cleaning and easing threads irrespective of whether the thread is single or multi start. No repairer should be without at least a 36tpi (turns per inch) internal thread chaser. The metric equivalent is 0.7mm pitch.

Chasers can also be used for cutting threads on the lathe in new material. They give the correct profile straight from the tool, so do not require finishing as would be required when using the 'V' tool. The codes of Parker chasers are stamped on the handles and are shown in the table at the bottom of this page.

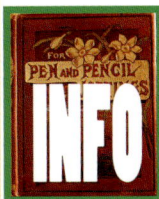

Chasers are the easiest way to cut 3-start threads on the lathe. If the lathe is set to 12tpi on the lead screw, the 36tpi chaser will cut the required three tracks in one operation.

THREAD REFERENCE DATA

General guidance

The 'standard' fountain pen thread is the V pattern with 36 threads per inch (tpi). The metric 0.7mm pitch thread is almost indistinguishable. Pen cap threads are commonly 3-start, so one turn advances the cap by 1/12 inch. Occasionally 2,4 and even 5-start threads are found on caps, so it is essential to check before making a replacement cap.

The easiest way to find the number of starts is to rotate the cap backwards on the barrel threads after binding the cap and the barrel with masking tape so that the position of each 'click' can be marked. The number of marks around the circumference of the cap is the number of thread starts.

Barrel section threads are usually single start 36tpi on early models, but with barrels that have to be removed in order to fill the pens, these are often multistart.
The left hand thread is used where parts must not unscrew in everyday use, such as in piston filling systems.

Finding the number of thread starts. The thread gauge (main picture) will enable you to measure the pitch, but it will not help determine the number of starts.

Specific detail for pen makes

Burnham, Chilton, Conway, Croxley, Esterbrook, Eversharp, Mabie Todd, Mentmore, National Security, Stephens, Summit, Unique, Valentine, Waterman, Wyvern all use 'standard' 36tpi threads.
3-start threads are frequently used, but many manufacturers did not adopt the same number of starts throughout their production run.

Mabie Todd is an example of this as early eyedroppers were single start or 2-start. 1930's models were 3-start and later pens 4-start.

Burnhams are 2-start, early **Conways** and **Watermans** are 4-start.

Dunn, Ford, Onoto, Parker, use standard threads with the following exceptions:-
Dunn uses 48tpi left hand threads for filler butto attachment to the piston (occasionally right hand **Ford** uses 3-start 36tpi threads on caps and 40tpi left hand threads for the piston components (occasionally right hand).

Onoto uses 4-start threads on caps and two star threads on the filler button of early pens. Later ones are single start. 5BA (British Association) le hand threads are used for piston components.

Parker has many variations: Vacumatics use 48t for pump attachment, **P51's** and **P65** Mk1's use 48tpi for shells and 48tpi 3-start for barrels. **P51** Mk3s use 32tpi 2-start for barrels. **P61** Capillary's **P65** Mk2s and **P45's** use 32tpi single start Acme threads with rounded peaks for shells and barrels **P75** barrels use 24tpi single start. **P51** jewel threads are 7BA on UK pens and 5BA on US pens (not 36tpi as on **Vacumatic** jewels).

Sheaffer is the different one; they opted for 30t with 3-start caps. Snorkel pens (including PFM) use 40tpi for attachment of nib sections and mos other internals.
Some left hand threads, and even some multista threads can be found on internal components, so beware of thinking that Sheaffer parts are alway interchangeable!

If you want to know something about pens or pen repair or where to get a part or some material, how do you begin? what are the options? do you 'google' before thinking? We appreciate the power of the internet and would not be without it. However, there are other ways which at times may be more instructive and accurate.

Information sources
People

Every repairer has to ask an expert, at some time, how to do something with a pen that they have not encountered before. In general, information is freely given but occasionally a person is protective of his/her sources of supply, his/her procedure or is just overwhelmed with work. It is perfectly understandable if he/she has invested time and money in perfecting something unique; they are not always keen to give it away. One must respect this but we can guarantee that, in most cases, the same person will willingly advise on general issues for as long as you want to listen.

Courses

Arthur used to have his famous day course, which has been sadly missed but the Writing Equipment Society has made great strides in estacblishing formal courses on repairing pens with the advantage of access to information and archives. Details can be obtained from their website, www.wesonline.org.uk.

Magazines old & new

There are some excellent articles in past issues of pen magazines such as The Pen Fanciers guides; Pen World (especially Fred Plewa's Clips); Pennant's repair sessions (originally with Frank Dubiel, Rick Horne, Victor Chen and Richard Binder); The Writing Equipment Society Journal's 'Two Doctors' pages and recently Stylus articles. There are often special themes or issues to treasure and some of Steve Hull's, Victor Chen's, John Mottishaw's and David Nishimura's contributions are reference works.

Most past articles on repair are as relevant today as they were in the 70s, 80s and 90s.

Booklets

The out of print booklet by Judson Bell is well worth buying if you can find it, particularly for Fred Plewas clips. Joel & Sherrell have produced a handy little guide. Specific pen guides, such as our Onoto guide, Laurence's special guide on the Swan Visofil VT as part of our new PP&PPG Pen Repair Monographs,

REFERENCE INFORMATION

which focus on less popular pen restoration. There is also Richard Binder's amusing but instructive exaggerated drawings - well worth looking at. Commercial booklets including makers promotional booklets are often treasure troves of special information, such as The Pen Sac Co's sac guide, John Mottishaw's 'Nibs', Jack Prices 'Introduction to pens' and Parker, Watermans and Sheaffer regular newsletters to their sales force.

Books
General pen books. It is important to have good reference books and a background on the history of pens. There are plenty of general books but which ones are the best? Which ones do we use?

The early books were peppered with adverts, but the quality of print and images of the soft bound books was poor compared to today's standards. Some books have a niche, and for older pens George Fischler & Stuart Schneider's Schiffer publications are still excellent reference books. For the 'golden age' and the transition to modern, Andy Lambrou's big book is our reference, but his early Sotheby's version was our first base for UK makers. For general reading Paul Erano's 3 books will give one a good foundation. Continental pens were first referenced by Regina Martini. There are now many others (see Bibliography) and the books of Peter Twydle, João Pavão Martins, Luiz Leite and Antonio Gagean will educate the collector in different ways. Have a look at reader's opinions on the internet and use your library's lending service, if you want to savour before buying!

Specialist books
Books that focus on makers or models or countries have been particularly popular in the last few years. The first specialist book was probably Paul Hoban's Esterbrook summary. Marc van der Stricht and Bernard Bernolet compiled a reference book for 'Limited editions' and Letizia Jacopini dealt with Italian pens. The trend was set, and the Parker 51 book of Mark and David Shepherd was followed by David Shepherd co-authoring more books on The Parker Duofold, The Parker Vacumatic and The Parker Jotter. David Moak cornered the US Mabie Todd shelves and Max Davis and Gary Lehrer dealt with Watermans. For ball pen enthusiasts Henry Gastony and Stuart Schneider and then Graham Hogg produced books and British pen manufacturers were not forgotten

with Neptune by Steve Hull and Mike Bryan and Conway Stewart by Steve Hull, whose book on Onoto and de LaRue is imminent. The classic Pelikan received attention from Jürgen Dittmar, Martin Lehman and recently D Schafer, while The Montblanc Diary and Collectors Guide by Jens Rössler became a collectable in it's own right as did Julia Hutt and Steve Overbury's book on Namiki. Fountain pens of Japan is a masterpiece by Andy Iambrou and Masa Sunami. The physics of pens has been elegantly dealt with by Geoff Roe in his booklet 'Writing Instruments' and summarised in the 2005 paper, 'Ink Reservoir Writing Instruments 1905-2005', read at the Science Museum, London in 2005.

Workshop Manuals

Not all manufacturing companies produced repair manuals, but most of the major companies did and these can be obtained from Society archives as well as trading websites. The PCA and WES have archives and copies of many manuals and these can be obtained on disc. One can also acquire copies of the major pen maker's old manuals from a number of websites or at pen shows (see bibliography).

CDs and Videos

We have not viewed many but they are available. Arthur was the star of two videos produced a few years ago. It can be interesting and instructive to see something being done and how hand tools are used, particularly if you are just starting.

Catalogues

Perhaps more for collecting than repairing but Bill Acker has a wealth of catalogues (see http://www.billspens.com) and some contain information on repairing.

Auction Catalogues

Bonhams, Cooper Owen, Bloomsbury, Christies and Phillips with the occaisional Swiss auction organised by Thierry Nguyen are always good to look at.

Libraries

Don't forget public libraries and also that societies have libraries and archives for members to access!.

Patent Offices & Design Registers

There is a wealth of repair information in the original patents. In particular diagrams that explain the function of the parts and how the pens are constructed. One can get most patents on-line, and extracts from 'Abridgement summaries' are available from Societies. These summaries are excellent for browsing but the original patents are much better for detail.

Internet

Undoubtedly this is the present and the future source of information. FAQ sections on repairer's web sites and links can lead one to knowledge unlimited.

Zoss, The Repair Forum of FountainPenNetwork, FountainPenGeeks and Bing, Google and Yahoo will keep one entertained. There is not much that is not detailed somewhere in an on-line magazine, web site or You-Tube and it is all free! However you may not necessarily agree with everything from such sources. What a site such as Wikipedia does is list the references and that is perhaps the most important part of the page.

Asking a professional repairer a question about a procedure.

We all need to ask help at times and if you are intending to ask an eminent restorer a question then think a little about it. How do I repair a Snorkel? is hardly a question to get the attention of a busy repairer. I remember Frank Dubiel's answer to that question - LEAVE IT WITH ME!

All the repair wizards that we have met are delighted to answer questions but choose your time to ask and make the question specific. This will make your reasoning clear and it helps you to get the best answer.

BIBLIOGRAPHY

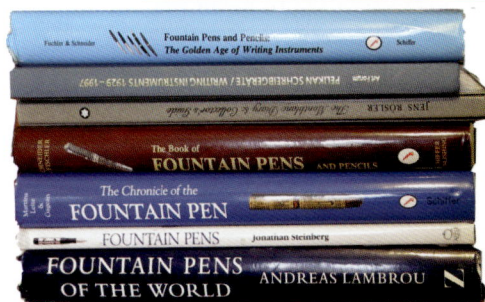

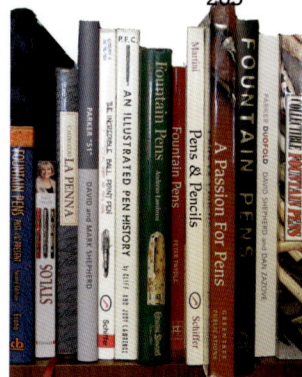

WEB PG 100 NOTES www.........

BOOKS
For specific Makers and Models

Parker 51	Mark and David Shepherd
Parker Duofold	David Shepherd and Dan Zazove
Parker Vacumatic	David Shepherd, Geoffrey Parker & Dan Zazove
Watermans	Max Davis & Gary Lehrer
The Montblanc Diary and Collectors Guide	Jens Rössler
Pelikan Schreibgerate	Jürgen Dittmer & Martin Lehmann
Pelikan	D Schafer
The Fountain pens of Esterbrook	Paul Hoban
Onoto pen (history & repair)	P Crook, S Hull, J Marshall, L Oldfield
The Jotter	D Shephard, G Hogg, G Parker, D Zazove
Mabie Todd	David Moak
Neptune	Stephen Hull and Mike Bryan
Conway Stewart	Stephen Hull
The Tibaldi Fountain Pens	Enrico Bettazzi and Letizia Jacopini
Fountain pens of Japan	M Sunami and A Lambrou
Namiki - The Art of Japanese Lacquer Pens	Julia Hutt and Stephen Overbury
A series of books on Wahl, Penol, Sheaffer	J P Martins, M Miloro, L Leite, A Gagean

General

Fountain pens of the world	Andy Lambrou
Fountain pens past and present	Paul Erano
The list	Bernard Bernolet and Marc van der Stricht
The Ultimate book of pens	B Garenfeld, D Geyer
The Incredible Ball Point Pen	Henry Gostony and Stuart Schneider
La Penna	Enrico Castruccio
Fountain Pens History and Design	Edited by Georgio Dragoni and Giuseppe Fichera
Fountain Pens and Pencils	George Fischler and Stuart Schneider
The Book of Fountain Pens and Pencils	George Fischler and Stuart Schneider
The Fountain Pen - a Collectors Companion	Alexander Crum Ewing
The English Fountain Pen Industry 1875-1975	S Hull
Fountain Pens - Their History and Art	Jonathan Steinberg
Collectible Fountain Pens	Glen Bowen
Fountain Pens - Collectors Guide	Jonathan Steinberg
Pens and Pencils - a Collectors Handbook	Regina Martini
Official PFC Pen Guide	Cliff Lawrence
Fountain Pens	Peter Twydle
The Chronicle of the FOUNTAIN PEN	Joao Pavao Martins, Luiz Leite, Antonio Gagean
The Parker Ballpoint Pen	Graham Hogg
Collecting Fountain Pens	Judson Bell
Collecting Fountain Pens -A primer...	Joel Hamilton and Sherrell Tyree
Ink Reservoir Writing Instruments 1905-2005	G Roe et al

.............and lots of others

Repair

Fountain pens – the complete guide to repair and restoration	Frank Dubiel
Sheaffers – Vac-Fil and Touchdown	Fr. Terry Koch
Conservation of Plastics	John Morgan
India Rubber and gutta percha in the Civil War era	Mike Woshner
The Amateur's Lathe	Lawrence Sparey
The Complete Metalsmith	Tim McCreight
Screw Cutting in the Lathe	Martin Cleve
Drills Taps and Dies	Tubal Cain
Inadequacies of writing instrument design and manufacture	G Roe
Writing Instruments	G Roe

Repair Manuals

Do you need to buy manuals if you are only a hobby repairer? This is a good question because often specific manuals can be obtained from the PCA or WES librarian. The Parker Service Manuals, Parker manual for UK pen mechanics, Eversharp Service Manual, Sheaffer's Manual for Trained Repairmen and a few older Duofold and Vacumatic booklets are all available in the archives. If you wish to purchase them, Pendemonium have a stock of reproductions in addition to Frank Dubiel's book; Lee Chait sells the 1970s Parker Manual and PPG offer the Sheaffer and UK Pen Mechanics manual. Bill Ackers site will give further information of the rarer manuals.

Repair Courses

There has been a resurgence of interest in courses after a vacuum of a few years created by Arthur Twydle's demise. He pioneered his repair courses based on the training that most pen dealers received from manufacturers in the 1940s and 1950s. The UK initiative has been taken by the Writing Equipment Society and seems to be very successful. Further afield others are commencing with beginners and advanced courses such as Auspens in Australia and there is always instruction at US shows given by the masters such as Osman Sumer and the US wizards.

Shows

The advantage of a show is that you can talk to people, ask questions as well as sell, buy and learn. The internet has had an effect on shows but a good social and commercial show is a feast for repairers. The bigger shows have been changing as a result of many factors, not least the hassle of dragging stock and items through security checks at airports. Nevertheless a show is one of the few places one can purchase parts. The Lott brothers cater for customers at US shows and Dale Beebe always has a fascinating display of repair items, small tools and parts. In the UK one can purchase parts at The London and Northern Pen shows and the recent smaller regional shows are excellent venues for that elusive pen -see the UK programme on www.ukpenshows.co.uk and the European Programme by Thierry Ngyen - http://www.freewebs.com/euroshows

Chicago, LA, DC, Columbus, Raleigh Durham, Dallas, Miami, Philadelphia and New York still thrive and are well worth the effort. Susan Wirth's authoritative list will give all the contact details for the USA and The Writing Equipment Society's web site will cover the UK and some European shows. The German shows such as Hamburg and Cologne are always well supported, France has it's regular meetings; Italy small shows; Melbourne is once a year; Japan has its regular events; Brazil, Poland, Tilberg, Waterloo all had shows this year and for the last few years the Spanish show in Madrid is a marvellous break from a cold December in the far North.

We have always been enthusiasts and participators as well as organizers and sponsors of some past shows. They are hard work, often without financial gain and if they disappear our hobby will suffer, so they do need your support!

INTERNET

The internet can be used for so many reasons but normally repairers use it to communicate, to acquire information, to purchase primarily tools, parts and materials and if one has time - to browse.

Information and searching

 If you want to advise someone what all these pen words and makers names mean then you can simply suggest that they browse about five or six websites and after that they will be either seduced or bewildered. Richard Binder's site has to be as good as it gets for anyone wanting to appreciate pens and understand brands and makers. His e-book glossary is a labour of enthusiasm for pens. David Nishimura, Penhero and a dabble with The Fountain Pen Network will entertain for hours.

There is an unselfish streak in most pen enthusiasts and those who share their knowledge freely rarely have a hidden agenda other than wanting others to participate in their hobby. We without their experience have to be grateful that such sites exist. Have a look at Uri Orland's site www. booksaboutpens.com or catalogues on Bill Ackers' site or US patent information and so on.

A few that we occasionally look at are listed below but most sites have lots of their own links.

Buying and selling

For buying items the internet can be a great help for pens, penparts and tools. We have noticed that in the last two years there are more sites selling pen tools and parts and this has to a healthy sign for pen collectors. Tools are at the centre of our activity so sharing sites that provide materials and intricate bits and pieces is beneficial to us all.

Although the pen auction sites are still crammed with pens, there are caveats when buying on line - we favour associations with dealers one can trust rather than a random lucky dip. However it is always fun to dabble and snipe! There are some interesting private auction sites such as Martiniauctions and The Saleroom is great for on line bidding for small pen lots.

The Internet can however be a nasty place and there are a few sad people, who delight in creating havoc. It pays to be aware of the pitfalls of selling and even repairing as your reputation can be badly damaged by someone who places defaming remarks without any substance. The internet can hardly ever correct anything once it is on-line, so if you have a dispute do be temperate and correct with your comments and criticism. It there is a disagreement it is usually most productive to talk.

Links

Most web sites will have links to other sites, and the best sites are ones most referred to e.g Richard Binder's list is very useful, David Nishimura's and so on. Use people's links they are meant to help. Some of these below are common to many sites

Pendemonium.com
Vintagepens.com
Vintagefountainpensinc.com
RichardsPens.com
Penhome.co.uk
Mainstreetpens.com
Cathedralpens.co.uk
Antiquewritingitems.com
Penpencilgallery.com
ThePenMuseum.com
Penpractice.com
Billspens.com
Booksaboutpens.com
Paulspens.com
Fountainpenhospital.com

Pensacs.com
Nibs.com
Agthomas.co.uk *(jewellery tools)*
Fountainpennetwork.com
Woodbin.ca
Onoto.com
Pencollectorsofamerica.com
Penhero.com
Sheaffertarga.com
Fivestarpens.com
custompenparsts.com
vintagepensacsandparts.com
ink-pen.com
oldpostofficepens.com.au
pentooling.com
martiniauctions.com

abclloyd.co.uk
auspens.com
classicpenengineering.co.uk
carneilpens.co.uk
arianantiques.co.uk
diamineinks.co.uk
ukpenshows.co.uk
thewritingdesk.co.uk
wesonline.org.uk

.....and many others worth browsing

268

271

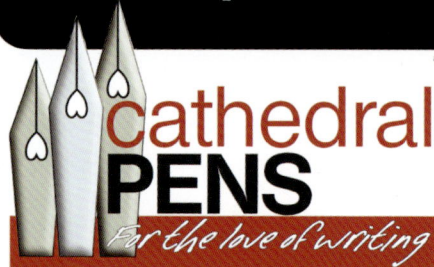

SIX OF THE SEVEN PEN SHOWS IN THE U.K. ARE ORGANISED BY US

UK PEN SHOWS have been organising pen shows for collectors and users of fine writing instruments for six successful years. Their regional events regularly attract most of the top dealers and collectors in the country.

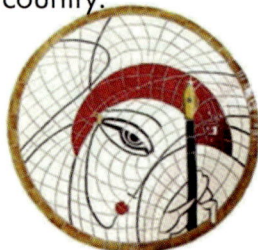

UK Pen Shows

EVENT PROGRAMME

South West Pen Show - February
Hilton Hotel, Bristol, BS32 4JF

Eastern Pen Show - March
Doubletree by Hilton Hotel, Cambridge, CB2 1RT

Northern Pen Show - April
Queen Hotel, Chester, CH1 3AH

Midland Pen Show -June
Guildhall, Lichfield, WS13 6LU

North East Pen Show -September
Copthorne Hotel, Newcastle-upon-Tyne, NE1 3RT

Sheffield Pen Fair -November
Channing Hall, Sheffield, S1 2LG

For full details and show dates please check out:

www.ukpenshows.co.uk

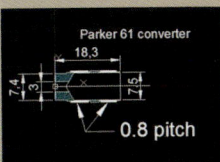

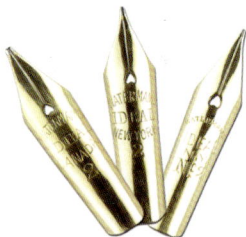

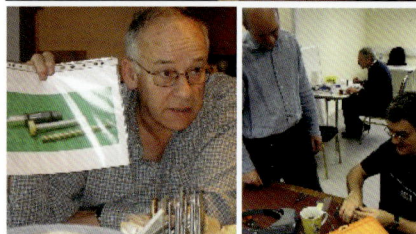

INDEX

A

AA Waterman	212
Adhesives	232
Anatomy	12

B

Ballpens	58, 90, 118
Barrel	21, 243, 244
Battleaxe	182
Bibliography	263
Blackbird BT	152
Body reservoir	54
Breather tube	18
Brenna	198
British pens	182
Burnham	184, 260
Button bar	26
Button filler	53

C

Cap bands	240
Cap lip	242
Cap puller	254, 255
Cap (steel finishing)	257
Cartridge	56, 71, 78
Centennial	88
Chatelaine	137
Chatsworth	182
Chilton	106, 188, 210
Clamp	28, 72,75
Cleaning	246
Clip	24, 39, 99, 130, 132, 139
Conklin	45, 211
Converters	57
Conway Stewart	166
Conway Stewart 700/800	168
Corks	170, 200, 203, 206, 218, 230
Cosmetic	246
Cracks	238, 242
Crocker	48, 52
Croxley	183
Cup washers	175
Curzon	185
Cutting seals	230

D

Decoband	158
De La Rue	(see Onoto)
Demonstrators	224
Dent removal	256
Doric	156
Dunn	45, 208, 260
Duofold	64, 82

E

Eagle	213
Engravings	247
Esterbrook	214
Evans	48
Eversharp Doric	156

Eversharp Fifth Avenue	164
Eversharp Oxford	160
Eversharp Skyline	162
Extraction inner caps	255
Eyedropper	120, 136, 183

F

Facilities	30
Feed	18
Filling a pen	14, 44
Filling system	15
Ford	194

G

Glass nibbed pens	217
Gold Starry	155, 225
Gripping section	20, 34, 252

H

Hard rubber	248
Holland	52, 182
Hundred Year	135

I

Imperial	114, 115
Information	261
Ink capacities	45
Ink Vue	124, 126, 265
Inner cap	29, 37, 255
Instructions	228

J

J-bar	24
Japanese piston	216
Jewel	182
John Bull	185
John Holland	182
Jotter (Parker)	93

K

Knight rider	181
Knocking block	28,36

L

Lady Ford	197
Lady Sheaffer	117
Lamy	97
Latremore	123
Lever	52
Lever box	133
Leverless	140
Leverfiller	49, 98, 138, 142

M

Mabie Todd	136, 138, 221
Mabie Todd eyedroppers	136
Machines	250
Materials	245
Macniven and Cameron	186
Mentmore	187, 260
Metal caps	254
Meteore	198
Montblanc	203

N

National Security	182, 193
Neptune	182
Nib general	17, 35, 41, 235
Nib grinding	236
Nib repair	238
Nozac	211

O

Omas	217
Onoto	170, 176
Onoto ink pencil	179
Onoto K-series	178, 225
Onoto Magna	173
Onoto Minor	177
Ormiston and Glass	183
Osmia	45, 55, 87
Overlays	134
Oxford	160

P

Parker	64, 88
Parker 17	83
Parker 25, 45	86
Parker 50	87
Parker 51	46, 70, 72, 225, 260
Parker 61	74, 76, 78, 260
Parker 65	80
Parker 75	85, 260
Parker VP/VS	84
Patrician	122
Pelican	200
Pen For Men	112, 225
Pencils	60, 94, 165, 180
Perry	185
Pilot	45
Piston filler	55, 100
Pitman	54
Platignum	187
Plating	249
Plevonia	97
Pressure bar	25, 65
Pullman	198

R

Relief	214
Repair procedure	33

S

Sac peg	37
Sacs	32
Safety pen	218
Seals	230
Section	(see Gripping section)
Sheaffer 444/506	116
Sheaffer	98
Skyline	162
Snorkel	108, 225
Soennecken	206

Spares/parts	46
Speedy Phil	167
Spot	187
Stephens	192
Stylographic	222
Stylomine	45, 155
Summit	185, 260
Swan	(see Mabie Todd)
Syringe filler	183, 194

T

Targa	119
Threads	244, 258, 260
Tools	27, 233
Touchdown	106
Tuning/Testing a pen	40
Typhoo	182

U

Unique	185, 260
Utility pens	216

V

Vac Fil	100
Vacumatic	66, 70
Vulcanite (see hard rubber)	
Valentine	190, 182, 260
Victory	65
Visofil	144, 146, 150
Visi-Ink	187

W

Wahl	156
Watermans	120, 122, 129, 220
Watermans CF	56, 128
Watermans pump	121
Watermans sleevefiller	123
Whytwarth	219
Wyvern	54, 191, 260

Y

Yard-o-led	226